TalkingPolitics

Political Conversations with Iain Dale

GW00469593

Talking Politics

TalkingPolitics

Political Conversations with
Iain Dale

To Alex

Best wishes

[signature]

biteback ˇˇˇ

First published in Great Britain in 2010 by
Biteback Publishing Ltd
Westminster Tower
3 Albert Embankment
London
SE1 7SP

ISBN 978-184954-065-0

10 9 8 7 6 5 4 3 2 1

A CIP catalogue record for this book is available from the British Library.

Set in Minion by SoapBox

Printed and bound in Great Britain by
TJ International, Padstow, Cornwall

*I dedicate this book to Tony Blair,
in the hope that one day he might
say yes to an interview.*

Other books by Iain Dale

Margaret Thatcher: In Her Own Words
(Biteback, 2010)

The Little Book of Boris
(Harriman House, 2008)

500 of the Most Witty, Acerbic & Erudite Things Ever Said About Politics
(Harriman House, 2008)

Margaret Thatcher: A Tribute in Words & Pictures
(Weidenfeld & Nicolson, 2005)

Prime Minister Portillo & Other Things That Never Happened
(Politico's, 2003)

Memories of the Falklands
(Politico's, 2002)

Contents

Foreword ix

Alex Salmond 1
Nigel Farage 18
Hazel Blears 25
Tony Benn 35
David Cameron 48
Ken Livingstone 64
Paddy Ashdown 78
Cherie Blair 92
Alan Duncan 104
Jacqui Smith 123
Ann Widdecombe 137
David Starkey 151
Vince Cable 165
John Bercow 178
Lord Pearson 191
David Owen 203
Nick Griffin 213
Adam Boulton 253
Andrew Neill 267
Alastair Campbell 283
Eric Pickles 298
Shirley Williams 309
Matthew Parris 325
Iain Duncan Smith 340
Peter Mandelson 365
The Miliband brothers – a GQ feature 378

Foreword

Let me make an admission. I have never had any journalistic training and I have certainly never had any training on how to conduct interviews. Some may say this will be manifestly obvious when reading this book, but I hope not.

The art of interviewing – and it is certainly an art – has always fascinated me. Listening to or reading a good interview ought to be a pleasurable experience, and for the most part it is. There are some brilliant interviewers around. For instance, each Saturday Rachel Sylvester and Alice Thomson in *The Times* are guaranteed to tell you something you didn't know before about their interview subjects. Gyles Brandreth's extensive interviews for the *Sunday Telegraph* (sadly discontinued) gave some fantastic personal insights into the rich and famous because he knew which buttons to press to get the most out of them. Andrew Neil is unrivalled as a TV political interviewer because he is able to quickly identify the biggest weakness in a politician's argument. On radio, Stephen Nolan on Radio 5 Live and Nick Ferrari on LBC both belong to the 'Jack Russell' school of interviewing: they nip away at a politician's ankles and aren't afraid of letting them know how ridiculous they are sounding if they just stick to a pre-prepared party line.

However, I cannot stand TV, radio or newspaper interviewers who think the interview is all about them or go into an interview determined for their own prejudices to be confirmed. Their egos get the better of them and you learn nothing new about the person they are interviewing. For example, I can never understand why anyone ever agrees to be interviewed by Camilla Long of the *Sunday Times*. Every week her interviews rip apart her chosen victim in a manner which leaves the readers scratching their heads and thinking: 'Why?' She's clearly a talented writer, but seems to enter her interviews with one aim in mind – to confirm a pre-existing public perception of the interviewee or to show how easy it is to ridicule someone. At times, they probably deserve it, but if you conduct every interview in that manner the reader cannot possibly judge which interviewee is genuinely a bad 'un. It's far more powerful to vary your approach. Lynn Barber is a perfect example of a tough but fair interviewer who, before you read an interview by her, you never quite knew what the outcome would be. I also hate the kind of interviews increasingly prevalent on TV and radio news programmes. Please don't think by singling out Camilla Long I am questioning her ability as an interviewer. She is a woman of many talents. And it may be that she is under instruction from her editor to interview in this way but, if so, it's a shame.

There's another type of interview I cannot abide. Next time you listen to *Today*, *The World at One* or *PM* just count the number of times you hear the phrase: 'I'm sorry, that's all we have time for.' Time after time nowadays in interviews, politicians or pundits are cut off in their prime just as an interview is getting interesting. Why? Because news producers think their listeners have the attention span of a flea. Yes, we live in a fast-moving society, but how can an interviewer possibly get anything out of a politician when the politician knows full well that he will be interrupted after ten seconds and will only be on air for a maximum of a couple of minutes? What happens is that the politician decides in advance what he wants to say and will say it whatever John Humphrys or Jeremy Paxman might decide to ask. And where does that get us? Nowhere. The listener or viewer is short changed.

It's time the media stopped treating its listeners like kids with attention deficit syndrome. Yes, the 8.10 interview on *Today* can last ten minutes – on the odd occasion longer, but where has the forensic thirty, forty-five or sixty minute interview gone? You won't find it on your TV and unless you're a non-politician, you won't find it on Radio 4 or Radio 5 Live. If we want to hold politicians and others to account the one-on-one, longer interview is the way to do it.

So to come to the point, this is what made me want to start a series of much longer, in depth, interviews for *Total Politics*, entitled 'In Conversation'. Even in national newspapers and magazines it is virtually impossible to find an interview with any politician longer than 1,500 words. Indeed, I have had several emails from political journalists confessing they are hugely jealous of mine because their editors won't let them do interviews of any great length.

So let me make a confession too. I very rarely do much preparation for these interviews. Yes, I do jot down a few notes and questions I want to ask, but the notes rarely extend to more than a few bullet points. The reason is simple. When I call these 'In Conversation' interviews that's just what I want them to be – political conversations. They're not meant to be rigorous grillings.

There's a trend in these interviews. I always ask for a minimum of an hour and a quarter because it usually takes about twenty minutes for someone to warm up and their tongue to loosen. After twenty minutes chit-chat the interviewee stops regarding me as a journalist on the lookout for a scoop, and instead regards me as a fellow politico wanting to chew the political fat. I have always believed that if you put people at their ease and ensure they don't feel on the defensive, they are more likely to reveal their real selves to you. By and large that approach works, but there's always the exception. And Vince Cable was that exception. Of all the interviewees in this book he was the only one I failed to bond with. Professional interviewers may recoil in horror at the use of that phrase – as an impartial journalist it is not their role to 'bond' with an interviewee. I understand that, but I stand by my reasoning that my approach gets far more out of people than if I was being intrusive and aggressive.

When a nationally known political editor suggested to me I should compile my interviews into a book, I was of course very flattered, but I wondered if it really would work. Reading some of the interviews again however, I understood what he meant. Put together I think they do give some very revealing insights into the minds of politicians and those who commentate on them. It's not a book which is meant to be read cover to cover; it's one of those you dip in and out of. I hope that it will be of interest to all those who study politics and are trying to find out what motivates politicians as well as those studying the political media.

I hope you get as much pleasure out of reading the interviews as I have had conducting them.

And, of course, you can read a new interview every month in *Total Politics* magazine.

Iain Dale
Tunbridge Wells
November 2010

Alex Salmond

Party affiliation: Scottish National Party (SNP)

Current position: First Minister of Scotland

Born: 31 Dec 1954, Linlithgow, Scotland

Education: Attended Linlithgow Academy before moving to St Andrew's University, where he acquired a joint honours MA in Economics and History.

Family status: Married.

Pre-political career: An assistant economist in the Department of Agriculture and Fisheries for Scotland before working for the Royal Bank of Scotland for seven years.

Electoral history: Elected as MP for Banff and Buchan in 1987 and then as National Convener for the Scottish National Party in 1990. He stood down from this position in 2000 but was re-elected as leader of the SNP in 2004.

Career highlights: Attaining leadership of the SNP twice.

Interesting fact: Consistently ranks in the top ten hardest-working Scottish MPs according to data from the Parliamentary Information Management System (PIMS).

Date of interview: July 2008
Extended version
Venue: House of Commons
Total Politics Issue 25, September 2008

This was the first 'In Conversation' interview I did for Total Politics. *I met Alex Salmond in his House of Commons office and talked for close on two hours. It was a strange experience as he twice had to go to vote, which meant that we continued the conversation walking through the Commons corridors with me holding my recording machine under his mouth. We finished off the interview in full public view just off Central Lobby.*

Alex Salmond is a politician's politician. He's deeply tribal, yet maintains genial relations with many people who don't share his views. He's got a very well-developed sense of humour and this shines through in this interview.

The interview created quite a storm when it was published, mainly because he committed the treasonous act of maintaining that Margaret Thatcher wasn't all bad. The Scottish media went into full 'outrage mode' and the story led the Scottish news agenda for a couple of days. It was difficult for Salmond to maintain he had been misquoted because the interview is a verbatim transcript.

When I saw what was happening I almost doubted my own recording so I went back and checked that the transcript was 100 per cent accurate. Luckily – for me – it was.

When was the last time you said sorry for something?
Personally, I said [it] to my wife on Saturday morning. The holiday we've just booked, may well have to be unbooked. I didn't say sorry once. I said it a hundred times. When you're First Minister you probably don't find it wise to own up to mistake after mistake…

But people quite like a politician who has the guts to say sorry, don't they?
That's right. If you do change your mind on something it's best to admit it. I haven't had many disagreements… Macmillan once got into some dreadful trouble with the Tory party and kept losing the Conservative whip until he became leader. After that, things became considerably easier. People didn't try to expel him anymore.

It didn't quite work for Iain Duncan Smith.
Well, it's been my experience in the SNP. I was always getting into trouble before I became leader. And then my troubles stopped! I got expelled from the SNP in 1982 as a rather brash young man and probably rather insensitive to other people's opinion. I've often reflected that there was a considerable amount of fault on my side. In 1988 I was given a seven day suspension from the House of Commons and all I was doing was intervening in the budget speech. I thought I was hard done by and it was very unfair … but I just got on with it. I lived to fight another day.

You are probably more forgiving now than others were to you at the time, possibly?
Yes, I've often reflected that you should avoid political disciplinary action for political reasons. Fine, if people run off with the church funds, you've got no choice in the matter, but wherever you can you should avoid using procedures of the party as a means of suppressing political dissent.

Why were you expelled?
The formal reason was for forming a political group within the SNP. This was called the '79 Group. We tried to get round a ban on this group by forming the Scottish Socialist Society. Seven of us were expelled – most of them have done well since! Being expelled can be no bad thing. It didn't stop me becoming leader.

Let's talk about leadership. When you decided to return to the leadership, did you really think you could end up as First Minister?

Oh yes, absolutely. I certainly thought it wasn't odds on but I thought we had a fair chance of winning.

How do you think you have changed as a leader second time around? You seem a lot calmer, a lot more at ease with yourself. You've shed the 'Chat Show Charlie' image. You had a reputation for enjoying life, being the life and soul of the party, whereas now we see a slightly different Alex Salmond.

Older and wiser. Certainly not sadder! Things could not have worked out better, but this was not calculated. Nobody calculates 'I shall resign'. I resigned when we were ahead in the polls, but I felt ten years was long enough. With the press reaction to the SNP, I was becoming the issue – they weren't seeing past me. Despite the fact that every newspaper was fiercely anti-SNP, they had never quite managed to stop me and I got the feeling that I had become a block on the SNP getting a fair shout. I thought someone else might get a fair shout. Actually, I was quite wrong because John [Swinney] got treated far worse than I was. Even Neil Kinnock used to moan about the papers but at least he had the *Mirror* and the *FT* on his side. We had nothing. I thought someone else would get a honeymoon, get a better press and it would be better for the party. I didn't calculate 'I'll resign, come back again, win the 2007 election', nobody can calculate like that.

You came back and stood for a seat for the Scottish Parliament which you might easily not have won. That, if I read it rightly, has given you far more of a mandate than you might have dreamt of.

I said I'd stand for a seat in the north-east of Scotland – so it's very familiar but it was the kind of seat we had to win to win the election. I thought we could win the whole thing and if I won my seat we'd do just that. I thought the party needed a fillip. We'd lost a lot of elections and we needed a boost. Winning Gordon would give us that boost. If I stood there it would encourage everyone else to believe we could win overall. I started from third place, after all.

When you walked into the First Minister's office for the first time what did you think? When Boris walked into the London mayor's office for the first time, there was this slight sense of disbelief that he had done it. Did you have any of that or did you immediately sit down and start barking out orders?

It was a bit different because it's not until twelve days later that you're elected by the chamber. That moment of saying 'my goodness, we've done it' doesn't come 'til some time later. Even though I knew there was no combination to stop us, it's not until you get the vote read out that it is the defining moment. That's the equivalent of Boris going into the mayor's office.

Emotionally, how did you feel? Euphoric? Tearful? A proud moment in the Salmond family...
My family were up [in] the gallery.

If it was me, I wouldn't have been able to look up to them as it would start me off...
My wife, my wee sister and my Dad were there. My Dad had never seen me speak in a parliamentary chamber. He didn't really approve of me setting foot in the House of Commons. My mother often came down, but it was the first time my Dad had seen me in the Scottish parliament chamber.

So proud on two counts.
Oh yes, very. It was a hell of a moment.

Were you daunted at all by the job? Most politicians, although outwardly self confident, have elements of self doubt. They think: 'I've got the job now. Am I up to it?'
I don't do daunted. The one moment I would say in my year in office that I did feel a bit daunted was the terrorist attack on Glasgow airport. It was the day of the Royal opening of the Parliament on 1 July. I had gone back to Bute House with a few friends – with Sean Connery actually – and was watching TV coverage when it came on. The daunting bit is, you might watch events but with this it wasn't just about watching; I was expected to do something about it. The civil service are very good at telling you 'what happens now, this is what you need to coordinate'. You don't have too much time to fret about being daunted. The decisions you have to make are quite interesting. You have to think about the consequences of what happened and how the rest of society is going to feel about it. So you take decisions like going to the airport the next day – something which wasn't universally applauded, but nevertheless you have to go, and then going from the airport to the central mosque in Glasgow with leaders of every religious group in Scotland and Strathclyde Police, making sure society doesn't fracture as a result of a terrorist assault. That's the daunting bit, when you realise it's not some other person that's behind the eight ball, it's you. It's not really a moment you can go and consult your special advisors; you've just got to get on with it. I suspect if you asked the present prime minister, or his predecessor, or his predecessor's predecessor [John Major] who was a nice guy, I suspect their 'daunted' moment was to do with war, deploying troops.

I suspect with Tony Blair it was Princess Diana's death, because if he had got one word wrong he would have been characterised by that for the rest of his term in office.
Quite. On the Glasgow attack, I did interviews at the airport and I wanted to get points across as carefully as I could, without prejudicing the investigation,

that the perpetrators were not part of the fabric of our Asian community in Scotland. It was a vital message to get across as early as possible to prevent any stories of 'the enemy within' developing.

The SNP gets quite a lot of support from the Asian community, doesn't it?
We get huge support from them, but whether we do or not, that message had to be put across. It was the duty and responsibility of the First Minister to communicate it in the interest of public order and the fabric and community of the realm of Scotland, regardless of what any junior minister in London might think.

Is there any kind of turf war in these circumstances between Edinburgh and London? Gordon Brown was seen to have reacted well to the incident, but it was on your territory.
None whatsoever. The transfer of the suspects south of the border was a law officers' decision, nothing to do with politics.

Did you and Gordon Brown talk?
Within seconds of it happening. He was literally just in office, his first few days. He arranged the COBRA meeting. I arranged our equivalent meeting in what we now call the Resilience Room. It was called the Emergency Room but it's very difficult if you are trying to be calm to do an interview in a room in front of a bloody big notice which says 'emergency'! We now have a Scottish Government Resilience Room!

How much contact do you have with Gordon Brown and how do you get on with him?
Quite a lot. Most recently during the fuel dispute at Grangemouth, but initially we had quite a lot of contact. More than I had with his predecessor. If you remember, he didn't phone or write when we took power.

You must have found that quite insulting.
No, I found it great. Another miscalculation. I thought for the master of presentation it was an extremely foolish thing to do. Maybe it was because he was demob happy so he didn't care anymore.

Your relationship with Brown is presumably businesslike rather than particularly friendly?
You wouldn't expect us to be bosom buddies, walking arm in arm to the pub for a wee snifter, let's put it that way. You wouldn't expect us to be bosom friends when we both have high stakes to play for. On national emergencies there's no question you have to operate together. There has never been any suggestion that I have noticed north or south of the border that – well, maybe the odd

junior minister in the Scotland Office – but for everybody serious, political differences get put to one side. Secondly, there are genuine political differences. I believe in independence for Scotland, clearly the Prime Minister doesn't. No amount of words or meetings or rapprochement will bring us together on that issue. And that applies to a range of other issues too. We have a genuine political disagreement. The best we can do is let the people decide. There is also a third area, which is why I have been keen to get the joint ministerial committees back, which is policies which are not essential to the ethos of either government. An example is the Marine Bill. Both governments believe in environmental control, clean seas. No one argues it is a bad idea, so for these things you need an institution which gets agreement where agreement can be achieved. I am anxious to avoid unnecessary disagreements as they are a complete waste of time. The Joint Ministerial Committee hasn't met for six years but it met again recently under Jack Straw's chairmanship and it was a good meeting. I am not expecting great things but I am hoping for progress in a range of areas.

If he loses the Glasgow East by-election, do you think he's toast?
I think there are people in the Labour Party who will be less than supportive of him in these circumstances.

I'll take that as a 'yes' then…
I have seen many people carry on under the same circumstances and even recovered so I am very wary about being certain. I think the problem is not so much, 'is Gordon close to his party,' it's whether he's close to the electorate. That's his underlying problem. There are aspects of Labour just now which look to me like John Major in the 1990s, and for some of the same reasons. I don't want to put words in to his mouth, but I suspect that Gordon is very aware of the problem he's got, with a track record stretching over eleven years. When Major came in at first, although he had been Chancellor of the Exchequer and Foreign Secretary nobody seriously believed he had been at the epicentre of the Thatcher project so he was almost there without form.

How many seats are you aiming to win in the next Westminster election?
A minimum of twenty.

That's a fairly high bar, as you have never got more than half way there.
Not quite true. We got eleven in 1974. As an economist I am good with figures. I think that is a reasonable objective.

From your agenda of independence for Scotland, what is the best result of the next election?
A hung parliament. Absolutely. Let's call it a balanced parliament.

It seems to me that the Conservatives are cosying up to the SNP in quite an overt manner in many ways and that you are showing a bit of ankle yourselves. Would I be correct?
[Affects to look affronted] Showing a bit of ankle?! We don't use such terms in Scotland!

I'm sure you have your own phrase!
It is certainly true that of the other parties in the Scottish Parliament the Greens – who have been very constructive – and the Conservatives have been the opposition parties who have understood best the advantages for opposition of minority government and they have got most out of the political situation in my opinion. The Labour Party has just been heads down and charging and usually missing, bypassing the matador and heading into the crowd somewhere. And the Liberals? I just cannot fathom the Liberal Party, but that may be a statement which can be applied generally. But in the Scottish Parliament I have no idea what they are doing. I don't think they do either. In politics you either believe for good reasons that circumstances will change in your favour at some point in the future and that principled opposition will get you whatever reward you are looking for or alternatively you take the opportunity for administration because you believe you can help change things for the better. The Liberal Democrats actually managed to turn down administration in three parliaments in the space of a few weeks.

Some sort of record.
They turned it down in Scotland, they turned it down in Wales and depending on how you interpret the Ming Campbell/Gordon Brown meeting, they turned it down in Westminster as well. It would indicate to me some sort of psychosis going on within the Liberal Democrats.

Your party has traditionally been very antagonistic towards the Conservatives but there has definitely been a change of mood. Is this because you can see David Cameron, to quote the famous phrase, as someone 'you can do business with'?
I have spoken about the Tories in the Scottish Parliament, where they have been more constructive than other opposition parties, but I think you wouldn't have to scratch very hard in London to see real anti-Scottish antagonism from many elements of the Conservative Party – there's a whole range of quotations, so I don't think the leopard has changed his spots.

Cameron has been very pro-Scottish in some of the comments he has made.
Maybe the wrapping has changed somewhat but I think the leopard is still there.

But if there is a hung parliament where the Conservatives are the largest party, is there any conceivable circumstance where you could see SNP MPs going into coalition with the Conservatives?
None at all.

So you completely rule that out.
We have a policy on that. We don't have a policy preventing a formal coalition with the Labour Party but I don't see circumstances where we would be in a formal coalition with the Labour Party either, right now. In a hung parliament we wouldn't be trying to enter a coalition, we'd be trying to exert influence. Believe me, the best way to exert influence in Westminster is not to be in a formal coalition.

So it would be on an issue by issue basis.
Yeah, you would maximise your influence. A good example of what is possible is to look at the DUP on the 42-day vote. The SNP could not have done a deal on this because we had a principled objection. You can't mortgage your political soul but the DUP weren't in that position. They could make a good argument for being in favour of 42-day detention. But without the engagement they wouldn't have been in favour of it as they turned out to be. Even in a Parliament with a majority of sixty-six, circumstances can arise where a small party can be extremely powerful in a vote to save the Prime Minister's bacon. In a Parliament with a much smaller majority or no majority at all it is going to happen more often, and that's what we would do.

I perceive that the SNP has changed a lot in the last ten years. The Conservatives were seen as a terrible enemy by you and the SNP was seen to be a very left-wing party by the Conservatives. It seems to me that you have copied Bill Clinton – I'll be careful where I go with this analogy – and tried to create a big tent for the SNP, so you can attract ex-Conservative voters who had previously felt put off by some of the more left-wing ideas of the SNP.
I suppose I have tried to bring the SNP into the mainstream of Scotland. We have a very competitive economic agenda. Many business people have warmed towards the SNP. We need a competitive edge, a competitive advantage – get on with it, get things done, speed up decision making, reduce bureaucracy. The SNP has a strong social conscience, which is very Scottish in itself. One of the reasons Scotland didn't take to Lady Thatcher was because of that. It didn't mind the economic side so much. We could see the sense in some of that. But we didn't like the social side at all. One of the most famous phrases in Scottish history is the 'community of the realm' – I used it earlier. This idea that there is a community of interest stretching across the population. It's a very Scottish concept and Scotland doesn't like people who rail against it.

Doesn't that illustrate the problem that Scotland is seen as having quite a big public sector, a bit too much of the Nanny State, and as the country of Adam Smith it is no longer seen as the country of enterprise? Or am I betraying English prejudices by even daring to suggest such a thing?

I think you are betraying Adam Smith. He was not just a friend of economics. He was a moral philosopher. Margaret Thatcher had only ever read the Penguin edition of *Wealth of Nations* and she missed out the moral sentiments. I would absolutely defend the reputation of Adam Smith against the Adam Smith Institute.

You're a better man than I am.

I said to Eamonn Butler [Deputy Director of the ASI], if Adam Smith could sue, you'd be in real trouble.

What can you do as a government to ram home the message that Scotland wants the world's business? We only ever see in London, mainly because the London media rarely reports anything about Scotland unless it's bad, things like the Donald Trump incident where it seems he wants to take his bat and ball home because he can't get planning permission for a a £2 billion golf project.

He hasn't quite taken his bat and ball home but I can't be conflicted by commenting on it because it's in my constituency and I am 'cup-tied'. I can't prejudice the results of the public inquiry. But on the broader point I don't think Scotland has an international projection problem welcoming business. We've had a very good reception in the US. Against a very difficult investor climate we have done spectacularly well in key sectors. That will be exemplified even more in our Year of Homecoming, and we expect you to take part in this, Iain. This is for first, second, third, fourth, fifth generation Scots.

I am a quarter Scottish.

There we are, we've got you. There are 100 million Scots around the planet.

I am a descendant of one of Robbie Burns' bastard children...

Iain, you are perfectly positioned to celebrate the 250th anniversary of your ancestor. That only happens every 250 years!

Indeed.

Therefore I am instructing, nay commandeering, 100 million people to come back to Scotland at some point during 2009 to enjoy the festivities.

Preferably not all at once.

No, because we have stretched the events from Burns Night to St Andrews Day. We have five themes. Burns himself, the Scottish history of enterprise and innovation – the enlightenment, Adam Smith – golf, Scottish history (genealogy, the gathering of the clans to Edinburgh). All the transatlantic flights have already been booked.

It's all becoming clear to me now. That's why you want the referendum in 2010 so you can sweep to victory on the back of this tide of nationalist euphoria which you will unleash in 2009.
You've got it. You've seen through me again.

That's why Wendy Alexander wanted it now. Now I get it!
I didn't get to the fifth theme, whisky.

We'll gloss over that one. I don't drink.
Can I welcome the change in direction of the Conservative Party, but I have to say the Conservative affection for whisky was about its only redeeming feature.

Don't take me as typical of the Conservative Party, in oh so many ways!
I think I had already worked that bit out, Iain.

What is the future of the bases under an independent Scotland?
One thing that never comes up when you talk about the Barnett Formula, in public expenditure terms, Scotland gets 7 per cent of defence expenditure, so if you held defence expenditure at the same level, you could generate more jobs. We won't have the next generation of nuclear missiles. Hans Blix wouldn't have much trouble in coming to Scotland and finding Weapons of Mass Destruction. He'd have managed that in an afternoon. I don't think it's reasonable to have that for the next forty years or so.

Nuclear power?
We're against any renewal of nuclear power for Scotland, but we'll have it until 2020.

The UK government is going hell for leather for nuclear power.
We're going hell for leather for renewables. We've also just signed a contract for £700 million with Scottish Coal. Scots' coal will now be burnt in Scots' power stations. We can get the clean power investment we're looking for. And at this rate we can get down to zero carbon emissions using clean coal.

You're not going to waste money on wind power, are you?
We'll have comparative advantage in wind power, lots of wind. Offshore wind has a lot going for it. In the Murray Firth we have a utilisation of 53

per cent – I don't know of any land-based wind turbines with more than 30 per cent. But we also have a comparative advantage in wave energy and tidal energy. It's going to be big in the future. The Pentland Firth is the Saudi Arabia of tidal power, potentially. I notice Gordon Brown has nicked that phrase – very naughty of him. I launched the world's largest innovation prize in Washington in April, the Saltaire Prize, which will be judged by scientific luminaries throughout the world. You have to demonstrate the device in Scotland. You can enter yourself, Iain

Hmmm. I can demonstrate good use of wind, but let's not go there.
The idea is to establish Scotland as the marine renewables centre of the universe. We had a full-page headline in *Fortune* magazine – 'Scotland Rules the Waves.' I loved that! My view on energy is that you position yourself where you have a natural competitive advantage. We don't have it in nuclear technology. We'd have to buy it from France or somewhere else. We'll get to 30 per cent renewable production, 50 per cent by 2020 and bigger after that if the technology fits into place. It will because the economics are dictating it. And we have to address the outrageous entry costs to connect to the grid.

Is it a frustration for you being First Minister that you only have powers over certain areas and not others? For example, you don't have full control over economic policy. You have limited tax-raising powers which you choose not to use...
Once upon a time they were called the Towering Heights of the economy...

You mean Commanding Heights...
Indeed. Yes, it is a frustration, of course it is. Can you do nothing about the economy, no I don't agree with that, but you are boxed in to enterprise policy, business incentives and supply side initiatives. However, we have done something dramatic for small businesses with the elimination of business rates for example. But for Commanding Heights intervention on adjustment of tax then you are heavily restricted and that is a real frustration, of course it is.

Do you think you will ever use the tax-raising powers you've got?
I don't see that in the foreseeable future.

A subject dear to my heart is an English Parliament, which you presumably approve of...
I am right behind you. I'm surprised at Ken Clarke's lily-livered report.

Are you? It's a compromise, isn't it?
I was being ironic. Certain compromises you can muddle through, but if I

was producing a way to protect the essential integrity of the United Kingdom – which, I'm not – I wouldn't produce that. This in and out rubbish is a lot of nonsense. You have to think about the whole constitutional structure and come up with something a bit more elegant.

Do you agree that there is a resurgence of an acceptable form of English nationalism and that a lot of English people feel disadvantaged?
I have huge sympathy with the political argument. As you know, by choice, SNP MPs have abstained from every vote on English legislation which does not have an immediate Scottish consequence. And when we have intervened it's usually on the side of the English majority. If you're asking me should people in England be able to run their own Health Service, their education system and a variety of other pieces of legislation then my answer is yes. They should be able to do it without the bossy interference of Scots Labour MPs. We had this in reverse through the 1980s. Because I believe in independence for Scotland I also believe in independence for England. I know there are a lot of doom mongers who say that England couldn't stand on its own two feet. I deprecate that sort of talk [laughs]. I have great confidence in England's ability to be self governing.

[Laughs] We are so grateful!
Sometimes it helps for people to see the wood from the trees to talk like that. Nothing makes me more angry than people who deprecate the abilities of their own country, their own people. You can't deprecate a country's abilities without having an effect on the people within the country. It's insidious and damaging. Patriotism is said to be the last refuge of the scoundrel. The reverse is the last refuge of the scoundrel in politics.

Does it irritate you when you read things in the English newspapers – and I get it all the time on my blog – about what a miserable Scottish bastard Andy Murray is? How the English shouldn't support him because he said he didn't want England to win in the World Cup?
I don't think that the plain people of England would think that. The sort of people who think that are the sort of people who go on your blog! [roars with laughter]

Thank you! But let me put the reverse point to you. I always want Scotland to win at any sport. It's partly my country too. But there are plenty of Scots who revel in an English defeat of any sort – even against the Germans, for God's sake!
I have form on this matter. You're not talking to the First Minister who supports other teams against England in the World Cup – that was my

predecessor [Jack McConnell]. I think that individuals have every right to a bit of banter.

But it goes beyond banter.
When you become national leader you're under a different set of rules. Anything I say can be interpreted as the view of the country. People should back your own country. No one is obligated to support anyone else, but I don't think you should get your kicks and thrills by some proxy. It's pathetic. I have never indulged in it. If you go into a TV room in the House of Commons when England is playing, all you have to do is look at the phalanx of Scottish Labour MPs cheering on whoever they are playing against. And you think to yourself, there's the Scottish Unionist Party. These are the people who want to have their country run from somewhere else!

In May 2011 you will be up for re-election. What do you want the Scottish people to be thinking about your four years in government? What will guarantee you your re-election?
Remember we will be having a referendum in 2010. I want our record in government to reinforce the popularity and trust in the SNP. By our deeds we shall be known. People do not expect miracles. They do not expect a minority government to have transformed the country in the space of twelve months but most people seem to be happy with what they have seen so far. The trust in government as expressed in the Social Attitude Survey has risen by twenty points – from 50 per cent to 70 per cent.

It was important for you in the first year to display competence, I suppose, as none of you had any experience of running a government department!
The SNP Cabinet has people in it who have worked for Standard Life, the Royal Bank of Scotland, Scottish Amicable. They've done a few things.

It must be a relief to have got through the first year with a reputation for competence.
It was a desirable objective. As you probably have noticed, I am not short of confidence, so relief is the wrong phrase, but I was determined that that should be done. So much so that I banned their holidays last summer and said look, you're Cabinet ministers, make your mark. And they did.

My point is that the Scottish media is against the SNP and apart from the Labour Party most other people in politics have said quite nice things about you.
If you get complimented by your critics then that is better than just being complimented by your friends. But we have a lot of achievements to be

complimented on. We have a new style of government. We slashed business rates for small companies, froze council tax, abolished tolls, saved the hospitals, reduced prescription charges. We're now trying to get to some of the more underlying structural challenges – reshaping the relationship between central and local government. If we can do that, there will be a big gain. We've already abolished more than sixty ring fences. We are attacking on the binge-drinking culture, which is an even bigger problem than it is in England. This is difficult because we are tilting against vested interests, the power of which you would not believe.

So how do you think you've done overall?
Well, I'm not going to do a Wendy Alexander and give myself ten out of ten [laughs].

Quickfire

James McAvoy or Sean Connery?
Has to be Sean Connery, but I would never pit two fantastic Scots against each other.

Oatcakes or Haggis?
Oatcakes win, but only marginally.

Favourite view?
Culloden Bay. If you haven't seen it, you must. A couple of Tory MPs have holiday homes there. It's fabulous.

Wendy or Douglas?
Wendy.

Last time you cried?
[Pauses] I shed a tear recently. There was an episode of *Star Trek* that was particularly poignant [collapses in giggles].

What music makes you dance?
My guilty secret is that I like country and western music. I am a devotee of Tammy Wynette. I went to Scottish Ballet recently. Wonderful, but in the interval I had to give a speech. I told them it was the first ballet I had ever been to so they were thinking I was a complete philistine. I then told them I was the only frontline politician who had once starred in an opera, and it's true. I had a lead role in an operetta. My musical tastes are wide. I have also done a duet with Sandi Thom.

Favourite food?

In the early part of June you can get Duke of York potatoes, fresh sea trout and Scottish asparagus. Usually they are out of sync, but sometimes you can get them all in season together.

Favourite comedian?

Elaine C Smith, the wife of Rab C Nesbitt.

Nigel Farage

Party affiliation: UK Independence Party

Current position: Leader of UKIP

Born: 3 April 1964

Education: Educated at Dulwich College, London.

Family status: Has two children from a previous marriage to Grainne Hayes. Currently married with two more children to Kirsten Mehr.

Pre-political career: Joined a commodity brokerage firm in London before running his own brokerage business from the early 1990s to 2002.

Electoral history: Became a founding member of UKIP (UK Independence Party) in 1993 and was elected to the European Parliament in 1999 and re-elected in 2004 and 2009. In September 2006, he was elected leader of UKIP with 45 per cent of the vote but announced he was going to step down from this position in September 2009. He has very recently returned to the position of UKIP leader, taking over 60 per cent of the vote.

Career highlights: Becoming the leader of the United Kingdom Independence Party in 2006, and later re-elected in November 2010.

Interesting fact: He was injured in a plane crash in Northamptonshire in May 2010, in which both Farage and the pilot were hospitalised.

Date of interview: October 2008
Extended version
Venue: Westminster Arms, Storey's Gate, Westminster
Total Politics Issue 5, November 2008

It's actually very hard for Nigel Farage to give a bad interview. He is the kind of character who always has something interesting to say. Indeed sometimes he says far too much for his own good. Politics needs characters like Farage. He clearly adds to the gaiety of our political life, but he's also the very definition of a conviction politician. Yes, like any other politician, he has an ego, but he is refreshingly honest about the fact that he likes a drink and has an eye for the ladies. I'm not sure if I can think of any other politician who'd front up like that.

Nigel Farage's trouble is that he is trying to do the political equivalent of herding cats. His party was once described by David Cameron as being full of 'fruitcakes and nutcases'. Cameron may have been exaggerating for dramatic effect, but there was an element of truth in what he was saying. Fringe parties are always open to fanatics being able to rise to positions of power very quickly, because they are often the only ones with the time and the money to follow their passion. They can be obsessive in pursuing their agendas and can be hugely disruptive and destabilising. Nigel Farage's first term as UKIP leader was full of instances where senior UKIP figures tried to destabilise him. Eventually, he decided enough was enough and left. There were other reasons too, but that must have been an important consideration.

UKIP needs to recognise that if they are to make any progress at all over the next five years Farage is the only game in town. He is the only UKIP figure to have a real national profile and he needs to build on that. But he also needs to recognise that he can't do everything himself. He needs a strong, closely knit team around him, and in particular a chief executive who can manage inter-party relations.

I published Nigel Farage's autobiography, Fighting Bull, *in March 2010. It's a brilliant read and every sentence is just so typically Nigel. A new paperback edition will be published during 2011, which will carry the full story of his air crash on election day.*

How do you think the role of UKIP has changed in the last five years?

The increase in MEPs we got was across the water. In terms of what we have done in the European Parliament we are without doubt the leaders of the Eurosceptic movement in the European Parliament. Our two biggest achievements were firstly the French referendum, and secondly the Irish referendum. We played a big part in both. The role in the Irish one was rather bigger than people have yet realised.

In what way?

The eight-page info booklet we, as the Independent Democratic Group (InDem Group), sent to every household in Ireland had a big effect. It was very well put together and very strong. While Declan Ganley is being portrayed as the CIA-funded bad boy [by the Yes campaign] we're not terribly popular either. I was quite happy when the Taoiseach got up in the Dáil and said that I and my fellow bunch of 'extremists' had subverted the political process in Ireland.

So you weren't part of Ganley's 'No Campaign'?

No.

Doesn't that illustrate the problem the Eurosceptic movement has always had, in that it is so splintered?

Quite the reverse. For years we have been told that you can't fight a referendum campaign unless you are all under one big tent. And then there's the argument about who is the person with the biggest ego who is going to lead the umbrella group. What the Irish campaign proved is that this view could not be more wrong. We had Sinn Fein doing their own thing, getting their vote out on the simple question of Irish nationality, you had Ganley fighting a completely brand new type of campaign in Ireland, talking about an overregulated European model, globalisation, the fact that the Treaty takes things too far and appealing to a business and conservative audience. You had the InDem campaign and we campaigned chiefly on the lack of democracy but we also went into the Charter of Fundamental rights because of the abortion issue. There were lots of different campaigns and degrees of cooperation. Ganley and the InDem group had discussions but they were separate campaigns and it worked a treat.

So in the unlikely event of a UK referendum do you think that would be the model here?
I am convinced now that there is no problem if we have four or five different No campaigns. The Political Parties, Elections and Referendums Act (PPERA) also allows for more than one campaign.

What is your prediction about what will happen now to the Lisbon Treaty and what do you make of the Conservative stance on this?
It's funny, isn't it, that David Cameron is doing what we expect the Conservatives to do – to try and sound sceptical enough to keep people in board.

Do you not believe that he is a Eurosceptic?
God, no. You must be joking! You've got to be having a laugh! I remember being on Eurostar when the Tory leadership election campaign was on and Dan Hannan was on the train. I told him I couldn't believe he would support Cameron. I said we all know what David Davis believes in private and really on this and many other subjects – localism and liberty etc. I said 'why on earth are you backing Cameron?' He said: 'Nigel, because Cameron has made the one deliverable promise. Not some vague idea about what might happen when he is PM, but a deliverable promise which will happen within weeks or months.' He ratted on it and he's saying it will happen after 2009.

Which is why David Davis never matched the promise – because he knew it wasn't deliverable.
It ain't going to happen after 2009 either. Secondly, we saw Cameron abandoning the Tory pledge to withdraw from the Common Fisheries Policy. Howard had been quite strong about it. I had pointed out that you can't do it without unanimity, but at least he was strong on it. Apparently,

Cameron says we are now going to negotiate the CFP from within. Well, the very best of British to him. He presents again and again things which he would do as prime minister, which are completely outside the jurisdiction of the British government and British Parliament. Never once does he ever say that in fact all of this is covered by EU law. So I don't believe he is Eurosceptic. If he was, then he could kill the Lisbon Treaty today.

I think you are missing the Realpolitik of this. In his heart and in his gut he is indeed a Eurosceptic, but because of all the traumas the Tory Party has gone through over the last fifteen years, it is a subject which dare not speak its name. I can understand and sympathise with that. There's nothing to be gained by him making a big song and dance over it at the moment.
Other than he has the power to kill the Lisbon Treaty. If he had said we do not recognise the legitimacy of it because the Labour government was elected with a specific manifesto pledge to have a referendum, he could kill it.

We can agree on that, but legally it was a different document even though the substance was the same.
The Labour manifesto didn't say the 'EU Constitution', it said the 'EU Constitutional Treaty'. How can anyone argue that this is not a constitutional treaty? Cameron has had the option of killing the treaty available to him for the last six months.

If Cameron wins the next election with a big majority he will have a mandate to do just that – and be far more trenchant than he could be with a small majority.
Look at his track record and the type of people he has close to him. I see no evidence to have confidence in that point of view whatsoever. He believes in EU membership.

That's where we part company. Your definition of 'Eurosceptic' means come out of the EU, whereas the normal definition does not mean that.
The world has moved on. We could have been having this conversation in 1992 and I would have accepted that view. Nearly two thirds of Britons say no to political union and yes to alternative trading arrangements. If Cameron says we should be part of the EU and says no to alternative trading arrangements, then how is that different to the Lib Dems or the Labour Party?

If your aim is for Britain to withdraw from the EU you will never achieve that with UKIP. You are never going to form a government and you're not likely to get MPs.
There are more ways of winning great political battles without forming a government.

But why not admit that UKIP is a pressure group, not a political party? The only way to achieve your aim of withdrawal is to do it from within one of the other political parties.

Oh Lord, that hasn't worked terribly well, has it? None of the pressure groups in this area have achieved a damn thing. The only person who achieved something was Jimmy Goldsmith. If he had worked from within the Conservative Party we'd have joined the euro in 1999. Because he worked outside the system, he put the fear of God into the Conservative and Labour parties, got them into a half nelson so they promised there would be a referendum before we joined the euro. It was that, and that alone which kept us out.

I can see the logic of that, but surely you would accept that the Conservative Party overall is a far more Eurosceptic party now than it was in 1992?

If UKIP hadn't been there, the Conservative Party probably wouldn't have reached that position. UKIP's achievement has been to take an argument that was considered to be mad and bad and to turn it into a mainstream political argument.

You talked about the mad and the bad. Were you talking about some of your own MEPs?

When you go from a small number of people to a larger number you attract a few people you would rather not have had.

You mean, 20 per cent of your MEPs? How did they get selected in the first place?

Well, I'd rather we got rid people who have transgressed than do nothing. It's part of the weakness of being a small, grassroots-based party where a con man can come along and con people. We have to accept what the weaknesses are. It's also the weakness of being a totally democratic party. We are completely one man one vote. There is no preferential treatment for existing MEPs or party officers.

So entryism is quite easy? You face it at the moment with the BNP don't you?

Entryism is one of the biggest dangers we face and we have to be very alert to it. We have had problems with the BNP but in terms of scale it is minute. If it was greater we would know. There is plenty of intelligence out there. We have been successful in dealing with the problem but it is depressing that the problem keeps coming back.

But people have been quitting UKIP because they say it's not the party they once joined and has been taken over at a grassroots level by people who do not have views they can associate themselves with.

I haven't seen much of that. I think I know what's going on in the party at grassroots level. The BNP issue is there, and I know it's there. We have made it clear that nobody with any past links or associations with the BNP is going to be a candidate or party officer for UKIP at any level. No exceptions, no exemptions. We have said to a lot of people, no, we're not having you. End of conversation. We are a non-racist, non-sectarian, pro-libertarian outfit. We are so far away from the image of the authoritarian right on issue after issue.

Apart from Bob Spink [the Conservative MP who defected to UKIP]…
Bob is an individual and that's fine.

What about the new Libertarian Party? That is a threat to you. You have lost people to it.
[Shrugs] Of course. People join organisations and they think that they are destined to lead these organisations and when it doesn't work out they seek pastures new. You get thwarted ambition. Outside the three main parties you find this all the time. It tends to be people who have got a lot of time and the reason they have got a lot of time is that they are no use at anything else. They haven't got a proper job, they have never achieved a damn thing in their lives and they see joining a political party as a way of putting something on their headed paper. It's human nature. When they find they don't do as well within UKIP as they ought to do, they are happy to go off somewhere else. You'll never stop that. We have suffered as a party from the angry old man syndrome – people with too much time on their hands and a wholly negative view of the world.

But isn't that a good description of many UKIP members, certainly a few years ago? Disgusted of Tunbridge Wells?
That's right! When UKIP started, it was exactly that! We were dominated by half colonels and the Second World War generation. They were fantastic people…

But they're not libertarians, and that's the point I am making…
And that's how the party has changed. You go to a UKIP meeting or the conference and you will see that the party has changed in quite a big way, especially in the last two years. Not in terms of numbers, but the type of people. It has become a lot younger and more professional. We have a youth wing now and we're setting up groups in universities. There will always be a libertarian–authoritarian division. I am encouraged by the quality of the people we are now attracting. I am forty-four, the chairman is thirty-one and the General Secretary is twenty-seven.

It's a very male dominated party, isn't it?
Too much so. I was critical of the Cameron approach to the European candidate selection and I have always felt positive discrimination was demeaning, but when I looked at our results I began to wonder whether we should have done a bit of it ourselves. Marta Andreasson is the one female

candidate we have in a winnable position. There are other women on the lists and there are more women on the NEC, so it is changing, but not fast enough... I have tried very hard to get us away from being negative and constantly outraged. I think I have achieved some of it but we have further to go. I have to think about this a bit more.

Is it a problem for you that you are the only recognisable face of UKIP? You're the only one who gets any media coverage.
Not quite true, but yes, it is a problem. If the punter thinks it's a one man band it's a problem, but it's also a problem in the organisation.

Have you ever thought to yourself since you became leader in 2006: why am I doing this?
Every month when I get my bank statement. What keeps me going is that I genuinely believe in what we are doing. The longer I go on, the more I see the true nature of the EU, the more I feel that someone has to stand up and shout about it. I believe if you want to change things and have an influence over public opinion you won't do it from within a major party. I could have said to hell with this, I want an easy life and go and rejoin the Conservative Party and bite my lip. But I believe in what I am doing.

Do you get a fair crack from the media?
From the broadcast media, when it's related to Europe, yes, I think we do. If the *News at Ten* are doing a European question then they will come to us. They wouldn't have done that ten years ago. But the media can be very ignorant on European issues. I rang the *Today Programme* about the European Arrest Warrant recently. The researcher hadn't a clue what it even was.

What personal strengths have you brought to the role of leader of UKIP?
The ability to work hard, the ability to communicate. Getting round the country doing meeting after meeting is hard work. Being able to enthuse. Hopefully, the ability to speak clearly and put arguments across that people can understand.

What about your weaknesses?
I have many of those [laughs]. I think ... er ... there are some within UKIP and outside who say that, well, he's a drinker and a smoker...

You have been in the papers a couple of times with regard to your drinking. Is that an issue?
No, not really. I live the way I live. To hell with it. If people don't like it... If I can't go for a pint or two after a hard day's work, then something's not right.

If I can delicately point out that there have been stories of it being slightly more than a pint or two…
[Giggles] Well, these things happen. There was one incident when I fell asleep in a bar, yes, but in my defence I had genuinely not got home until 1am the previous night after a meeting in Hampshire and had been up at 3.15am to get the first plane out, and I was done for.

Do you get embarrassed by those sort of stories, or just think, oh sod it?
I don't let it worry me too much.

I can tell. Sticking on the leadership question, there seem to be some plots to oust you at the moment. Is this BNP inspired? Why do people want rid of you.
Not totally. But there are people who think the BNP should move on from the immigration issue to take over the anti-Europe argument too. So some people are doing whatever they can to destabilise UKIP. There are many in the BNP who believe that if UKIP disappears the BNP will be the main beneficiary. In truth, it would be the Conservatives, or the Don't Votes. So there has been a campaign, chiefly through email, to undermine everything we do. And they have managed to pick up one or two useful idiots along the way. It has been a problem and I could give you a couple of names of people who are not UKIP members but they are doing this and fomenting discontent from within. But what do you do when the person causing the problem is an unemployed and unemployable misfit? I have a reputation for ignoring it and getting on with the job, but there are other people in the party who it has really upset.

You were delighted when Bob Spink defected to you, but he doesn't share all your views, does he?
No. Absolutely not. We had a long conversation before he joined and I wanted to be clear about what we were getting. I knew his stance on 42-days, but we are not a party that wants to whip everybody so there are issues where Bob and I don't agree, but there are many where we do.

Is he a rival to you?
I don't know, is he? If he is, that's great! If we have some proper competition within UKIP, that's great. We need it.

What are your realistic expectations in the 2009 European elections? You got 16 per cent and 9 MEPs last time. You're not seriously expecting to beat that, are you?
That depends. The potential to do it is there, because there are a greater number of people out there who agree with the stance that we've got. We

have been around for a few years, people have seen us in the local papers. It's too early to say. The biggest single factor is whether we can raise enough money, early enough, to fight the right campaign.

Now, a very important question. Have you and President Medvedev ever been seen in the same room?
This is a great one, isn't it? I wondered how long it would be. When I first saw him I knew what would happen.

He's not exactly a libertarian, is he?
Not exactly! Although I am very strongly opposed to the policy we are pursuing towards his country; this desire to expand the EU and NATO to take in the Ukraine and Georgia is mad. I have felt this ever since the wall came down. I am not a supporter of Putin or Medvedev but we shouldn't be trying to provoke them.

Hazel Blears

Party affiliation: Labour

Current position: MP for Salford and Eccles

Born: 14 May 1956

Education: Attended Wardley Grammar School in Swinton and then Eccles Sixth Form College before graduating from Nottingham Trent with a BA (Hons) in Law and later from the Chester College of Law.

Family status: Married to Michael Halsall.

Pre-political career: Senior local authority solicitor and a local Councillor for Eccles.

Electoral history: First elected as MP for Salford in 1997, and continues to hold this, a constituency which is now Salford and Eccles. She was appointed Alan Milburn's Parliamentary Private Secretary in 1998, Parliamentary Under-Secretary of State for the Department of Health in 2001 and later promoted to Minister of State in the Home Office in 2003. In 2007 Gordon Brown made her the Secretary of State for Communities and Local Government.

Career highlights: Gaining and holding her seat in Salford for over ten years and reaching such high positions as Minister of State for the Home Office.

Interesting fact: Member of the parliamentary tap-dancing troupe known as Division Belles, along with Caroline Flint, Meg Munn, Jacqui Smith and other female MPs.

Date of interview: October 2008

Extended version

Venue: Secretary of State's office, Department of Communities & Local Government

Total Politics Issue 6, December 2008

There's little doubt that Hazel Blears has become one of the most unpopular politicians of modern times. It's mainly to do with her expenses claims. The image of her brandishing a cheque at the TV cameras came to symbolise the whole expenses scandal. She and her friend Jacqui Smith became cover girls for it.

I first met Hazel back in July 2005 when I was working as chief of staff to David Davis. In the aftermath of the 7/7 bombings I attended meetings with her at the Home Office, where she was Charles Clarke's number two. She was a very effective minister and I remember her being particularly impressive when she chaired a meeting of Muslim groups. She wasn't backward in telling them they had a responsibility to meet.

The thing about Hazel is that no matter what happens to her, she appears to remain cheerful, displaying her trademark chirpy grin at every opportunity. But there's no doubt that her constant happy demeanour winds up a lot of people.

She's always reminded me of a little chipmunk, and that's what I affectionately started to call her on my blog, back in 2006. Someone then Photoshopped a picture of me in a sweatshirt with the slogan 'Nuts About Hazel' on the front. People actually believed I had one.

To my mind, she is a sad loss to frontline politics. She was a good minister, even if I disagreed with her much of the time.

I'd better start with an apology, because it was me that dubbed you the 'ginger chipmunk'. It seems to have caught on a bit.

When David Dimbleby mentioned it on *Question Time*, I had no idea. I thought 'where's this come from?' The upside was that a man called Trevor emailed me after the show and said I was cuter than any chipmunk he had ever met.

Chipmunks *are* cute. They're also very positive.

But they have pudgy cheeks. I haven't got pudgy cheeks! [she pulls at her cheeks]

That's not what I meant. On that programme you seemed very embarrassed at David Dimbleby's suggestion that you might succeed Gordon Brown as Prime Minister. Politicians always seem embarrassed about ambition, yet they encourage everyone else to have it.

There is something disingenuous about people saying they are not ambitious. I am ambitious. Goodness me, think about where I come from, brought up in a two-up, two-down terraced house, parents left school when they were fourteen...

Never got change out of a farthing...

Precisely, lived in a shoebox on the motorway, eighteen of us! My Mum and Dad told me, Hazel, you can be anything. Now that does something to you as a kid because you believe them. It took me three goes to get into Parliament. I have spent eleven years looking for the next job. I'm now a Secretary of State sitting round the Cabinet table and I think, wow. I haven't had a political upbringing and I haven't had that much patronage, I have done it on my own.

A bit like your hero, Barbara Castle.
Absolutely. Everything for Barbara was a fight. I tend to pick my battles, though. I don't think she did. She had guts, she had courage, she was brave

When I told a friend I was interviewing you, he said 'You'll be charmed, she's more normal than most politicians.' Do you think of yourself as normal?
Sometimes I think the word normal is a double-edged sword because if you are normal you could be really boring. I like to think I am in touch and that I have retained through thirty years of political activity a sense that I am a human being, I am a woman and I experience the same things that everyone else does. I have joy, I have despair, I have laughter, I have sorrow. I am quite an emotional person and I am in touch with my feelings. If that makes me a bit different from most politicians then so be it [giggles].

Most politicians think showing emotion is a weakness. Have you ever found it a weakness when you have been in a negotiation and felt angry or howling your eyes out with frustration?
I think if you accept the traditional frame of politics then you will worry about your emotions. It's masculine, macho, tough and the way that you get credit in politics is if you are a tough negotiator and stand your ground. It's 'wild west' stuff. I don't burst into tears or lose my temper in meetings. I am a good Taurean with a very long fuse. I am patient but when I do lose my temper it's not pleasant.

What makes you lose your temper?
[Pauses] I hate rudeness. I like good manners. If people are rude that does something to me. My emotions manifest themselves best in passion. Passion is a much maligned thing in politics. What we have lost over the last few years is a sense of people who care so passionately about what they want to do that they are never going to stop, they are never going to go away, they are determined to get where they want to be because they are driven by wanting to make a big difference. It becomes a prize rather than a tough negotiating stance. In order for you to win, you're winning for someone else. Sometimes I am very, very determined.

Do you think you are a tribal politician?
I think I am! [roars with laughter]

Because you're seen as a Blairite, and they're much less tribal than most. They seek consensus. You strike me as more tribal than most of your Cabinet colleagues.
I got characterised as a 'Blairite' which I think was a convenient label. A lot of commentators and politicians like to think they have defined you, because

then you are easier to deal with. I try not to be put in a box and I try to be me. I have been in Labour Party politics since 1979. For quite a long time I didn't feel at home in the Labour Party with that very traditional Old Labour semi-Marxist analysis – that's not my politics. I am from a working-class background, I wanted to get on. I was ambitious and I make no apologies for that. When Tony Blair and Gordon Brown articulated that ambition and aspiration were OK, I thought, 'at last, this is my home'. It took me twelve years to get into Parliament. I didn't get a seat three weeks before election. By the time I got in, by God I was going to do it and I went out and advocated passionately what we were doing. People said I was toeing the party line, just being a robot. Actually, I believed it. I have always been who I am, I'm Labour. You cut me in half, it's like Blackpool rock. I'm Labour, but I am New Labour.

Do you see any redeeming factors in the modern Conservative Party?
Redeeming factors. Hmm [giggles]. I am a sceptic about all this stuff about repositioning and compassionate, caring Conservatives, but if I am pushed I think the stuff about well-being and about not just always being concerned about the bottom line is welcome, if it's true. But I would not be surprised to see the Tories come out with some really strong tax-cutting lines. Those on the right who believe in a small state, who believe in the survival of the fittest, devil take the hindmost, get down to your core and put more money in people's pockets, and don't invest in public services. They are going to come back because the Tories haven't fundamentally changed.

How do you remain permanently optimistic? You must have thought in the last six months that the game was up but you go on the media and radiate optimism. How on earth do you do that?
I am not arrogant at all, but it is a bit of a gift. It is something I have got. You used the word radiate. I do feel physical. I have been blessed with a cheerful optimistic, positive temperament. I believe in the power of positive energy to change things. If you wake up in the morning and put the duvet over your head then you're going to have a bad day. We all do it! But if you wake up and think, right, what are we going to achieve today then you'll get there. Secondly, I am not unrealistically cheerful. I am not Pollyanna, I am not stupid. I wouldn't be where I am if I were stupid, and it does annoy me if people caricature you as somehow not clever just because you are cheerful. I have a fundamental belief that in the darkest of times people are capable of the most fantastic things and I believe in people.

You sound like Margaret Thatcher! She used to say that!
Oh my God! [laughs]

[Adopts Thatcher voice] Trust the people, Hazel!

But I do! They're clever, they are bright, they have got common sense, they don't expect you to change everything.

Do you understand why some people find you quite irritating and your permanent optimism irritating?

[Pauses, as if genuinely shocked and slightly hurt] I don't know why they find me irritating. It's sad for them if they can't deal with optimism. If you find an unusual person and you find that irritating and you set your framework only to respond to certain types of people then that means you are missing out on an awful lot in life. It's their loss. If people caricature me, who've never met me … that's the bit I really dislike. If you've met me and I have really wound you up, and you think 'God, she's a pain', fine, by all means.

People find it odd that I like you as a politician, but I like the fact you're always so cheerful. But cheerfulness in politics is something many people can't deal with, isn't it?

It depends on people's mindsets. You don't walk in and go 'ha ha ha'. People walk in here with difficult issues about hundreds of millions of pounds. I make big decisions, I take my time, I drill into things, I analyse, I test, I challenge but I do it in a polite, courteous and respectful way.

Do you ever feel daunted by the decisions you have to make? I'm thinking of the aftermath of the 7/7 bombings, for example, when you were at the Home Office.

It was almost a physical shock. I will never forget learning about it from Sky News. The only think that saved me was that by sheer coincidence we had had an exercise a couple of months before about 'what if'; I just thanked God for that. It meant we knew what to do. You just had to take decisions and get on with it. You just do it. Some of the harder decisions you have to take are about the relationships you strike up with people – who you are going to engage with, and how you are going to tackle, particularly in terms of counter terrorism, the biggest threat this country faces, and how you are going to move the country on. It is a big, big responsibility on any politician. I am not daunted, I don't think 'I can't do this'. Every politician has to have an ego. You don't go into politics if you don't have an ego. The danger is when the ego takes over from the intellect. If you're frightened then you're not going to make decisions. The thing I learned in the Home Office is that you have to take decisions. Sometimes you get them right, sometimes you don't. The world is not going to cave in on you just because you get one decision wrong. The worst thing is prevarication.

What do you think of the accusation that you are the most authoritarian government in living memory?

It doesn't irritate me but I find it a bit schizophrenic from Tories. The Tory Party has a real problem with liberty at the moment. It's trying to be on the side of a liberal, libertarian analysis that forgets that everybody's liberty impinges on other people's freedoms. You need to get to a proper balance of individual and collective freedoms and that if you simply say you want to err on the side of individual liberty in every single choice you make, then there will be an awful lot of people who become vulnerable and exposed. It is a fundamental fault line between our parties.

What do you think of the political media? Do we get the political media we deserve?

Twenty-four hour news is really difficult. It's boring and repetitive so it devalues news. It then inevitably deteriorates into comment. We should be clearer about what is news and what is comment in this country. The commentariat – and there are some great columnists – have stepped over the edge of exercising political power. They are not elected. They've never even considered it. In many cases they seem to have more power, certainly than backbenchers and probably as much as Cabinet ministers. I am uncomfortable with that.

Isn't that partly the fault of politicians? Sky News doesn't want to interview a backbencher who will toe the party line, they'd rather have a pundit with an opinion.

I don't know. Ten years in we haven't got many of that sort of backbencher anymore! The days of the pager message and the line to take are long gone![laughs]

What effect is the new media having on the old media?

I think it's having a big effect, bigger than traditional media give it credit for because they feel a bit threatened. Newspapers are doing much more online. I loved seeing *Guardian* print journalists struggling with podcast machines at the Labour conference. In a way I wish the new media had more influence because it is a way of reaching a younger, more diverse audience, people who are not engaged with politics. But there is a danger in blogging that you have always got to be against something. We were in opposition for eighteen years and when you are making tough decisions, some of our Labour Party members would rather be there. There's a corrosiveness to it, if you're not careful. The beauty of new media is that it is much more subversive, more challenging, you can be more informal, but the downside of that is that it can degenerate into just being 'anti'. As you say, I am a positive person. The challenge is to get the new media to be more positive.

Do you swear much?
Very rarely actually.

What makes you swear? A phone call from Gordon Brown?
Certainly not! I'd be purring! [makes a rather erotic purring noise]

What a shame this is a written interview! You recently said that if you weren't in politics, you'd be running a local authority. Doesn't that display a lack of ambition?
[Roars with laughter] If I wasn't in politics and I wanted to be a manager I could be chief executive of a local authority. I was a principal solicitor in local government for fifteen years and without being immodest I am sure I could do it. That's probably where my career path would have taken me, but I always wanted to do politics.

You are now in a position where you could devolve a huge amount of power down to local government. Every local councillor I meet complains that they have no real power and it's all decided centrally. Why haven't you done a bit more of that?
I'd say to you that quite a lot of local councillors who say that lack ambition. If you look at the framework they have got now they have got a huge amount of power. You've got the framework I set up through local area agreements, which allow councils to prioritise locally, but in the end it's taxpayers' money and I make no apology for wanting to know how it is being spent. We've also un-ringfenced £5 billion. It's partly our fault because we created a culture where people had to ask permission and that's deep in the psyche of local government now the challenge is to persuade people to think big. They've got the powers to do things if they want to.

What about the idea of local referendums, which the 'Our Say' campaign is advocating? They do it in other countries, why not here?
We don't do it because it's never been in our culture. Some people will say you have a representative democracy and therefore you elect people to do it on your behalf. I think that is a strong argument. I personally think you shouldn't just elect people every four years and shut up shop. I think you should be able to take more power yourself but I don't think that's just through referendums. Parish councils, of course, have the power to call a poll. But it's a bigger challenge to get involved with, for example, participatory budgeting where local people get to decide on street repair priorities, for example, or which projects are priorities for community punishment teams, dressed in their 'high vis' jackets...

You got into trouble over them, didn't you?
Well, do you know, they are wearing them now. You see, I'm a prophet in my own time!

Are there too many one-party states in local government? Don't they breed corruption?
Well there are less of them now! [laughs] Having someone challenging you is quite important in formulating ideas and getting things to happen but it's too broad to say they are corrupt. Manchester is a Tory-free zone but the leadership of the Council there has transformed the City. It's got ambition, it's got aspiration and it's incredibly well led. That isn't the case in some areas which are dominated by one party and they can be as dull as ditch water.

But with annual elections it is sometimes difficult to remove an incompetent and corrupt council in one fell swoop. Why not abolish annual elections?
There are arguments on both sides, but local authorities now have the power to do it if they want to. My personal view is that if you have an all out election there is a clearer choice. There's a clearer mandate, there's a platform, a manifesto. But equally, all the evidence is that if you do that, the parties stop campaigning in the intervening years so you have less political engagement.

Some people thought you were behind some of the moves to destabilise Gordon Brown over the summer.
The things you read in the paper that come from briefings are often a complete and utter surprise to you. It's not something I do, I have never done it and I am not sure it's effective. The people who do it don't achieve what they set out to and I think what they do is even more damaging so I have very little patience with it.

There must have been a time over the summer when you thought to yourself, is he [Gordon Brown] going to be able to pull it off.
[Pauses] What I was concerned about was that there was a time when I don't think we were as decisive and focused as we needed to be. What you have seen in the last few months is a recognition of that and an absolute determination to lead from the front, make decisions, get on with it and address the fears and anxieties of the British people. There has been a major shift in the last few months about where we are. My overriding desire is to win for Labour, right? I have seen what a Tory government does and I remember what it was like. I want to keep a Labour government in power for as long as I possibly can. That's why I wanted us to get a sense of energy out there.

What's it like having Peter Mandelson round the Cabinet table?
It's more fun! There's a bit of banter. When people have a relationship that goes back a long time they will have been through experiences with you, they've seen how you respond, they'll wind you up a bit and make you laugh. Peter also brings a great stillness at the centre of him, an anchor, and I think that's partly because of what he has been through in politics. He's recognised what's dross and what's important. He has a real centre to him.

A little bird tells me you subscribe to a magazine called *Ride*. My mind is working overtime. What kind of magazine is it exactly?
It's a motorbike magazine! There's another one called *Bike* which we take as well. It's full of stories, brilliant writing. Some of it's written by a guy called Dan Walsh who by pure coincidence lives in a flat 100 yards from us. So my hero lives almost next door!

What do you get out of riding a motorbike?
Freedom, a bit of anti-authoritarianism, a bit of thank God I've got home and I am still alive, and if I am honest, it's a bit of posing. I do like to look in the window of the shop as you go past. You've got your leathers on, your bike's glinting a bit and you think, hmm, not bad.

I hear you are taking dancing lessons? Is this because you want to be on *Strictly Come Dancing* with Vince Cable?
I'd love to do it. I can't do it while I am in government – you have to take seven weeks out. Vince Cable is keen to do it but they won't do it unless there's political balance so Vince and I may well be up there one day. I watch it every week. We're also reforming the Division Belles [a tap dance troupe of female MPs] and we're having lessons every Monday night doing songs from the shows [collapses in a fit of giggles].

Isn't tap dancing one of the most pointless forms of dance?
No! You get to move around and make a lot of noise [giggles].

It's not exactly *Riverdance* is it? *Riverdance* was phenomenal.
It's better than *Riverdance*! At least you move your arms in tap. Have you never danced? Why not? There is an inner dancer in you that needs to be liberated. I'm going to get Brucie to talk to you!

You said recently that you rather fancy Gene Hunt from *Life on Mars*. You like real men, don't you, and think David Cameron is a bit of a wuss.
[Giggles] That's interesting. My husband's not very tall and he's cleverer than me. He's a man's man and not given to great emotional flourishes. I have

more than enough for the both of us. He is a lawyer now but was a physicist so he has a very enquiring mind. He doesn't really do a lot of 'feelings'. There's a bit of me with Gene Hunt that, well, I know it's terribly politically incorrect but I just love the 'let's go out there and get 'em' approach. One of my first boyfriends had a Lotus Cortina – basically a Ford with a Lotus engine. It went like stink.

Tony Benn

Party affiliation: Labour

Current position: President of the Stop The War Coalition

Born: 3 April 1925

Education: Educated at Westminster School and later studied Philosophy, Politics and Economics at New College, Oxford University.

Family status: Was married to Caroline Middleton DeCamp until her death in 2000. They had four children.

Pre-political career: Joined the air force and served in South Africa and Rhodesia, after which he worked for a short time at the BBC.

Electoral history: In 1951 Benn was elected as an MP for Bristol South East and was, at the time, the youngest Member of Parliament. He continued in a variety of roles, from Minister of Technology to Secretary State of Industry and in both 1981 and 1988 stood for election as deputy leader of the Labour Party, losing on both occasions. He retired from Westminster as an MP in 2001.

Career highlights: Only losing his 1981 contest for leadership by barely 1 per cent and then eventually becoming President of the Stop The War Coalition.

Interesting fact: Oversaw the first commemorative stamps and changed the Queen's head to just a silhouette.

Date of interview: January 2009
Extended version
Venue: Holland Park, London
Total Politics Issue 8, February 2009

When I was growing up and first became politically aware, to me, Tony Benn was the political devil incarnate. In the early 1980s he and his adherents came very close to ruining the Labour Party. And yet twenty years on he became a political hero to millions. He left Parliament in 2001 to, as he put it, 'spend more time on politics'. His one-man theatre shows have played to audiences of thousands up and down the country.

I first met Tony Benn when I was running Politico's. He would come in and call me his favourite Thatcherite entrepreneur. We made two videos together (back in the days when VHS was still watched), one of his best

parliamentary speeches. He was a pleasure to work with and we struck up a good rapport.

Harold Wilson once said of Tony Benn that he 'immatures with age'. I'm not sure I would put it that way, but he has certainly become more left wing the older he gets. Has he got more principled? I'm not so sure. He's certainly changed his mind on a lot of things. Although he decries the politics of personality, Tony Benn is very adept at using populist language and positioning to his own advantage. Nothing wrong with that, but it can lead to charges of hypocrisy.

Tony Benn's legacy will be his wonderful diaries. I have read every word of each of the eight volumes. The last one was especially evocative as he described the death of his beloved wife, Caroline. It also made painful reading as he catalogued his own declining health.

When you stood down from Parliament did you think you would enjoy your post-parliamentary life?

Before she died, my wife Caroline said, when you do stand down (and we had agreed I would) you should say it's to devote more time to politics. It was a joke but also serious, and that's exactly what I have done. I have never been busier. Last year I did 161 public meetings, 175 broadcasts and I go round supporting the causes I believe in and do my theatre performances, which are the equivalent of a constituency meeting. You are not asking people to vote for you but the people who come are generally not of your opinion. I get from that something I used to get from constituency work. I was seventy-six when I gave up and the strain of getting up at 5am every Friday to go to the constituency to do your surgery was getting a bit much. I don't have a secretary. I do all my own letters and emails so it's a busy life, but I am enjoying it very much.

Do you miss the parliamentary side of politics?

The Speaker gave me and Ted Heath a pass called the 'Freedom of the House' and I go there a couple of times a week. What I miss is the constituency. I miss the surgeries. They were very emotional events because people would often burst into tears and unload their problems. If you are a conscientious constituency Member you are really in touch with what people are thinking. You're not there to lecture them on your ideology. You're there to help, and that's what I miss most.

The constituency side is a big part of the job, but it's largely ignored by the Westminster media, isn't it?

They say MPs are out of touch but most MPs are diligent and hold regular surgeries. No journalist does that – it's not part of their job, of course, but the idea that journalists are in closer touch with public opinion than MPs is wrong. I once filmed a surgery. It will never be shown, but I wanted a reminder of what surgeries are like. A man who had had a stroke burst into tears, a mother told me of the sexual abuse of her child. It was so moving. It would make a fantastic television programme, but you couldn't use real people because it's secret, but it does show the relationship between real life and politics.

You were quite outspoken about the Damian Green arrest, partly because of the dangers of that confidential relationship between constituent and MP apparently being breached.

It was an outrage to go into a Member's office and go through his files. If you write to an MP it's like going to a doctor or a lawyer. It's a confidential relationship. If people thought the police could get hold of what they said to an MP the whole thing would come to an end. They have turned the House of Commons into a government department. Originally the House of Commons used to control the Executive, but now the House of Commons is a government department with the Leader of the House in charge.

Whose fault is that?

The pressure from underneath has been defused in a whole series of ways. It will come right again when the pressure builds up. All progress has always come from underneath, by demands that are made that can't be resisted. That's why I spend all my time now on grassroots things, supporting pensioners, students, firefighters or whoever it happens to be. When the pressure gets to a certain point the guys at the top have to listen.

Isn't it partly the fault of MPs themselves? They have allowed the Executive to get so many powers and to bypass Parliament.

Yes, I agree. The Damian Green case is a good example. I went to speak for David Davis because I felt so strongly about the 42-days issue. It was a principle. I must be the only Labour candidate to have had a letter from Winston Churchill endorsing me. He wrote it when I was thrown out of Parliament because he saw it as a principle. I photocopied 50,000 copies of it!

So your cross-party alliances go back nearly fifty years!

On issues where we can agree, yes. I think politics has become far too tribal. There should be less hostility and more of the argument and then you would find people coming together from different sides on different issues.

Do you think the age of the political party is drawing to a close?

I have heard that said, but on the other hand how do you get anything done?

I joined the Labour Party in 1942. I have seen it swing from left to right. It isn't a socialist party, but it is a party with socialists in it. When you look at all the alternatives, all the left groups – Socialist Labour Party, Socialist Party, Socialist Workers Party, Communist Party and the rest – there's no future in ideological splits so you work with the people with whom you feel most comfortable, and that's the Labour Party. The whole idea of leaving everything to the market is discredited. The effect of a slump is not only economical but political. It produced Mosley in the thirties – I had tea in his house at the age of three in 1928. The next time I saw him he was in a black shirt in Parliament Square. That, plus war, radicalised people. But the Labour Party didn't surge to the left ideologically in 1945. Attlee was a practical man, he said let's utilise the wartime spirit to deal with the problems of peace and provide food, homes and health for the nation.

Do you think that's what Gordon Brown is doing now, trying to evoke a wartime spirit using the language of Churchill and Roosevelt?
He's talking in that way yes, and I think public opinion is ready to accept that now. It's a realisation that when it comes down to it, the things that really matter are very simple and you have a responsibility as a government to address people's problems. British politics has never been dominated by ideology pure and simple.

Keith Joseph said he only realised in 1974 he had not, until that point, been a true Conservative. Did you have a similar epiphany when you lost office in 1979 and only then did you become a real Socialist?
Not really. I think office turned me to the left. I realised when I was there that shouting 'Thatcher Out' didn't get you very far. But when the American Ambassador delivered a note about energy – and in diplomatic terms, when one government sends a note to another government, Whitehall quivered. And he came to see me. You realise that when you are there you are locked into a system that you don't control, and that was what really radicalised me. Europe makes laws we have to obey. We don't elect the Commission. They decide the agenda. So this wasn't a swing back to my faith from being in office, it was the development of my understanding in office which gave me the confidence to put forward my arguments when I was out of office.

It's difficult as a Minister, when you are bound by collective responsibility, to drive forward an individual agenda. You are always compromised by the system.
Not really. I developed a way of dealing with that. I realised that collective responsibility applied to the present parliament, so I would say 'looking ahead ten years this is what we will have to think about…' so I could open up a whole area. They couldn't get me on that. I would also say 'I'm getting

an awful lot of letters at the moment saying this, that or the other...' It didn't please colleagues but I think that on the whole a government where it is known there is a debate going on is more credible than the pretence of unanimity. The idea that a Cabinet is unanimous on every issue isn't true and everybody knows it isn't true.

That boxes you in as a minister because you are never going to get one of the top jobs if you are seen as a maverick.
It isn't about that. I was defeated many times. The biggest of all was in 1976 over public spending cuts and the IMF. I thought it was wrong. The oil was bubbling ashore and I tried to persuade the Treasury to publish the gold, oil and dollar reserves every month, in which case we could have said boo to the IMF. I lost the battle, but I give full marks to Jim [Callaghan]. He allowed the debate. The Cabinet was a really interesting, clever group of people. It was riveting. At the end of it all I was able to say, well, you know my view, but this was a decision and I am a member of the government and I accept the decision. I never minded being defeated as long as I had a chance to put my case. There's a credibility about that position.

And you never came close to resigning?
I went to my local party in Bristol. I am probably the only Minister who ever did it, and I said I want you to tell me whether I should resign. If they had asked me to, I would have stuck to it. In the end they said 'stick it out, say what you think, and if you are sacked, we will support you'. I did think that through very carefully. If you're in Cabinet you lose half the time and win half the time, but if you resign and then there's a vote of confidence, do you then vote for the government you've resigned from, or not? I came to the conclusion that if I had argued my point and lost it was a credible position to accept the decision and move on. I could never have voted for a war. In 2003 if I had been a Minister I just couldn't have stayed in the government, but it's very rare for it to be of that degree of magnitude.

In your eleven years as a Minister what is the one achievement you'd single out?
Maybe the creation of the Giro Bank. By the time Mrs Thatcher abolished it, it was the fifth largest bank in Britain. But I would like to be remembered for having encouraged people. It sounds very innocent, but if you have given people confidence that they can do something, that is a real achievement. I look back and think, have I always explained things to people truthfully? Have I always said what I meant and meant what I said? And as a result of that, have I encouraged people to have confidence in themselves? All I would want on my gravestone would be: 'Here Lies Tony Benn: He Encouraged Us.'

Do you think about death? Is it something you fear?
Well, I'm eighty-four. I don't mind being dead. I don't want the circumstances to be too unpleasant. Until about a hundred years ago, no one knew what they were dying of. They just felt unwell, got into bed and died. Death is a natural part of the process of life.

Does the physical limitation manifested by old age frustrate you?
I haven't the energy I had. I was on a march in Trafalgar Square and holding a banner, and being pushed by the people behind. That made me reach the limits of my physical capabilities. I'm trying to write a book with a brilliant title of 'A Letter to my Grandchildren'. It details what I have learned about war, violence, religion and the economy. It's not my life story, but it's the things I think I have learned. It's a challenge because it has to be credible to that generation when they read it. I'm not trying to force them to share my views but I am using my experience to explain.

Your granddaughter Emily is standing for Parliament at the age of nineteen. What do you think of the continuation of the Benn dynasty, and do people of that age have enough life experience?
I didn't get elected to Parliament in 1950 because my Dad had been an MP. She's doing it on her own merits. She's a very clever girl and very active. She's fighting Worthing, which is not a Labour seat. When I came back from the war I was twenty. I had been a pilot for three years and I was furious that I wasn't allowed to cast a vote. The principle of no taxation without representation is a good one. I am in favour of votes at sixteen. It would radically alter things at school. If teachers had to respect that pupils had the same vote as they do, it would change a lot. We don't apply criteria to voting, do we? We don't have an education test, or a literacy test, you have an inherent right to have some say in the laws you are expected to obey. Why should someone aged sixteen obey a law passed by someone he didn't elect and can't remove and who doesn't need to listen? It's the European argument again, on which you and I would agree.

How would history have been different if you had become deputy leader of the Labour Party in 1981? After all, you only lost by half a per cent.
I took the view that an election campaign was an opportunity to present an argument. I wasn't motivated by the single-minded hope of winning. Obviously if I had won I would have been thrilled to have won, but I don't know how it would have changed things. I know people find it hard to believe but I don't think about that particularly. I stood, I campaigned, I said what I thought and I lost. The people who defeated me all joined the SDP, so without them I did defeat Healey, but that's by the by.

Do you think the Labour Party in power and the Labour Party in opposition are two different parties?
Not really. If you look at the Labour Party in the thirties Cripps was expelled, Foot was expelled, Nye Bevan was expelled but they still played their part when an election came. Government is hard work and you are locked into a system you don't control and even more so now, where 80 per cent of our laws are made in Europe. I find the role of European Commissioner even more offensive than the House of Lords. The Commissioners can do what they like and can't be criticised. When I was President of the Energy Council of Ministers I found I couldn't even put in a document. Only the Commissioner could. It's as if I had gone into the Energy Department and only the Permanent Secretary could say what should happen. You could veto it, but you couldn't put in another paper. The whole European argument for me is a democratic one and not about nationalism. I am not a nationalist at all. I was very pleased to go to Ireland and see the Lisbon Treaty defeated.

What's the solution?
There are three solutions. The status quo, which is fundamentally undemocratic and will crack up. There's a United States of Europe which would be democratic but cumbersome. But I have always favoured a Commonwealth of Europe. Get rid of the Commission and have a Secretary General. The countries would adhere to it from their national parliaments. It would be slower, but more democratic. I would like to see the Russians brought in. It's ridiculous that they are not included in the European family of nations now that the Cold War is over.

Do you think the Cold War would have ended if Britain had adopted the unilateralist agenda you advocated in the 1980s?
I saw Gorbachev a few years ago at the TUC and I said to him, if we had been friendly to Russia after the revolution would Perestroika have come earlier? He said it was an interesting idea. I gave a talk to seventy senior defence staff at the Defence College at Shrivenham recently to talk about alternatives to war. I thought they were going to chew me up for breakfast. But it was a riveting discussion. I asked how many of them believed that it was because we had nuclear weapons the Soviet Union didn't attack the West. Only two put their hands up. There never was military threat. There was an ideological threat from Communism.

Sorry, but you cannot seriously say there was no military threat from the Soviet Union...
There was no military threat to the West, no.

Well why did they have all the missiles?
Well why did we have all the missiles? We had them before they did. What's the point of nuclear weapons? You can't use them. They didn't help the Americans in the war against Iraq. The Israelis have got them but they're not helping them in Gaza.

My point was that the Cold War would not have come to an end, or the Communist system brought to its knees without the policy of multilateralism in the 1980s and indeed rearmament on the part of the West.
I understand the argument but I don't believe that. It's an illusion. The European Union was set up to save capitalism in Western Europe and NATO was set up to protect capitalism. They were really a diversion.

Wasn't it a scandal that Tony Blair committed us to renewing our own nuclear deterrent without any sort of debate about Britain's future strategic defence needs? Didn't that illustrate what is wrong with our politics today?
The existence of nuclear weapons destroys democracy. You can't ask any questions. There's no accountability. Do you really believe Gordon Brown would ever press the button? I don't. I resigned as a front bench defence spokesman in 1958 because I said I couldn't support the use of nuclear weapons. Perhaps that's what we should do – press Gordon Brown on whether he would press the button. He would be put in a very awkward position.

Keynes once said, when the facts change, I change my mind. What have you changed your mind on?
Many things. Nuclear power, for example. In 1955 when Eisenhower said he was going for 'Atoms for Peace' I became a passionate supporter of it. Having been brought up on the Bible I liked the idea of swords into ploughshares. I advocated it as Minister of Technology. I was told, and believed, that nuclear power was cheap and safe and peaceful. Having been in charge of nuclear power I discovered it wasn't cheap, wasn't safe and when I left office I was told that during my period as Secretary of State for Energy plutonium from our nuclear power stations went to the Pentagon to make nuclear weapons. So every nuclear power station in Britain is a bomb factory for America. I was utterly shaken by that. Nothing in the world would now induce me to support nuclear power. It was a mistake.

Israel is another one. I was rowing on the Sea of Galilee in May 1945 when the war ended. I was all in favour of a Jewish homeland, but now I see what has happened and it was absolutely wrong.

Why do you go on demonstrations against Israel, yet say nothing against the launching of rockets into Israel by Hamas?
The Israelis have blockaded Gaza for two years. They have arrested ships that

bring supplies. They occupied Gaza for many years. Israel is the American instrument for the domination of the Middle East. Hamas is an elected government. Hamas won but no one will talk to them.

What do you hope for from Barack Obama?
He raised hope among the American people. He built a movement. He transformed American opinion. America is a declining empire. In the end it will change. Obama is imaginative. Attlee was an imaginative leader managing a declining empire too. How declining empires decline without bloodshed is the great task.

Do you think people are hoping for too much from Obama, are their expectations of immediate, radical change too high?
Well, how does change occur? It occurs when the demands get so strong that the guys at the top cannot resist. It can't come from the top, it has to come from underneath. You're right, Obama is locked into the Pentagon. Remember that Roosevelt was elected on a very conservative programme in 1932 but when he got there he effected change...

But government was so much smaller then. The state is like an oil tanker now, so vast, so intrusive and all pervasive, partly because of technology, that it's difficult to put it into reverse. And there are so many vested interests ranged against you.
But it is possible. Look at history. I've been thinking about world government and if you had a world government based on the normal principles of constituency members, China would have two billion votes at the UN, India would have two billion, the USA four hundred million and the UK sixty million. That transformation would be fantastic, wouldn't it?

If you say so! [laughs] I don't wish to be governed by the Chinese.
But that was the argument used in 1832. You cannot let the poor have the vote. They will challenge the rich.

No, no. It's nothing to do with that. I would love the Chinese to have the vote in their own country, but I do not wish to endorse a system which would give China any powers over my life, thank you very much!
The most revolutionary idea is democracy. Nobody in power likes sharing power with anyone else. Democracy transfers power from the market place to the polling station, from the wallet to the ballot. Stalin wouldn't allow it, Bush isn't all that keen on it and you're not wildly enthusiastic about it...

I am totally enthusiastic about democracy...
Not globally.

No, because I believe in nation states, not world government. You admit you are disillusioned with the EU, why should a world government be any different to that? Globalisation is spoken of in such a narrow sense. We live in a world which is now a village, where news travels quickly but without any democratic control. Fear is what makes the guys at the top concede power. The only reason we ever got democracy was because they thought that if they didn't concede it there would be a revolution.

Did you, as a Cabinet minister, ever feel you had real power – that you could change things with the stroke of your pen?
No. The only way you could change something was by arguing for it. The internet is where the power is nowadays. That's why the Chinese are clamping down on Google, and why the Americans are altering entries in Wikipedia.

You like your gadgets and you are quite internet savvy, aren't you?
Not as much as you, but my grandson keeps me up to date. He can get on my computer if it goes wrong. I just sit here and watch the mouse whizz round. The internet is great for organising meetings and protest marches. It's a formidable organisational power. My 12-year-old granddaughter just emailed me a paper she has written on the Chinese policy of one child per family. She had Googled all the information. It was fantastic. I have a lot of time for the younger generation yet the old treat the young with arrogance, but it is we who made such a cock up of the world. One hundred and five million people killed in two world wars, yet we lecture them on violence in Africa. We lecture kids about hideous stabbings, yet compared to what we have done... A little bit of modesty by the old is not inappropriate.

Do you think the internet is a force for good in democratic terms?
Yes, it's empowering. People talk a lot about inaccurate information on the net but there are also a lot of bad books around. You have to make up your own mind. Access is the key. I am an optimist. This is the first generation in history which has the technology to destroy the human race, but it is also the first generation to have the ability, technological knowhow and the money to solve the problems of the human race.

Does the spontaneity on the internet and the 24-hour news agenda damage democracy? Everyone wants an instant reaction. There's no time to think.
I know what you mean, but ignorant people have played leading roles in world politics for a long time! Read some of the Victorian speeches on the Empire. Ignorance should not be a barrier to discussion and we have to hope that good ideas will beat bad ideas. It depends on the media. The BBC has a rule never to report a speech on a public meeting, unless of course it is in

support of Greg Dyke. If the public could ever hear anything directly which hadn't gone through Paxman or Humphrys or Jon Snow it would undermine their authority.

Who's your favourite interviewer?
I like Jon Snow very much. I get on well with Paxman.

If you were Chancellor of the Exchequer, what would you be doing now?
It's very difficult, but the all-party market philosophy running from the monetarism of Callaghan and Thatcher through to Blair has failed. I am not looking for scapegoats but it has failed. The case for the banks, like the army, police and health service to be publically owned is unanswerable. If you put it like that people think it's sensible. Thatcher was a very clever woman. She realised that if you were going to reverse what had been done after the war you had to destroy trade unionism, which she did with the miners and then made trade unionism illegal.

She did nothing of the sort, apart from GCHQ.
Well, no, but the legislation is worse than in 1906. She then said to people you don't need a wage claim, borrow. She created a debt slavery then she destroyed local government and began privatisation. She understood that local government, trade unionism and public ownership were the foundations of the Labour Party. Blair was a Thatcherite. She even said that her greatest achievement was New Labour! She's right and that's why Blair had such a wonderful press. That whole philosophy crumbled with the credit crunch. You now have to intervene publically. Look at the rail fares and energy companies. How many people really think those privatisations were sensible? If you could make such huge profits, why doesn't it go to the Treasury?

It does, in business taxes.
A lot of the things we argued for I could make a case for. But the big thing is recognising that it is global in character and how you cope with that. That's why in the end there will have to be some form of global system. The IMF and WTO, like the EU, are run by people who are not elected and cannot be removed. They don't listen to you or me in Brussels, or the WTO or IMF. They are running a global dictatorship of the wealthy. How can you have any system which calls itself global without any form of accountability to the people who have to obey it? The older I get, the more idealistic I become. Now I know what the world is like, I realise the importance of having a dream.

So Harold Wilson was right. You have immatured with age!
That was one of the nicest things ever said about me! You have to retain

some dream. I have a dream of a non-aligned, non-nuclear Britain with a special relationship with the UN.

What do you make of David Cameron?
I have only met him once. He told me his interest in politics began when he read my book *Arguments for Democracy*. I saw him at the unveiling of the Mandela statue and told him it was a pity he didn't read *Arguments for Socialism*! I do try, seriously, not to think in terms of personalities.

I'm going to take issue with you because I think personality is incredibly important in politics. Personalities define which direction a country goes in. Blair would be doing very different things now to Brown, partly because of his personality. Thatcher was a force in politics because her personality drove things through. Churchill's personality was vital to Britain winning the war.
I'm not sure. It wasn't Churchill's personality but what he said. He articulated something which gave us an understanding. Blair didn't give us any understanding of anything and he won't be remembered. Mrs Thatcher will be remembered. The idea of a spin doctor controlling Mrs Thatcher was laughable. She was a signpost, not a weathervane, although she was a signpost which pointed in the wrong direction.

You always got on quite well with her, didn't you?
She came to Eric Heffer's funeral. There was someone behind me coughing. I didn't know who it was but after I had gone up to speak I saw it was her, so I thanked her for coming. She burst into tears.

Who were the two or three parliamentarians you think made a difference during your fifty years there? I know you have been quite kind about Enoch Powell.
He said what he meant. Someone once said that Enoch Powell had the finest mind in Parliament until he made it up. The last time I spoke to him, he said, you do realise that Lord Mountbatten was murdered by the Americans, don't you? He said it to me in the library in the Commons. I said, what do you mean? He said, well, Mountbatten was against nuclear weapons and that wasn't acceptable. I'm just reporting to you what he said as an illustration of his judgment. The 'Rivers of Blood' speech was a speech of a professor of Greek. It did enormous damage, I don't think he meant it to, but it released something which was very dangerous to society. Compared to the thinkers, though … I mean, why do we still study Moses, Jesus, Mohammed. It's because they explain the world. In so far as I have any function now, it is to try to use such experience as I have to give my best explanation. I describe myself as an untrained classroom assistant to the nation.

What's your everyday life like?
It's a bit of a struggle to be honest. I come down here to my basement office in the morning and there are up to 150 emails waiting and then there's the letters and organising engagements. My family are very supportive.

Do you get lonely?
Yes, but I have lots of friends, but it's nine years since I have been alone and Caroline died.

You're still keeping up the diary, I assume?
Yes, but it's not very interesting at the moment. I have been writing it for sixty-seven years now. I was looking at some previous entries the other day and came across a funny story. I had just come out of my publishers in Vauxhall Bridge Road, and at my age your bladder can play up a bit. It was clear I wouldn't make it home in time. So I got out of the car, opened the hood, looked in and, well, did what I needed to do. A man came up and said: 'I think I know your problem.' 'Oh yes,' I said, 'what's that?' 'I think your radiator is leaking.' I zipped up, closed the hood and drove off [roars with laughter]. People are so kind. I've never mentioned my bladder problem, but from all over the world I get emails offering me Viagra. Isn't that sweet of them?! I tell this at my theatre shows and I can see the audience not quite sure if I am joking, or if I know what Viagra is.

A good note to end on.

David Cameron

Party affiliation: Conservative

Current position: Prime Minister

Born: 9 October 1966

Education: Educated at Eton and Brasenose College, Oxford, before graduating from Oxford University with a first class honours degree in Politics, Philosophy and Economics.

Family status: Married with three children.

Pre-political career: He was Head of Corporate Affairs at Carlton Communications

Electoral history: Elected Conservative MP for Witney, West Oxfordshire, in 2001, later becoming deputy Chairman of the Conservative Party and then shadow Secretary of State for Education and Skills. He became leader of the Conservative Party in December 2005 and became Prime Minister to a coalition government with the Liberal Democrats in May 2010.

Career highlights: Becoming Prime Minister of the United Kingdom on 11 May 2010, making him the youngest prime minister for nearly two hundred years.

Interesting facts: David Cameron chose Benny Hill's 1971 hit 'Ernie (The Fastest Milkman in the West)' on Radio 4's *Desert Island Discs* because, as he told Sue Lawley, it was the only song he knew all the words to. Also, he is a direct descendant of King William IV.

Date of interview: January 2009
Extended version
Venue: Leader of the Opposition's office, House of Commons
Total Politics Issue 9, March 2009

My relationship with David Cameron could have got off to a better start. Back in 2003 I wrote a magazine article which sought to predict who would be at the top of politics in 2013. Of David Cameron I wrote that although some people were predicting he would be a future Tory leader it was hard to work out what he had achieved during his first two years in the House of Commons. And guess what? Two weeks later I was sat next to him at a Policy Exchange dinner. I brought the subject up and he roared with laughter, saying it had made him think about just what he really had achieved in his first two years in Parliament. He easily defused what could have been quite an awkward situation.

A few months later he drove up to North Norfolk in his battered old Skoda to spend a day supporting my election campaign. He had a great time and told me I had got him more local press coverage than anyone else had managed to achieve.

Had my old friend David Davis not run for the Tory leadership (I was his chief of staff during his leadership campaign) I would have undoubtedly supported David Cameron. Easy to say now, but it's true.

Sitting in the reception area of David Cameron's House of Commons office suite, I observed two pictures on the wall of Baldwin and Disraeli. A consolidator and a social reforming radical. As I walked into his office he immediately told me that he'd just been looking at my blog. I tried desperately to remember what I had written earlier that morning. He was fascinated by a County Court fining Labour MP Ann Keen for being lazy. 'Is she really lazy?' he asked, displaying a neat penchant for Commons gossip. As we sat down, I reflected on the fact that the last time I had sat in that seat was in July 2005, when I was meeting Michael Howard's confidante Rachel Whetstone to discuss the transfer of power if David Davis won the Tory leadership election. At that point David Cameron didn't figure in many people's calculations. Three years later, he was tipped by Ladbroke's as a racing certainty to become Britain's next Prime Minister.

It's 5 June 2010, you've just done your 'where there is discord, may be bring harmony' bit, you've opened the bottle of Newky Brown which Gordon Brown has left you as a welcome present. What's the first thing that Prime Minister Cameron does on day one in office?
I sometimes get that question at my Cameron Direct town hall meetings. I never have a satisfactory answer because I don't think like that.

But when you started out in politics there must have been one thing, which you thought, if I ever get the chance, I'm going to do this.
I don't think, literally, at five past eleven I appointed this person, or fired that person. I know exactly what I want to do in the early part of a Conservative government, if we are elected, and that is education reform and the family policies we have set out. Those are the things that I am most passionate about. But we will face an enormous economic challenge so our first task will be sorting out the finances and getting the economy back on track and restore confidence. We won't be able to do everything else that we have set out in vast detail, we will have to be clear about the early priorities. Education will be absolutely right up there. That's the thing I have a personal passion for, as well as a political one.

Boris's answer when I asked him that question was that he would 'rejoice'.
[Laughs] I think you are allowed a small moment!

What made you decide to do your Cameron Direct town hall meetings?
I'm genuinely a bit bored of the routine of going somewhere, having a meeting with some people, going to see local worthies, and then going home again. I found the McCain New Hampshire meetings riveting. I enjoy them, I like public meetings. It's a great way of getting around all the marginal seats, helping them...

But you only get to 200 people at a time at these meetings.
The deal is that if you want a Cameron Direct in your constituency you have to deliver 8,000 leaflets and get the local media to cover it. So everyone does a lot. The idea is that after you've been to, say Chatham & Aylesford, half the people will have known about the event, even if they couldn't come. Politics is getting more personal. People want to make a connection from their area to a political party and the person who wants to be Prime Minister and say, 'Yes, actually he made the effort. He came here, he listened to particular issues.' That is an important connection to make. When it comes to the election you're asking people to vote for a party they didn't vote for before and to give up the MP that maybe they quite liked. You've got to help them over that and say, 'Look, OK, Joe Blogs might have worked for you, but if you want change in Britain, if you want a Conservative government, if you want Gordon Brown to leave Number 10, this is the step you've got to take. Although I've done twenty-six or twenty-seven of them, I really enjoy them, they're good fun, and a very good way of keeping in touch with what people's concerns are, because they vary from time to time. And it's also a good way of testing out your arguments and seeing where there are gaps in your approach.

What's the question you get where your heart sinks and you think, oh no, not again?
[Long pause] The question you get which you always give a disappointing answer to is university fees. There are always young people there who are worried about debt, and it would be lovely to say we're going to get rid of all these top-up fees and tuition fees, but you can't, so you have to give an answer that is truly disappointing. That's another good thing about these meetings; they make you confront the fact that you have to give people some straight talk, as John McCain would say. If you haven't disappointed a few people when you've left the room, you're not doing it properly, in a way. Increasingly people are asking about the economy as we face this enormous economic and fiscal crisis.

Do you fear the economy is going to derail a lot of the things you want to do, because the situation is so serious?

I think inevitably it is going to change what a government can achieve. We've got to be honest about that. We are going to be facing a situation where we are already borrowing 8 per cent of our GDP. If the economic forecasts change at the budget it could be a lot more than that. It is a fiscal crisis. It won't be possible to do all the things we want to do. We have set out a lot of policy detail in a lot of areas but we can't do everything at once so we will have to be rigorous in prioritising. And we will have to do tough and difficult things as well. We have to prepare people for that over the coming months. I'm really getting a sense that people understand that. Six or nine months ago people were saying: 'Get rid of them, they're hopeless.' Now, it's much more 'Gosh, this is going to be incredibly tough, you've got to do it, but it's going to be tough'. There's a mood change. The country senses the state of the economy.

Mark Field wrote on ConservativeHome that there will be three stages to this recession: fear, then anxiety followed by anger.

There is an anxiety, which is turning into anger. Before Christmas, people were very anxious. To start with, they turned back to the government for a bit. The first thing you do when you are anxious is 'what's the government going to do to get us out of this mess?' They got the benefit of the doubt. It's changed since the New Year. I have a clear memory of going home and watching on the *Ten O'Clock News* the announcement of the second bank bailout. As a citizen, not as a politician, I just thought 'God, this government has completely lost control of things.' They don't know what they're doing and they are behaving like headless chickens and the things they have done don't seem to be working. I think what's happened since the beginning of this year is that the Conservative Party has pulled itself together in a good way. The reshuffle was very important. It is good to have Ken Clarke back. I think our campaign on debt and helping savers has been a positive thing. I think there has been a mood change. At the same time, the government is not saving the world, they are trying to save their own skins and they don't know how.

Do you worry that the move back in the polls towards the Conservatives is more of an anti-government vote than a pro-Conservative vote?

I always worry about that. My big thing is that we don't have to show that the Labour Party have failed. People know that. We have to show how we are going to succeed. Of course, the exchanges between me and Gordon Brown get quite heated over the economy, but if you look at the three years and what I have done as leader, I would say it's been pretty aggressively positive in terms of getting the Conservative Party to focus on environmental issues, social reform, educational reform, tackling poverty. It's very positive and that's what wins and loses elections – your positive vision for the way in which you want to take the country. You can never quite tell if it's Labour doing badly or the Tories doing well, you just get on with it.

How have you and your family been affected by the credit crunch?
Without inviting an enormous *Daily Mail* investigation… Anyone working in a commercial business, as my wife does, notices that the pressures are much greater. You notice in every contact you have with almost any business – large, medium or small. The credit crunch has affected businesses right across the piece. There are enormous swings in prices, particularly diesel and fuel. I do still fill up the car every week. I'm not that out of touch! At £1.30 a litre, suddenly it was seventy-five quid to fill a tank rather than fifty. But as a state employee, paid by the taxpayer I am insulated. Politicians in general have to understand that they are insulated in a way that people who work in the private sector aren't. That's why I felt so strongly about freedom of information about MPs' expenses and allowances. We are very lucky. We are not under pressure to hack costs away like everyone else in the private sector is. That's why it is not a bad time to say that the next few boundary reviews should be looking at shrinking the size of the House of Commons. We should be more productive, like everyone else is having to be.

Have you noticed a difference in the way people talk to you. When you're popping down to your local supermarket to get a pint of milk, and people approach you, are they talking about different things now?
People do indeed come up and talk to me. They're always very friendly. I get very little abuse, although I am sure that will change if I am successful! The things they say do change with the times. It's now all about the economy, their concerns, their anxieties. There is now a mood of anxiety turning into anger. People see their friends losing their jobs, they see their own pay being cut, the expectations they had being taken away.

What can the internet bring to your campaigning over the next eighteen months?
We ought to be doing a lot more and a lot better. Let's look at the positive side. The Conservative website is now good. Webcameron was at least a start and ahead of what some other parties have done. We use quite a lot of internet devices to launch policies, but we still have a long way to go before we are up with the best. It's boring and trite to say it, but what Obama achieved with bringing together both campaigning and advertising and fundraising all in the same place was fantastic. So often in politics people think these things are all separate. We'd really like to do more of that.

That's not happening on the Conservative website.
No, but we are working on it. Could we do more in terms of people who want to help through internet contact – ring these ten numbers, organise a house meeting? Clearly yes. Can we really go to a small, individual fundraising model? Well, we can try, and we should try, but actually when you look at Obama, he did still raise quite a lot of big money from other sources.

But if you want to impose a £50,000 donation cap, you've got to make up the shortfall somewhere and the internet is the only way you can do it.
It is. There is no enthusiasm for state funding. I would like to have the cap at £50,000 and I have always argued that if you can deliver that then there might be some legitimisation of some limited state funding, but at a time of straightened public finances it's about the last thing you want to spend any money on. So I absolutely recognise we will need to do better on small donations. Could that be accompanied by some sort of tax relief on donations to encourage giving? Maybe that's one answer. We have to ask what we are trying to achieve. We want healthy political parties as they are an essential part of our democracy and politics. In funding reform we want to make sure we are not encouraging parties to be reliant on either big unions or big business for donations, or indeed, big fat state money. What we want is parties that have to, as a matter of course, engage massively with people in order to win support and win donations at the same time. Any reform has got to be focused on that. I would still argue that we have made big, big progress in terms of broadening the base. Yes, we do still take some very big donations because we have to compete with the Labour Party who can literally pick up the phone to three unions and get the money, but we have massively broadened the number of people giving £50,000.

Do you regard having to meet donors to get the money in as one of the least enjoyable parts of your job?
No, I don't. It is a voluntary activity that people join a party, give their time and give their money. They are part of the team, part of the great coalition I want to build. Spending time encouraging them is part of the job. It would be like a farmer complaining about having to plough the fields.

Some farmers like combining, but not ploughing!
Well, they still take part in ploughing competitions in my constituency! Fundraising is important. You've got to do it and encourage and inspire people, believe in what you're trying to do and just get on with it. I like a challenge and the challenge of expanding the base of funding, the challenge of paying down the massive debts that were in place in 2005, the challenge of raising enough money in a recession to fight a really good election campaign

– those are all challenges I am quite enjoying. But one of the things you learn is that there is absolutely no pleasing people [laughs]. On this you can't win.

Do you think the reason politicians don't embrace the internet is that they fear it? They see the threats rather than the opportunities?
Yes. That's true. It's a problem. I am of a generation that didn't grow up with the internet. My first job did not have a PC on the desk but I am now completely computer literate. I spend a long time on the internet – shopping, I buy holidays and presents on the internet, a lot of the family shopping is done on the internet. I enjoy the political blogosphere. I think it's enlivened things. There's an awful lot of crap and gossip…

That's enough about my blog…
[Laughs] No, no… I think if you look at some of the stories you have broken, or Guido, it has enlivened politics and debate and democracy. It's great. So then the politician thinks, well, how do we make sure we avoid the danger of getting left out of the picture unless we use all tools of communication? We've got to work out how we do it. You do have to be a bit careful because politicians do have to be responsible for the words which come out of their mouths. You are expected to give an instant opinion on everything, but it's important for politicians to stop and think and try and get it right. So there are dangers and we have to be alert to those dangers. Being a politician is not the same as being a journalist.

Would you encourage candidates and MPs to have blogs, recognising the risks that there are?
Yes I would, but I would encourage them to be responsible. The one person they can be absolutely sure is reading their blog is Derek Draper and his team of henchmen. I want MPs and councillors and MEPs to be fully online and engaged online, having good websites, consulting about policies and ideas online, doing Q&A sessions online, but they have got to be responsible and recognise that everything they say will be taken down and used against them.

What sites do you look at apart from the obvious ones?
I use the BBC site a lot. What I try to do in terms of consumption of media is try and make sure I am getting a good flavour of what's going on without getting too obsessed by one thing or another. You see lots of stuff written and you have to develop a hard skin.

Are you ever tempted to comment, even anonymously, if you see a particularly vicious attack on you?
No. You get frustrated when someone misses the point, particularly in a complicated argument. In politics you've got to have a feel for what's going

on – the comment, and the mood and where things are going – but you mustn't allow yourself to get obsessed by any one thing. The BBC site is good, I look at Guido, your blog, and I think the Spectator Coffee House is bloody good. I also love Willem Buiter's blog on the *FT* site. I tend to look at them on the BlackBerry in the back of a car after I have done my work. It's time to look at what's occurring, as they say.

How much of a priority is House of Lords reform for you?
If you mean, can we please throw out people or suspend them if they are touting for business, then that's a very high priority. That needs to be done. In any legislature there has to be a way of suspending or expelling people who break the law. In terms of reform, having a more elected chamber, which is what I favour, to be frank that is not an urgent priority. The urgent priority is to sort out the economy and introducing social reform programmes. But I will sort out the egregiously broken things in politics like expenses, pay and pensions and the House of Lords – I will do that early on.

You made frontbenchers declare all their interests and if they have family members who work for them. Are you going to expand that to all MPs?
Yes. There were only four who didn't fill in the Right to Know form in the end. I am proud of the fact that a reform pioneered by the Conservatives is now being adopted by the rest of Parliament. It's right that the man on the Clapham omnibus can see what his MP is spending money on and who he is employing. I designed the Right to Know form myself. I took a piece of paper and wrote down what should be on it. The front bench had to fill it in, and in the event only four of our MPs refused to do it. Parliament then came along and decided to produce the same form for all MPs. That's great. If for any reason this gets delayed we will still publish ours and it will be a condition of being a Conservative MP. Some MPs were nervous about it. They feared local papers would just go through their expenses looking for scandal, but you know, sunlight is the great disinfectant. We've also done it with our MEPs. I sent our compliance man off to Brussels. They publish more detail than any of the Liberals or Labour MEPs.

Some people think that with David Davis out of the shadow Cabinet and Chris Grayling being appointed to be shadow Home Secretary, that the Party's approach to civil liberties is going to change, and the Party will revert to its more traditional authoritarianism. What do you say to that?
I don't think so. There's a strong strain of conservatism that is about civil liberties. We believe on limits to state power, we do believe in the importance of individual liberty. I think when you've got people like Dominic Grieve and Oliver Letwin sitting round the table you will always have strong voices standing up for civil liberties. I don't think it's fair to say that Chris Grayling isn't interested

in those things either. Look at the response of the whole Conservative Party and the instinctive response I had to the arrest of Damian Green. This is a party that does understand that you need limits on state power. A lot of stuff gets written about who really argued for what on 42-days and other things, but look at the number of times I challenged Blair and Brown on issues like this across the Despatch Box – that shows a pretty strong personal commitment.

Without using a four letter word, what was your reaction when David Davis told you that he was going to resign his seat?
When someone brings me a very bad bit of news I don't throw my toys out of the pram. Confusion – no, confusion is the wrong word [long pause]. What is the right word? I'm trying to think. Incomprehension. Because I am quite a logical person I couldn't get the logical connection between the loss of a vote in the Commons and a decision on something the whole Conservative Party was united about and the decision to resign and fight a by-election. I am very fond of David. We worked extremely well together. Perhaps better than many people predicted. He is an extremely talented politician. He fought his by-election campaign very well and got an extremely good result. It did demonstrate, and perhaps surprised some people, that the Conservative Party cared so much about civil liberties, but we do. I tried to persuade him out of it because I didn't think it was the right thing to do, so I didn't think it was something the Conservative Party could say, well that's our policy – when we disagree with something we'll all fight by-elections. You can't do that, so that's why I had to say quite rapidly that I'm going to have to get a new shadow Home Secretary.

Having decided to move Dominic Grieve in the reshuffle, why didn't you reappoint David Davis as shadow Home Secretary?
Any leader has to be able to shuffle their team and put round pegs in round holes. I've got a great team. I wanted to get everyone in the right place. I think Dominic Grieve is best suited to the Justice role, with his great knowledge of the law and legal processes, and I think Chris Grayling will be very good at making sure we have very strong and tough approaches to the crimes that really matter to people like burglary and knife crime and the guns on our streets.

I guess the point is that in government you've got a choice to make. You either have a Cabinet or shadow Cabinet of the biggest beasts and best talents like Ken Clarke or David Davis or a Cabinet made up of lesser known people who've done the legwork in opposition. Maybe it was too early to bring David Davis back, but the electorate would have seen it as a good thing.
It's a very good question. You've got to get the right people in the right jobs and forge a strong team. Those things shouldn't be in contradiction but that's the way I approach it.

Do you think you take advice from a wide enough circle of opinion? Some people think you don't.

[Becomes very animated] Yes I do! And I'd really like to get this across. You are right that some people think I don't, but you're wrong to think they're right! [laughs] I think people haven't seen enough of this from me. If I think about how I make decisions and who I listen to I would say that first of all I have a wide range of advice from the wise heads in our party. I have Heseltine on City policy, I get the former chancellors in to talk about economic policy, not once or twice but a lot. Geoffrey Howe has been in here two or three times this year already. I got Peter Lilley involved on international development, Dorrell on health. Over the Damian Green affair I said to the office, let's get all the wise heads who have been in parliament for a long time together, because this is such an extraordinary event and it's important the Conservative Party makes sense of it. I had Michael Jack, Bernard Jenkin, Ken came in, John Gummer came in.

Fine, those are all initiatives you've instigated from this office. If people want to feed ideas in to you a lot of people, especially backbench MPs, feel they can't penetrate the inner circle.

Any backbench MP can come and see me, and they do. Oliver Letwin's role in policy coordination is crucial. He's one of the most user-friendly and affable and interested people I know and I think he's very good at sucking in ideas from people. Look, every leader in history has been accused of not having an open enough door, not listening to enough people. I have strong opinions and convictions, but I think I do listen. I run the shadow Cabinet with quite a team approach, so I don't think the accusation is particularly fair. Maybe I haven't demonstrated, or shown enough about these things.

Last year I had a civil partnership. I have little doubt that a previous Tory government would not have passed the legislation enabling me to do that. How can you assure the however many million gay voters there are that a Cameron government won't just not discriminate against them, but will deal with whatever policy concerns they have?

I stood up in front of a Conservative conference, my first one as leader, and said that marriage was important and as far as I was concerned it didn't matter whether it was between a man and a woman, a man and a man or a woman and a woman. No other Conservative leader has ever done that. I don't think any Labour leader has done that. Even since then. The good thing was that they applauded. On civil partnerships, Oliver and I talked about it a lot … not that we were going to have a civil partnership, I hasten to add [roars with laughter]…

There, I've got my headline from this interview!

…We talked a lot about it because there was a real problem which needed to be overcome. There was a series of ways in which gay people were being discriminated against because they couldn't get married, so there was a strong, logical argument for civil partnerships. I think most Conservatives voted for it. The argument was getting stronger and stronger because the only other alternative was to try to deal with all these instances of discrimination – inheriting property, visiting rights etc – individually, and I think civil partnerships were the right way through it. If you believe in commitment, as I do, then the argument is even stronger. I totally agree that on some of these issues the Conservative Party had some work to do. Individually, some of us had some work to do and we needed to do it. I am not saying it is done but big progress has been made.

How will you defend the right to offend?
It's about balance. It's a difficult issue. This goes back to the 'do you listen' question because on the one hand you don't want someone inciting hatred of gays but on the other hand you want to live in a society where people don't feel their free speech is restricted if it is about humour. So there is a balance. Over the Waddington amendment, I got Nick Herbert, who was handling Justice but also a gay man in a civil partnership, Dominic Grieve and David Davis and we sat round and tried to thrash out a fair way through this. We thought the Waddington amendment wasn't right.

Nowadays almost anything you say can be construed as offensive by someone, somewhere. It's dangerous road for society to go down.
Yes, it's illiberal. We all rage against political correctness and there's lots of political correctness which is ridiculous – silly health and safety worries that stop children grazing a knee on an outward bounds adventure. We have got to get rid of that. But there's one bit of political correctness which is terribly important and that's about politeness. I have a disabled son and I don't want people to call him a spastic. You are a gay man, you don't want someone to call you a poof, if you have a black friend, you don't want someone to call them something offensive. It's about manners and I think what we've got to do is frame this debate in a sense of what is good manners and politeness and what is common sense. It's about saying things which are not unnecessarily offensive. Then there's a sense of responsibility and proportionality. If someone does say something offensive, what do we do about it?

You're accused of being a bit of a focus group politician, of being an opportunist...
[Almost leaps off the sofa] Bullshit! There are lots of misconceptions in politics and you shouldn't worry too much about them, but I would argue that this Conservative Party which I am leading is one of the least focus group, opinion poll-lead parties for a long time. Did I ask a focus group before saying I am a marriage nut? Did I ask a focus group about gay marriage? Of

course not! I just don't! I have never pre-tested a speech, which I know other politicians do. I think our Prime Minister does. Of course we hold focus groups to try to find out what the mood of the nation is and understand it. Of course we have regular reports and opinion polls. It would be crazy not to. But I really don't think this party, this leader, my team are obsessed by focus groups, and it's a great misconception that we are. It's frustrating.

How can people be confident you are not just another Blair? We had the 'heir to Blair' comment which I think has haunted you.
Yes. You shouldn't worry about these things too much. I've been doing this job for three years. People have seen I have some very strong views about things that not always everyone agrees with – marriage, or reforming the police. A lot of people have wondered where that one has come from. The line we took on the VAT cut. I mean, since when did the Conservatives not support a tax cut? We did not sit round and ask a focus group whether it was right to cut VAT. We thought it was wrong and said so.

So you'd describe yourself as a conviction politician?
Yes I would. Because my conviction was that the Conservative Party needed to reconnect with its compassionate conservative roots and have more to say about social policy and be a nation party, some people took that to mean that it must be poll-driven. It wasn't. So I am a conviction politician. It is a misconception that people have but it's not the most worrying thing in the world.

Do you think the BNP are a left-wing party? And do you think they should be ignored or actively taken on?
I think the first thing to do is recognise that it is an excrescence rather than a party. Don't ever run towards it, but the way to defeat it is to campaign actively on the ground. Pavement politics. People turn to extreme parties if they think they have been forgotten by the mainstream parties. That doesn't mean running towards issues they are campaigning on, it means running towards the people that they are talking to and showing you are listening to their concerns, taking up their issues and working for them. You have to show that no part of the country, no part of your constituency, no ward, that no housing estate is forgotten. That's the key thing. Eric Pickles is an expert on this and has helped teach me this lesson.

Do you think it is time to show UKIP a bit of love and attract some of their voters at the European elections?
I don't believe in showing the party [any love], about which I have said some things that turned out to be fantastically true, actually. If people want to have

the biggest vote in June for a party that wants a referendum on the European Constitution then it is self-evidently obvious that the right thing to do is vote Conservative. That's the way to maximise pressure on the government to do what they promised.

Do you think Nick Clegg is in the wrong party?
[Pauses] I don't really know him well enough. I don't know his views well enough. I think it is very exciting what they are saying about education because our education policies are very close together. That's a good thing. I'm a liberal Conservative so I think there is always going to be lots of common ground between liberal Conservatives and Liberal Democrats. If you look at what we are saying about decentralising power, passing power down to the lowest level, if you look at what we are saying about the environment, opposing identity cards, the priority given to education, I think there are a lot of people in the Liberal Democrat Party who would agree with that, so that's encouraging. Is he in the wrong party? I don't know enough about his views about other things.

On your relations with Gordon Brown it seems to me that there's an absolute mutual loathing there, which sometimes goes beyond where it should.
When we meet each other at state functions we're perfectly polite and we get on.

But when you were walking together to the House of Lords for the Queen's Speech you had a complete poker face and didn't say a word to him.
I couldn't! I couldn't get a word in edgeways! He launches into a long conversation and that's it. I would have loved to have said something, but I didn't get the chance. Maybe next year.

Describe Gordon Brown in one word.
[Long pause] Wrong [giggles].

Describe Simon Heffer in one word.
[Sighs] God, I don't know. The same applies! The last time I described him in a few words it set off this great tirade, so maybe I won't. Oh, alright then. Misunderstood! [roars with laughter]

Do you think that your questions at PMQs have become far too long. Gordon Brown seems to be flummoxed when an MP asks him a five-word question.
It's not about the question being long. He often asks me a question and I don't want to turn it into Leader of the Opposition's questions, but if he makes a point I'll respond to it too. I like answering the charges and engaging in

a debate rather than having a series of short pithy questions. I do think that some of the things he says need to be rebutted. Luckily, most of them are so ridiculous that I don't think anyone believes them. The 'do nothing' thing is ridiculous. I don't think anyone really believes the Conservative Party would do nothing. He has this habit of saying things which are self-evidently not true but he doesn't realise that it does enormous damage to him rather than the person he is saying it about. I managed to explain that at PMQs a couple of weeks ago but I am not sure anyone noticed apart from me! The most important thing is to get your point across and sometimes it takes a few more words. But perhaps I should vary it a bit more.

Have you ever thought about your life beyond politics? If you become Prime Minister and stay in the job for six or seven years you will be younger when you leave the job than Blair is now. What will you do?
I haven't really thought about that. I am so focused on the task in hand of marshalling the party towards the next election.

How will you make sure you don't outstay your welcome, because most politicians do?
Yes, they all do, even if they say they're not going to. What you have got to do is to keep a perspective on life. This job requires an enormous amount of application and hard work. I thrive on hard work. I love it. If I am fortunate enough to be elected Prime Minister I will thrive on the hard work and throw everything into it. I very much believe that in politics what matters most of all is your judgment, your character and your ability to listen and then make a decision. You lose that if you lose what makes you who you are. If what makes you who you are is your family and the rest of life, and the little bit of time when you do switch off then you'll lose your character and your judgment and all the other things. How do you know when it's time to go? Hopefully you just have a perspective and you try to avoid that seemingly inevitable process of losing touch.

Your current job has an effect on your work-life balance and family life. Do you worry about how things would change if you were Prime Minister?
Yes of course you worry about it. But I would not have put myself in this position if I didn't think there was a way of handling it. It must be possible to be a good Prime Minister and a good father and husband.

When my niece sees me on TV she rushes up to the screen and kisses it. What does your daughter do? Does she comprehend what your job is?
She does. She doesn't kiss the TV, but she refers to it as 'politicianer'. It's a bit like doctor, lawyer, you're a politicianer. She has come to the conclusion that

what politicianers do is talk a lot. She said to me the other day, 'oh, you're always fixing a speech' [giggles]. My children are very young but they have an idea of what's going on.

Quickfire

Jack Bauer or James Bond?
Both! But James Bond, just.

Book you are reading?
I've just finished Robert Peston's book, which ought to be called *Who Ruined Britain?* rather than *Who Runs Britain?* I'm now reading *America and the World* by Zbigniew Brzezinski and Brent Scowcroft.

Are you superstitious?
Not particularly.

Food you hate?
None. They haven't invented it yet. Abolone, a weird fishy thing in Chinese restaurants. I was made to eat it once in Hong Kong. Other than that I have yet to find a food I don't like.

Most embarrassing song on your iPod?
There's some hot competition for that accolade. 'You Don't Bring Me Flowers' by Neil Diamond and Barbra Streisand.

Sarah Palin or Bree Van de Kamp from *Desperate Housewives*?
Bree, every time [said with just a little too much enthusiasm]. And the rest of the cast.

Favourite view?
From the top of the road from Dean to Chipping Norton looking into the Wychwood Forest.

Worst present you have given your wife?
A plant.

Worst one she has given you?
The worst was when we both forgot our tenth wedding anniversary and we only remembered when Alastair Stewart sent us a card. We both forgot, so it was alright.

Last time you cried?
Watching the *Sound of Music*, worryingly recently.

Swedish schools or Swedish films?
Schools! And not to confuse the two!

Have you ever sampled a slippery nipple?
No I haven't! Of either variety!

Ken Livingstone

Party affiliation: Labour

Born: 17 June 1945

Education: Educated at St Leonard's Church of England School and Tulse Hill Comprehensive, and later studied for his teacher's certificate at Philippa Fawcett College of Education.

Family status: He has five children, two of whom with his current wife Emma Beal.

Pre-political career: He was a technician at the Chester Beatty Cancer Research Institute from 1962 to 1970.

Electoral history: Elected to Lambeth Council in 1971 and later to the Greater London Council in 1973. He then became Labour candidate for Brent East before running as an independent in the election for London mayor, after losing to Frank Dobson in the battle for selection by Labour. He won and became London mayor in May 2000, and in January 2004 rejoined the Labour Party. After two terms as mayor he lost out to Conservative Party candidate, Boris Johnson in 2008.

Career highlights: Becoming the mayor of London on 4 May 2000 and retaining the position at the subsequent election.

Interesting fact: He was briefly suspended from his office as the London mayor for remarks he made comparing a Jewish journalist to a concentration camp guard.

Date of interview: March 2009
Extended version
Venue: Ken Livingstone's house, north London
Total Politics Issue 10, April 2010

For someone who the right regard as the equivalent of the political devil, Ken Livingstone is surprisingly popular across the political spectrum. Yes, he's one of the few remaining out and out lefties and unashamedly so.

I first met Ken in the late 1990s when he would come in to my bookshop, Politico's. He turned out to be a very good customer and liked nothing more than to have a political gossip over the counter. But it was Ken's introduction of the congestion charge that contributed to my decision to close the shop in 2004, as it led to a 15 per cent reduction in customer footfall. To this day he can't see that the charge had any effect on business at all, but I know different. I was at the sharp end.

The thing about Ken Livingstone is that he is a real political enthusiast. I've joined him in the studio on his Saturday morning LBC radio show from time to time, and he's someone you can have a really sensible argument with. And a pleasant one. I think that comes through during this interview.

The interview was carried out in his very unassuming Cricklewood home. And it really is a home. The whole time we were interrupted by his kids who he clearly loves to bits. And from what I saw, he's quite a disciplinarian too! As you would expect, there are quite a few reptile tanks in the living room. It's quite disconcerting asking a question and then seeing a reptilian eye staring at you from behind some glass.

How long's the recession going to last then?

People see this as a short to medium term recession. I think it's seminal. In the aftermath of the war there was a real scathing attitude to business people. That was the generation that had been through the depression. They thought they were idiots. For thirty years we've been told these people are better than us and brighter than us and deserve more money than us, and they've proved to be complete idiots. There are going to be films, serious books about all this for several years to come. There will have been a huge cultural shift. A lot of it will depend on how far Obama shifts the political spectrum. I'm optimistic. You should be pessimistic!

I am very pessimistic because I don't think people have the faintest concept about what's about to hit them. When it really hits the middle classes, they are going to get a nasty shock. People like me feel let down by the private sector, just as I suspect people like you felt let down by the behaviour of the unions in the 1970s.

I felt let down by Callaghan. Trade unions are defensive institutions. They are never going to innovate. They are protecting what their members have got already and you can't look to unions to set the next agenda. That's what politicians are for. But the tragedy is that in all parties, politicians are just focused on the short term. Blair and Brown's agenda in 1994–7 was controlled by the thought: 'What do we need to say to win the election.' They should have been thinking: 'What sort of Britain do we want to have in 2015?' and then work back from that. That's what I tried to do. My assumption is that Cameron won't be as out of his depth as Blair was. I think he is alert to the danger of wasting a term finding out how to do the job.

Do you think you lost the mayoralty, or did Boris win it? Because there is a difference, isn't there?

You had two candidates with high positives, committed supporters but with high negatives from people who loathed them. London was fractured. There was a huge swing to me in some parts and sadly, in more parts, a huge swing to Boris. If you could have taken away the national dimension I think I would have won because Boris's negatives were more than mine. We did monthly polling and from the moment Boris announced [he was running] my ratings went up and up and up. It was only in November they started coming down. I then realised it was just tracking the national party's polling. Immediately after the budget Labour's figures and mine just went off a precipice. The figures slowly came back and if we had had another two months we might have pulled it back.

When did you realise you were going to lose?
From the moment Boris announced I thought he was the one Tory candidate who could defeat me. The real trouble initially – not among my immediate staff, but amongst the wider Labour movement – was that people thought he was a bit of a joke. I always thought it was neck and neck and it was only really when I woke up on the Friday morning and switched on the *Today Programme* and heard that Labour was on 24 per cent nationally, with the Tories on 44 per cent I realised I couldn't overcome that. I came in and started clearing my desk. It was a disastrous period. Even though GDP was still going up, it felt like a recession already. If ever any of my kids want to go into politics I'll sit them down and say look, if you go into any other career and you're bright you can achieve a lot. Politics is the one profession where you can be at the wrong place at the wrong time. Poor old John Major didn't deserve to lose the night I won in Lambeth in 1971. That Tory council was the best for thirty years – highly imaginative and I agreed with almost everything it did. All those people like Hattersley and Kaufman whose careers were snuffed out in 1979, or Ken Clarke in 1997. This is the one career where the question of luck is so overwhelming, but I really can't complain. I've had two periods of power on a basis only just below that of what the Prime Minister has. I would have said Cabinet minister twenty years ago, but Cabinet ministers today have been reduced to rubber-stamping.

What you are saying is that Gordon Brown lost you the mayoralty. Why were you so gracious to him afterwards? I thought you might launch a bitter attack on him.
When you have had a defeat like that and you start blaming everyone else you diminish yourself. It wasn't like sudden death. I had been intellectually prepared for defeat from the previous July. The campaign had been horrendous, with all the *Evening Standard* stuff. It wasn't like a Portillo moment where the whole nation is cheering and glad you've lost, so I didn't feel it was a personal humiliation. I had gone through the election thinking the impact of the *Standard* will be to squeeze my vote closer to the Labour vote, but if the Labour vote had only collapsed to 27 per cent I would have hung on. There we go…

Was the campaign strategy against Boris wrong? I couldn't understand the tactics of accusing Boris of racism right as soon as he was selected. You should have kept some of that ammunition for the campaign itself. You shot your bolt too early.

I don't think there was a strategy towards Boris.

Maybe that was the problem!

Throughout my life I have run positive campaigns about what I believe in. Back in 2004 when I got back into the party I was suddenly made aware Labour had printed a million newspapers attacking Steve Norris personally. I told them I would denounce it if they put it out and they had to pulp them. In 1981 a reporter from the *Standard* came to me with stuff about Horace Cutler's private life – they had found his love nest, and all that crap – and I said I was more interested in cutting fares.

Why didn't you adopt that attitude in this campaign because some of the things you said about Boris were vicious.

No it wasn't. Nothing was orchestrated by me. Boris's problem, and he has no one to blame but himself, is that he spent fifteen years writing for *The Telegraph* and *Standard*. Both he and [Andrew] Gilligan seemed to think it wasn't fair that people went back and read all this. I still get people recycling things I said in 1981! Boris seemed genuinely hurt. But he wrote a load of racist, reactionary, negative, neo-con piffle. The only thing Boris had never taken a right-wing position on was immigration. How were we to know he was just writing for his audience? I believed he genuinely believed all this. It's only after the last ten months as I have watched him desperately trying to govern from near the centre that I realised Boris doesn't believe in anything at all, except that Boris should rule the world. If I were one of those BNP people who gave him a second preference and then I listened to him saying that illegal immigrants should have an amnesty, I think I would want my vote back!

But you never seriously believed Boris was a racist, did you?

I had never met Boris. Where would I know Boris? All I had ever seen was Boris being a buffoon on *Have I Got News For You*. All I can do is believe that the stuff he spent fifteen years writing, he might actually believe. Who else in politics has ever used the word 'piccninnie'? Or 'water melon smiles'? You might know he's a lovely engaging chap because you might have met him. I have never met him. We have still only ever exchanged a few words in passing. I know he was genuinely hurt that people thought he was a racist. He's not a racist in the sense that anyone would make that point, but he shouldn't have written that crap. He can't help himself. I have to be careful about revealing sources, but the thing about Boris is that everyone around him gossips about him all the time. Apparently when he meets foreign mayors with distinctive language patterns, he's mimicking them almost as soon as they are out of the bloody door! He doesn't mean it in any unpleasant way, but it is very easy for people to misinterpret that.

I had a group of people who were totally loyal to me and the agenda. Some of us had been together for twenty-five years fighting internal party campaigns. Boris was never involved in internal Tory Party struggles. His people all have their own agendas and he's having to learn how to administer something for the first time in his life. He's trying to work out what to do with a job he had never thought about before he decided to run. People ask if Boris will be good or bad. In my view we won't know until after the general election, when he will be in his third year.

Do you think he's done better in his first year than you thought he would?
God, no one could do worse than I thought he would. I thought we were getting an unpleasant piece of work who believed George Bush was right on global warming and had written all these nasty articles. If someone writes millions of words you assume they probably believe them, but Anthony Browne [Boris Johnson's director of policy] was revealing when he was asked about all the nasty stuff he had written about migrants. He said he didn't really believe it but was writing it because he was told to by the paper he was working for. I respect Richard Barnbrook more. He does actually believe his racism, whereas Anthony Browne and Boris were paid to write it.

I don't think Boris has done as badly as you thought he would.
It would be hard for him to have been as bad as I feared he was going to be. Why do you think I fought so hard to keep him out?! Boris's weakness is that he doesn't have an ideology. Every leader I have watched try to govern from the centre has failed.

Aren't we in the age of pragmatism now, not the age of ideology?
No, you have got to have an ideology to have a framework to construct a strategy about where you're going. People in the centre are, by definition, devoid of ideology. They make what appear to be rational decisions at the time, but are usually too late, and stumble from crisis to crisis. Tell me a centrist leader who has been successful.

You sound like Margaret Thatcher.
I completely disagreed with so much of what she wanted to do but I did respect her because she believed in something and drove towards it. You

look at poor old Neil Kinnock, always trying to accommodate to the right, keep the left happy. Also, another weakness is that Boris is not a workaholic and you have to be as mayor. *Private Eye* do a spoof about me blaming Boris for everything, but I do actually. My office was always pro-active. Boris's failure to act when we had all the snow was symptomatic.

That wasn't Boris's fault, that was Peter Hendy and Transport for London. Hendy was the operational guy in charge. He's the roadblock to reform. If you want to get from a Livingstone transport agenda to a Boris one you have to get rid of Hendy.
A bureaucracy isn't pro-active. The political leader has to call people in, hold immediate meetings, give clear instructions and expect them to be carried out. Hendy says it's nicer working under Boris. Of course it is. I told the bugger what to do, but Boris doesn't. The Tory Party's problem is that Boris is learning from making the same sort of mistakes I made on Lambeth Council at the age of twenty-six. It's like Tony Blair. Blair hadn't run anything before he became Prime Minister. This is very late in the day to work out how you start handling civil servants.

Is this a wider problem, where you have people going into politics at an ever younger age. It's the age of the career politician, isn't it?
That layer of successful businessmen who went into parliament in their fifties, or trade union leaders who did much the same and could say 'bugger off sonny', there are just none of them left. It's not just that all we are getting is career politicians, it's also that they haven't had a chance to run anything until they get to run a government department. American or German politicians get to run their cities or states before they go into Federal government. It's a terrible weakness in our system. Obama is only the third President to be elected from the Senate. Every other President has run a state or been a successful military commander. Every German Chancellor with the exception of Adenauer and Erhard has run a Bundesland. No one in Germany would think you can play with the national government until you have demonstrated you can run one of the smaller bits. Only here do we think that posing against your opponents in parliament is a preparation for government.

What would your advice to David Cameron be?
I think he has already made the fatal mistake which will sink his government. He's not really going to devolve power away from Whitehall. He's already told local government there will be no great change or shift in power. He'll try to run all the schools from the centre. When they talk about localism it's a sham. Neither this government, nor a Cameron one will empower people. Labour's

real mistake was to micro-manage everything and try to run everything from the centre. Nowhere else in the world does this work. If Cameron had any sense he would devolve about half of what Whitehall does to regional and local government, but he doesn't believe in regional government. But you can understand it – all those years in Opposition waiting for power. When you get it, it's very difficult to give it up. What I discovered when I became leader of the GLC was that previously everything crossed the leader's desk. The senior civil servants, like Treasury civil servants worked to the leader, blocking off their Committee chairs. At my first meeting with the Director General, I said I do not want any officer coming to see me other than the Director of Finance or yourself. They should work to the Committee chairs we have appointed. Immediately, all these things were happening. If it had all had to come across my desk, half of it would never have happened. Although there will be mistakes, a real, massive devolution would start bringing good people back into local government, but there's got to be financial change as well. Ninety-seven per cent of all tax collected in Britain is collected by Gordon Brown. When I told the mayor of Moscow that, he said: 'That's worse than Russia under Stalin.' From the moment Thatcher got power everything was sucked up to the centre and it got worse under Blair and Brown. Civil servants try to keep ministers busy with endless meetings and trivia.

Perhaps you should go and talk to Cameron's implementation team.
Whatever he thinks of my policies, the main lesson Cameron should draw from my time is that if I made a decision it was carried out, and carried out quickly. The civil service is a malignant conspiracy against the national interest. A Cabinet minister is the executive head of the department, able to remove the entire top tier. They probably couldn't bring in a Bob Kiley figure from outside, like I did. When I took over we removed twenty-seven of the top thirty people in London Transport. A government minister can't do that. It's tragic. The civil service is filled with crap. I met a government minister every week for eight years. There were a handful who were in charge. Ed Balls obviously was, because he was backed up by Mr Big. The one who impressed me was John Spellar. He and I had fought viciously from opposite wings of the party, but I had loads of meetings with Transport civil servants and they always expected him to endorse their position. When he said 'I agree with the mayor on this' they were shocked. I saw government ministers read the brief which had been prepared for them and on one occasion I told the minister: 'Your civil servants are lying to you' and I demonstrated why. They didn't have an answer. The tragedy is that everyone below Cabinet level knows that the Permanent Secretary in their department does an annual assessment of their performance and sends it to the Chief Whip. It should be the other way around. They know if they go out on a limb, the civil servants

will undermine them. Even if you're John Prescott and all else fails, they'll bring the Treasury in, or the lawyers to tell you you can't do something. We've just got to break this. The civil service has its own agenda. In the end most ministers and most prime ministers go native and get sucked in by it.

What were you most proud of in your eight years as mayor?
It is so difficult to narrow it down. It was the shining apex of human civilisation! Clearly the congestion charge. I am not aware of any other IT system that big that's been brought in on time and on budget and that works.

Was expanding it a mistake? If it was truly a congestion charge you would have expanded it where there was congestion. By doing what you did it actually encouraged more cars into the centre.
There was congestion. West London was by far the most congested. The extra cars were under 1 per cent.

Looking back, what do you think you got wrong?
I don't think we got any of the major decisions wrong. All the things you could say were mistakes were things about being rude to journalists…

It was a bit more than being rude to a journalist, wasn't it?
I have been rude to journalists all my life. Every time a journalist has displeased me I make an allusion to concentration camp guards, or Nazis. And just because some reporter is Jewish, they're not getting any special treatment. My biggest failure was not finding a way of forcing the *Standard* out of business. I know the giveaways played a part, but under Max [Hastings] it had a circulation of 400,000, increased to 500,000 after the merger with the *Evening News*, and she [Veronica Wadley] leaves it at 160,000. The *London Paper* was positive about London and the *Standard* wasn't.

Do you think you mishandled the Lee Jasper issue?
If I had known he had written some salacious emails at the beginning I would have handled it differently. We'd had two investigations by the Director of Finance at the GLA, two by the LDA auditors, the Assembly went over everything. We have had ten months of police investigation. One or two organisations may have been set up to steal from us but that's a problem everyone in the public sector has got. What there isn't is anything that links Lee Jasper to any criminality. That justified a couple of stories. It did not justify twenty-five front-page leads and thirty-five double-page spreads. They finally got Lee Jasper for something that was contrary to our code of conduct. If you access the emails of everyone on the BBC or any newspaper you'd find something similar.

Why do you keep going back to City Hall? You even attend Mayor's Questions at the Assembly. It makes you look sad.
I was uniquely lucky in that I got to set something up from scratch. Watching Boris come to terms with what I created is absolutely fascinating. I do intend to seek the Labour nomination again and if I am selected, I want to know more about Boris's administration than he does.

People think it's demeaning.
But they're the ones who aren't going to vote for me. In the debates next time I want to be able to hit back at Boris when he's wrong. Because I am there I can say with authority that the Tory group on the GLA are disappointed he is not more right wing. You can see it in their body language. It's a bit like all those Labour lefties who have waited years for a Labour government and then they get Blair! Boris was going to keep the western extension [of Labour's congestion charge] until they went and sat on him. If he had had more experience he might take more risks and do his own thing.

He's taken a lot of risks. The amnesty for illegal immigrants is only one example. But moving on, why do you want to stand for a third term when you gave a clear commitment to only stay for one term?
I change my mind all the time on the issue of term limits. The defining thing was George Bush. If America hadn't had term limits, Clinton would have been elected for a third term. I said I would also retain my seat in Parliament because I didn't think the job of mayor would be any more demanding than that of a Cabinet minister. I assumed I would then be well rewarded by Blair for having got it all settled down. Once I got elected, by the first autumn, I realised there was huge potential and I had to give up my seat in Parliament and decide it would be the last job I did in politics.

Don't you think that if people are in power for a long time, the risk of corruption increases?
There's no more risk of corruption if I am in power for twenty years and when I get there. You are corrupt, or you are not.

But there are one party states in local government which are incredibly corrupt.
Then the answer is proportional representation so no one holds absolute power. I'd also have a primary system because the party machines become so small. You get more rapid political change in America than you do here. Insurgents can capture the party machine. Here, you have to brown nose your way up. That's the killer.

The Tories have introduced open primaries for candidate selection.
But not of all the voters…

Yes, absolutely. Anyone can turn up.
I didn't know that. That's excellent.

Do you not think the Labour Party machine will be mobilised against you? You can already see it with these articles about Alan Sugar – they want anyone but Ken in 2011.
This was foretold in the Bible. If you look in the Old Testament in Proverbs it says 'the dog returneth to its vomit as the New Labour fool returns to its folly'. It will be twelve years. It's time to return to a Frank Dobson moment – the only question is, who is it going to be? [smiles] It's an Andrew Gilligan story – that sad loner who gets off on destroying other people's lives. Gilligan wrote a piece recently broadly suggesting I was responsible for the credit crisis, calling me Livingstone Brothers. He, and others like [Nick] Cohen are obsessed. Yes, I would love to be mayor again. I am as certain as you can be, two and a half years ahead, that I will run for the Labour nomination.

If you didn't get it, would you commit now not to do what you did before?
I wouldn't have run the first time if I hadn't won, but I won and it was rigged. There was a huge amount of ballot stealing going on. Piara Khabra [former Labour MP for Ealing Southall] was going round boasting about how he had personally collected 300 postal ballots. They have to have one member one vote. I will be happy to submit myself to one member one vote and abide by the result. I was happy to do that last time, but they changed it.

Have you never been tempted to go back to the House of Commons? You'd stand quite a good chance of succeeding Gordon Brown after a Labour defeat!
That's most probably why they wouldn't let me get a nomination! [roars with laughter] If I thought I could get to be Prime Minister I would do it, but I don't think so. I would be seventy in 2015. You'd all be saying that this man's too old to be Prime Minister.

You're probably right…
[Laughs loudly] Getting back into Parliament? I don't know. Don't you think I am perfectly made for London politics but not for the rest of the country?

I might have said that a few years ago, but not now. But the way you're talking about it, it's almost as if you haven't considered it before and I have just put the thought into your head.
When I left Parliament, people like Diane Abbott said, no, you must stay and go for the leadership when there's a vacancy. I thought, no, that could be forever. I have a big, demanding job to do. At the next mayoral election

I may still look forty-five, but at the following general election I may look like a pensioner. And I love the London job. The Labour Party tolerates me because I only get to play with London. If they thought I might get my hands on the whole country I think they would be very serious about stopping me. It's just as well Barack Obama is there now. If I looked like becoming Prime Minister while Bush was in the White House then I am sure I would have had an accident. I believe in a neutralist Britain. I'm what Bill Cash calls a 'Federast'. I believe in the euro, a united Europe. That plays OK in London, but not the rest of the country. I am not in favour of any parental choice in education. You will go to your local school.

That's a pretty bold statement. You've got young kids.
They go to the local school and they will go to the local secondary school.

Even if it's a terrible school and you know it's a terrible school? Surely a parent's duty is to get the best education possible for their kids?
Tom's in his first year at school. In his class there are only three kids who were born in this country, and one of them is called Mohammed. He's doing fine because he has parents who read to him and he lives in a house full of books. A school can screw up kids if it's got a bad head who has lost interest and loses control. The home environment is far more likely to screw up kids. The illusion of educational choice has been a disaster for most kids and most parents. So you say, all things considered, I might have some trouble getting elected outside London!

Yes, possibly! What did you think when you heard the news that Peter Mandelson was returning to government?
He's a formidable operator but I am not certain it sends the message of renewal that we want. I had fundamental disagreements throughout my eight years as mayor. I hoped when Brown took over things would change more than they did. But I have not been massively surprised.

You were never a great fan of Brown, were you?
I was very critical of the first two years. The passage of time has shown me to be right.

What role do you think the internet is going to play in the future in politics?
I don't know how rapidly the papers will continue to decline. I regret their decline because the really good papers are providing a good range of news. But you get good stuff on the blogs too. The blogs, even those on the right, have been more balanced about Boris than the *Evening Standard* was. They were just cheerleaders. I tend to find out what's going on from what I am getting off the blogs.

Have you ever been tempted to start your own blog?
Once I have finished writing my autobiography I might. I've written 40,000 words and I am only up to the age of thirty. It will be out in time for the party conferences. Once that's finished I shall be twittering all over the place!

How do you best fight the BNP?
Do you expose them for what they are or ignore them? I've always been in favour of exposing them and taking them on. The far right do well when a Labour government is failing. It's basically working-class voters who would be inclined to be our supporters who become disillusioned. They don't want to vote Tory. If Brown gets a fourth term it will grow as a problem, unless Brown's policies become more popular with the working class. There is a lot of anger out there. If Cameron wins, it will be just like when Thatcher got in. The BNP will rapidly fade away. It's a problem for incumbent Labour governments. It's never going to be a problem for a Tory one. But the BNP are not the sharpest knives in the drawer. We've got to do everything possible to stop them, but it was like this in the Callaghan government when the National Front rose to prominence. The BNP will continue eating into the Labour vote until the government realises it needs to do something for working-class people.

You went out on a limb to support Sir Ian Blair, when you used to have a reputation for being rather anti-police.
The Metropolitan police were a deeply reactionary and racist force in the 1980s. They were intensely politicised. I don't know where it changed but when I started running for mayor I saw the police operating in a wholly different way. They knew the sort of policing they had been used to wasn't working. Peel set up the police force because you couldn't use the army on the streets, and when a police force starts behaving like an army you're going to lose it. The Met had changed long before I was elected mayor, or the process had at least started. Stevens and Blair were seemless. There were no policy differences, although they had very different styles. They both pushed forward an agenda of change. You judge a person by the quality of their enemies, and when you have got *The Telegraph* and the *Mail* leading the campaign to get rid of Ian Blair you know he must be doing something right. What they wanted was a good old racist copper.

Oh for goodness sake. You can't seriously believe that's the case. You seriously think they would like to have a racist head of the Metropolitan Police. Get real.
I do. I think they are racist. The *Mail* is a deeply racist paper. Just read *Flat Earth News*. I was shocked. Dacre comes over as a bullying racist thug in the book.

Why are the British so negative about the Olympics?
I don't think they are. Every poll we have done in London shows two to one

support. There was a wave of euphoria when we won, especially as we beat the French. There will be more euphoria when it happens, but in between you get seven years of crap. The success in Beijing has meant that it has died down a bit. It's all on budget.

Why are you such a fan of Robert Kennedy? He was one of the cheerleaders for the Vietnam war.
Politicians make mistakes. What he learned from his mistakes would have led to him being a truly great President, much better than his brother. There was nothing between Robert Kennedy's assassination and Obama which ever made me think: 'This president will change the world.'

I did think that about Reagan, and I was right!
Unfortunately Reagan didn't live long enough to see where it all went wrong.

I am talking about ending the Cold War.
Kennedy would have ended that.

If he'd been elected in 1981 he might have. He could not have ended it in the 1960s. The Russians weren't in a position to end it.
Yes they were. They knew they had economic problems. Scaling down their nuclear programme would have been of huge benefit to the Soviet Union. They only achieved parity in the 1980s. Kennedy would have offered a deal which in real terms would have been of huge benefit to the Soviet Union.

In that scenario, that would have entrenched communism in the Soviet Union.
It would have released military resources so communism could have evolved and changed without going through the collapse which has been so damaging and so catastrophic.

What's your prediction for the next general election?
Labour has only one real chance. Providing Brown continues to look as if he knows what he's talking about on the economy and he gets on top of the problems, and Cameron and Osborne continue with the line they have got, you have the mirror image of the 1992 election. You're in a recession but the party of government is re-elected because it looks as if the opposition will make it worse. Kinnock said he would increase taxes. If Cameron says he will put up taxes and cut spending people won't go for that. Everyone else except the Republican right will be saying it doesn't work.

Not exactly a great rallying cry to the electorate, though, is it?
Neither was John Major's but it got him another term.

The difference between Brown and Major is that Brown can't connect with people on an emotional level.

In a time of economic crisis people don't care whether you connect with them emotionally. They care about what's going to happen to their pocket. In 1992 the Tories said, very successfully, the only thing stopping us coming out of a recession is Kinnock. That's what Brown will say about Cameron.

Cameron is no Kinnock. People rather like Cameron in a way they never warmed to Kinnock.

Quickfire

What are you reading?
Harold Nicolson's diaries – the condensed version.

Most formidable political opponent?
Boris Johnson.

City Hall or County Hall?
County Hall.

Most romantic thing you have ever done?
That's an intrusion, but it involves a log fire and a mountain retreat.

Favourite music?
I have a very catholic musical taste. Classical, Katie Melua, Alexandra Burke, Stones, Scott Walker, Byrds. I am promiscuous about music.

Last concert?
El Sistema, Venezuelan Youth Orchestra.

Favourite view in London?
Parliament Hill, Hampstead Heath.

Paddy Ashdown

Party affiliation: Liberal Democrats

Born: 27 February 1941

Education: Educated at Bedford School, Ashdown before enlisting in the Royal Marines.

Family status: Married with two children and two grandchildren.

Pre-political career: Served as a Royal Marines Officer, went to Hong Kong to undertake a full-time course in Chinese and then commanded a Commando Company in Belfast.

Electoral history: Joined the Foreign Office in 1972, then stood as Liberal parliamentary candidate for the Yeovil constituency in 1979 and was elected eight years later. After being appointed spokesman for Trade and Industry Affairs and then Education and Science, he was elected leader of the Liberal Democrats in July 1988 with over 70 per cent of the vote. He stood down as leader of the Liberal Democrats in 1999 and retired from the Commons in 2001.

Career highlights: As well as becoming leader of the Liberal Democrats, Paddy was knighted in 2000 and made a peer in 2001.

Interesting fact: He is fluent in Mandarin Chinese.

Date of interview: March 2009
Extended version
Venue: Kennington, London
Total Politics Issue 11, May 2009

Paddy Ashdown is the very definition of an all action politician. When he was party leader his staff had great trouble keeping up with his energetic schedule. He was similar to Gordon Brown in thinking nothing of ringing people at 6am. And now that he no longer has a front-line political role, you can almost feel him itching to be at the centre of things again. A life tending roses in Norton sub Hamdon is not something I can see him relishing.

This interview was conducted shortly before Ashdown's autobiography was published. It was not a book for the fainthearted. The chapters on his early life and career in the armed forces and Foreign Office were riveting – more interesting than the political chapters, I thought. What a pity it was that

*Ashdown couldn't have talked more about his life in the special forces while
he was leader of the Lib Dems. I suspect the electorate would have found him
more appealing that they did.*

I invited Paddy Ashdown to be a member of the Total Politics *magazine
editorial board, as I knew he wouldn't be shy in voicing any criticisms.
And so it has proved. And he's a font of ideas too. But there is a part of me
that wishes he had had to resign from the editorial board in May. I heard
a rumour that David Cameron wanted him to be Defence Secretary in the
coalition government. Sadly, it never happened. I think he would have done
an excellent job and it would have been highly entertaining to watch. It would
have been a great last mission.*

Why is there a disconnect at the moment between politicians and those who elect them?

It may well be that one of the reasons people feel so upset about the
disconnect is because politics has become a profession rather than a calling.
Service seems to be a long way down the spectrum of qualities that you need
to have and experience of the way people live their lives for people whom
you are legislating seems to be rather thinly spread.

When did you first think about going into politics?

When I was a young officer one of my jobs was looking after the welfare
of marines on board a ship. I found the pastoral care side of it immensely
satisfying, slightly to my own surprise as I was quite a rumbustious, physical
kind of guy. I think I decided to go into politics at the age of thirty-one,
although my wife Jane tells me she thinks I had decided at the age of twenty-
seven. Special Forces was a seminal experience and formed my politics. I was
leading people in quite difficult situations, who were by any standards better
than me at the job we were supposed to be doing. I was in charge of them
because of the class structure, which I have always detested. I started off as
a socialist and was a declared socialist during my time in the Royal Marines
– a very unpopular thing to do among fellow officers in those colonial days.
I parted company with the Labour Party over *In Place of Strife*. I was always
worried that Labour couldn't be tough enough on the unions. When Callaghan
caved in, I changed. By 1965, when I was commanding the SBS in the Far East
I had shifted from standard corporatist, socialist ideas to very much more
meritocratic ideas. I remember being attracted to Labour by Jenkins, Owen
and Shirley Williams. By 1967 when I was learning Chinese and was getting
a very strong internationalist view my belief in Labour was seriously shaken
by the Wilson government and the devaluation. I was in Hong Kong. By 1970
I had parted company with Labour. I looked at the Liberals but I thought no,
too small, too zany, nothing to do with me. After 1970, when I was in the

Foreign Office, I counted myself as one of the great disconnected. Indeed, in 1974 I was digging in the garden and a canvasser called. He was a funny little man. My mind has him in an anorak and with a squeaky voice. He possibly had a beard but my memory may be playing tricks.

So all he was missing were the sandals...
He said 'Hello, I'm a Liberal.' I said 'Don't be ridiculous. Go away.' I was being very grumpy but I invited him in and we sat down and talked for about two hours. It was an unlikely epiphany but at the end of that conversation I discovered that I was indeed a Liberal and had been a Liberal all my life. I then went to Geneva, pretending to be a diplomat and doing things which I describe as 'in the shadows'. On my birthday, 27 February 1975 I went back and called in to see Yeovil Liberals and said some day I'd be happy to help. Coincidentally, their candidate had resigned that day and gone to fight Newbury which he regarded as a better bet. I resigned my job and went off to Yeovil. It was the most irresponsible decision I have ever taken. I had no idea what it was like. The Tories had won Yeovil for more than seventy years. Liberal candidates were famous for losing their deposits. And my party leader was about to be arraigned for murder at the Old Bailey. I had a wife and two children. It took me eight years to win Yeovil, with the aid of homemade wine and a printing machine but leaving a well-paid career for unemployment on two occasions and a job with half the salary I had been on was a hugely irresponsible decision but it was the best one I ever made.

How did you justify it to yourself, and your wife?
I don't think I needed to to Jane because our kids were coming up to the time when they would have gone to boarding school and she just did not want that to happen. This was a means by which she could be with the kids. Jane was enthusiastic and so was I. I am a romantic and the temptation I find completely irresistible is when someone says it's impossible, you can't do that. If I was being pompous I'd say that there was no point in living this sybaritic existence – a very nice house on the shores of Lake Geneva – if the country you were representing was going to hell in a handcart behind you. I suppose there was also a bit of egotism. I wanted to have the ball at my own feet. I didn't want to be kicking around other people's footballs.

So why did you join the Liberal Party then? You've led people. You know what power means. Why did you pick a party which was never, in a month of Sundays, going to wield power?
Because I believed in it. I do believe it will wield power. This is the romantic in me. It does have power governing Britain at the local level. I knew I couldn't be a Tory. It's alien to my nature. That's not to say there aren't some very good

people in the Tory Party. I love people like Ed Llewellyn [David Cameron's chief of staff] and Chris Patten, probably the best prime minister we've never had. But I couldn't look myself in the mirror if I became a Tory, I'm afraid. The main reason I am so anti-Tory is their visceral anti-Europeanism.

There's a difference between being Eurosceptic and anti-European.
I think they are anti-European. They are not internationalist in the way I think will be necessary for the age. The right thing to do is deepen our integration in foreign affairs and defence because the next few decades are going to be even more difficult and turbulent than the last few. This issue will come back to destroy them in government. I am a Liberal. I am comfortable being a Liberal. It is the only answer to the conundrums of our age. Fifteen years ago Blair was heading to be, broadly, a Liberal. He didn't end up there for all sorts of reasons. He was casting around trying to find a home for his ideas but he never found it. Labour is now hollowed out. There's nothing left of the Labour Party. What does it exist for? Its organisational base has become decrepit; its ideas base has been sold down the river. They are an instrument for government, but that's about it. There's a real opportunity for us under those circumstances.

Why is it that the Lib Dems haven't made progress since the last election?
The other two parties have conceded that it is the Liberal Age. They are all liberals now. They are all trying to be Liberals. David Cameron even proclaims himself to be a liberal Conservative, so here's the conundrum. If this is a Liberal Age, why the bloody hell aren't I Prime Minister? That's the real question! But that's what happens. People see the ground, they occupy it and you are squeezed under those circumstances, but I remain completely convinced that the party's day is coming, provided it manages its affairs effectively.

I still think a likely outcome of the next election is a hung parliament. That presents the Lib Dems with a real problem. There are many Lib Dems who are hungry for power, but others who see the party as a permanent opposition check on the Executive. They can't imagine sharing power with Conservatives.
You are dangling elegant temptation before me, but I shall resist it inelegantly. If a Lib Dem leader is successful, they always get dealt this hand of cards. Jeremy Thorpe, David Steel and I all had to play that hand. Every circumstance is different and presents difficult choices. I had to take the risk of working with Blair because it delivered things Liberals believed in like devolution for Scotland and so on. How the party plays that hand is really up to the party. For example, in 1992 I absolutely didn't want a hung parliament because I thought that combining with Neil Kinnock would give a one-shot Labour government and we would suffer even more. I thought the biggest

advantage to us came from a Labour defeat and I was planning my Chard Speech well in advance of 1992. Whichever choice the Lib Dems make before an election or after it is very difficult and I'm not intervening in it. In my day a hung parliament was a statistical near impossibility. The alignment of mathematical constellations was almost impossible. We talked a lot about it and so did a lot of other people. Nowadays the size of the Lib Dems and the breadth of the no mans' land across which Cameron has to travel to get a majority makes a hung parliament almost a statistical probability.

Nick Clegg is a risk taker, you were a risk taker. I get the impression that he may well lay his cards on the table in advance of the election.
Yes, I was a risk taker, and I laid my cards on the table in 1997 very clearly when I abandoned equidistance. That was always an uncomfortable position for us but it gave us cover in '92. But even then people knew that we couldn't have combined with Major. In '97 we said we would form a partnership government. It all depends on the unpopularity of Labour. If Labour is popular and the toxic effect of voting Liberal and therefore assisting Labour in our seats, i.e. Tory seats is minimised – and Blair minimised it – then it is possible to do that. I am not going to say whether Nick should make his hand clear. I'm not going to go further than saying these two things. Nick is a remarkable political talent and I think the more people see of him the more they will like him in the context of a general election. I really do. He is a risk taker and you have to be as a Liberal Democrat. One thing you can't do is play for safety. The second thing is that when people vote for the Lib Dems I think they ask themselves two questions: what does it mean for me, and what does it mean for my country? The closer you can get to giving clear answers to both those questions the better you are. It is a very difficult conundrum but Nick will be the person who makes that decision and I am confident he will make the right one.

Have you found the role of ex-leader rather trying? You have generally resisted temptation to make any intervention.
There are three kinds of ex-leaders. Those who say: 'I've been a brilliant general and to prove as much I will wreck things before I go and throw in hand grenades afterwards.' They think what they are doing is improving their standing as leader but they almost always diminish it. I fear that happened to Margaret [Thatcher]. The second type is: 'Thanks very much, I had a great time, I'm off to do my garden, please don't trouble me again.' The third is: 'I'm off to do my garden, call me when you need me.' That's what I have tried to be. I have tried to be for Charles, Ming and Nick the same kind of leader as David Steel was for me. He was always available when I needed him. I could always ring him up and say, David, 'I need a comment from you, I

really need to win this battle.' He would always come out and do it and that's what I do too. Being a model ex-leader is also part of being a leader.

Do they call you much?
If they did, I wouldn't tell you! They ring me when they feel it is necessary.

How do you think the Lib Dem membership views Paddy Ashdown ten years on?
Probably more kindly than they once did. People often asked me why did I stand down. Nice people say that. The truth is I was getting grumpy with them, they were getting grumpy with me. Perhaps the party has been lucky in that it gets the leaders it needs at the time it needs them. You needed David Steel's unique positioning skills, you needed the sort of commando trained, cliff-assault person when we were coming out of nothing and then I think it needed Charles. The party felt much more comfortable with Charles than with me. It would not have been a good thing if I had stayed on. I would have almost certainly tried to persuade them that the position they took on the Iraq War was wrong, and I would have found myself at loggerheads with the party and have had to resign. I wrote Blair a private letter a week before the invasion and said 'I think you're right'. With the benefit of hindsight that looks like a mistake. The war was not the problem. I personally think the war was probably justified – still. It was over quickly. It was a success. It was what happened afterwards that was the problem. That does not excuse me very much because the truth is that I, of all people, should have known the war wasn't the problem but our complete failure to prepare for what happened afterwards was. I should have spotted that and made more of it at the time. I believed the Weapons of Mass Destruction stuff and maybe I shouldn't have done. I regard it overall as a failure, but I regard it as a failure of mine and an error of judgment of mine, but I have a suspicion that with a long view of history, this will look a little different to what it does now. I would not be surprised if the Iraq we see eventually emerging – messy, uncomfortable, untidy, but broadly a democracy – doesn't have a considerable influence on the countries around it, which was part of the Bush/Blair calculation. I wouldn't be surprised at all if one of its national days isn't the day it was liberated from Saddam Hussein. History will bless this with a slightly different view from the one we see at present.

I guess like me, you believed a Prime Minister who told his people he had intelligence.
I remember being at a meeting with Blair in 1998 when he said he had seen intelligence reports on Saddam Hussein and he said: 'We're going to have to deal with this guy, there are weapons hidden under his palaces.' I accuse Blair of misjudgment, I accuse him of fatally misunderstanding it. It was

hubris. He believed he could do with Bush what he had done with Clinton over Kosovo. He didn't realise he wasn't dealing with Bush, he was dealing with the people behind Bush, like Cheney and Rumsfeld. But I don't accuse him of lying or deliberately deceiving us.

Do you think he misled you over including Lib Dems in his government?
That's for people with a little more distance than me to judge.

Reading your diaries, which I found gripping, it read like a seduction routine and you were seduced with your legs akimbo!
I remember saying to Richard Holme towards the end of this process, do you think he means it? Richard said, ah, the best seducers always do! [roars with laughter] If you believe that, and it is tempting to do so, and we all prefer conspiracy theories to the truth, I think you have to explain a number of things. As a new Prime Minister, with a huge amount on his plate, why did he devote so much time to this? Hours and hours with me, and Roy Jenkins. Why did he do that? If this was all part of a seduction routine, how come Gordon Brown and John Prescott really believed it and went out of their way to try and stop it? I remain of the view that he was intending to do it and the problem was far more that it was the big thing he wanted to do, but it was never the next thing. But I think I was too close to it to give you a judgment, but I am very clear on one thing. As the Lib Dem leader, inheriting a party who had believed in partnership government, and with the prospect of many of the things we had stood for for a hundred years being delivered, it would have been derelict of me not to pursue the greatest opportunity we had to achieve those things.

I think the greatest achievement was that it didn't leak.
It was indeed extraordinary [chuckles]. I love taking the media by surprise. I did it on my resignation as well. But I remain of the belief that the realignment will happen. The big event is for the centre left to realign. Then you guys [the Conservatives] are in real trouble.

What were your relations like with Margaret Thatcher? I got the impression when you first became leader you were in awe of her.
I was a disaster when I first became leader. I see some of the criticism of Nick Clegg and think, just go back and look at my first year. Of all the experiences in my life, which have included some quite hairy ones, the one I would prefer not to repeat before any other is standing up on a weekly basis and being regularly handbagged by Mrs Thatcher at Prime Minister's Question Time. She said to somebody: 'Who is this Ashdown fellow? Glittering military career, why isn't he in the Conservative Party?' [laughs loudly] She always used to treat me with

a slight air of incomprehension. In the mid 1980s she had all those qualities of leadership which second lieutenants are taught in the army. When the House was sitting late at night she'd be in the tearooms geeing up the troops at three or four o'clock in the morning. David Steel would be nicely tucked up in bed in Dolphin Square and Maggie would come out. That's just worth a million dollars to her troops. She was an impossible person not to admire, even though I opposed her. I didn't deal with her one to one very often.

In that first year as leader, did you ever think, this really isn't for me, I don't want to do this anymore?
[Chuckles] I had only been in the House for four years. I don't like the chamber and I wasn't good in the chamber. I had a tendency to be hectoring and I found PMQs very difficult until I got to learn the technique of it. We had to fight the battle with David Owen, then we came behind the Greens [in the 1999 European elections]. Yeah, there were occasions when I thought, is the party of Gladstone going to end with Ashdown? Am I really good enough to do this? It was very tough.

Do you think most politicians suffer from self doubt at some point?
Sure. I think you have to be a slightly misshapen personality to go into politics anyway. Why would you want to have your name plastered on posters? There is a certain strange quality that sustains politicians, which is probably related to ego, I suppose. Every politician suffers from this. In government, when you take decisions – and by the way I love decision taking and it's the thing I miss at the moment – I remember Tony and Cherie Blair coming to our house for dinner before he was leader and we were talking about all this stuff and Cherie said to me that Tony was thinking of giving up politics because he didn't think John Smith would hack it. She said: 'He thinks John Smith will win the next election but he's not being radical enough and Tony doesn't want to spend the rest of his life sitting around as an Opposition MP, he might as well go and do something else.' So we can all suffer from a lack of confidence.

Do you think it's a coincidence that a lot of quote flawed personalities become great leaders?
That's an interesting thought. Great political leaders and probably great military leaders too, have some bit of them that is magnificently misshapen, which enables them to do it.

But nowadays, if you have some character defect or you are away from the norm, it means it is unlikely you will get to the top.
But there's the ones we know who shouldn't be away from the norm, which the tabloids always have fun with, but there are all sorts of other ones which are a distortion of character of one sort or another. Is Gordon Brown a

normal human being? No he's not. Everybody can see that. He is a very abnormal human being. That doesn't make him a bad prime minister.

Do you think he is a bad prime minister?
[Pauses] I think I have to say that the answer to that is that history will probably say so. It's a combination of the hand he has been dealt…

Come on, he dealt the cards himself, mostly…
Well, yeah, he did. But part of that hand is coming in after ten years of government. He will go down as not a successful prime minister. But it is not irrecoverable for him. It's unlikely, but not irrecoverable. He has open to him what I call the Captain Ahab strategy, which is that he lashes himself to the wheel, he faces, granite-faced, into the storm, he should never smile, and just stick there until a light appears on the horizon and he can convince people he can see them through the storm. That is his only hope. He has partially done this but there are ways he could have done it better. If he can convince people that he has been guiding people through the worst while Cameron and his crew have been sheltering down in the hold, there's a possibility. Is it likely? No. The most significant thing about the British electorate at the moment isn't who they're supporting, it's the volatility. They are all over the place. Cameron's support looks wide but it is not deep.

Why did you decide to write an autobiography? I am sure you told me once that you wouldn't.
You're right. I thought the diaries would be enough. But Jane and my friend Ian Patrick, who worked for me in the leader's office, persuaded me it would be worth doing. I have enjoyed writing it and it represents a certain act of closure. It's quite an anti-climax when it's over. I've tried not to be too serious about it. You need to be a bit light hearted and not take yourself too seriously.

I hope it's not one of those autobiographies which someone once defined as a work of fiction about oneself!
I hope not! But it's a real danger. Inevitably you are tempted into that but I know there's an element of self criticism too. There are plenty of things I have done wrong. This is my sixth book and writing a book is the nearest a man can get to giving birth. I love writing. I adore it. I do it on trains and planes and in waiting rooms. I don't do it in a disciplined fashion.

You'd be a great blogger.
[Laughs] I love the process of putting a book to bed – choosing the photos, and then you have to go out and sell it. I've already started the next book. I hate having nothing to do. That's the greatest fear I have.

What's the next book?

I'm going to see if I can do a thriller. There will be a bit of spying in it! [laughs conspiratorially] I am not sure it will work. It may never happen!

How would Afghanistan be different now if you were there?

I am not sure it would be yet. When they asked me to go there I really didn't want to. People don't believe me when I say that because I didn't think it could be done. My worry is that we have passed the tipping point. I hope we haven't and we have to keep on trying but it is difficult to pull it back from where we are. Either I'd have gone in there and thrown the furniture about a bit and then become intolerable to the international community because they didn't want it to be like that or we would have succeeded in bringing some focus to it. The real scandal about Afghanistan, which is far worse than the lack of equipment for our troops, is that young men and women are losing their lives because politicians can't get their act together. Not only is the British government completely failing to have a comprehensive strategy out there. Once our soldiers take a town, DFID (Department for International Development) should be in there the next moment, taking advantage of what they have won. It's taking six weeks for DFID to get in, because they can't go in until it's safe. We are completely failing to connect the political with the military. We have a disastrous failure in a lack of coordination and a lack of planning. We love to blame Karzai and everybody else, but the reality is that if you provide more troops but no coordination, unity, priorities or a plan we are going to lose. Lives are being wasted because politicians are not getting their act together. It's a scandal. If I had gone in there I would have got an agreement to concentrate everything on three key priorities but we are all over the place.

Why did Karzai veto your appointment?

I know why Karzai vetoed me because he knew perfectly well that one of my three priorities was to establish the rule of law. The powerful are always the corrupt. You embed corruption in your society instead of taking the longer, tougher road, which is to construct the rule of law. Karzai knew I would launch an attack on those structures because his people told him that's exactly what I had done in Bosnia. It's corruption which is eating away public support for his government. He's not corrupt but the people on whom he depends are deeply corrupt. We are associated with that because he's our man.

At what stage do we admit we have failed and make the decision to get out?

I don't know. Either you do it by some rational decision-making process or you leave from the roof of the American embassy like in Vietnam. I don't think it will come to that. It is not irrecoverable and we are now taking the decisions which need to be taken and we are lowering our ambitions. We're saying containment may be enough for a bit, though how do you explain to a mother of a young marine that her son died for 'containment'? It may be that [Richard] Holbrooke and his magnificent muscular bullying fashion can get the international community more coordinated. If that's the case, there is still a chance to pull this round.

What gave you most satisfaction – bringing the Lib Dems back as a serious political force, or what you did in Bosnia?
The pinnacle of my career was getting elected as an MP and being leader of the party I love. Bosnia was a tremendous experience too, but doesn't compare.

But in Bosnia you were doing things, running things, as opposed to saying things and talking.
Yes, I was, but I was doing them in someone else's country. What I loved about Bosnia was taking decisions every day which genuinely changed the nature of people's lives on a day to day basis, in a way which isn't given even to a Cabinet minister. And I was gradually winning people's support for that, but it was in someone else's country. I have had a wonderful life but I am pretty pissed off at not being prime minister! I really would like to have been prime minister. Whatever you do, that's the measure of a life. Did I manage to achieve that?

Which prime minister would you have most been like?
You're not going to draw me into that. Every prime minister is different.

I think you are a bit of a dichotomy. Quite strategic and calculating, but also quite emotional. That's not necessarily a good thing in a prime minister.
I never said I would have been a good prime minister! [laughs] The thing that makes me passionate about that is that particularly today and the conundrums of our age, there is only one answer. Only the Liberals have the belief in individual freedom and internationalism. I would have liked to have been prime minister but I also think it would have been quite useful for the country to have a government genuinely informed by the Liberal ideal as it is, rather than for it to be imitated.

What does that word 'liberal' mean anymore, because it can mean what you want it to mean, can't it?
It has been taken to mean what you want it to mean. It means placing power as close to the individual as you can, allowing them to govern their own lives and take decisions. I hate it when I hear Liberal Democrats stand up and talk about post code lotteries. If you believe in local determination then you have to accept there will be differences in delivery according to what people think

they need within their own community. It also means an internationalist approach to what we're doing. The nation state is failing. The interesting thing to me are the intermediary institutions between the nation state and the citizen, and the supra international institutions above the nation state, which enable us to govern the global space. We can only make sense of our politics if we think of those structural changes. What you are talking about is a redistribution of political power. I don't see much understanding of that among Labour or Conservative politicians, although the Conservatives have understood the importance of intermediary institutions.

There's a problem there. If you believe that power should be as near to the individual as possible, yet you then talk about supranational institutions, they are inevitably remote from people.
There isn't a contradiction at all. I see no reason why my local health service shouldn't be run, according to norms set by the state, with its priorities set by me and my fellow members of the local community. But I worry about my children and their future when global warming is round the corner. Neither my local community nor the state is going to be able to deal with global warming, so I have to create the institutions able to do that. The real question is how you create democratic accountability. Those institutions are unlikely to be formed within the United Nations structure, they will be formed by treaty-based organisations like the WTO. That's the line of accountability. How do you deal with international terrorism or crime unless you are able to create some kind of international framework? Where power goes, governance must follow. It's an old liberal principle, and power has now moved onto the global stage and if that is the phenomenon of our time, our challenge is to create the institutions which can bring power to regulation, law and governance.

How can the word liberal be used in the context of Chris Huhne's decision to cheerlead for the government over their decision to ban Geert Wilders from entering the country?
I am not in the business of criticising my parliamentary colleagues.

In other words, you agree. Why do you think some people view you as a bit holier than thou? I know you are great company, yet before I met you I had this image of you as being very sanctimonious.
It's fear. A combination of fear and passion. I talk about it in the book and I admit that it really damaged me. It comes out in the House of Commons. If I get quite frightened, and the chamber does frighten you, my voice has a habit of going shrill, and I have a habit of over-painting the clarity. It comes from Bosnia. I was passionate about the immorality of Bosnia and people

interpreted it that way. Quite a lot of people took a lot of satisfaction over the Tricia Howard affair, the famous Paddy Pantsdown affair took place and the joke going round was that my answering machine said 'please leave a message after the sanctimonious moral tone'. By the way, I had never made any comment, and nor would I, about the morality of public figures, but even so, I think it's a fair criticism.

That affair could have ruined you, but you emerged from it with your reputation enhanced because of the way you handled it.
I don't think my reputation was enhanced! I was the first politician to hold my hands up. What people dislike is the lying.

I think people felt you were honest and even your opponents saw a side of you they hadn't seen before.
That's very kind of you, but I wouldn't recommend it as a way forward in politics – or with your family, for that matter!

Quickfire

What are you reading?
Obama, *Dreams from my Father*. I'd like to think I was a writer. This man makes me feel inadequate.

Your latest gadget?
I have a Sony e-Reader. It's completely fabulous. I don't just read books on it. I also convert all my papers to PDFs and dump them on it.

Favourite interviewer?
Andrew Marr.

Most formidable political opponent?
Margaret Thatcher.

Most trusted political ally?
I have friends rather than allies. I am not very clubbable. Archy Kirkwood. We are as different as you can get. I used to call him Chicken Lickin'. He would often persuade me not to do something and he was usually right.

Most romantic thing you have ever done?
Stand as a Liberal candidate for Yeovil in 1976! I'm not very big on romance to be honest.

Favourite music?

Classical music is a great source of solace. Strauss's four last songs, especially the third.

Last concert?

Sarajevo youth orchestra in 2006.

Favourite holiday destination?

I bought a chalet in the Savoie in France with my kids, where we go twice a year with my grandchildren. It gives me great pleasure.

Favourite view?

Looking out of the window of the chalet in the Savoie.

Jack Bauer or James Bond?

Who's Jack Bauer? Never heard of him. I have never seen an FA Cup Final. I have never seen an episode of *Coronation Street* and I don't know who Jack Bauer is.

Are you superstitious?

I like to think I am not but I discover in small ways that I am. I find myself avoiding cracks in pavements.

What food do you hate?

Tripe and bread & butter pudding.

Last time you cried?

It is one of my afflictions. I do it far too easily. When I saw *La Bohème* in January. I cry whenever I see a refugee camp because I see my own family there.

Cherie Blair

Party affiliation: Labour

Born: 23 September 1954

Education: Educated at Seafield Convent Grammar and then graduated from London School of Economics with a first class honours in Law.

Family status: Married with four children.

Career: She became a barrister in 1976 and was later appointed a Recorder (a permanent part-time judge) in the County Court and Crown Court. She is a founding member of Matrix Chambers in London from which she continues to practice as a barrister.

Interesting fact: Ruth Lang, a pivotal character in Robert Harris's fictional thriller *The Ghost* is said to be inspired by Blair and people who have met her claim the portrayal is spot-on.

Date of interview: June 2009
Extended version
Venue: Colman Getty, Soho
Total Politics Issue 12, April 2009

I had never met Cherie Blair before conducting this interview, and it came about in a rather curious way. It coincided with the paperback edition of her autobiography being published. Nothing odd in that, of course, but having been, shall we say, fairly critical of her on my blog over a number of years, you might wonder why on earth she would agree to be interviewed by me. Quite simply, she read a review of her book, which I had written on my blog. Here's a short extract…

> *I hope you are sitting down for this, but I cannot remember the last time I enjoyed a book so much. It is well written, pacy, informal, gossipy, full of wonderful anecdotes and, contrary to what I expected, did actually tell the reader a lot of new information. It is not a book which seeks to skate over some awkward truths. Cherie Blair seems to be a woman who is fully aware of her own weaknesses and penchant for embarrassing moments. She must be as she gleefully recounts them all, sometimes in a little too much detail, but she does it in an engaging and almost endearing manner.*

A few days afterwards I got a handwritten note from Cherie saying words to the effect that I was the only person to have reviewed her book and understood her. You could have knocked me down with a feather. So I thought I'd chance my arms and ask for an interview.

And I have to say I was completely charmed. Cherie is very flirtatious and proved to be a very good laugh. I didn't have as long with her as I'd have liked, so it was a little rushed, but I think it worked. Judge for yourself.

After I wrote a review of your autobiography on my blog, you wrote me a note which effectively said I was the only person who understood you.
[Laughs] Well maybe it's true…You were an unusual person to write a review and enjoy the book.

How did you find the whole experience of writing a book?
I think you may have even said this in your review, that I felt a lot of people were expecting me to write a certain kind of book. I didn't write that kind of book because I didn't want to write a political book. The political story isn't mine to tell, it's Tony's story to tell. So I wanted to write much more of a woman's book, which I'm unapologetic about. I wanted to write about the human side. There were lots of people who said 'oh she's going to write this sort of book' and so they wrote a review about that sort of book even if I hadn't written it.

Before I read the book I doubted whether you could be as honest as I hoped you would be, but in the review I wrote that it was warts and all. And it really was.
Well I think I'm absolutely entitled to be honest about myself but I also think, not least because I'm a lawyer, that I know about privacy and things, that I'm not entitled to be honest about other people's private life.

Did you in retrospect think that maybe you put a little too much in about certain things?
[Laughs] I don't think so. I don't mind talking about my pregnancies and talking about Leo and where he was born. I thought it was quite a nice story actually. I still do. All those experiences of going to Balmoral – who would have thought that a girl like me would ever get to meet the Queen – and she was always so kind to me, she really was. You know I can remember going to the White House and seeing Stevie Wonder and Elton John perform, I mean this is kind of surreal.

Were you conscious that when you went abroad you were always representing the country? Did you ever fear letting the side down?
Well absolutely, very much so. And that's partly why I wanted to make sure I looked my best; I don't claim to be a fashion model, and never have done. I have

always been a clever girl, a girl who makes her living by what she says and her brain rather than by her wonderful face and body, so when you are suddenly representing your country it's a big challenge for everybody as none of us are perfect. I think even models find it difficult. I am so glad I don't have to stand next to Carla Bruni; nobody's going to win that competition are they? That's why I paid to take Andre, my hairdresser, with me because I wanted to make sure I looked my best. It's OK for men. They just have to have their suits pressed.

What a sexist thing to say!
[Laughs] No, it's true, they don't have a problem with their hair. Anyone who goes on a plane knows that your hair goes flat. You come off and all the photographers are waiting. You are representing your country and you have to try and look your best.

Did you ever go on any trips where you met a foreign leader and you just thought, 'I really don't want to meet this person' and afterwards you just wanted to have a shower?
No, not really, I think I was much more curious. The strange thing about meeting foreign leaders is that there's always something you've got in common. If nothing else, you can always talk about the press [laughs], or you can always talk about your children. It's just fascinating to meet some of these people.

What about the Bushes? You had a really close relationship with the Clintons. It must have been a bit of an odd feeling, the first visit to the Bushes. I got the feeling any preconceptions that you had were shot away fairly quickly.
I was apprehensive because we'd known the Clintons so well. We'd obviously known them before Tony became Prime Minister, and Hillary was very much a mentor to me. When we first met the Bushes it was they who were the new ones on the block. Anyone who meets Laura Bush will say what a lovely person she is. I'd been around for several years by then, so she and I had a more equal relationship than I had with Hillary, because with Hillary I was always the one who was learning from her.

So if Hillary was a mentor, you don't have any desire to follow her into elected politics?
It's so different in our system, isn't it?

Well, it is, but you stood for Parliament in 1983, and you're clearly a political person.
Well, like you, I enjoy politics but I also enjoy the freedom I have of not being in party politics.

But when Tony finished being Prime Minister did the thought never cross your mind 'well actually I could do something now if I wanted to'?

In elected politics, no. When your husband has played the political game and reached the top, there are so many other things you could do. Why would I want to repeat his journey? We've both been there and we've done that.

Do you think that since you left Downing Street your reputation has changed and that you have had a rehabilitation in the public eye? Because you were a bit of a lightning rod weren't you?

I think that's probably the case. Sometimes when you have been such a successful politician like Tony was – he's the consummate politician, and someone who has won three election victories – it's often quite hard for his political opponents in the press to attack him because, after all, the public have voted for him, so it's easier if they want to attack him to attack me.

And was there a stage in Downing Street where you just thought 'if that's the way it's going to be, I just have to accept it'?

Absolutely, and I think there comes a point when you just have to realise it's not about you at all really. You can't take it personally and you try not to read a lot of the stuff. The truth is, even if you don't read it people tend to tell you about it, so you can't pretend it's not there. You have to understand that it's not really personal. Because I'm a political animal myself, I can look back and think I had views about what Mary Wilson was like – the first prime minister's wife I ever knew. But I also had views about Norma Major which reflected the sort of image she had in the press and I'm sure you probably know Norma Major…

Lovely hair.

…and the image she had is not actually the same as the reality of someone who is a considerable woman in her own right, does a lot of work for charity and has her own views. I got to realise that just as I had these views about people, so lots of people who absolutely don't know me, haven't seen me, have views about me. It's just the way it is.

Do you mind being described as a Marmite person, you either love them or you hate them? I put on my Twitter this morning that I was going to interview Cherie Blair and I had lots of responses, half of which were 'oh my God, how could you' and half of which were 'she's an absolute idol to me'. A friend of mine said 'I read her book and am now absolutely besotted with her'.

[Laughs] Is he tall, dark and handsome?

He is actually.

Oooo [giggles].

Do you mind that stark contrast or would you really quite like to be one of these people who actually everybody quite likes but nobody has any strong views about?

It's very difficult for me to choose because it does appear that opinion is divided and that it's partly just because if you say nothing and do nothing then no-one's going to criticise you, but once you start doing something – and some things I do believe in; I feel very strongly about making sure that women get a fair deal, and talking about that.

Because of my legal career I feel very strongly about making sure the law is open to everybody, not just so that people can get their rights in court but also so that the legal profession itself is open to everybody. If you start expressing views on these things, and people are going to have different views, then that's why I say it's not about you the person, it's about your views inspiring either criticism or approval.

Do you think your public profile has harmed your legal career or helped it?

It's one of those imponderables. When Tony became Prime Minister I couldn't do government work anymore, but ironically I used to do some government work for the Tory government before. That obviously didn't stop me being able to take cases against the government. It was like the time when I was pregnant with Leo and I had the case about parental rights, which was quite funny really in one sense.

What's your ambition in the legal world? Where would you like to end up?

That's, to some extent, not up to me. When it comes down to it I'm a lawyer and I'm good at law, I do the law, I understand the law. It's my world. A lot of the book is about the law and trying to explain a little about what it's like, so who knows where my legal career will take me next.

You've evaded that question. Everyone in every field has an ultimate goal they'd really like to achieve. Most people in politics say they'd like to be Prime Minister. There must be something in the law that you would ultimately like to do?

The great thing about the law is it's a big challenger. You are only as good as your last case and so you're always competing about the next case, performing the next challenge, but I also like law as an academic discipline – the way you can shape what happens in the law.

There's still a lot of work to be done in that field. I am enjoying what I have been doing. At the moment I have been doing a lot more international arbitration and that's interesting, that's a new world. It's a good challenge and I enjoy it. I'm quite interested in arbitration and mediation, and how you can solve legal problems not necessarily by the traditional court system. We absolutely believe we have the Rolls Royce system but it is of course expensive and time consuming so things, alternatives, like mediation and arbitration are also worth exploring.

You talk quite a lot in the book about the fact that you didn't want Tony to go when he was originally planning to?
No, he never originally planned to go at that stage. There may have been talk about whether he should go but I felt very strongly he did the right thing over the Iraq war, I still do. I also felt that the British public would sense that and by winning the election, if he'd stepped down before that election he would never have had the chance to take his case to the electorate.

Do you miss it all?
I don't really miss the big events but I do miss some things. It was a privilege. What a fantastic opportunity, especially for someone coming from my background. You make friendships not just with world leaders and all that but with the people, the staff who were around in Number 10. We still keep contact with the staff that were there and the staff at Chequers and a lot of those people became part of our extended family, and leaving them was sad.

Everyone makes contrasts between one prime minister and another, and I'm not going to try to get you to slag off Gordon Brown at all…
Would a person who's been a member of the Labour Party for so many years do such a thing? No way! [laughs]

…but you were quite clear that you weren't 100 per cent sure he should succeed Tony. How do you draw the contrast between the two? What do you think he's brought to the job that maybe Tony hadn't?
Well one thing of course is experience. When Tony came in in 1997, he was very unusual as he was probably one of the few prime ministers who, in recent times, had had no ministerial, let alone Cabinet, experience. Not only didn't Tony have any experience, but most of his Cabinet didn't either. Now Gordon of course has had the strength of being ten years in the Cabinet and there's a vast wealth of experience that we need now.

But do you think in retrospect Tony was right to give him complete control of the economy?
Well, [laughs] I think that Tony might disagree with that.

Well that's the impression given in all the books. It was part of the deal.
Tony is writing his own book and will no doubt give the definitive account of that, but Tony and Gordon had a very strong relationship along with a group of people that made New Labour the success it was. Tony and Gordon were pivotal in that and no relationship is black and white. It's a lot more complicated than that.

But there were huge rows, weren't there?
But again, I didn't witness many of them but in so far as we are talking about Tony's character, Tony is very much a conciliator, that's for sure. It's one of his strengths. It's more likely me who's the one who's likely to put her foot in it [laughs].

But when he does lose his temper, how do you calm him?
He tends to only do that at home [laughs].

I can't think why.
He has been known to lose his temper with me.

Surely not. Was there a point when he first became Prime Minister when it became obvious to you that life had changed; you wanted to do something and you thought 'actually I can't do that anymore'?
Well there was the famous time, for a start, when I opened the door in my nightie [laughs].

Yes we all remember that one…
We all remember that one and that was a lesson. I was still at that time thinking 'shall we move into Number 10?', 'won't it be easier for the kids to stay at home?' Actually they were the ones who said 'no let's move now'. And when I opened the door that morning, I realised we needed to have some distance, some protection so we could have some privacy.

Describe the feeling as you drove out of Downing Street for the last time.
There was a sense of sadness. Definitely. Partly because we had to say goodbye to some people that had been so kind to us. A great sense of achievement. That last Prime Minister's Question Time was an extraordinary thing and the House was very generous to Tony when they gave him that genuine tribute. So few prime ministers get that opportunity.

Were you there?
Oh yes, we were there, we were all up there, me and three of my four children. We got dispensation from the Speaker for Leo to go and that was a great thing. It really did mark the end of an era. I knew also that Myrobella [the Blairs's constituency home] had been the one stable home my children had known – all of these things were coming to an end. But at the same time there was this feeling that now we were moving on to this new phase, that there would be a new challenge, something to look forward to.

From my point of view the best thing now is that I am able to speak for myself, although I am always conscious, because I am Tony's wife, what I say isn't just about me. There are consequences for him too, but I can talk about things a lot more than I was able to when I was the Prime Minister's wife.

If one of your kids came to you and said 'Mum I think I want to go into politics'?
I'd say go for it. Politics is a noble thing and I think one of the worst things we have these days is a cynicism about politics – about all these politicians only being in it for themselves. I am not saying that every single one of them is a saint, but people who do go into politics do so because they want to make a difference and they have a sense of public service. My husband had it, and I like to think through my law that I also have it. If my children feel it too, then I would think that that's a job well done.

You are more tribal than Tony, aren't you?
I'm probably more political with a big P, or more Labour with a big L than perhaps Tony is. But Tony is an amazing politician. I always say that I'm the better lawyer but he's definitely the better politician.

Paddy Ashdown told me recently that he had you both over for dinner at his flat just before John Smith died, and Tony was expressing great frustration with the way things were going and was almost at the point of quitting politics. Did you play a role in persuading him to stick at it?
I think that may have been the impression Paddy got from that but it's not actually where Tony was at that time. He was frustrated because he genuinely believed that the Labour Party had to fundamentally change. John, however, thought that we could still sort of finesse our way back into power. I don't think there was any question that he was going to give up on that. The question was: how was he going to push forward the agenda for change that he felt mattered at that time – and it really did matter! I personally believe that that change made all the difference between Labour not only winning but sustaining power as we have done now for these last twelve years.

When Gordon Brown took over did you give Sarah Brown advice on the role at all?
I didn't give her advice, but obviously knowing Gordon and Sarah and them living in the Number 10 flat already, there wasn't a lot I needed to tell her. I certainly offered to show her around the flat and in fact when I first left, Sue, who works for me, stayed for a month to help the transition between the two offices. And we left them gifts as John Major had very kindly left us a gift. So we left a gift for Sarah, a gift for Gordon and a gift for the two boys.

If Samantha Cameron rang you up and said 'Cherie, I need to know what do I do', what would be the two things that you would say to her, on the premise that she might possibly get there?

I think that the first thing is – and I think Sarah Brown does this very well – you've got to hold the family together, especially when you have children. Number 10 is two separate journeys; there's the political journey and what the Prime Minister does, and then of course there's a personal journey and for that you know the family is very important. Number 10 is a strange place. Tony and I are like most modern married couples. It's an even-stevens relationship.

People make compromises, but when suddenly your husband becomes leader of the government then little things have to give. I used to cook and still do cook, and Tony would come home from work and I'd be told 'he's coming up to the flat for his dinner'. Tony liked his dinner ready. He's very traditional and he liked to come and put Leo to bed so we'd get ourselves geared up so that he could put Leo to bed, and then suddenly he wouldn't come and half an hour or an hour would go by.

And his dinner was in the dog...

When we were in Richmond Crescent the dinner would have been in the dog, but once you're in Downing Street you can't do that. He'd come up and say, 'I'm sorry I had to take a quick phone call or a long phone call from George Bush' or 'some crisis has come up'. You've got to accept that that's going to happen.

Does it frustrate you that people don't understand that you don't have a lot of help in Downing Street and also have to pay your own way?

Well we don't pay rent but what we are is taxed on the benefits, so basically on top of the salary they assess the value of the flat and then you're taxed, so you pay the 40 per cent tax of the value of living in the flat and the cost of the cleaner and the cost of the electricity and all of that is taxed. You don't have a chef. I always loved the story about when Ted Heath became Prime Minister. When he moved in and started to form his Cabinet, it got to about 8 o'clock at night and they had been working all day. He asked if there was anything to eat and the civil service turned round and said well, no actually, there are no facilities here. They literally had to hunt around to find some sandwiches and in the end they came up with some stale sandwiches. The system wasn't geared up for that.

One of the themes throughout the book is the importance of your faith which I think a lot of people would have been slightly surprised by. They remember Alastair Campbell famously saying 'we don't do God'. Talking of Alastair, he's

become a Facebook friend. I told him I was coming to see you today and I said 'got any questions for her then?' and he said 'I think you can think of your own'...
[Laughs] Fiona's just written a book of course.

She has, I just did _Woman's Hour_ with her about her book a few weeks ago
Yeah and I think it's going well, I think it's great, she and I were always interested in that theme about how you keep things going.

Yes well she certainly had a challenge...
Yes [laughs], he has his good points as well, does Ally.

Well indeed. You recently said that Christians were being marginalised in the UK, what do you really mean by that?
Did I?

Well, so I'm told.
No, I don't think so. What I learnt when I was in the Young Christian Socialists in my teenage years as a Christian, was that it's about what you do. The church needs to be there when people need it. It needs to be there among the homeless. It needs to be there among the people who are finding things tough at the moment, and it is. That's what I believe and I said that if they don't do that then you become marginalised. I also said that you have to engage with women, particularly at a time now when society is much more about groping towards equality between men and women.

Some say that for 2,000 years you men have had control, so now we're going to spend 2,000 years controlling you. That's not what it's about. It's actually about men and women with equal respect for each other doing things better together. The church needs to think about that.

I guess what I meant was I think a lot of Christians feel that, I mean bearing in mind that Britain is in effect a Christian country, other religions are getting priority from government in a way. It's understandable that government has to engage with Muslims but we are actually a Christian country. Do you agree that there's that sort of feeling out there?
It's not something that I am conscious of myself, but I think it's important that we reach out, not just among Christians themselves but also between religions because I think what people in faith share is much more important than what divides us. I don't think that means we should agree on everything, because obviously we don't agree on everything, but it's actually more important to highlight what we agree on than what we disagree on.

How much of a role should religion play in politics? In America it plays a huge role and here I think it is beginning to play a bigger role, but I'm not sure that that's a very good thing.

Personally, I am a huge believer in the secular state and I think it's really important that the state is a place where everyone comes as equals and there is no sort favoured, whether it's class, whether it's sex or whether it's indeed religion. Because of that the common meeting place, which is the state, has to be secular but to pretend that people 'don't do God' ... When I come into the secular space I come in with all the baggage I bring with me and that includes my beliefs, as it does with everybody else, because if you are a believer then these things matter to you.

Tony's role in the Middle East is effectively all about religion isn't it? Isn't that proof that religion has played such a divisive role in politics?

Where religion meets politics they aren't always happy bedfellows. The challenge is to try and make sure that you respect each other. In a secular state, it's important that we don't oppress any religions and we allow people to have their beliefs but we don't allow anyone to say that only people who share this religious belief are the right people.

Do you worry when Tony is in the Middle East that he is a target, or is that something you gave up worrying about years ago and have learned to accept?

Yes, to some extent that is true. Tony has a lot to offer in the Middle East. I think both sides respect the fact that he is a person of belief himself. Because of what he did in Northern Ireland and because he's very persistent and persuasive I really think he can make a difference there and that's very important.

Quickfire

What's the worst present you have ever given Tony?
Shoe polishing kit [laughs]. Actually he loves polishing shoes. I get him to do mine.

What's the most romantic thing you have ever done?
I can't think of anything. I'm sure I have done something. That's ridiculous. Obviously I have done romantic things.

Favourite comedian?
This will really date me, but I still really like Morecambe and Wise.

Favourite foreign leader?
Well, I have a big soft spot for Bill Clinton actually.

Most hated food?
I love food, I was brought up by a grandmother who would make me eat everything on my plate, but I remember we went to one state banquet where we were served sheep's eyes and I couldn't do that. No thank you!

Favourite holiday destination?
I like a bit of variety in my holiday destinations, so I like to try new places.

Favourite Cliff song?
He's such a nice man. 'Living Doll'.

What are you reading at the moment?
I have just finished a book called *The Girl on the Landing* by Paul Torday. It wasn't what I expected at all.

Jack Bauer or James Bond?
Who's Jack Bauer? I don't watch TV.

Gordon or Alastair?
Gordon or Alastair who? I'd really rather not choose [laughs]. Well, what would you rather me do with either of them?

Alan Duncan

Party affiliation: Conservative

Current position: Minister of State for International Development

Born: 31 March 1957

Education: Went to Beechwood Park School, Herts and Merchant Taylors' School before going on to read Politics and Economics at St John's College, Oxford.

Family status: Entered into a civil partnership with his partner James Dunseath in July 2008.

Pre-political career: Lived in Singapore and subsequently worked as an oil trader for an independent commodity company.

Electoral history: Elected for MP of Rutland and Melton in 1992 and later re-elected in 1997, 2001, 2005 and 2010. He played an integral part in William Hague's successful campaign for the Conservative leadership in 1997 and held a variety of shadow Cabinet positions during Labour's time in power. Following the formation of the coalition government Alan was made Minister of State in the Department for International Development.

Career highlights: Being given a significant position upon his party's ascension to power.

Interesting fact: The BBC and Metropolitan police received complaints after his appearance on *Have I Got News For You* after making an ironic joke about Carrie Prejean, Miss California 2009, and her public opposition to gay marriage: 'If you read that Miss California has been murdered, you will know it was me, won't you?'

Date of interview: June 2009
Extended version
Venue: Gayfere Street
Total Politics Issue 13, July 2009

Alan Duncan is a politician who is irrepressible. Just when you think he can't take any more he bounces back. There's no doubt that he is not a politician without enemies, but show me a good politician who has no enemies and I will show you an ineffective one.

When we conducted this interview it was in the immediate aftermath of the expenses scandal, in which Alan Duncan figured prominently. His

gardening expenses became a national story. There's little doubt that the whole episode was deeply damaging to him – a fact he quickly recognised. But he still feels he is deeply misunderstood. Indeed that question provided one of the most interesting responses in the whole interview.

The interview also took place shortly after Alan Duncan appeared on Have I Got News For You where he made a joke about killing an American beauty queen. For many Conservatives it proved the last straw. They viewed it as the latest example of misjudgement by a politician who should know better. Unfair, maybe, but that's politics.

Not long after this interview took place it was announced Alan Duncan was leaving the shadow Cabinet but would remain on the Tory front bench covering prison reform. It must have been a shattering blow to his pride, yet Duncan bore the blow with equanimity.

On this day, he remains one of the Tories' best TV performers and it remains to be seen whether his undoubted talents will see him restored to the top level of party politics.

What is it with you and Harriet Harman?

On a personal level I really like her. We joke, we spar and we tease but I think it shows two very important things about Parliament. One is that just non-stop, ding-dong, yahoo biffing and bashing across the Despatch Box is just not very good box office and people think 'just get real, get a life'. But the other thing is that in the House of Commons, particularly at the moment, there has to be the ability to work on two levels.

One is the level of political combat; but the other is of people having to discuss lots of detailed things behind the scenes. For instance we sit on the House of Commons Commission together and that's been in the thick of it recently. You've got to have a proper working relationship.

There's another lesson. I've got far more out of her by introducing a bit of wit and not being ferocious than if I'd gone hammer and tongs. So although it is humorous it is also serious, and I think it's much more effective politics than just throwing grenades across the chamber.

You're naturally quite a combative politician and I suspect if it had been somebody else in that job you might have adopted a different approach.

Well I'm capable of being combative because I don't like just backing off, and I think in politics you should fight your corner. In that sense – and perhaps in many senses – I'm a misunderstood person in politics.

I believe in the theatre of the House of Commons, I love the House of Commons, I love Parliament, but it's not working at all well at the moment but I think that courteous and powerful exchanges are better than scrapping in the playground.

You said you were misunderstood, why did you say that?

Well we can come to that later [laughs]. I am always being caricatured as a short little terrier but those that know me know that life isn't as simple as that.

But do you think sometimes people deliberately misunderstand you?

Of course.

And do the caricatures hurt sometimes?

Yes, they do actually. I am quite easily hurt but I'm quite good at not showing it. The trouble is that as soon as you start discussing it people start saying 'pathetic little self-pitying wimp', which is not me either. I think discussing one's inner feelings in politics is almost impossible because we live in a pretty malicious political climate at the moment and there's insufficient generosity of spirit to ever expect people to be understood. I'm sure Blair had feelings and felt that he was being ripped to bits all the time. That can't have been nice. I think it's better to be tough on people for their politics and their decisions and not their personality.

Why do you think it is often the case in politics that it is people on your own side that are the most vicious? In your case, you get far more thrown at you from your own side than you do from the opposition.

Maybe. I haven't seen it recently but maybe it's there. I suppose last January there was a lot flying around in the run up to the reshuffle, but why? If people want to have a go at me they can. I can't quite work out what their motivation might be but that's up to them.

Do you think it's got to do with money, that people think you're filthy rich and that people in this country still have a chip on their shoulder about that sort of thing, whereas if you were an American politician there would be absolutely no problem?

I remember about twenty years ago Peter Luff, who used to work for Peter Walker, said that the one thing Peter Walker regretted was that he got labelled rich before he ever really made any money. I really find it irksome to be labelled a multi-millionaire. I am not a multi-, multi-millionaire…

Just a multi…

…I suppose I am if I'm dead, but I can't just sign a cheque for a million quid or something. It's one of those modern labels where fifty years ago 'millionaire' was like billionaire today, and still newspapers just stick it in as a label. And yes, it creates resentment. I actually spent a lot of my own money, about three or four thousand quid ten years ago, to prevent a magazine from putting me on a rich list because it was totally untrue. I had to spend money simply to establish the truth. There were no other means of doing it. I can't escape the label and compared to lots of politicians I'm nowhere near what they're worth. I certainly would have been if I'd stayed in the oil business, so you can imagine it gets up my nose that not only have I given up being super rich but I'm accused of being super rich when I'm not. It's one of those crosses one just has to bear in this game.

If you had your time all over again would you have still made the decision to go into politics?
If I was starting now, it really saddens me that I would probably recommend to a young professional that they should not do it.

Why?
The lack of reason, the vilification – it's almost impossible now in politics to retain one's self-esteem. I'm not just talking about the allowances and expenses issue, I'm talking about in general and from my own point of view. To quote someone I have met once or twice, 'I'm not a quitter and I am seeing this through'.

Looking back I would have started later, but the trouble is you never know what the political cycle is going to bring. Nineteen ninety-two to 1997 was a miserable period and we've been in opposition ever since. If I had come into politics ten years later I'd be more secure and in a much better position in many ways, but you can never judge that. Ninety per cent of success in politics is luck and timing.

But funnily enough, the more we are under attack as politicians and because the country is in such a mess, the more determined I am to try and play my part as a politician.

That's how I feel, I had almost decided not to do it but with all that's happened over the last few months I thought, sod it.
What motivates me? I had a traditional family background. My father was in the RAF, and inevitably when you are the child of a serving officer you get instilled with a sense of country, a belief in certain institutions and good manners and educational advance. Throughout all my teenage years I just saw Britain going down the economic plughole and this made me want to go into politics, so here we are thirty years on from my last year of university when Thatcher was elected. It was her wish to put Britain back on an even economic keel that inspired me to go into politics. Thirty years later we are going down the economic plug hole again and that is what drives me to play my part in politics, because in the end if you have a strong view about the poor, about people who can't pay their bills, if you have a view about elderly people who can't afford their care, the fundamental building block

under everything is a sound economy and Gordon Brown's blown it. The man has completely busted the country, he has spent ten years spending other people's money as if there was no tomorrow and now is hitting us all in the gob and I am actually a very angry politician because of that, I think he's blown it and it's going to hurt people for generations.

How well do you know Gordon Brown?
He is so tribal and so antagonistic he rarely engages any Conservative person in conversation. I used to bump into him in the street when he lived in his flat in Westminster every now and again. He only ever stopped in the street for a chat once and it was a begrudging few words as I was off to the laundry with all my shirts in a black bin liner. He said, 'Oh, what's that? Your manifesto?'

You got a joke from Gordon Brown?
I thought, bugger me, he's got a sense of humour tucked away there somewhere but it was said with a scowl. But that was it. I find him worryingly odd.

But for such a tribal politician do you think he is physically and emotionally capable of building consensus?
I think he has no leadership qualities whatsoever in the sense of those qualities that unite a country. He is the most decisive, antagonistic political figure I have ever encountered in my life. His only political motivation is to get one over the other side. He is incapable of any kind of general consensual action, and he is pathologically divisive. I think the same goes for Ed Balls; he's the little mini-me who has inherited all the qualities of the man whose boots he has licked for the last ten years or more.

By the time this comes out he may have gone in one way or another I suppose.
I always say I have never had a political patron really and one of the reasons I am quite easy to be shot at is that I am what I am and it's just me. William Hague and I are very good friends and we have mixed and matched for nearly thirty years but I would never ask anything of him. Hague–Duncan is not the same as Cameron–Osborne but as I said to someone over a decade ago who was very closely associated with a senior politician: 'Beware. Those who hitch themselves to someone's coat-tails normally go the way of the coat.'

Do you think Brown will lead Labour into the election?
I think if he survives to the summer, yes he will lead them into the election but I think the Labour Party is in a long, slow miserable decline. Everything they say they stood for, they haven't done: equipped people for old age? Helped the poor? No, they have abused their position to raise money and

hide and disguise things over the last ten years. They have wasted a decade of growth and they are now going to cause great pain for some of the most vulnerable people in the country. Despise is a strong word but I do have a lot of contempt for the deceit of their politics. They have governed by headline and propaganda for ten years. I don't see any proper action and decency and I think that is at the root of people's disillusion with the forces of politics at the moment. They just feel completely deceived at every turn. Look at equitable life – no compensation; look at what it took to get the Ghurkhas properly rewarded; what has happened to everybody's pensions pot? We used to have what was the biggest pension pot in all the European Union put together, and then Gordon Brown went and dynamited the whole structure. This is the man who has doubled your council tax and destroyed your pension and he thinks he's fit to govern.

Is there anything you think they have done well over the last ten years?
Well obviously I think some of their social legislation has been alright – civil partnerships, for example.

That would have never been introduced under a Tory government now would it?
No, probably not, so I think that is a definite achievement that Blair can lay claim to, but I think that it's belittled by so many of the other things that they have got wrong. I think that it boils down to money, they have squandered a decade of growth, they could have recalibrated the British economy, they could have equipped us for global competition and the next phase of economic activity. Instead they have just spent everything. After fourteen years of consecutive growth we should have had lower taxes, higher savings, low unemployment, a massive pensions pot and a large government surplus. Instead the opposite is true in all of those cases. We went into a recession with unemployment, headline unemployment starting at 1.7 million, it's burst through two million and I fear it's going to go up to three. There's nothing left. The kitty has been squandered, PFI debt hidden, a mountain of debt, bigger than Everest times twenty, I mean we are up a gum tree big time. And the man who I think is largely responsible for this bubble of illusion is the man who is now prime minister.

I guess the solution to that is to be completely upfront before the election and say 'Look, these are the sort of things we are going to have to do but if you do that you risk losing support before the election.'
Of course this is a very difficult dilemma. We have had about twenty years in which no journalist or broadcaster, bar one or two have ever turned round to a Labour politician and said 'How are you going to afford that?' But in a trice they will turn round to a Conservative and say 'Oh that's cuts, isn't it?'

So given that all economic decisions are a balance between tax and spend, money in and money out, our critics or the country's economic observers in the media tend only to look at one side of the equation. So, no, it's not going to be easy.

Does it fill you with a certain amount of dread that it's actually you and your colleagues that are going to have to clear up the mess because in some ways it's a worse situation than in 1979?
In '79 a lot of the problems were physical in terms of strikes, directional in terms of inflation and on this occasion they are massively substantial which is squillions and squillions of government debt and in that sense the scale is greater and its going to take longer to resolve but do we relish the prospect. Yes, but with some foreboding because it's going to be difficult. Put it this way, people have short memories, we are going to go in and we are going to open the box and say 'Oh my god is it that bad!' Labour will have a new leader who will start getting up to all their old tricks and we will have a massive challenge in remaining democratically popular whilst having to do the right thing and that's not going to be easy as it's going to need continuing real acts of leadership and courage on our part to try and solve the problem. It's almost like open heart surgery without anaesthetic, you cannot put the voters to sleep for three years while you go through the necessary surgery; they are living voting beings who are going to be open to a Labour party who are saying: 'Oh look horrible Tories, they've had two years and they haven't solved the problems.'

However you dress it up, it means cuts. Isn't it better to spell it out in simple language that people understand and explain roughly those areas where those cuts will have to be made?
Labour always play with words. What's called spending is now called investment, as they think it's a cosier word and they brand us with cuts. You cannot go on as a country spending beyond your means, or living beyond your means so there is going to have to be a massive effort to pay off debt and then to balance things out over the long term. Whether that means high taxes or less spending or completely dramatic radical change that suddenly gives us the growth to pay things off quickly remains to be seen. George has got some big tasks ahead but he's a very thoughtful guy and he understands the magnitude of the challenge that is going to be dumped in his lap.

Whereas thirty years ago you had a clear difference between left and right, you had high tax and high spend, basically pro-inflation pro-trade unions pro-socialism in Labour and then you had a distinctive Conservative Party under Margaret Thatcher, which even in opposition laid down the broad building blocks of its proposals in terms of wanting to tame the trade unions, encourage more enterprise, have lower taxation and have freer markets. We don't have now what we have then which were massive nationalised industries in the great sectors of the economy such as coal and steel. So the differences between the two parties now does not appear as stark and if ideologies have converged people's decisions become less clear and I think that's another ingredient in the problems we have had over the last few months.

Right, now, I have to ask you the obligatory question about legalising drugs.
Thank you for asking me the question.

Do you still stand by the libertarian philosophy that you outlined in *Saturn's Children*?
I saw on your charming blog that this question was likely to come up.

Well I'm not going to ask most of the others…
I might ask you a question in a minute about the good manners of the people that contribute to your blog.

Oh yes, do!
By and large *Saturn's Children* outlines my philosophy; I probably get a couple of letters a week from people who say they have read the book and they like it. You can't take things away from people who are expecting the state to give them so I'm not suggesting, and never have, a sudden big chop of government. You can't leave people beached and bereft, but in looking at what makes a free rich and moral nation I think the principles in that book had a lot to commend them. I think if people had looked at Britain today from the perspective of forty years ago they would say in many respects we are a socialist country because basically half of everything you earn goes to the state, more or less, and that's a massive percentage. We actually have a very centralised state in terms of public services, a very centralised media unlike America which has a much more diverse federal structure. No one newspaper is as powerful as the newspapers here and I think Britain has lost a lot of its individuality and freedom. The surveillance state is beginning to take over, I think the civil liberties agenda is growing in importance.

In a way you ought to feel vindicated by what you wrote then, because I think the Conservative Party now has adopted far more of that agenda than it ever would have done ten years ago when the authoritarian side of the party still had a grip.
Yes, there are some areas where you need authority rather than authoritarianism and in that sense I think in our criminal system people don't fear any of the sanctions that might be brought against them, particularly for younger people and near violent crime. So in that sense we need proper

authority, but that's not the same as authoritarianism and I do worry that young people are getting sucked into going to court whereas it would be much better if they just feared authority to some extent, and were told not to do it again and were sensible enough not to.

That's actually a difference between now and then but also David Cameron to the public seems to appear much more a centre ground consensus figure than Margaret Thatcher was. Might that be a problem because people don't see him as the conviction politician they saw her as?
David puts it this way. He says whereas then, thirty years ago, the problems seemed primarily economic, now they seem mainly social, if you look at things like teenage pregnancy, poverty, violence and the lack of social mobility. Of course in the last six months the economic agenda is firmly back on the map, so that means we have both these things to handle. But I think that the way we've turned the argument is to concentrate on debt and I think that's right. Debt is the legacy of Labour. Labour governments always run out of money. They hide everything under the carpet, they buy your vote by spending other people's money and they dump this whacking great big bill on you when they get shoved off into the sunset and it's going to cost us for ages. They always run out of money.

When you look round the shadow Cabinet table do you not think there's an argument for bringing in some people who have got a bit more experience of government because it's going to be such a huge challenge?
Well Ken Clarke is in the shadow Cabinet and I am sure there are other names. I think going straight into government without ever having ministerial experience is more of a challenge. On the other hand, you're not there reminiscing, you have a fresh start.

I suppose the point I am trying to make is that Tony Blair always said he thinks he wasted his first term because they were so intoxicated with actually getting into power that they didn't quite know what to do with power once they got it. Whereas if you have got people who have experience you're more likely to have the agenda to do things.
Well, I think rather than just turning to people who have been in government I think the question you're really asking is about our processes for preparing for government and they are going on in depth and detail and that is probably more important than anything else. Maybe after two years in we will have a bumpy patch, Margaret Thatcher was helped by General Galtieri otherwise she would have found it very difficult. We're not going to have a Falklands War, I don't imagine, but it means that assuming we win, as we are not complacent as we can't just assume we are going to win. But there will

be a big parliamentary party with a lot of new faces who are going to need a lot of handling and inspiring and driving, so perhaps you need all sorts of people in the team to be able to do that in different ways.

Why should the tax payer fund your garden?
I think the outburst of fury is understandable and must be understood. We've reached the absurd and vulgar state of affairs in which a lot of people can't pay their basic bills and MPs look as though they are being paid in luxury items. Public opinion says: 'I don't care what the rules were. You should have applied a better moral code yourself.' I refused to use expenses for TVs and cookers and things, and I declined ever to use the allowance to buy food. I didn't have to, but I insisted on giving receipts. That is why *The Telegraph* was able to say that what was pretty basic maintenance – which is what the allowance was designed for, love it or hate it – was for pruning the roses which it wasn't . If you take Nick Clegg, wasn't it £800 on a rose garden, another £900 on his garden, £800 on curtains, and £1,400 on food? Where was the coverage for that?

I don't think a taxpayer's money should be used to pay an MP in things; you should just let an outside body decide what they should be paid and get rid of a lot of these allowances. MPs should not be deciding on their own pay and allowances. That is the fundamental thing and we are paying the price for prime ministers over the last twenty years not being able to stand up and accept the recommended pay rise and through a skunky little deal with the whips hiding it under the carpet in this disguised allowance system. The world has changed; it's called expenses but it was an allowance – tough. MPs should have seen this coming. I tried to set up my office in a model way, I tried to set a high standard for myself and I think if you look at everything else those of us in the shadow Cabinet have done, I think we have set a very good example by early on in this trouble recognising the public outrage and getting out a cheque book and saying we don't care what the rules were, even if we were within the rules as all of us were, we are going to sign a cheque where it hurts to show we understand.

But some would say that's all very well for you because you can do that. There are other MPs who are in a very different financial position who are finding it incredibly difficult.
I know, it's a nightmare.

Do you feel that your own reputation has been besmirched by all of this?
Yes, and you have this standoff between politicians who are annoyed and upset that their reputation has been damaged when they don't think it should have been, and the public who say how dare you think you deserve any sort of reputation at all and this is a very corrosive period in British politics.

What reaction have you had?

I mean initially, because the shadow Cabinet was first in the line of fire, I think we probably got it very intensively, but even now, even though the public might generally be getting more bored and just dismissive and fed up with it all, it still can explode at the local level for anyone whose name was in the *Daily Telegraph*, unfairly or fairly. There's little difference between the goodies and the baddies in all of this.

Have you been shouted at or abused?

No, it hasn't been that bad. Two or three weeks later it was already getting better. People were coming up in the street saying 'sorry you are going through such a hard time recently and now that I look at it I think they've overdone it on you'. But it's given people across the whole country an excuse to be utterly venomous and condemnatory.

You said before that you sit on the House of Commons Commission. You've got a role in putting it right. What kind of reforms do you want to see instituted? The public are demanding some quick action rather than putting it into the long grass with committees and all the rest of it.

Within two days of my becoming shadow Leader of the House I, with David Cameron, forced the government into a u-turn as the government wanted to stop the publication of our years of receipts. David and I forced them to do so and that was a very big step. David has already announced lots of things to dramatically restrict any of the items a Conservative is going to claim for. So within this second home allowance, that's where the focus is and there's already significant improvement. Within the House of Commons there's already significant improvement because of the new green book and having to provide receipts, as bear in mind everything we are looking at is three or four years old. The system has changed since then. Ultimately, if we are to be true to our view that we should not determine our own pay and allowances we must ask Sir Christopher Kelly to do something about it.

If he comes back and says actually I think MPs should be paid £99,000 a year, what's going to be the reaction to that because then Cameron, Brown and Clegg have got a real test of political courage because who's going to be able to sell that to the electorate?

Sir Christopher Kelly will have to.

What would you say, looking back on your career in politics so far, what do you think you have achieved?

My generation, the 1992 intake, has helped keep the party afloat through a very punishing decade. In terms of specific achievement, getting stuck into William Hague's leadership campaign and making that work was a very dramatic moment. We were working in the complete wreckage of the party after eighteen years in government. There was no press apparatus to speak of in central office and I pretty much drove myself to the edge of a nervous breakdown for the six months after William became leader just trying to do the work of ten people in the press office. No one appreciates what was happening behind the scenes there. When I helped William get elected I didn't ask for a job in the shadow Cabinet or anything like that, I just got on with the real nuts and bolts stuff in Central Office and tried to build up a press capability. But it was too much. The phone would start at six and finish at one in the morning. I just couldn't do it.

There are those who think he didn't treat you particularly well.
Well, he had a lot on his plate. I didn't keep a diary or anything but I think I can look back on that and say if I hadn't flogged myself to bits for that year after the election I think a lot of the apparatus would of completely fallen to bits. There were some other players in there too, there was Charles Hendry – George Osborne was in William's office later. But in that period William kept the show on the road. He had some pretty horrid, torrid moments, but look where he is now. He's deeply respected, powerful, assured. The phrase I use is 'combat trained', as you have got to go through the mincer sometimes to come out as a strong politician and few people in Parliament are combat trained in that way.

Do you think in retrospect it was therefore a mistake for him to do it at that point?
The argument I used with him at the time was maybe that the postman only knocks once, and when everyone says 'oh he got it too early' his reputation now is very strong because he has gone through what he went through. For instance, would he be the leader now if he hadn't done it then? Who knows? Politics is about grabbing opportunities and like I said earlier, 90 per cent of success in politics is luck and timing or bad luck and bad timing [laughs].

Indeed. Going forward to the 2005 leadership campaign you famously ended up supporting David Cameron in quite a public way; do you regret how you handled that?
No, not at all.

Because you were seen by many people as rather duplicitous over it.
Quite the opposite.

How?
I was under enormous pressure from David Davis and people like Andrew Mitchell but then journalists started coming to me to say: 'Oh, I gather you have pledged'. I said 'No that's not the case' so I was not at all duplicitous. Some people think I am, but when you talk about being misunderstood I'm straight down

the line. At my birthday party, William [Hague] told this joke: [adopts a Hague-esque accent] 'The thing about Alan is that you get what you see. He doesn't plot, he just comes and tells you to your face that if he thinks you're bloody useless, he will tell you if you're bloody useless. He's gone and done that to two leaders. He did it to me.' I tell it straight. In 2005 I was absolutely straight down the line and I think the absolute moment of clarity came on Radio Four at the Party Conference when they said 'Mr Duncan you've declared your support for David Cameron, why is that?' and I said 'Well I didn't before' and then I realised the only thing that was stopping me doing so was jealously as being from an older generation.

Because you had said some very rude things about him a few months before.
I'm quoted as such, but to be honest I can't ever recall saying it.

That's a very convenient memory loss.
A very convenient memory loss! Again, I have been teased about that!
 It was just as I said though. We guys who are a bit older and who naturally thought it was our turn had to overcome that and say right, these guys are up to it and for the good of the party off we go, and I think that that was the right decision.

But when you recognised the reality was there a little bit of a light that switches off because you know if somebody is younger than you they are going to be around for a long time and therefore there's a slight edge that goes off it all?
You're suggesting one has to recalibrate ambition, of course, but that's a good thing so long as you come to terms with it. And I have.

So what is your ambition now?
I want to be part of a successful, restoring and reforming Conservative government under David Cameron which can put this country back on track.

Any part?
Well… [smiles enigmatically]

It seems to me in all seriousness you are enjoying your current job in a way I don't think you enjoyed your previous job.
Well I did enjoy my previous job but there were a lot of frustrations about getting heard. But yes I am enjoying my current job as I like the theatre of the House of Commons; I think there's a very important agenda ahead that needs to be approached with real sanity and I think a lot of the trouble with politics is about the collapse of the House of Commons as a functioning institution. I think that the Blair/Brown destruction of the House of Commons with the timetabling and

different timings, the itsy bitsy holidays have just stopped it. It's ceased working as an institution capable of playing its proper part in the government of the country.

You talk about blaming Blair, as I think he's more to blame than Brown in this, but isn't this what governments do? Governments have one agenda, to get their legislation through and if the House of Commons lets them do it in the way they want to then they will just carry on regardless. How can you know that a Conservative government will be different?
Well we have always opposed timetabling and that kind of thing, so at the moment bills are getting through with half of it completely undebated.

Well that happened in the Major government.
No, not true.

There were guillotines.
They were unusual, but not leaving things completely undebated and not as a matter of course for every piece of legislation which we have now – a completely different order of timetabling.

But we all know the House of Commons and indeed the civil service are probably the conservative, with a small c, in the country and they are what Blair would of referred to as 'the forces of conservatism' so if you come in with a radical agenda of reforming the way Parliament works, the way government works, how would you make sure that you would swipe away these forces of conservatism?
I would like to see select committees elected. It's not forces of conservatism that are the problem, as much as the forces of inadequacy which have been elected and the way individuals behave in the House of Commons. Nothing makes me wince more than someone standing up and saying 'does the prime minister agree with me that he is the most wonderful prime minister since Winston Churchill'. You get some lick spittle, ghastly sort of slurp slurp question and what purpose does that serve for anybody?

I just think the collapse of competence amongst so many of the characters that are now elected is desperate. I am all for having lots of different fields of life represented. That's what a healthy House of Commons should contain, but not people who have no understanding of the bigger impact of economics or the world and global affairs. I would love to do a survey of Labour backbenchers and find out how many of them have not ever moved an amendment to a piece of legislation. It's probably about 80 per cent.

Why do you think the new intake of Conservative MPs would be any different?
I hope they will be [laughs]. We should encourage them to be so. If we encourage them to be automatons it will come back and harm us. We all

need a bit of grit in the oyster, we need people who are characterful and occasionally awkward because without them people at the top become detached and deluded actually.

How conscious are you of being a bit of a role model for gay people in politics?
It cuts both ways. I probably get about three or four letters a week quietly saying thank you. I have never been anyone who parades this and I regard it as something that ought to be a matter of fact issue. But I do regularly get letters saying 'you have really made a difference to my life' and that's very heartening even though I don't like to go and jump up and down about it. In a way I would just rather be shot of the 'gay' label. I've done my bit. I hope it's helped, but the trouble is, over the past few weeks exactly the opposite has happened. I've had letters that I know come for BNP-type people and some older people which are vicious. I know exactly what they are saying. You can read between the lines.

There's a lot of hatred and nastiness tucked away beneath the surface and I think that actually political leadership had been very important on this and on racism and on other kinds of religious discriminations be it anti-Islamic or anti-Semitism. It's very important for political leadership to have consensual dominance of this issue so that it doesn't go wrong, but when there is an eruption such as we've seen recently, it becomes a pretext for some really nasty stuff. I can never understand why, but people quite often want to have a go at me. It's probably one of the subliminal reasons why, but I have never complained. It's better not too.

I have always thought that this is the reason why that in some ways you have been held back in the Conservative Party and I think your reputation has been affected by this issue.
People accuse me of certain things which are not true because what they are really doing is getting at me because of that. Do I care? No, should I care? I don't know. I once joked with a friend that in politics you should never fall prey to jealously or self pity. Sheer hatred on the other hand… [laughs].

But ten years ago could you ever of foreseen that the Conservative Party would embrace civil partnerships and encourage gay people to get involved in politics? Could you have imagined there would be two people who have had civil partnerships in the shadow Cabinet?
I couldn't have foreseen it and I could never have foreseen my role in it or the way that it turned out. I have no regrets about what I have done and I hope in a way it's helped others as that's what politics is all about. I only have one serious regret though, which is that it is seen as my main label, whereas it should be my secondary label. For thirty years through Oxford and business

I have learnt about global economics, global politics, I have strong views about the economy and the way the state ought to be structured and I have built up a reputation of being media friendly let's say. And I have played my part in helping the Conservative Party survive with William's election and all that kind of stuff. I was very slow to get into the shadow Cabinet but that never bothered me at all, but what does irk me is I am sometimes not taken seriously on these bigger issues because of my prominence on other issues and I have been there, done that and got the t-shirt. The big picture of what this country ought to be about drives me more than anything else.

You had ten years as an MP before you formally came out. Why did you wait?
I would have fired a blank if I had done it earlier because the age was different. There was a bit of 'why should I, its private' but then my view on all that changed because if you are in public life you get forced into these things. People say 'you have to' and then say 'why did you – why didn't you keep quiet?' The truth is in public life that honesty is the best policy. I didn't want to do it too early because I would just be a junior MP who said he was gay and that would be it forever, end of story. It was much better to do it when I was more senior and therefore able to say there's more to me than just this but it is an important issue and it is part of the apparatus of the Conservative Party that is endorsing and embracing this as something they understand and support – not just some irrelevant little backbencher. So I think I got the timing absolutely right.

And you got civil partnered last July; do you regard yourself as 'married'?
I don't use the word because exactly as I said in the civil partnership bill, we must respect the distinctive faith and belief of churchgoers and other religious believers who feel that the word 'marriage' is owned by them really, and that's fine by me. So although people use it as shorthand, I don't. It would be useful if we could find another word for it. But as I said in the debate these are two parallel lines – very similar but distinctive. Parallel lines do not meet, yet nor do they collide, and we must respect the church in my view. In my view there's room for both and no need for friction between the two.

How has your life changed because you and I have spent twenty or thirty years on our own living independent lifestyles. Have you noticed any differences in your own attitudes?
Yeah it's fantastic. It's just so easy going and comfortable and happy and when the bullets are flying and the shells are exploding all around you it's much easier if you are with someone than not as we spend the whole time laughing and having fun. It's great. It all works perfectly.

Is being media friendly a double-edged sword? Would you say your recent experience on *Have I Got News For You?* rebounded on you?
I try to be media friendly rather than a media tart, I'm not just rent-a-quote, I try to lift a discussion to more thoughtful territory.

Like shooting beauty queens...
We will come on to that in a second. One of the deepest frustrations of modern politics is where interviewers think 'how can I trip up a politician today' rather than get them to say what they think. I have been on *Have I got News For You* four times. Two were great, one was an absolute classic triumph with Brian Blessed and the fourth was a complete almighty disaster because when it was recorded no-one could have foreseen the fury that was about to burst. They recorded longer than ever before, over two hours, and I was knackered by the end of it and it was in the last five minutes that I goofed. I had faith in the editing and they edited it in instead of editing it out. Then of course all the blogs completely distort what happened and you get attacked for what was never said. I think it's a pretty sad world that doesn't any longer know how to distinguish between a comedy programme and real political comment.

But as a politician you aren't allowed to have a sense of humour are you?
We must be allowed to have a sense of humour, although I think there would have been a better occasion than that programme [laughs]. I admit it, it was a disaster but it's all in the editing.

You had a double whammy with making light of all the expenses stuff and murdering this beauty queen.
There's no point in going through this [laughs]. I did not say she should be murdered and funnily enough blog and media outrage can sometimes head up to the stratosphere and it doesn't actually bear that much relation to what most people in their daily life think.

I watched that and I thought you were pissed!
At the end I had a headache coming on.

No, at the beginning.
At the beginning, I hadn't had a drop; I'd been sat around the studio for two hours drinking water.

So you would do it again?
I doubt it [laughs].

Do you regard the internet as a threat to the political process or an opportunity?
It must be seen as an opportunity but at the moment there are too many tantrums and not enough arguments on the internet and on blogs. But it's an increasingly important part of politics.

How do you think Conservative sites will change once the party has got into power?
I have no idea; I think we have to go back to minsters and government departments resisting government by headline, pretending they are rescuing the world by spending £50 billion on something.

But is it possible? With 24-hour news people want an instant reaction and if you don't give them the material they will fill it with what they want.
In which case, we are all doomed.

Quickfire

Jack Bauer or James Bond?
Definitely Bond.

What are you reading at the moment?
A book on the Middle East by Alastair Crooke.

Abba or Kylie?
Oh, Abba.

What makes you laugh?
Being interviewed by you. [laughs]

Who's your favourite superhero?
Superman probably.

What's on your iPod?
So much, but I am hopeless at remembering names, James Blunt and all that lot.

Your credibility is shot. Favourite meal?
Tagliatelle carbonara.

Sarah Palin or Bree Van de Kamp?
Who's Bree Van de Kamp?

You know the one from *Desperate Housewives*.
Oh God, anyone but Sarah Palin.

Favourite Labour politician?
Alan Johnson.

Most hated Labour politician?
Sorry Gordon, but you're it.

Most formidable opponent?
In terms of me being up against them it was Alan Millburn when I was shadow Health spokesman.

Thing you most like about Harriet Harman?
Her cheerful dippyness.

Most romantic thing you have ever done?
It's a secret.

Last concert you went to?
My brother, playing in a charity band.

Favourite view?
From the top of a Scottish mountain.

Favourite comedian?
It's got to be Rory Bremner.

Jacqui Smith

Party affiliation: Labour

Born: 3 November 1962

Education: Attended The Chase School in Malvern and later graduated from Hertford College, Oxford.

Family status: Married with two sons.

Pre-political career: Took up teaching in 1986 at Arrow Vale High School and then taught Business Studies and Economics before rising to become Head of Economics at Haybridge High School.

Electoral history: Entered Parliament as an MP for Redditch, Inkberrow, Feckenham and Cookhill in 1997 and then served for two years as Parliamentary Under Secretary of State at the Department for Education. She was later given the prestigious positions of Minister of State for Health, Minister of State for Schools and as chief whip in the Cabinet, before being named Home Secretary in October 2008. She stepped down from this position in 2009.

Career highlights: Becoming the first woman in British history to fill the role of Home Secretary.

Interesting fact: She is a season ticket holder at Aston Villa Football Club.

Date of interview: July 2009
Extended version
Venue: City Inn Hotel, Westminster
Total Politics Issue 14, August 2009

I met Jacqui Smith barely a month after her resignation from Gordon Brown's government, after some of the most turbulent weeks of her political life. Like her friend and colleague Hazel Blears, Jacqui Smith had become one of the poster girls of the expenses débâcle, having been pilloried for claiming 88p for a bath plug, claiming for a second home which was clearly her family home and the cost of renting a soft porn film, ordered by her husband.

This was the second time I had met her, the first being in the Durbar Court of the Foreign Office where she was giving a talk to FCO staff with David Miliband, who I had been interviewing. Spying me in the first row during her talk she came over afterwards and asked what on earth I was doing there. I had no idea she even knew who I was. She was incredibly chatty and friendly and I came away thinking what a nice woman she was.

The thing about Jacqui Smith is that she is perfectly able to laugh at herself and can see humour in most situations. I like that in a politician. Our conversation here was punctuated with uproarious laughter throughout. But that should not detract from the fact that she is, or was, a serious politician who was dealt an incredibly difficult hand when she was made Home Secretary by Gordon Brown. No one was more surprised than her. In those situations, you either sink or swim. And for a long time Jacqui Smith swam. That she was sunk by some ill-judged expenses claims is something which will live with her for a long time.

She lost her Redditch seat at the general election. That would have happened anyway due to her wafer thin majority. But there's nothing so ex as an ex-politician, and it is difficult to see any way back for her in front-line politics. I find that a shame.

So what's it like having your freedom back?
After ten years as a minister it's very strange in one way. The first normal Saturday when I woke up without a red box appearing on my doorstep was very weird but at the same time it's what I wanted when I made the decision.

You've been in government since 1999, now you're not and you have your life back, does it slightly horrify you all the things that you know now that you missed out on while you were a minister?
Oh, it doesn't horrify me. Somebody said to me just the other day, 'If you knew everything that was going to happen to you, including the bad bits in the last six months would you still have done it?' And I said: 'Without a doubt, yes.'

Do you think it's a weakness of our political system that there is no kind of career path planning at all and that people are plonked into jobs, sometimes for absolutely no reason, it's just there's a gap missing and there's a person there, 'right let's stick him in that ministerial job' and some people get put in the wrong jobs?
Yes, if I ever describe the process of becoming a minister, moving from one ministerial job to another, to somebody in almost any other job outside they think it is, frankly, pretty dysfunctional in the way that it works. That's not just this government…

No absolutely, it's the system…
The idea that you have people who have a lot of talent and a lot of experience and different styles but they very rarely have the opportunity to say 'actually,

I think my particular style would be best suited to X or Y', is a problem for government. To be fair, Gordon had talked to me about whether or not I wanted to do a different job but you have to get to a pretty senior position in government and you have to be pretty powerful as well before you can even express a view, let alone expect to influence where you go. I think we should have been better trained. I think there should be more induction. There's more now than when I started as minister but it's still not enough. I think there should be more emphasis given to supporting ministers more generally in terms of developing the skills needed to lead big departments, for example. When I became Home Secretary, I'd never run a major organisation. I hope I did a good job but if I did it was more by luck than by any kind of development of those skills.

When you were appointed as Home Secretary, did you think 'Oh my God, this is the big time now, am I up to this?'
Well every single time that I was appointed to a ministerial job I thought that, Iain [laughs]. I didn't sleep for a week in 1999 when I got my first ministerial job.

Yes but you admit it. Most politicians wouldn't admit that...
Wouldn't they?

No I think there is something in a politician's psyche, that it's seen as a bit of a weakness to admit any kind of self doubt.
Please note, I didn't admit it at the time, though, did I?! [laughs]

No, well you had a bit of a baptism of fire so it probably wouldn't have been a good idea! Going back to your first job when you first went into government: education. Having been a teacher was that the job that you really wanted or did you feel 'I was only given that as I had been a teacher'?
If you had asked me what job I didn't want, it would be to have gone into education and been typecast as an ex-teacher. I had spent a year on the Treasury Select Committee, and I'd done that explicitly because I didn't want to be typecast as an ex-teacher. Having said that as soon as I started doing it, I absolutely loved it. It was a fantastic job, one of the reasons was because of the people I was working with – Minster of State, Estelle Morris and Secretary of State, David Blunkett. That was a fantastic team to be working in.

It's an interesting point you make about the team because if you compare that team to some of the ones that there are now, you get the feeling that – and I think this happens to all governments when they get to a certain point – there's just no one else to promote. I think Gordon Brown's problem in his

last reshuffle was that that meant at the Minister of State level there wasn't
the level of talent that Tony Blair had in those days and this happened to the
Conservatives as well in the 1990s.

It's part of the reason as I said, not only for thinking about how you train
people when they become ministers, but perhaps to think about how you
develop that talent amongst your back benchers for example. We've only ever
dipped our toe into the net. When I was chief whip it was one of the things
I wanted to develop and we were never able to do that, but I think you need
to acknowledge that you are managing your biggest asset, people, and you
need to keep replenishing talent. There is no idea that in your parliamentary
party you should be managing them, supporting them, trying to bring on
talent, giving people projects to do, succession planning, the sorts of things
that would be basic in any other workplace. None of that goes on. I'm not
naive but I think there is more that we can do.

You were chief whip for just over a year.
An interesting year though! [laughs]

**I would have thought you were the most unlikely chief whip in the history of
chief whippery.**
Why's that?

**Well, I think you've got to be a bit of a bastard and I don't think of you as being
a bit of a bastard.**
That's because you take this you've got a very, dare I say it, traditional view
of how you manage people.

**No, actually I haven't, but I've got a traditional view of what the chief whip's
role is.**
My experience from 1997 was that people felt they had to behave if they
wanted to get on but that wasn't actually the way that chief whip Nick Brown
behaved. There are now too many people who have had a ministerial job
and are out of it, not interested, or who are a bit semi-detached from the
government. You've got to find other ways to handle them. I think the reason
Tony Blair asked me to do it was because I had done the education bit, I'd
done quite a bit of what was the handling of difficult issues in that, I think
that's why he chose me. I got the job in May 2006 straight after the local
elections. We hadn't done very well. There were already questions about how
long Tony was going to stay. So I had that run up to the summer, which is
what I suppose you call the calm section. Then we had all of the summer
difficulties [laughs] as I call it.

[Laughing] Tom Watson visiting Gordon Brown with presents, that sort of thing…
Yes. All of those things, Baltis and goodness knows what else. After that, the
job was to calm people down when they eventually came back to Parliament
and then effectively manage a transition from one prime minister to another.
I quite often say about my time as chief whip that although I never lost a
vote, I did lose the Prime Minister!

**Do you think part of the problem with our political system is that the
government payroll vote is just too big? Why has Peter Mandelson got eleven
ministers in a department that the Liberal Democrats think should be abolished
because it doesn't do much? Could we not reduce the number of ministers?**
That's two separate questions. Could we reduce the number of ministers? It's
easy for me to say that now after ten years as a minister, but probably yes.

**You've been in the system, you've been a Cabinet minister, you've seen how it
operates, it seem that sometimes there are ministers with not much to do.**
Actually I think in some departments there are people without an enormous
amount to do, but parliamentary under-secretaries, ministers of state in all
of the departments I've ever been in, big spending departments, those with a
big lobby or a lot of stakeholders have to work incredibly hard doing the basic
stuff of government. There has been a very interesting history at the DTI, for
example, which had been pretty well downgraded, with the Treasury always
wanting to take over quite a lot of its responsibilities. It has now been well and
truly reinstated as a leading department. I think it makes sense if what you're
doing is making an argument that 'in order to get through the recession we
need to build for the future'. You need a department that has a more active
industrial policy and ensuring that the innovation and higher education links
are there. Plus Peter Mandelson is an important and powerful politician…

He's the new chancellor…
I'm not sure that's true [laughs]. He's certainly the person who the Prime Minister
looks to much more broadly than simply his brief. When I was sitting in Cabinet,
and I sat next to Peter, the Prime Minster would look to him for some of the
broader political analysis. Good, I say. One thing we know about Peter is that he is
a consummate political strategist and communicator and the fact that the Prime
Minister brought him back into government last year lifted everyone, even those
of my colleagues who either don't like him or who feign to dislike him. I think
even they thought 'actually this is pretty much a master stroke'.

**Well, certainly the opposition thought that and presumably as a Blairite you
welcomed it from that point of view.**
I did [smile followed by laughter].

When you first heard on your first day in the job about the terror bombs what was your first reaction? Apart from 'oh, shit' [laughter].

I'm not sure I understood, I'm ashamed to say, when I first heard it, quite how serious it was. When somebody rings you up and they say 'a car has been found in Haymarket and it seems like it might have been set up to explode' and your first reaction is 'oh, that's interesting'. You then think 'well now I'm Home Secretary, so I have responsibility for that'. The point at which I felt a bit of cold run through my veins was on the Saturday in the office when the Jeep ran into Glasgow Airport. Even though we knew that there were other people involved, that they were travelling up to Scotland, at that point you ask yourself, 'How big is this? Are there more? Are they going to be more successful? Is it getting out of control? Do we actually know the extent of what's going on?'

Did you realise that your performance in the media over that 48-hours was going to be absolutely crucial in the way that people viewed you as Home Secretary in the future?

No, I was absolutely amazed that they were surprised that I was calm. What did they think I was going to do? Come running out of Downing Street shouting 'don't panic, don't panic!' [laughs]

I think because you had gone straight into the Cabinet as Home Secretary. I think it was understandable that people thought, we don't know this person really. They were asking 'is she up to it?'

I suppose so.

But you weren't thinking that way? You didn't think when you did the first TV thing 'my God, I had better get this right'?

Well, I did think I've got to get this right because I was the Home Secretary and everybody expected me to know what was going on be able to explain to them what we were doing to keep them safe. That was the mindset that I started the job with and though that was tested over the weekend, it didn't feel difficult at the time – I wasn't going to start screaming or crying or saying it was all too difficult.

Why do you think that Gordon Brown appointed you?

Somebody said to me the other day that they had talked to him about me – and he's in fact said this to me – I think he wanted someone who he felt was able to communicate in a reasonably down to earth way about issues that really are up amongst the top three that people are concerned about, like crime and immigration. I think he wanted – and he was right to want this, incidentally – women right at the very top of government. I think my CV in terms of the other jobs I had done in government sort of made me just about qualified to do it. I hope he trusted me and thought I would be loyal and supportive and I think I have been.

There was the theory at the time that it might signal a change in policy in the Home Office, but actually you carried on the policies of Blunkett, John Reid and what I would describe as fairly authoritarian polices with ID cards, 42-day detention and the rest. Were you not tempted to change tack with a new prime minister and new government?

I believe in those things – the ID cards and 42-days. One person's authoritarianism becomes another's emphasis on supporting those who are actually least able to protect themselves. I think I did change style, not only by being a woman but also in the same way as I wasn't an authoritarian chief whip. Helena Kennedy said to me the other day something about the water in the Home Office that turns you all authoritarian, but actually I think it's something about knowing the threats out there and your responsibility that makes you want to do everything that you can to protect people. I've always been pretty – to use your word – authoritarian.

I never felt your heart was really in 42-days. You must have realised the level of opposition within the Labour Party.

We did compromise in various different places. In fact, I arguably conceded too much and actually made what we were trying to do less clear to people. I still believe that there will come a time when an investigation will run out of time. But we couldn't convince the people that we needed it. Having said that, we won it in the Commons.

You mean by bribing the DUP...

No, there was no bribery involved, and don't forget we had to get quite a lot of our people. That was hard work!

I know one Labour MP who was offered any committee membership he wanted by Gordon Brown, but everyone said 'oh no, nothing was offered to anyone at all'...

Is he on the committee?

I couldn't possibly say.

I'm sure he's not.

We all know these things go on and it's what happens in politics but to maintain this facade that nothing was offered to the DUP or rebel Labour MPs just won't wash.

I didn't offer anything. I was solely concerned in making the argument and making concessions where necessary to reflect people's understandable concerns, and to make it acceptable. I think that we did do that, although I think we overcomplicated it. It was clear that it wasn't going to get through the Lords and that was the point at which we conceded. But we got it through the Commons where people thought we wouldn't.

And you got rid of David Davis at the same time…
Absolutely! David Davis is a talented politician but he made his whole raison d' être to get rid of Home Secretaries. Well, he didn't get rid of me… In fact I got rid of three Tory shadow Home Secretaries.

The Damian Green issue is a period which a lot of people thought of as the low point in your time as Home Secretary. Looking back on that now do you think you should have been told about his arrest? John Reid certainly says that he would have been told if he was Home Secretary and Michael Howard agrees. Why do you disagree?
Interestingly the Select Committee said that they didn't think that Home Secretaries should be told. John was in a similar situation during the cash for honours inquiry and I don't think he was told when the Prime Minister was going to be questioned or others were going to be arrested. Sometimes there's a little bit of rewriting of history. What did these former Home Secretaries think they would have done had they been told? I often ask myself this. They said, 'we would have asked questions'. Well, frankly, as a minister if I ask questions it's not only because I want an answer, it's because I want something done. If I had asked if they were sure they were doing the right thing I would have expected somebody to take some action on it. But it would have been wrong for a Home Secretary to interfere in the case. Part of me is frustrated that I didn't know, but I think it would have been more difficult to know and not to take action, or to know and take action because that would have been wrong as well.

Thinking back on the whole thing now, what went wrong ? What was done wrong?
I don't think that they quite understood the political significance of arresting a senior opposition politician and doing it in Parliament.

What does that say about the police, then?
It says that they are not sufficiently savvy when it comes to political matters.

Do you think Damian Green is owed an apology?
No.

Should the government implement the European Court judgment to give prisoners the right to vote?
It certainly is the case that there has been a European judgment about votes for serving prisoners and up 'till now, and in my opinion quite rightly, the government has resisted doing it.

It is something that they will have to do at some point.
I'm not sure if we will have to do it and I think it is one of those things we should refuse to do.

Drugs policy has been a disaster for years hasn't it? We have more drugs on our streets now than ever before.
No we don't. What we have is less drug use in both adults and young people – it might not be the perceived wisdom, but all the research in all the surveys suggested that that's the case. I think we have been more successful than your question would suggest. The reality is that it's not as out of control as people fear and I think we've got a handle now on what we need to do to control it and to keep it down. We have massively more people going through drug treatment. It's a fair criticism that we focused to begin with on getting people into treatment as opposed to getting them successfully out of the other end and back into life. I think we are doing better on that now.

Would you say that the last few months have been the worst of your political career? Has there been any time in the last few months when you've thought why do I bother?
Yes, in the middle of the night, most nights. If your reputation and family life and career were being dragged through the mud then you wouldn't be a human being if you didn't lose sleep over it.

Describe on a human level what it is like being at the centre of a media storm, not just for a few days but for a sustained period of time?
Horrible. It's probably even worse for the people around you than it is for you because while I was still Home Secretary I was reasonably cocooned. You've got a job to get on with, you've got civil servants and advisors around you and, because you're Home Secretary, you don't generally – though I sometimes still did – go to the supermarket an awful lot. However, you can't open a newspaper without seeing stories about yourself. I think the scale of it was brought home to me when I was sat at home one night in London with my sister. I said that it had been an awful day, and I didn't want to watch the news. Instead, we turned over to a comedy quiz programme chaired by John Sergeant, which started with 'welcome to the programme where people get sticky and uncomfortable, just like Jacqui Smith's husband'. I can laugh about it now but it was one those moments when I thought that I wouldn't ever get away from it. I felt I would have it hung around my neck, and that's part of the reason why I had to resign. The other thing that was deeply frustrating about it was that I knew the things we needed to do as a government in order to stand a chance of winning the next election, which were convince people that we can tackle crime and anti-social behaviour and that we could control immigration. That's the job

of the Home Secretary and that's what the Prime Minister wanted me to do, particularly in terms of being able to get out and talk to people. I couldn't do that because every time I did interviews I spent two thirds of the time talking about my expenses or the expense system generally.

Had all that not happened then you would still be Home Secretary. You wouldn't have resigned, would you?
No.

That's a pretty heavy price to pay. To a normal person in the street it was ludicrous that you were claiming your home in Redditch as a second home.
I had a choice in the matter but I had followed the rules. I had sought advice. I had lived with my sister since 1997 for a very short period of time. I wasn't in a box room up the top of the house with a shelf in the fridge if I was lucky – it wasn't as it was characterised.

No, but your main home has to be where your husband and kids are. It's just logic isn't it?
Well, this is the interesting thing. I thought that it was strange that you could have a main home that wasn't where your family lived. That was why I wrote to the Fees Office to ask if they could clarify for me that your main home isn't where your kids live. The other problem with that, of course, is that I did have to make a decision. So when I became a minister, my husband and I sat down and we discussed the fact that I was going to be spending all this time in London. I did then make the explicit decision that my main home was going to be different to where our family home was. I stuck by the rules, I never flipped. I thought that I had done the right thing both by the spirit, and by the letter, of the rules. Hopefully within the next few weeks the commissioner will determine whether or not I was…

But you did commit the heinous crime of buying an 88p bath plug. Is that something you bitterly regret and have apologised to the nation for?
Somebody, an MP who is also an accountant, said to me the other day: 'What the hell were you doing putting in such detailed receipts?' I thought it was a good idea to be transparent, putting in the receipts which of course included that 88p bath plug…

What do you think it says about politics or people's perception of politicians that it is actually the comparatively small things like that that people have really got angry about, rather than some of the bigger figures?
I can understand that, because it just looks piddling and it just looks like you are in it for everything you can get out of it. We shouldn't have had a system

in which you could claim for all of those little things and we shouldn't have had such a system in which so much discretion was necessary, because then you can always identify the thing that, on its own, looks ridiculous. One of the things that I regret is that we didn't grasp this earlier. I can remember us vaguely discussing the fact that the accommodation allowance didn't really make sense when I was chief whip and Jack Straw was Leader of the House. It was all a bit tricky and we discussed whether perhaps this was the time when we should just increase MPs' salaries. I can remember thinking that it wasn't a priority for my constituents and it wasn't a priority for me to make that kind of reform – it's not something that people were worried about. Well, I was wrong.

If Sir Christopher Kelly came out and said we are going to do away with some of these allowances and put MPs' pay up to ninety-five grand or something – that the public would stand for it? I don't think they would, would they?
They might not, but I think it is probably the only answer.

When you found out about this film package did you think 'that's it'?
Yes.

Can I ask what you said to your husband?
'I'm going to have to resign' was the first thing I said. I then had to go into a meeting which was the hardest thing I have ever had to do. However, it was the Friday before the G20 and people said to me – not the Prime Minister, you understand – that they didn't think the Prime Minister or the government were going to thank me for resigning just before the G20 which was so important for the government and so important for the Prime Minister. That and I suppose a certain amount of inertia meant that I didn't resign at that particular point, but it more than crossed my mind I have to say. I felt the situation would be exactly as it is, which is that people would be sympathetic to me but they would always remember it, and that this would make it difficult for me to get on with the job that I needed to do.

What does the future hold for you? You have a very marginal seat, and if the polls are right, you're stuffed. You're definitely standing then?
Yes.

You wouldn't be human if you didn't contemplate defeat...
Well I've contemplated defeat at every election since 1997. It's a pretty straight forward Labour–Tory marginal that becomes more difficult in the next elections because of boundary changes, so I have always operated on the basis that the next election will be my last. To that extent it's nothing new, and I think it's also the way that you think nationally as well as the way

you think of your constituency. I'm not out applying for jobs, put it that way, because you've got to be in it to win it.

In the unlikely event that Labour wins the next election, would you want to go back into government?
Yes.

That's a straight answer! Were you angry with Hazel Blears, doing what she did?
Hazel is one of my best friends in Parliament so on any occasion when I have been angry with her I have got over it pretty quickly.

She was clearly annoyed at what she felt was a briefing operation against her from Number 10. They were accusing her of leaking your departure. It was astonishing that a Cabinet minister would resign the day before important elections.
She's been very hard done by. One of the problems of this whole expenses thing is that the pain has not necessarily fallen where it should have.

You mean that the laws of natural justice have gone out the window.
And people feel hard done by, and with some justification in some cases.

Are you going to write a book?
I'm not going to write my memoirs, because if you want to make any money out of them you have to bad mouth your colleagues. If there's one thing I've always been it's a team player and I'm not willing to do that.

You've worked with two prime ministers, both of whom are obviously completely different characters. Caroline Flint accused Gordon Brown of a lot of things when she resigned. She made a lot of allegations about the way that he conducts government and said that she felt that women were excluded from his circle. Did you ever feel any of that?
I think because I was Home Secretary I wouldn't have done. I had quite a big job to do and Gordon was always willing to listen to me. I didn't have an input into broader government policy apart from what happened around the Cabinet table, but he was always willing to listen to me about Home Office stuff and change his views on occasion if we disagreed. I wouldn't have any complaints. I thought Caroline was badly done by and I think that almost had more to do with distrust by people around Gordon than it had to do with her gender. I think the trouble was that for some people if you got on the wrong side you could never get on the right side. You need to be more inclusive, because you're the prime minister and you've got to bring in all sorts of people and not test their loyalty in a way that means they're almost set up to fail.

Is he too tribal? Even the hard left found it almost impossible to dislike Tony Blair on a personal level. He had that magnetic personality that enabled him to draw people in and get people to do things that maybe they wouldn't normally have done and Gordon Brown just doesn't quite have that.

He does one-to-one. The thing about Tony is that he could do it through the TV, in a meeting, in Q&A and one-to-one, although he was more powerful in a larger group than in a smaller group. Gordon is very different. If you're on a one-to-one with Gordon Brown he is more relaxed, more personable, more clear in his thinking but not in an aggressive way. He communicates with you really well. If you could just bottle that and use it for the sorts of forms of communication that you need to use now...

Would you ever take on an outside interest whilst an MP?
Yes.

It seems at the moment that it's the new thing to beat politicians with and it's a myth that it's just Tories – you don't see anything wrong with taking on outside interests?
Well over the last ten years I've had three jobs effectively and I think I've done them pretty successfully and I haven't let my constituents down. That's being a minister, being a constituency MP, and being a mum. I've probably done the last one worst of all really... If you're organised I don't think it's impossible to do other things as well. I'm not averse to people doing jobs alongside being an MP and I think there's a certain amount of double standards between the idea that it's ok to do interviews and write books but not ok to be in business. It's whether or not you've got the energy and ability to do those things and not let your constituency down – that should be the determining factor.

You said that of those jobs you were the worst at being a parent. Do you really think that, and if so, do you have any regrets that you've spent so much time on politics?
It was partly flippant. I don't think I've been a bad parent. Although I haven't been a very 'there' parent I've been there more than a lot of dads in similar situations probably. However, it's the thing that I've missed out on because the kids live in Redditch and there have been times when I haven't been there enough for them and I haven't been able to attend events. When my 11-year-old says to me – because they knew I was going to resign – he said 'Mum, when you are not Home Secretary any more what does that mean? Does it mean that when we go on holiday you won't be on the phone so much?' and I said, 'Yeah that's just about what it means'. He's never known any different because he was born in 1998, so I've been an MP or minister most of his life. I don't think there are permanent scars – or I hope there are not.

Quickfire

Jack Bauer or James Bond?
James Bond.

What makes you laugh?
My kids, TV, my colleagues – sometimes for the wrong reasons. Steven Pound is the funniest Labour MP.

Favourite meal?
Christmas lunch.

Most hated politician?
Nick Griffin.

Most formidable opponent ?
David Davis.

Most romantic thing you've ever done?
Probably not making my husband sleep on the sofa in the last six months.

Last concert?
Girls Aloud, it was brilliant.

What book are you reading?
Kate Atkinson – *When Will There Be Good News*.

Favourite view?
The view of Harlech beach, from just above it, near where our caravan is.

Favourite comedian?
Catherine Tate.

One word to describe Tony Blair?
Brilliant.

One word to describe Gordon Brown?
Equally brilliant [laughs].

Ann Widdecombe

Party affiliation: Conservative

Born: 4 October 1947

Education: Educated at Royal Naval School, Singapore; La Sainte Union convent, Bath; Birmingham University; and Lady Margaret Hall, Oxford.

Family status: Shared a home with her widowed mother, Rita Widdecombe, in London until Rita's death in May 2007.

Pre-political career: Worked in the marketing department of Unilever before becoming an administrator at London University.

Electoral history: Became a Conservative MP for Maidstone in 1987. She has held a variety of government positions including Minster for Employment and Minister for the Home Office. In October 2007 she announced her intention to retire at the next general election. She recently said she would like to take over from Michael Martin as Speaker of the House of Commons, but lost out to John Bercow.

Career highlights: Attaining the position of shadow Home Secretary under William Hague.

Interesting fact: After her second appearance on the BBC's *Have I Got News For You* she vowed never to appear on the show again after comments made by panelist Jimmy Carr. She wrote, 'His idea of wit is a barrage of filth and the sort of humour most men grow out of in their teens...'.

Date of interview: July 2009
Extended version
Venue: Ann Widdecombe's office, 1 Parliament Street, Westminster
Total Politics Issue 15, September 2009

I first met Ann Widdecombe in 1997 when she came into the Westminster bookshop that I owned called Politico's. We stocked a nice line in novelty political underwear at that time. We had the Margaret Thatcher knickers with 'no, no, no' across the front. We had the New Labour knickers with 'Things can only get wetter'. And we had a nice black pair of knickers with 'Something of the night' across the front. They were the Ann Widdecombe knickers. I presented her with a pair and to her credit, she roared with laughter. But as she was leaving the shop I noticed the knickers were on the

*counter. 'Ann,' I shouted. 'You've forgotten your knickers!' And there can't be
too many men alive today who've ever said that to Ann Widdecombe!*

Since then we've become firm friends. We do a theatre show together, called
A Night with Ann Widdecombe. *Of course, if you talk to her, she'll call it* An
Audience with Ann Widdecombe. *We tour provincial theatres up and down
the country and always get a good audience. They like her because she tells it
as she sees it. There's very little spin to Ann Widdecombe, except of course if
she's on a dance floor with Anton du Beke. You may not agree with what she
says (and I often don't) but you know she isn't following any party line.*

*I tried to persuade her not to stand down as an MP as I feared her media
might dry up if she lost the letters M and P after her name. She's certainly
proved me wrong on that. She's on her way to becoming a national treasure.*

How much of your time are you thinking about and preparing for retirement?
Quite a lot, but the plans have been in place for a long time. I've bought
a house on Dartmoor. I know exactly what I'm going to do. The office is
beginning to gear up. We've got twenty-two years of archives which we're
pruning through. People here are beginning to think about what their own
futures are going to be. Meanwhile, the ordinary stuff is happening as well.

Why on earth choose Dartmoor? It's a very solitary place.
That's precisely why I've chosen Dartmoor.

**Having gone from a life with lots of people around you, you're going to be on
your own all the time.**
That's what I want. I don't want to be a hermit but I want a much more
solitary existence.

Why?
The great attraction of Dartmoor is that it really is possible that if you get
out deep in you really can go a whole day and if you see anybody else it will
only be in the distance. And if, as you rightly say, you've lived a life when you
never have a spare minute away from people, then you do really appreciate
your own company when you can get it. And I think it's one of the reasons
– and I don't want to overplay it – that I've been very contented not to have
married and not to have had a family. Because what I've always been able to
do is to go home at night and shut the door and then I've got peace and quiet.
And the most I've ever had is a couple of cats or in latter years my mum. I've
always valued that, I've always actually liked my own company. I like time to
think. I like time to ruminate gently.

It's quite rare for a politician to say that they're comfortable in their own company.
I don't think that's true. Why do you think that Winston Churchill used to just go quietly away and sketch? Not writing. Writing's actually quite a tumultuous business because you're heavily engaged in what you're doing. But he used to paint and that's a very solitary pastime.

You're not someone I'd describe as clubbable. Is that a problem in politics: that you have to go through all the social niceties, you have to smile at people and pretend that you think they're wonderful, if you actually don't get right to the top?
I've never pretended to think people are wonderful if I haven't thought they're wonderful. I'm perfectly pleasant to people. I think you have to be clubbable in the sense that if you're a complete stranger to the bars and restaurants of Westminster you will just miss out on the ordinary gelling that goes on between colleagues. So you do need some of that. I do think I'm a clubbable person. Last night I was taking on the Carlton [Club] and saying 'come on: we need a club table where ladies and gentlemen can mix'. I do feel a part of the team, but I've got my own views. I've always known what I wanted to do and under William Hague certainly I was allowed to do it.

You quite like a good gossip don't you?
Er, I quite like a good gossip, yes. Depends where it's leading of course [laughs]. Maybe leading in directions one wouldn't want to go.

So when you're sitting in your study, in your house, on your own, in Dartmoor, what will you be doing?
I shall write more novels. I shall try my hand at a detective novel. Now, you may well say what do I mean by 'try my hand at' when I've already got four novels published? But the way I write and have always written is that it is a work of exploration. So I invent a situation, introduce some characters and throw the two together and I see what happens. And therefore in three of my four books at the end I have been surprised. When I sit down to write I very rarely know what's going to happen by the time I stand up. You can't write a detective novel that way. You actually have to know from the first sentence who did it and why and how. You can't wait to see what happens at the end. So it's a completely different discipline and I'd like to see if I've got it.

What about your memoirs?
I've decided after a lot of vacillating. I was never entirely certain I was going to write them – I've always said facetiously that the best time to publish them is posthumously. Because if you are to tell the whole unvarnished truth you'll upset friends as well as enemies and I don't fancy the prospect of a

friendless old age even though I am going down to Dartmoor. So I was never entirely certain I was going to write them.

I remember you telling me that you definitely wouldn't.
I don't think that I said that. But I very often said that I thought not. That I thought the balance was against it. I always held a little chink open and of course it's a chink through which agents and others have tried to climb. I think I have been persuaded that it will be a good idea. But it won't be the sort of memoir which produces very juicy gossip.

It won't sell then, will it?
Maybe not. Maybe you're right. But it will be a genuine set of memoirs.

Have you started?
I've made a start. Even at the point of starting I was profoundly unconvinced that I was necessarily going through with the project. I don't think now that I shall abandon it because I am loathe to have wasted that work. But I was never gagging to write my memoirs. I am not longing to expose something. I don't have anything like that in my mind.

Would you like to go to the Lords?
That's entirely within the gift of David Cameron. It's not within my gift. So I have no idea whether it's going to be offered or not. If it's offered, I shall take it. If not, I shan't bury myself in a handkerchief.

What kind of peer would you be?
A pretty good one I would think [laughs]. I don't want to be a minister: red boxes, days that begin with the *Today Programme* and end long after *Newsnight*. If I'd have wanted that sort of life, realising that we're going into government, I'd have stayed on. I don't want that sort of life. I've done that, been there, got the t-shirt. On the other hand, I don't think that one can take a peerage and treat it as an honorific and do nothing whatsoever. So I think the answer to your question is that I would be a moderately active but not obsessively active peer.

I think Baroness Widdecombe of Widdecombe in the Moor in the county of Devon has a certain ring to it.
I haven't given that any thought. That would be presumptuous [laughs]. And anyway I couldn't be 'of' anything except Maidstone. That would be a terrible insult to Maidstone. I'm pleased to say that Maidstone would have priority.

When did you decide to throw your hat into the ring for the Speakership?
On the day that Michael Martin resigned, two colleagues came up to me – Nigel

Evans and Mark Pritchard – and asked me to stand. My reaction was polite but inside I was laughing. It was ridiculous. I was standing down. Who wants a Speaker for a maximum of a year? It seemed a silly proposition. However, I became convinced that, because of the extraordinary situation that we were in, there was merit in that suggestion. Then some Labour people approached me and said they thought it would be a good idea as well. People were ringing up my office saying go for it. And of course, as ever, the public were behind it. I won just about every opinion poll very convincingly. But as usual, and we saw it over the leadership in 2001, the view of the public is not necessarily reflected in Parliament. I was actually pleased with the result: it was a respectable result.

Do you think if you hadn't been standing down, things might have been very different?
I don't know the answer to that. A lot of Labour people who were prepared to support would only do so if I agreed to stay on. I said no. For many reasons: I have a successor who's worked the seat hard.

You could have gone for another seat.
That I would not have done. That's unfair because you'd just be a token in another seat. You wouldn't know it or anything. I had a successor who had worked very hard for a year. My own private plans were well advanced – I'd bought the house on Dartmoor; I had the column in the *Express*. All my plans were in place. But far more than that: I simply want to go. There have been straws in the wind for some time. I now prefer the countryside to the metropolis. I prefer the whimsy of *Countdown* to the bash-bash of *Question Time*. And these straws have been arriving over some period and I know I want to go. There would have been a terrible upheaval to have faced supposing I had decided to stay on and supposing Maidstone had agreed that I should stay on. I could never express a view again. I would have had to have disappeared into that – I nearly called it a mausoleum – into that place over there [laughs and points to the Speaker's Apartments] and not come out and mixed with colleagues – your clubbable point. In the end I thought I just don't want any of that.

You clearly considered staying on, though?
Not seriously, but I had to keep justifying why I wasn't staying on. So all these things that I'm saying to you now – my successor, my own plans were advanced – these were arguments I was deploying the whole time. But I knew inside me that the major reason was I simply wanted to go.

Is that because you become disillusioned with politics?
No. There isn't a great shaking the dust off my feet, brushing down my robe. There isn't any of that stuff. But things have changed: I came into this place as

a Member of Parliament, I leave it as an employee of the House of Commons, and they're completely different. And if we're not careful, we are going to end up with a Parliament full of professional politicians, with precious little contact in a sensible way with the outside world. We're going to end up with rules and targets and all the things that currently paralyse so much of British life. And it has no appeal at all. We're moving away from a loose gathering of people from all professions and none who get together to make law and make decisions of state. We've passed from that to becoming actual employees. Now that might suit some people well. It doesn't suit me. I do not believe that in the end, it's going to suit the country. I think we're going to have a thoroughly third-rate Parliament. Already the quality's declined but I think this will precipitate a Parliament full of career politicians. If you're a dentist for example, you must pull teeth, you cannot stop pulling them after a ten-year gap. You must pull teeth. And so you need to keep your hand in.

Literally.
Yes. You have to do it. You're told you have to come in to a place where you cannot practice, you won't come in. But it goes beyond that. It's all very well to talk about professional politicians but if you're in a profession, you make a reasonable assumption: you train and from the end of your training until the day that you hang up your hat, you practice that profession. You can't do that in politics: we have this thing called an election every five years. We have this thing called a Boundaries Commission which can wipe you out with one stroke of the pen. You can't do that; it's not a profession. And we're trying to set up something which simply won't work and which will give a very poor service.

But in the end, isn't that the fault of the House of Commons of which you have been a part?
Of course it is. But one of the things is, we're just very panicky here. It's the internal equivalent of the 'dangerous dogs' legislation which was a load of nonsense. Of the gun law which I – poor muffin – had to take through parliament. It was a load of nonsense and wasn't going to do anything to stop gun crime. We panic in response to a deep public reaction. And that is, as far as I'm concerned, an abdication of responsibility. We shouldn't. But that is not the reason I'm going. It's part of a great mix of reasons and at the end I've simply had enough. The straws have been arriving which say you want to go off to a different set of pastures. I do not want to grow old in office. I've still got some of my vigour left and I might even discover more after I've retired! [laughs]

God help us all.
I want to go off and use it elsewhere.

In the next parliament there could be three hundred new MPs. What effect do you think that will have both positive and negative?

I think it will actually be quite a difficult parliament to run. I don't envy David Cameron. It isn't so much that we've got new MPs, but we've got a vast number with no experience at all. It is profoundly desirable that you always have in parliament people who've come in completely fresh because they're the ones who have the fresh perspective. But it's also crucial that you're anchored. And there's been an attitude in the Conservative Party for some time that grey hair isn't worth anything. Never more so than in candidate selection. We have some very good [ex] MPs who lost their seats in 1997. Those of us who survived in 1997 were lucky. We were blessed. We were not somehow superior beings. And yet that is how we reacted and we started passing judgments on colleagues who'd lost. They didn't desert their seats when they lost in 1997 and go off to green pastures, they stayed with them. Those people have been treated with contempt by the party. I think the party is wrong and it's going to rue the day. It isn't going to have the experience that it ought to be able to call on. Not just in forming a government, but also in running a parliament.

How do you think Mr Bercow is doing?

I think John's got an uphill task. It's a situation no one foresaw. The irony is when you're standing you have to produce three names from parties other than your own. Nobody ever said 'you need three from your own party as well' because nobody ever assumed it would be necessary. And what I think any Speaker needs is cross-party consensus in the House of Commons because then they're the servant of the House of Commons. If they're a simply partisan appointment, it stores up trouble. That was Michael [Martin]'s problem. John's begun against a huge tide of resentment because it's seen as a partisan appointment. But he is now the Speaker of the House of Commons and I think whether or not he's successful will depend entirely on him and how he decides how to discharge the office.

Your face during his speech was a picture.

Yes. It was not my wished-for appointment. But I take the same line with the Speaker which I've always taken with party leaders. There's got to be losers in any election by definition. When somebody's won, you want to try and make it work and get behind them. If we keep turning on this Speaker, we'll turn into a rabble because he's the authority figure in the House of Commons. So you've got to try and make it work. I said that when Michael Martin was appointed and I say it now John Bercow has been appointed.

And if it doesn't, should he be challenged?
I do hope not, because if we get into the habit of turning on our Speaker we really do become a rabble. It happened with Michael after 300 years. I would willingly wait another 300 years before we do it again.

What did you make of David Cameron's plea for anybody to come forward who wants to be a Conservative candidate a few weeks ago? Apparently 4,000 have.
I think he's wrong. It's been well known for a long time that David and I have not agreed on candidate selection. I think he's a fantastic leader; he's winning. But all leaders get some things wrong and I think our approach – which hasn't just been David's – to candidate selection over the last few years has been completely misguided. We have gone for category rather than ability. We're looking for more women. I'm all for more women, I'm all for more members of the ethnic communities, I'm all for more anythings as long as they get there on merit. I believe as a woman, that every woman in Parliament should be able to look every man from the prime minister downwards in the eye and to think she got there on exactly the same basis that he got there. And if she can't she's a second-class citizen. We're going to have a Conservative Party full of second-class citizens.

You are calling your successor in Maidstone a second-class citizen.
No. I think – and she would say – she wished there were no A-list. That she wished she'd been allowed to compete on merit because the fact is she'd have got through anyway. But what was happening was that we were told – and that moment in the selection process stands out in my memory – that we had to have in the final, two men and two women regardless of the assessments we'd made. Helen [Grant, Conservative PPC for Maidstone and The Weald] was going to go through anyway. And one of our Association said to the Central Office agent 'are you telling us that we may not select on merit?' And with admirable honesty the Central Office agent said 'yes'. Now that is lunatic: it is putting cart before horse. First you look at merit, then you look at category. I think we've actually insulted a lot of women who would have got there on their own merit. Instead we've insisted on equal numbers on the shortlist, fast tracking on A-lists. I'm very glad it didn't happen in my day.

What do you think is the best thing that David Cameron has done?
To win. And I'm not being facetious.

He hasn't won yet.
He's well set to. That is the best thing he's done. Because as I say to everybody: if you want to do anything about anything, you actually need to be there.

We've got virtually the whole of Britain behind us on fighting post office closures. What can we do about it? Nothing. We've got a vast majority of the population on our side on having a referendum on the Lisbon Treaty. What can we do about it? Nothing. It doesn't matter how good your policies are, how popular they are, how much on side the public is. You can't do a darn thing about anything unless you're actually in Number 10. And what Cameron has done is to get us in a position where it's now assumed that we're now getting into Number 10. That, to me, is his great contribution.

Do you find yourself having to bite your tongue from time to time? You have spoken out on a number of things – specifically Home Office issues, civil liberties – where you're not in tune with the party's agenda. Do you find yourself having to think, 'I just can't rock the boat on this'?
That balance is normal. You always have that balance and the pressure it produces always intensifies the nearer to an election you get. The reason that Michael Howard was able to get away with sacking Howard Flight was that we were so close to a general election, the party wasn't going to go into rebellion. And nor should it have done, if you've got your eye on the big things. Sure, as an election gets closer you button your lips a bit more. But I do believe that one of the roles of MPs who've served in senior office and who've got the experience is not to rock the boat for the sake of rocking the boat, but occasionally to deploy that experience in argument.

Give me an example.
It so happens that I know that an awful lot of people in our party – and by that I mean a lot – are deeply unhappy with the way that we've signed up apparently quite blindly to the climate change agenda. It isn't that they don't want sensible things like recycling, it isn't a silly rebellion. But there is a deep unease that we're rushing in virtually to a theology: those who asked questions are 'deniers'. The language is theological. We're rushing in to what has become a theology imposed by the equivalent of what has become the mediaeval church and that nobody's allowed to question it. And that even by questioning it, you're doing the world a massive disservice and bringing it under perdition. A lot of us are very unhappy but when it came to a division on climate change; three of us actually opposed the bill. I was almost surprised that there were that many. Supposing instead of three of us, there had been so many of us that there were a few votes in the balance. That becomes a much bigger question. It's easy to be one of three. It's very difficult to be one of three who make a difference and embarrass the party big time by doing so. That I think is a subtlety that often isn't appreciated. It's easy to be part of a small minority that is making a racket; it is very difficult when what you do will have an adverse effect on the party.

You have a reputation for going against the grain and standing up in a very lonely way sometimes. You did it on 'something of the night', fox hunting, climate change. What's it like being in that fairly lonely position?
It is a lot more comfortable than people outside think. The whips always know when they're on a winner and a loser. They always know when it's worth putting pressure on somebody and when it's not. And sure they went through the motions with me on fox hunting and I said 'no this is the view I take and it's supposed to be a free vote'. 'Something of the night' was phenomenally difficult, it was the only time that I remember when Betty [Boothroyd] called my name I didn't want to stand up. But I set my hand to the plough and wasn't going to turn back. If you feel very strongly about something, you are not sent to [Parliament] simply to act as a lackey. While you're in government or in the shadow Cabinet, you bear collective responsibility. You've got to think very carefully before resigning in protest, because if you resign in protest you've resigned a lot more than that position then. You've resigned your reputation as a reliable person. There will be circumstances in which that is still the right thing to do. But on the whole if you want stability – and everyone accepts that when you want to speak as a member of the government or the shadow Cabinet, you're speaking for the government and for the opposition and not for yourself – when you're a back bencher people assume the exact opposite: you're representing yourself. And therefore you can't betray yourself by taking a line that actually you don't take.

Is there a modern day politician of whom you would say they have something of the night about them?
If I did, I wouldn't say so. I think once in a lifetime is enough for most people.

It was a sound bite that over the last fifteen years has resonated more than most.
You have to put it in the context of its time. Everyone knew what I meant when I said it. Now everybody says 'what did you mean?' But back then everybody knew exactly what I was saying. That's why it was so successful at the time.

Do you regret any of the more trivial TV shows that you've done?
No, not at all. I'm very comfortable with the ones I have not done. Huge pressure was brought on me this year to try *Big Brother* and I said no and I wouldn't even meet the people. I disapprove of it. It's not that I don't want to do it, which is a different issue altogether. I actually disapprove of it. I wouldn't ever do *I'm a Celebrity Get Me Out Of Here* because I'm too squeamish. I'm not going to eat slugs. Eugh! No thank you! I resisted *Strictly Come Dancing* right up to this year when I took the request slightly more

seriously; maybe because I'm retiring. But the ones that I've said yes to on the whole, (in retrospect) either I'm glad I did: as in *Fit Club,* which was a huge balance of judgement, I nearly didn't do it, or as in *Louis Theroux*: I'm not unhappy that I did that, even though I'm not rejoicing and bouncing up and down about it. But there is one I regret. Way back, shortly after I'd come in, when I was still a back bencher, I gave a profile which involved coming round with me for a day to Simon Sebag Montefiore. I deeply wish I hadn't. That journalist will never interview me again. Indeed many years later when I was in the 'shadow Home' job, I had great joy in turning down a request.

Strictly Come Dancing: You're not doing it, but you've thought about it?
I did very seriously consider it. I won't deny that John Sergeant gave me quite a lot of reassurance because if he can galumph around the floor well I can galumph around the floor. I've always thought that cavorting around with those frightfully elegant mortals, I'd look a complete idiot. But what I've realised from John's performance is they do let you go at your own pace. If I'm allowed to go at my own pace, it's not such a horrible thought. [giggles]

So you're still in the running for it?
Certainly not this year but once I've retired. They may come back, they may not; they may never come back. I don't worry about those things.

I remember before you said you adamantly wouldn't ever go on *Have I Got News For You* and now you've presented it twice with astonishing success.
I've had two completely different reactions to *Have I Got News For You*; the first time I did it I was nervous but thoroughly enjoyed it and I came out and said 'Oh, I'd love to do that every week.' The second time I did it, we had Jimmy Carr on the panel and of course to get the show that you see we have to record for a couple of hours. And two hours of non-stop vulgarity from Jimmy Carr was more than I could stand. I came out with exactly the opposite reaction that 'I am never ever going to do this again. No amount of money is worth sitting through that'. I've mellowed [laughs]. Now I remember the first one with some fondness and I think why not try the best of three and see what happens?

What question have you always wanted to be asked in an interview?
I'd just love a TV interviewer to say 'what is the purpose of this policy' and listen to the answer. They never ask that. They always assume they know the purpose and go in on some abstruse angle, and it's such a waste of time. So it would be quite nice if just very occasionally they said to you what is the purpose of this? Having said that, there were two occasions when I was in office and was giving an interview to the *Today Programme* where I actually

said to them at the beginning: 'Look I know we've only got two minutes or whatever it is, but please give me at the start the ability to set the context of the policy and I will only do it in three sentences.' And I stuck to my bargain and kept it short and they stuck to theirs and didn't interrupt. It's worth knowing that. You can sometimes negotiate a little bit with them.

Do you nowadays feel that whenever you go into an interview, you have to be combat-ready? Because there is an automatic assumption on the part of the interviewer that you're a politician and therefore – in the words of Jeremy Paxman – 'a lying bastard'.
I think I understood more the position of the interviewer when I did a week's stand in for Nick Ferrari on LBC, and I was interviewing a lot. And suddenly you realise there's a pressure on the interviewer to 'win'. A good interview is when you haven't got that gladiatorial attitude. And the most sensible interview I ever did in my entire political life was in the days when Jonathan Dimbleby had a Sunday lunchtime programme with fifty minutes devoted to one subject and, in those days, one spokesman, one Minister. I was then the shadow Health Secretary. I'd said at party conference that I didn't think the health service was going to last in its current form, that we couldn't do everything that was asked of us and therefore we must look for alternative ways to look for health. I don't mean herbs, I mean alternative mechanisms for delivering health. It was a controversial thing to say but people were willing to debate it because it was 1998. We weren't going to go into the office the next day. Instead of cranking up a great opposition to it, people were willing to debate it. I spent fifty minutes with Jonathan Dimbleby and an audience of national health workers, which should have been hostile. Yet actually it was the most sensible interview I'd ever had. Because he was unpeeling the onion instead of being in a position of challenge and I had time to answer fully and time to come back. It was the most sensible interview and the most memorable interview I've ever done.

But a Conservative health spokesman nowadays wouldn't even agree to do that.
I know. Unfortunately – and it's an inevitable consequence of party politics and was probably ever thus – we actually sacrifice real hard truth and real big leadership. We should be saying that just as the founding fathers of the NHS had a vision, we should be saying we've got a vision: we want to deliver health, we want to deliver it properly, we can't go on pretending that we can deliver. We're rationing health all over the place: you can't get Lucentis, you can't get Avastin, you can't get this and that. And we're still pretending that the NHS can deliver everything oblivious of what's about to come on stream and make ever greater demands. They won't face it, won't start the debate. Do you think they're all fools out there? They know that, and they're yearning to hear a politician start it.

This policy of ring-fencing the health budget: it seems to me that's being dishonest in many ways?

Well you can ring-fence the health budget, but no matter how much you ring-fence and how much adding to it you do, you will never meet every last demand that's made upon the health service. That's the crunch point. It's not who's willing to spend, it's no matter what you spend you won't sort it all.

What's the worst bit of sexism you've experienced in politics?

I don't think I've experienced much. I don't think I've been looking for it of course. I find that women do go looking for it. About six months after the Blair babes came in, one of them came up to me in a corridor and said, 'Ann isn't it horrible how the men are so rude to us?' And I said 'Yes and isn't it so horrible how they're rude to each other?' She'd never thought of that. She'd be roughed up in the chamber, she assumed it was because she was a woman. It was actually because she was useless. I've been roughed up in the chamber before and I've roughed others up. That is the cut and thrust of politics. You don't take it personally. I've never gone looking for [sexism] and therefore I've never found much.

What would you do if you were Alistair Darling?

I don't know. I'm very glad I'm not Alistair Darling for all manner of reasons. I've never aspired to be the Chancellor. I can tell you exactly what I'd do if I were Jack Straw or Alan Johnson. I do not know exactly what I'd do if I were in the Treasury but I know exactly what I'd do if I were in Number 10, which is to take a fair and square look at the amount of bureaucracy and its cost in this country. I have never known a period in my lifetime when the state was so intrusive on the ordinary individual. If you happen to have a leaf in your recycling bin, this is an offence. The state is taking an interest in your rubbish, the state monitors your journeys, and all the time you've got a bureaucracy which is backing up this vast intrusion. David [Cameron] said quite rightly that he would demolish a lot of the QUANGOs. So he should. He should also reduce the sheer scope of Whitehall – which is vast – and the amount of money we spend in this country on things that we shouldn't be spending it on. It's a bit like a housewife: if you've got a very tight period you look at your whole budget and you say, 'What do I have to spend?' Frankly, if we asked ourselves, 'Do we really have to spend this money', we'd come up with the answer 'No'.

What would you like your political epitaph to be?

Go tell the chief whip passers by that here alack unpaired I lie [laughs].

Why have you decided not to be blonde anymore?

Very simple. When I retire I want to spend a lot of time swimming. Chlorine and hair dye produce some rather odd results [laughs].

Quick Fire

What book are you reading?
Sisters of Sinai by Janet Soskice.

What songs do you like on your iPod at the moment?
'How Great Thou Art' by Aled Jones.

Favourite comedian?
Ken Dodd.

Favourite view?
From my study in Dartmoor.

Should one kiss on a first date?
Well it depends what sort of kiss one is talking about. I don't wish to go into that any further!

Political hate figure, excluding Michael Howard?
Idi Amin.

Last concert you went to?
I'm tone deaf. I don't go to concerts.

Last film you saw at the cinema?
It's a 40-mile round trip to the cinema from Dartmoor. I buy the DVDs!

Most formidable political opponent?
Frank Field.

Most admired opposition politician?
Frank Field.

Favourite holiday destination?
The Arctic.

Best friend in politics?
David Alton.

David Starkey

Born: 3 January 1945

Education: Went to Kendal Grammar School and won a scholarship to read history at Fitzwilliam College, Cambridge.

Family status: In a relationship with his partner James Brown.

Broadcasting career: Acquired a reputation for abrasiveness on BBC Radio 4's *The Moral Maze* before presenting a current affairs show on Talk Radio UK. As well as being known for his television series on Henry VII, Elizabeth I and other lesser-known Tudor monarchs, he has done a multi-year series called *Monarchy* on Channel 4.

Academic career: Taught history in the University of London (London School of Economics).

Career highlights: Appointed CBE in the Queen's 2007 Birthday Honours List.

Books: Involved in or written eighteen in total, including *Crown and Country: A History or England through the Monarchy* in September 2010 and *Elizabeth* in March 2001.

Interesting fact: At the age of four he suffered from polio.

Date of interview: September 2009

Extended version

Venue: David Starkey's house, north London

Total Politics Issue 16, October 2009

This interview came about in a most bizarre way. A couple of years ago, I was sitting on a train heading for Tonbridge, when David Starkey sat down opposite me. I had met him once before but it had been a long time ago and I knew he wouldn't remember me. So I then did something I shouldn't really have done. I tweeted: 'Am sat opposite David Starkey on a train. Should I leave him in piece or risk an eruption?' I had some very amusing replies, but in the end decided to leave him in peace.

An hour later I had an email from David's partner who, unbeknown to me, is an avid follower of my blog. 'You should have said hello. Have just shown David your tweet and he thinks it's hilarious.' And that, ladies and gentlemen, is how this interview came about.

David Starkey is supposed to be Britain's rudest man. Well, that may be part of his public persona, but face to face it would be difficult to find anyone more transparently charming. But you'll see when you read the interview, that he loves a good gossip and has a very impish personality. And I love that he is not afraid to be critical of his fellow historians, many of whom have an ego far greater than David Starkey's.

Starkey is a man you could talk to for a whole day without becoming bored. He's certainly not a fence sitter, and will have a view on everything. In short, he's an interviewer's dream.

How did you first get into history?
Almost accidentally. It was by no means a subject I was most interested in. Most people thought I was going to be a scientist. My best subjects were physics and chemistry. The reason that I made the choice I did is simple: I am not a natural mathematician. Numbers only mean something to me when they have a pound or dollar sign before them, which is when I become quite good with them. From a very early age I had very high verbal skills. The only thing I was ever any good at at school outside of the curriculum was acting and in particular, our public speaking competition – in those days called elocution. By the time I was fifteen I was a practiced performer in what was then called 'the stump speech'. Once you'd done that, you were never ever frightened of public speaking.

Perhaps your next TV thing should be the *X-Factor* of public speaking!
It would be interesting wouldn't it! And most people are so bad at it, including those who are supposed to be good at it. Most university lecturers and teachers are awful.

What do you think of politicians as public speakers?
Very few are any good at all. I can't really think of any current ones who are. I was never impressed with Blair. Cameron is alright.

Blair was quite a good platform speaker because he could act.
Yes, but if you are to be a really impressive public speaker, there's got to be content, and of course there never was. There was a blather of commonplaces. And also, I don't think with really good public speaking you should be too keen to please. Blair has a Labrador quality.

Isn't that endemic in politics though?
Well it's endemic in current politics. I don't think Churchill fell over himself in his desire to please. I suppose what has really happened is that the idea of the major political speech as sustained exposition – explanation, policy – that has largely vanished, because most of them don't have any policies to explain. By no means all the 'great' nineteenth-century speeches are great speeches, but some of them are.

Wasn't that because they had no other way of explaining things, whereas nowadays there are?
But how often are they used? How often is there any real exposition of policy at all? What's astonishing is that we have a prime minister who is supposed to be an intellectual – I've never seen any evidence of this, but we are told all the time that Brown was a brilliant student and briefly held a university position. I've never heard one word from him that suggests connected thought. If you look at the alleged 'great rescue' of the economy there are two ways you can explain it. One is that he was grounded in serious understanding of Keynesianism and all the rest of it, and the other is that Brown is doing what he's always done best which is throw money at things. And nothing he has said has persuaded me that it was anything other than the latter.

Is there a figure in Tudor history you would liken Gordon Brown to?
Gordon Brown actually reminds me more of a figure of modern literature, there is a real feeling about him of Kenneth Widmerpool from Anthony Powell's *Dance to the Music of Time*. Widmerpool is the dreadful, plodding figure, whose only good sport at school is cross-country running. While all his brilliant, charming contemporaries bugger it up, Widmerpool rises! It seems to me that with Brown there is a complete sense of humour and charm bypass. There is that relentless bludgeoning quality with his alleged 'brilliant performances' as Chancellor, the machine-gun fire of statistics that were always at least ten degrees from the point. But no charm, no wit.

Do you think there's something Nixonian about him? I've always thought that, and what he said the other day about the Megrahi case gave me a sense of 'there was no conspiracy at the White House!'
Yes, nobody believes a word. Again, there's a lovely story I was told by a couple I know who know Mandelson rather well. And one of them said to me: 'The only time you ever doubt a word Peter says is when he tells the truth.'

When did you first become entranced with the Tudor period?
Very early. When I was at Cambridge there were two really dominant figures in the history faculty: Jack Plum and Geoffrey Elton. Plum had already handpicked Simon Schama at that point, and so I suppose I gravitated to Elton. And in many ways I discovered myself by doing history seriously in my third year, when Geoffrey supervised my special subject class and was a wonderful teacher.

Some people have always wondered why you tend to stick with the Tudors and don't do any twentieth-century history. Does more contemporary history not appeal to you?

I am mildly into it. I think the real problem is that there are loads of people who are very widely learnt – from Anthony Beevor to Andrew Roberts – in twentieth-century history. Why start from scratch? Whereas what I can do, is use some of the insights and patterns of knowledge that you have from the Tudor period to illuminate certain aspects of twentieth-century history. I have after all, written quite widely on the twentieth-century monarchy, where I think my understanding of the earlier period can give me different sorts of insights that are useful. The real test of how good you are as a historian is how well you find it easy to remember the privy council members of the 1540s than the current Cabinet! I wouldn't want to present myself at all as a specialist in modern history. There are good reasons to stick with the Tudor period. It's a kind of Goldilocks period, in which you've got just enough information, but not too much.

When you started writing books about the period and doing television, did you set out to popularise it, because that's what you've achieved. People have settled on that period as one of the most interesting in British history, I think in large part because of what you've done on TV and in your books.

Well that's very nice of you to say so. Obviously if you're doing something on television, you expect to be getting an audience of a couple million plus and when we started we very comfortably exceeded that. I've been looking at my own dissertation, which I wrote in 1972–73. And what struck me about it was that I was quite pleased with it – he said smugly!

Did you feel as if you were reading something by someone else?

I am very masculine in my approach to writing. Writers fall into either two groups: you're either a mother or a father. If you're a mother you remember every word, you care passionately about them. But if you're a father, once it's done it's done. There was a wonderful remark by Elizabeth Russell, that's Conrad Russell the last Earl Russell's wife, that 'old Conrad views the responsibilities of fatherhood as ending at the moment of conception'. That is pretty much my view of writing – once it's done, it's done. Most of it was written in six weeks. That's how I write most things – like a railway train. Once I get going…

Do you do all the research and then start writing?

No, I find huge holes. It's why I think it's so important with kids at any stage – but particularly at university and particularly research students – to get them writing. It's only once you've started to connect the material that you realise what you need to know. And you invariably discover huge gaps and things that you thought you knew you don't know, and I am very sceptical of these people who claim before they write a book to have structured every paragraph.

That's what Andrew Roberts does doesn't he? He literally does all the research and then goes to France for six weeks, sits down at five o'clock, finishes at nine o'clock in the evening. I don't know how you can do that.
I certainly don't, because that's not how my mind works. I find myself questioning the material.

You've made the period very popular in one sense, but what about shows like *The Tudors*, that in some senses…
Vulgarise it! The nice line of division between popularisation and vulgarisation!

But there is a positive to programmes like that in one sense isn't there, because it means if people are fascinated by them – even if they're historically inaccurate – they think, oh, actually I'd quite like to find out a bit more about that.
They write to David Starkey and say, is it really true that Anne Boleyn slept with her father?! And you reply no, but if you are interested in finding out who she did sleep with, then see David Starkey's *Six Wives of Henry VIII*, pages so-and-so to so-and-so!

So they clearly didn't employ you as an advisor on this series!
No no! It's the higher tosh. But the real question is: why does it work? And what is the foundation of this interest? I was actually asked this question by a schoolteacher in the exhibition yesterday and I said I thought there were two reasons, and the first – *The Tudors* simply is this – is that it is a most glorious and wonderful soap opera. It makes the House of Windsor look like a dolls house tea party, it really does. And so these huge personalities, you know, the whole future of countries turn on what one man feels like when he gets out of bed in the morning – just a wonderful, wonderful personalisation of politics.

Compared to how you learnt your history, do you think today's school age kids and students are being short-changed in how history is taught today?
Yes I do. The core of history is narrative and biography. And the way history has been presented in the curriculum for the last twenty-five years is very different. The importance of knowledge has been downgraded. Instead the argument has been that it's all about skills. Supposedly, what you are trying to do with children is inculcate them with the analytical skills of the historian. Now this seems to me to be the most goddamn awful way to approach any subject, and also the most dangerous, and one of course that panders to all sorts of easy assumptions – 'oh we've got the internet, we don't need knowledge anymore because it's so easy to look things up.' Oh no it isn't. In

order to think, you actually need the information in your mind. It's going back to what we were saying about the construction of an argument on paper – it's only once you've got all those pieces together, and see the holes I was describing. The 'skills' basis misunderstands what education should be about. I am really old fashioned and think that education is about the introduction of the young to the best of what is known and has been known. In other words it's a cumulative process, and that's not in the least conservative or sterile. If I were made 'God' of the curriculum, I would want people to do a really broad course in the history of the last two thousand years in general, and the last thousand years of British history in particular. They should have a sense of a map of time – know where you place yourself, know the broad intellectual, economic, political movements. You should realise that to assume democracy and freedom are synonyms is the mistake of a tyro. You should know that there were free societies that weren't remotely democratic, and many democratic societies that were certainly not free. To do that you need broad patterns of both comparisons in time and comparisons in place.

Do you think we're now seeing the results of that type of education, where very few politicians seem to have any sort of historical knowledge or perspective at all?
I think that's absolutely right and it also goes along with a particular type of society – if you like the Californisation of the world. One of my American friends said many, many years ago – decades ago – that what you've got to understand in California is that with that blue sky and eternal sunshine and lonely beaches, the concept of the past can't exist. We're all Californians now! And I think a very interesting example was someone like Princess Diana – from the grandest, upper-crust English background – and yet her references, modes of behaviour, appearance and dress suggested she was born in Orange County. Didn't she think that Duran Duran were more or less the best thing since sliced bread?!

And she was right! Couldn't you actually come up with a character from any age of whom you could say that about?
Well, the airhead isn't a new phenomenon. But what was still particularly interesting was what sort of fecundity she represented. And most of the young women on television, it seems to me, seem to belong in this kind of Orange County 'never never land'.

Talking of women in history, you've come in for some flak recently for your comments about the so-called feminisation of history.
I can't imagine why. It seemed to me such a sensible, gentle comment. If you have a large number of women historians, writing for a readership where a very large percentage are women, you will get a certain kind of editing and presentation of history. It was no more than that.

Couldn't you make the counter argument that if men are writing about history there will be a particular slant to it also?
Of course you can. That's precisely what I was saying: that certain sorts of things are put into the foreground like personal relationships, the role of the wives and so on – and I have after all written the definitive book on Henry and his wives – but certain other things are put into the background, like war and religion.

But aren't you impugning the ability of female academics and historians?
I wasn't talking about academics at all really. What 99 per cent of academics do doesn't make any difference outside of their own university, let alone have any impact in the wider world.

You also sparked controversy with your remarks on *Question Time* about Scotland being a 'feeble little nation'.
It was a joke! The question was did I think the English should treat St George's Day the same way the Scots and all the rest of them treat their saints' days – St Andrew, St Patrick – and my answer was no. That would mean we would become a feeble little nation like them and we're showing every sign of doing just that. The English were – H.G. Wells has this wonderful phrase – 'the English are the only nation without national dress'. It is a glory that we don't have such a thing. If you want to be academic about it, there are two completely different patterns of nationalism in the British Isles – the Celtic nationalism of Scotland, Wales, Ireland, which is entirely typical nineteenth-century European nationalism, an invention based on folklore, supposed authentic peasant cultures which are entirely fictional, national dress, national music and some goddamn awful national poet like Burns. English nationalism went through that phase under Henry VIII.

But if you do really want me to go back to being abusive – I would say that Scotland's decisions with the Libyan bomber confirms everything I said about them. If you want to see what happens when a country becomes 'little' – when you have a government that wouldn't make county councillors in England, and a Minister of Justice that is an underemployed provincial solicitor – that's what you get. And I am not anti-Scottish, I love Scotland – my childhood holidays were there, apart from that fact it pissed with rain all the time. But Scotland's greatness took place not in medieval history when it was a catastrophe of a place, but in its long, long association with England and Britain. The transformation of Scotland from this deeply backward Presbyterian horror of the early seventeenth century – where you still hang a lad in the 1690s for denying the existence of the Devil – to this extraordinary 'Athens of the North', the Scottish enlightenment, the amazing products of Glasgow University in the eighteenth century, is when Scotland looks out as part of a greater whole. What's happened of course is that Scotland is now looking in. It has become exactly like medieval Scotland – the clannishness, the introversion, chucking money at the Edinburgh Festival to make it 'more Scottish', that awful Parliament, the dreadful Parliament building. The self-indulgence of the whole thing, the complete sense of in-growing toe-nail; I mean Edinburgh has turned into a city where you can see its toes growing in.

As someone who is contemptuous of nationalism in the Celtic nations, how do you reconcile this with your own English nationalism, and the fact that most of the glories of England were achieved under the rule of the Welsh, (Tudors) Scots (Stuarts), before England was finally put out of its misery in 1707 and the Act of Union?
Well England wasn't put out of existence, and the Tudors were not Welsh. The term 'Tudors' was only used as a term of abuse, remember. Elizabeth I, 'glories in the name of English' and being 'mere English'. And of all the dynasties that have ruled England, I think the Tudors and particularly Elizabeth – Edward and Elizabeth – have to be extraordinarily unusual amongst our rulers in having both parents born in England! I think what's important to realise is the extent to which England – and I only care about England, really, not as a domestic culture, which was exactly the point I was making, I said I don't want us to become a little nation. England only matters because in a funny kind of way, it has been for the last three hundred years, the world historical country. It's given a language to the world. Concepts of security, of property and law – although they have largely vanished here – began here, and it's perfectly obvious that these are the foundation of economic growth and the freedom that comes from it, the extraordinary efflorescence of English literature which is now a world – if not the world – literature. That's why I care. It's not Morris Dancing. It really isn't. It's not even Elgar or *Last Night at the Proms*.

What do you make of what this government has done to the Constitution?
Catastrophic. One of the great problems is that when you have no written constitution, there is nothing that is actually entrenched. It's only respect for convention that holds you back, and Labour has a very bad record in this regard – going back to the Parliament Act – of forcing major constitutional change unilaterally, always, of course, in the name of 'social justice' and 'nice' things like that. I think the situation that we find ourselves in now is that our structure of government is broken.

So what's the Starkey recipe for fixing it?
We need a version of the American constitution. When you think of all the silly fuss over the office of Lord Chancellor – when did a Lord Chancellor

last do any serious harm? The alleged confusion of political and judicial functions. What's been so striking about a lot of Labour constitutional reform is that on the one hand it's done big things that it shouldn't have done, and it's also done little things that there was no need to do like fiddle around with the position of Lord Chancellor. The catastrophe is one body being both the executive and the legislative. It means that it does neither job very well. In particular our Parliament is useless as a legislature. It's why our legislation is so awful. It's why, of course, MPs have actually got no function. MPs now are at best overpaid social workers.

What we need, I think, is something very much like the American model, and I would go the whole hog. I would have a directly elected Prime Minister. The emergence of somebody like Gordon Brown, who is so totally unsuited to the office and never actually been subject to the test of election, would be absolutely unthinkable in America, because from Primaries onwards you are subject to this test. So I think we should have a directly elected Prime Minister. We should have something very much like the American cabinet, which is outside the legislature. We should have an elected Lords. The obvious basis for the Lords are the old counties. The catastrophe of the semi-abolition of the old counties under Heath was a catastrophe. Incidentally, there's only been one government that's as bad as this and that's Heath's. Heath and Joseph together were a catastrophe. Every single thing they touched turned to something brown. I would go to a Lords that has two members elected from each county.

And the monarchy?
I'm not a Republican, I actually think that constitutional monarchy has served us well.

You were quite rude about the Queen recently. What about Prince Charles, what's your view on him?
I wasn't rude about the Queen...

You called her a 'provincial house wife'.
Well that's right. It's what she is. And provincial house wives are not without virtue, my mother was one. They are not without virtue at all, and...

Why were you happy to receive your CBE from a 'provincial housewife'?
I didn't, I received it from the crown. [Laughs] She's had the virtues of solidity, of good sense, of rugged determination to stick at the job, and she's had the vices of a complete lack of imagination, of style, of no interest in anything but horses and farming.

I learnt the other day that she's a supporter of my team, West Ham United.
Well there you are that's even more of a problem then isn't it? [laughter] Charles, you know, is almost the mirror image. I like the idea that somebody gets excited about things like architecture and the environment. Far too few people in Britain do. He's also got an extraordinarily impressive track record, which really is worth thinking about, in organisational terms. Think of things like The Prince's Trust. It's one of the few bodies in Britain that's got any kind of serious record in genuine rehabilitation, of *genuinely* getting the young out of this dreadful rut of three-generational unemployment – and as you know we now have getting on for 20 per cent plus of the nation stuck in that rut. Anybody that can help [them] get out is a good thing. I mean, poor Prince Charles, he is in one sense profoundly conservative but like me he's a child of the '60s. And you know he found himself like Henry VIII, shipwrecked against concepts of marriage as a kind of public act, and the desire for private happiness – and he didn't have Henry VIII's available methods of solving the problem. [laughs]

What do you think of Nick Clegg?
[Sighs] Do I think anything at all of Nick Clegg? Quite a good-looking young man but I mean… There's a sort of 'who he' quality about him isn't there?

What punishment would Henry VIII have meted out to Gordon Brown for all he's done to the country?
Well, when a previous Chancellor of the Exchequer named Thomas Cromwell, had his come-uppance it is alleged that Henry arranged for especially incompetent executioners. [laughter]

Alan Johnson! [more laughter]
But at least he knew how to wield the blade, yes.

Going back to the Scotland, Wales issue, are you in favour of an English Parliament?
In the current arrangement you certainly need something like that. We probably need a genuinely federal system. I can see lots of reasons why, for historic nations that have come together as Britain did, this would actually be a rather good way of managing things. What I think is much more important, and I care about much more, would be a revival of local government. We've recently acquired a house in America in a little town on the Chesapeake called Chestertown. It's 4,500 people, it's a retirement community. I was entranced by the town. The core of its eighteenth and nineteenth century – lovely and safe and handsome and a civilised community – but what strikes you about it is that it's like going back to my childhood in a rather bigger town, Kendal in

Westmorland which was then 20,000 but is probably a bit bigger now. When I was a boy Kendal had its own fire service, it had its own police force, it had its own mayor and council that were responsible for virtually everything that mattered. Chestertown still has. Now we have this ludicrous argument for the professionalisation of services but if you're in Kent, where I am, they're all 30 miles away. Ditto police. Four thousand, five hundred people is twice the size of medieval York. London under Henry VIII was 50,000. Medieval York was capable of sustaining its guilds, contributing to the building of its cathedral, that vibrant civic life. Again one of the reasons for the kind of disease and sense of atrophy in national politics is that politics should build itself from the grass roots up. The roots have withered because people genuinely don't control their own lives. It's absurd that the basic unit of government in London now is well over quarter of a million. Antony Jay published a little while ago a quite interesting book arguing that the natural human unit is about a legion or a regiment – it's about 1,000 people. [He argues that] a group like that, where a high degree of common knowledge is possible, is the obvious unit. I think it's too small. And again you see what's so different about America is that the federal government can't change local government. Local government – the county, city structure – is an absolute given. It's embedded within the law. Look at the number of different arrangements that have been made for the performance of justice in the last fifteen or twenty years. There's a complete disconnection between units of local government and how the judiciary works, whereas in America there are the courts at county level, the courts at state level, the courts at federal level, and there is a very close relationship between those areas and political boundaries. Again, look at the courthouse. We've spent all our time knocking wonderful Victorian crown courts and magistrate's courts down. In America the courthouse is nearly always one of the great centres of a town or township with an immense pride and history to it. Whereas we've gone in for perpetual deracinating change. I mean look at the National Health Service, the millions, billions, trillions that have been squandered on perpetual re-jigging, re-jigging, re-jigging.

Oh come on, you're not allowed to criticise the NHS. You've almost committed an act of treason if you do that.
There's this ludicrous notion that an accidental set of arrangements from somebody who I think was basically deranged. Bevan I think was basically deranged. Why should that particular set of arrangements become the definition of patriotism?

Particularly after sixty years.
It bears about as much relationship to modern Britain as, you know, the Christianity of the Bible does [laughter]. It's a joke, but we've touched on a

very interesting point. With the loss of belief in real political institutions what you do is you retain belief but it becomes a kind of mere sentimentalism. The most powerful force in English public life at the moment is an absolute sentimentalism. And the worst sort of sentimentalism is that which surrounds the National Health Service. It leads to a refusal to think seriously about things. Again the embrace of certain types of multiculturalism and whatever, they're forms of gross sentimentality. Refusal to analyse, refusal to look fairly and squarely at consequences.

What do you think your public image is?
Do I have a single public image?

I don't know, you may have two or three.
I don't know. I think, in so far as it's possible to read, and after all I am the last person in one sense who is necessarily aware of it, I don't watch myself very much, I don't necessarily read everything that's written about me, in fact much of the time I deliberately avoid it [laughter]. I would have thought that I'm a bit of an amalgam aren't I? One the one hand dear old George Austen's remark about the rudest man in Britain, Doctor Rude, which periodically gets refreshed as with little remarks about Scotland and the Queen. On the other hand I suppose there is a rather cuddly figure who is Britain's best-loved historian.

Do you think nowadays though that there is a pressure on people in the public eye to be slightly more controversial than they might otherwise be in order to keep in the public eye? You have a reputation for being controversial and therefore are in the media a lot. It's an advantage to you as a historian, as a TV personality, to be in the headlines, or do your controversial remarks just come out? [laughter]
I think they just drop out on the whole. I mean I don't consciously work on it, but it seems to me that there are rules to be observed. You don't go too far. I also think that it's terribly, terribly dangerous only to live in that particular glare. It's particularly dangerous I imagine if there's nothing else to you. I also think that you've got to remember – and poor dear Diana… the first time in history that we've known about a Princess's bowel movements and vomiting – the terrible danger when the whole of yourself goes public and there's nothing left that's private. That sort of celebrity is like the turning inside out, that which should be private becomes public.

Do you sometimes think your fellow historians slightly look down their noses at some of the things that you do or say?
I'm sure some do. On the other hand I think that the more intelligent of them realise that the subject will not survive simply within the grooves

of academy. That the only way that you'll get students, and the only way you'll get people doing A-level, the only way you will in fact sell books, is by history that can be a proper part of public discourse, which is of course where the subject naturally belongs. History and historical writing is much older than the academic study of history. The academic study of history is a complete Johnny-come-lately. It doesn't get going at Oxford and Cambridge until the last four decades of the nineteenth century. It's just not taught. Cambridge has nothing by way of a degree until the 1840s. Right through from Newton's period, well the beginning of the eighteenth century, to well into the nineteenth century there was one degree at Cambridge which was mathematics. The diversification of the university curriculum in Britain is totally a child of the later nineteenth century.

Do you think there's room for every type of history, analysis, writing, historical fiction? What do you think of Philippa Gregory's books, for example?
I wouldn't know I've never read one. But I know who she is. I'm a believer in letting it all hang out. I am a libertarian, a liberal. Let it all fight for its place in the sun. There are certain things actually that I think are part of responsible government. I mean the Victorian sense of the preservation of archives, of the making of the same freely available to anyone interested, I think that's a wholly proper part of state activity.

Do you ever switch off, or are you sort of constantly thinking about what you're writing or what you're about to write?
I'm very good at switching off, I like cooking. I like gardening, I like faffing about. I'm very, very domestic. Equally, what can quite often happen is I do my best work when I'm cooking dinner. You know, get something going and then 'oh gosh, yes that's a very interesting idea'. I then put everything on hold, rush off, do another hour. [laughter]

'Is dinner going to be a bit late tonight?'
'It's going to be very late tonight.' [more laughter] 'Sit down with those crisps.'

Quickfire

The monarch whose reign you would like to have lived through?
The present one because of modern medicine.

The most incompetent monarch?
James II.

Which of Henry VIII's wives would you have most liked to have married in the unlikely circumstances…

Catherine of Aragon, as we could have both agreed she'd go to a nunnery and I'd go to a monastery.

What are you reading at the moment?

I don't actually read. Confession: I do not read. I lost the habit of reading once I really started writing. I only read to write.

Last film you went to see?

I can't remember. I don't go to the cinema. Probably *The Go-Between*. That tells you how long ago it was.

Favourite historian?

Pass. It is interesting, I've never really been influenced by fellow historians at all. I don't know, I don't really have one.

Least favourite? Beginning with A and A?

Well no. No, no, no, no, no. I think those said historians have their merits. I mean, I happen to find them completely unreadable, but lots of people enjoy them.

If you hadn't been a historian what would you have been, or what would you have liked to have been?

I always used to have fantasies when I was young about being an architect.

Your favourite view?

Standing in my garden in Kent, looking through the trees at the bottom and imagining that it's a great park, when in fact it's just a field that looks like a great park.

Current day politician you most respect?

Sort of Vince Cable, but they are a very unimpressive lot.

Best British prime minister in history?

I suppose it's a kind of cross between Pitt the Younger and Churchill.

And worst?

A cross between Edward Heath and Gordon Brown.

Vince Cable

Party affiliation: Liberal Democrats

Current position: Secretary of State for Business, Innovation and Skills.

Born: 9 May 1943

Education: Studied Natural Science and Economics at Fitzwilliam College, Cambridge University, before doing a PhD at Glasgow University.

Family status: Married to Rachel Wenban Smith with three children by his late wife, Olympia.

Pre-political career: Lectured at Glasgow University in Economics and worked for Shell International from 1990, becoming the company's Chief Economist in 1995.

Electoral history: Entered Parliament at his fifth attempt in 1997, joining the Liberal Democrat shadow Cabinet in October 1999 as spokesman on Trade and Industry. He was the Liberal Democrat shadow Chancellor from November 2003 and the party's deputy leader from March 2006 before being appointed Business Secretary in the coalition government in May 2010.

Career highlights: Becoming deputy leader of the Liberal Democrats and later gaining his position as Secretary of State for Business.

Interesting fact: In January 2009 Cable revealed, on BBC Radio 4's *Desert Island Discs*, that he wears wedding rings from both his marriages.

Date of interview: October 2009
Extended version
Venue: House of Commons
Total Politics Issue 18, December 2009

I have never been a fan of Vince Cable. And I am still not. I never quite understood how everyone seemed to come to the view that he is some sort of economic messiah. It's astonishing what a bit of populist rhetoric can achieve with a media too lazy to dig beneath the surface. When Andrew Neil cornered Vince Cable on the BBC's Straight Talk *programme, I sat watching, cheering him on. For the first time an interviewer dared to question this apparent economic colossus.*

I'll be frank. When I do these interviews I always seem to connect with my interviewee. But with Vince, it just didn't happen. Maybe he had read some of my blogposts casting doubt on his status, or maybe he's just not clubbable. No matter how I tried I just couldn't break through the inscrutable shell that he had erected. I still think it was an interesting interview, but I left his office feeling that as an interviewer I had failed. I didn't want to have a row with him, but I did expect to get more than I got. You can't win 'em all, I suppose.

You've published one book already this year. Two would seem to be a bit much, what's *Free Radical* about?
The second one is personal. It's different experiences of life, and it's partly a written version of the *Desert Island Discs* stories. It's a personal account, it's not an economic commentary and it's not a political text.

So it's more autobiographical?
Yes, but with a bit of a twist, and the central character I suppose is my late wife.

What made you decide to do that now? Isn't it the sort of book you would normally publish at the end of your career?
Well that's right, the timing is different. I started doing it several years ago, partly, I think, because I wanted my family to know how I'd originated, where they came from, so there were very personal motives. After the Radio 4 programme a lot of people expressed a lot of interest, so I thought there would be a wider public interest, and my publishers encouraged me, and that's how it has now seen the light of day.

Were you surprised at the reaction that Desert Island Discs got?
Yes, I was. I was surprised. But it was broadly good.

Because you've got a reputation of, obviously economics is your portfolio, and apart from the *Strictly Come Dancing* stuff people don't actually know an awful lot about you as a person, do they? Are you trying to give a more rounded picture of you as a person?
Yes, I don't enormously enjoy exposing all, you know. I have a private kind of life which I value. But I think I was warmed by the general reaction, which was about things that most families experience – how you deal with bereavement and long terminal illnesses, and a less common issue, but an increasingly common one, which is cross-cultural, cross-racial marriages and all the issues around that. I think there was such a degree of interest that I thought I should write this up properly. Not everybody will like it, but, going back to your question, I think being seen as a human being rather than just a number cruncher and a party politician is important. I think it's quite helpful to have that dimension.

How important is that in a modern day politician, to be willing to bare your soul a bit and actually show that you're a human being just like any other voter, and you're not on this pedestal, you've experienced life just the same as everybody else?

I think it is important, and increasingly so. We can speculate as to why it is, but I suspect it has a lot to do with the decline of ideological politics and the traditional tribal class dividing lines. People are looking at parties which are populated by personalities and they want to know who they are. There is this search for authenticity. It's tricky. Obviously one has to strike a balance between being open about your feelings, but at the same time we all have a private life, and nobody wants every single detail of their life from year one exposed to the public gaze. The book is an honest one.

Was it difficult to write?

It was quite difficult, yes. You're writing about other people as well as yourself, obviously, and the key people in my own drama are dead, but one has to be sensitive about it, particularly if there are critical things. Yes, it was a very difficult thing to do, but it is a recognition that if you are out there in public life people want to know a bit about you and what motivates you.

And can I ask what your wife made of you doing it?

My current wife?

I didn't want to say your current wife because it sounds a bit odd doesn't it...

It sounds like a sort of harem or something, but no, my second wife, Rachel, was very supportive. She typed it up for me and made comments as we went along.

She bought into it?

Yes.

It must have been quite painful to write about your late wife in the sense that it brought back some very good memories but some very painful ones too?

Well it was a happy marriage overall, and a good marriage, so in that sense it was an easy thing to do, but she was a very strong personality and I think that probably comes across.

And what experiences do you relate in the book about being married to someone of a different race?

These days it's quite commonplace, not controversial at all, but when I was first married it was highly controversial and both my family and her family were strongly opposed. In my father's case it was on very straight-forward racial grounds. With her family it was a bit more complicated, but it had to do with a different culture. She had a young man lined up, as was traditional in Asian families. So for the first four or five years of our marriage we had no dealings with our parents at all. Eventually they came round, as often happens. When they see grandchildren they become much more positive. Eventually Olympia became really quite close to my father despite his vehement prejudices. So it was, in many ways, quite a heart-warming outcome.

When you first got into Parliament what was your ambition?
Having got in aged fifty-four, I didn't see it primarily in terms of a greasy pole and climbing to the top of it. Like most newly-elected MPs with small majorities, my ambition was to get re-elected, so during most of my first term, as well as caring for Olympia my other preoccupation was doing local things and being a good constituency MP. I wasn't looking at all beyond that. It was only in the second term that I started getting a profile. Charles Kennedy had already appointed me as our Trade and Industry spokesman. I made a bit of a splash with one or two issues like abolishing the DTI. I got a headline I was rather proud of. It was Richard Littlejohn identifying what he described as the first Liberal Democrat policy he'd ever agreed with [laughs]. But my profile was overwhelmingly local and it was only in the second term that I started doing more stuff that got national attention. I went into the last election campaign as our Treasury spokesman. I wasn't thinking about ambition in terms of leadership and the rest of it. I was, I think, pleasantly surprised to discover that I was, A, in Parliament, and B, had been re-elected with a big majority and was starting to get national attention for some of my ideas. Although I admit I am an ambitious person, otherwise I wouldn't be where I am, I guess.

Was Parliament a culture shock? You'd been in quite a senior position in Shell, and a lot of people who have been in business come into Parliament and are shell-shocked by the way it operates.
It is a completely different world. I suppose the difference in my case was that I had had earlier immersion. I had been involved as a councillor in Glasgow and stood for Parliament four times before I got in. So Parliament was new but politics wasn't new.

You say you are an ambitious person. I think you can divide Liberal Democrats into two categories: those who are quite happy to be in Parliament, do the job of an MP and make the case for liberal democracy, and then there are others who actually want power. In the end, if you're in politics, you've got to be in power to change things. Does it frustrate you that, being in a third party, power is fairly elusive?
Yes, it is, and I suppose that of the two categories you've mentioned I am probably in the second, because that is why we're here ultimately. It's not just to have views and make speeches but to actually try to do something. So yes

in that sense, but I'm not thinking of it just as an individual. My ambitions are for the party.

I'm not going to ask you the normal questions about coalitions because…
You know what the stock answers are, don't you? [laughs]

In the event of a hung parliament, wouldn't going into a coalition with one of the parties be a good thing for the Liberal Democrats, because then you can actually prove, you're running a government department, you can prove that you can do it and then move on from that?
Well it might be, and we're not ruling that out. But I think the point we emphasise is that it's not our call ultimately. If you get a government with a minority then they have a choice. They can run as a minority government, or they can turn to other parties and ask for help. The spirit in which we approach it, and I don't mean this in a pious way, would be to act in the national interest, because we still do have an emergency situation. It's their call, it's not our call.

Forget which party it would be, but if the day after the election there was a hung parliament and you got the call saying, right Vince, we're in a terrible situation, the country has more confidence in you than it does anybody else to sort us out, we want you to be Chancellor of the Exchequer, you'd find that a bit difficult to turn down wouldn't you?
I wouldn't, because I've made it very clear from the outset that I'm not acting as a freelance individual.

No Jeremy Thorpe here [laughter].
What's that? I can't remember that era.

Well, that's basically what he did in '74. He couldn't take his party with him.
OK, well I'm not acting as a freelancer. It would be up to the party leader and our team to decide what they do, and I'm part of that, but I'm not going off on my own, that's very clear.

Do you see the Liberal Democrats as a centre-left party?
No, I don't use that description, I know some of my colleagues have in the past. There are some areas where we are, to use the jargon, centre-left progressive. A redistributive approach to taxation is obviously one of them, but there are other respects in which we are genuinely liberal, which puts us on the other side. Lots of the writing I've done on economics is very much about a liberal approach to economic policy, free-trade and open markets. I don't use that term because, although some of the things we say can be very clearly put in that box, in other respects we are economically liberal. I think

the other thing is, a lot of the things we're about have nothing to do with the traditional left/right spectrum – localism, environmentalism, civil liberties, you can argue these from either a libertarian or a leftist perspective.

I was going to say, you sound like David Cameron there for a second [laughter].
Did I? Hopefully that's a compliment.

What do you make of him? Do you have much to do with him?
Not on a personal level, no. He's very professional, and he's obviously done a lot to decontaminate the Tory brand, and as a political professional one observes that. I think there are some problems with the position he's got. It isn't entirely clear how deep and sincere all of this is. We've moved a long way from hugging huskies, the environmental stuff has gradually sort of disappeared, and I suspect it isn't all that deep. They've got themselves into this problem recently with these loony European parties, which suggests he does feel he has to give his right-wing red meat. It may indeed be that's what he believes. So, I think they have a bit of an identity problem. He's taken them so far that some of the nasty Tory stuff has been neutralised, but I think there is a genuine issue now about what he really believes, and the way he really wants to take them. I see locally, also, the old nasty Tory stuff, and quite a lot of it's still there at a grass-roots level.

Does Nick Clegg have a problem with David Cameron in that he's seen as a 'Cameron-lite'?
Well, he's the same generation but I don't think they have much else in common. I suppose they are both nice-looking, youngish leaders, but politically I don't think there's much in common. This was said of Nick when he first became the leader, but he's trodden a separate path. He's now got a very clear sense of identity. He's come well out of the last year and on a whole series of issues he's carved out a distinctive position – on expenses and the Ghurkhas, for example. I think he's now much more publically identified than other leaders we've had at the same stage, and the image is a positive one.

Did you regret not standing for leader?
No, I didn't. You probably know the story. It was never actually an option in the circumstances where the issue arose, when Ming Campbell stood down in a hurry. I just got on with the job.

So you don't do what Ming Campbell used to do every morning when he was shaving and think, God, I wish I'd stood against Charles Kennedy?
No, absolutely not, I genuinely don't. I quite enjoyed the 'acting leader' period, and did quite well, but I've got a very full role. I have a dual role.

One is the economics stuff, which I enjoy and have a competence in, and I wouldn't, frankly, have been able to do it if I'd been the party leader. I wouldn't have been able to write that book which has, I think, been quite influential. I get round the country for the political stuff. Every weekend I go off to some exotic place. So I get the high level politics and the economics, and without a lot of the stresses that you have in a leadership role.

Do you feel that there's sometimes a danger that you slightly overshadow Nick Clegg in some ways? I mean, in some ways that's a good thing because it means there's more than one Liberal Democrat with a national profile, but I wonder whether sometimes he's frustrated by that?
I don't think so. I've never sensed that and I think it's helpful to the party, and to him, and to me in a way, that we're a team. The Tories are putting themselves forward in a presidential way whereas we're presenting it much more as a team approach and I think that goes down well. But he's very clearly the leader now. That image has been very clearly marked. He's got some distinctive issues that he's done very well on. I think people did say that a year ago but I don't think it's an issue now. It's an inevitable consequence of the fact the economy has been at the top of the agenda.

What do you think the most important thing Nick Clegg has done since he's been leader?
I think there's an overall climate of professionalism in the way that we do things. He's a very good team leader. The way he deals with the party and the public is very professional. I think that's what's now coming through: we're serious. It goes back to your earlier questions about whether these people are capable of exercising power and responsibility, and I think that he has got it across that he personally and we as a team are able to do that and I think that's probably the biggest achievement.

There's five months before the election will be called. What do you think is the overwhelming priority for the Liberal Democrats in those five months? How can the Liberal Democrats differentiate themselves in five months?
If it all has to be done in five months then that's difficult. But there is a hinterland of policy and record which is what we're building on, so it isn't starting from scratch. There will be clear dividing lines with the Tories over fairness in taxation. We're very distinct from the Labour government in our approach to radical reform of the banking system and economic institutions, and on their centralisation of power and contempt for local government. We'd certainly argue that we were greener than the other two major parties. But these are things that haven't just come out of nowhere.

Is Afghanistan the issue that's going to do it for you?
It's certainly increasingly important. In the last few weeks – starting at our conference – Nick has carved out a position which is much more critical of the position that the government is in; you just cannot continue to go along with a deeply corrupt, undemocratic government and continue to send troops to die for that. We're raising questions about future strategy in a way that the other two parties are not willing to do.

But can you imagine a scenario where you go into the next election campaign saying, 'we think we should pull out'?
I think we have to be very careful about how the whole issue of withdrawal is dealt with, because it's different from Iraq – Iraq was an illegal war. We all supported intervention in Afghanistan. It's quite different in that sense and a lot of British troops have already been sent and died there for this cause. But certainly we have raised and will continue to raise the basic question of how much longer can you send British troops to die for a cause when there's no clear strategy at present and where the government we're trying to protect isn't defensible politically. Where that leaves us in six months' time I can't speculate on.

Every extremist politician in Europe has been elected by proportional representation and we're seeing that here now with the BNP. Doesn't that make you stop and think about the merits of PR?
You can argue this both ways. The BNP started making inroads into British politics under the existing system, and they've got a significant number of councillors elected on first past the post at local government. The systems vary across Europe as you know. I don't think the emergence of the extreme right is a function of the electoral system; there clearly is a constituency in almost every European country that is very nationalistic, xenophobic and it expresses itself in different ways.

They wouldn't have two MEPs under first past the post and Nick Griffin wouldn't have appeared on *Question Time*.
They might not have done, but under our existing first past the post system they could have laboured away at one or two constituencies in Britain and got an MP, and under our system that would give them much more exposure than they'll ever have with two MEPs. I don't think we can blame the system. The fact is there is a strand of public opinion which is responsive to what they're saying and that's very worrying in itself and that's what we've got to deal with. Where we've seen proportional representation in action in Britain – as in Scotland – where there's much healthier politics, much more diversity at local and national level and you've got parties that are willing to work together, it hasn't actually unleashed extremism.

What was Susan Kramer's response to your mansion tax plan?
She was critical of it.

Because that could have lost her her seat couldn't it?
No, I don't think so. Our position on the mansion tax is that we think it's a good idea that people with large amounts of personal wealth should pay a bit more in order to cut taxes for people at the bottom. We've taken it through our party's federal policy committee that determines policy, so it will be there. But how exactly it applies is something we're working on. Obviously we have to be sensitive to the concerns people have raised.

That sounds a bit like backtracking.
No, I think you'll find it will be in our election manifesto.

But you will know from your own constituency, particularly in London, there are lots of houses that have a high value, but the people who live in them are not cash rich.
Yes, there are some in that category.

But how do you differentiate between them and the people who are genuinely rich?
Well that's an issue that arises at the moment in the council tax system, which the Tories bought in. We've expressed unhappiness about it and that affects every single household in London. We're talking about a very minor subset of an existing problem, which is for people who have very large assets but don't have very large incomes. We've suggested that if people have retired we would roll up the tax payments, which is what councils are already doing if people have very large commitments and residential home fees. There are ways of dealing with it, but we are looking at the details of how you would deal with that genuine practical problem.

Wasn't that announcement a victim of the fact that you needed a big announcement at conference and you actually made it a bit too quickly? A lot of your colleagues were incandescent with you about it, weren't they?
Well, one or two of them were concerned about it.

Your local government spokesman [Julia Goldsworthy] didn't even know about it!
It was a national tax policy, but as I said at the time she should have been told more about it. I actually raised it two years ago at one of our party conferences and got predominantly positive reactions to it, so the concept was already out there and had already been floated.

You've got this tremendous reputation in the country as someone who's interpreted the economic crisis well and come up with some solutions and all the rest of it – but the media love to build someone up and then knock them down. I was watching the interview you did with Andrew Neil, which you didn't look particularly comfortable in. Did you get the feeling that that was the start of people trying to chip away at the reputation of Vince Cable as an economic guru?
Like everyone else you get some things wrong but I think I've been predominantly right. I don't think that's been in anyway changed. I think I had two interviews with Andrew Neil, one of which went perfectly well, the other of which there were a couple of areas where he got selective quotes of things I said, but in so far as I recall I had perfectly good answers to. But it's quite right that over a period of years you take a different position on things.

Do you enjoy that kind of combative interview?
Yes and I certainly don't look out for soft interviews. Some of the interviews I've found least interesting are some of the ones where you are just given an opportunity to say your piece.

But he pointed out that you've changed your position on Quantitative Easing.
No I haven't actually, he got that wrong. I'd probably been a little bit too clever in an article by using irony.

Always dangerous!
It is always dangerous, and I said that potentially large scale printing of money could lead you down a hyperinflationary route and it was said in a kind of semi-jokey way. But from the very outset I have argued very strongly in support of what the Bank of England was doing, and it clearly is a very necessary part of the monetary response. There was no inconsistency; you'll find a passage in my book which is very supportive of it.

In September 2008 you said the government must not compromise the independence of the Bank by telling it to slash interest rates, and then a month later you urged the Chancellor to write to the Governor of the Bank of England demanding a large cut in interest rates.
Yes that is true and I think like a lot of other people, I realised in the autumn of 2008 that we were on the verge of a completely catastrophic failure of the system – a once in a lifetime experience. The whole banking system was in danger of going down and this was a system for which the Bank of England had not been prepared. The mandate of the independent Bank of England, which I supported was not just concerned with those issues, it was concerned with a broadly stable environment. I had supported the independence of the Bank of England and I still do and I think its role will be increasingly

important in future years when we get a lot of inflationary pressure. But that moment in September and October when they had to do something dramatic and where their existing mandate was simply about responding to and anticipating inflation rates, this was not actually the primary concern. And I was certainly the first person out of the traps saying that, although it was a departure from the line I had been giving before.

Do you think in retrospect that it might have been better to let one bank go under? Wouldn't that have made the bankers 'get it'? Or would the consequences of that have been so catastrophic as to have been unimaginable?
When the Northern Rock crisis broke, my view was that that probably should have been what happened – the government should have rescued the depositors and let the bank go. That was how I responded to it for precisely the reasons you implied. But once the government had decided to put in taxpayers' money, it seemed inevitable and right that you had to take it over, because you then had the problem of the public taking the risk and the private donors taking the profit. But the moral hazard argument was and is a powerful one. The problem with it in practice is that in the panic environment you had last year, any sense that our government or the American government were just going to back off a major institution would have just fuelled the run. And we all know what happened with Lehmans. The principle of moral hazard is this: if a bank has got itself into trouble through chronic mismanagement then the senior management and directors and shareholders have to take a big hit. And that's the principle. Whether or not the institution is then taken over by the state or run down – there are different techniques of dealing with it.

Imagine you have six months as Chancellor of the Exchequer. What's the one thing you'd like to look back on and say, I did that in my six months?
I would put sorting out the banking system at the top of the list. I think the government did the right things in October last year. It behaved well in the emergency – it was prompt and the rescue operation was necessary. I acknowledged it at the time and it's still true. But they've let the situation drift, and if I had six months as our Lib Dem Chancellor, I would first of all be much more proactive in making sure that the semi-nationalised and nationalised banks are lending to solid British companies, because they're not doing it at the moment – they've lurched from extreme recklessness to extreme conservatism. So they've got to use the directors on the bank to make sure that they lend to good companies.

Why aren't they doing that?
The government is obsessed with not being seen to interfere. I suppose I can see where they're coming from – they didn't want to be accused of

over-loaning and steering money to workers' cooperatives, so they had an ideological thing. But it's totally wrong and it's done an enormous amount of damage and British companies are suffering from it. But I think the thing is to act on what the governor of the Bank of England has been saying about splitting up the banks. He's quite right: that has to happen. This government has bottled out of it and the Tories have been very ambiguous about what they think, but I'm quite clear that that is the right route.

Quickfire

Dirty Dancing or _Flash Dance_?
Dirty Dancing.

Arlene or Alesha?
I'd take both.

That's just plain greedy.

What book are you reading at the moment?
I'm reading this Swedish trilogy by Stieg Larsson – his crime thrillers. I've just finished the second and I'm going onto the third. It's a wonderful series of crime thrillers.

All women shortlists: good or bad?
Bad.

What's your favourite view?
From the top of Lake District mountains.

Most formidable political opponent?
Ken Clarke would be fairly high up on that list.

What makes you laugh?
Good comedians – Rory Bremner.

Has he done you?
Yes, though it wasn't a major part of his routine. Jasper Carrot's another one.

What's your favourite meal?
South Indian curries.

The thing you most like about Nick Clegg?
Good, open, honest – good colleague.

What's the most romantic thing you've ever done?
Married two lovely women.

Which was the best year of your life?
Probably 1997.

Worst PM in history?
Probably Chamberlain.

The political decision you most regret?
I think probably going back to York in the mid-eighties and fighting for a second time. It took a terrible toll personally and was completely futile.

Abba or Kylie?
Abba definitely.

Your favourite Tory and Labour MPs?
Ken Clarke and Frank Field.

John Bercow

Party affiliation: Conservative

Current position: Speaker of the House of Commons

Born: 19 January 1963

Education: Educated at Finchley Manorhill School and then graduated in 1985 from the University of Essex with a first class honours in Government.

Family status: Married with three children.

Pre-political career: Worked briefly at Hambros Bank and then had a time in public affairs and lobbying.

Electoral history: He became a Conservative councillor in the London Borough of Lambeth in 1986 and then, in May 1997, was elected as a Member of Parliament for Buckingham. In May 2005, he was later re-elected with an increased majority. Since then he has held a variety of positions, including shadow Chief Secretary to the Treasury and shadow Secretary of State for International Development. In June 2009, he was elected as Speaker of the House of Commons.

Career highlights: Being elected as the 157th Speaker of the House of Commons.

Interesting facts: He is a qualified lawn tennis coach.

Date of interview: December 2009
Extended version
Venue: City Speaker's Office, House of Commons
Total Politics Issue 19, January 2010

I was at university at the same time as John Bercow. He was at Essex, I was at UEA in Norwich. I didn't know him well, but on the occasions we met I found him to be engaging company and an absolutely spellbinding speaker. Never has anyone ranted to so few. He was, and is, an astonishingly talented mimic. His Tony Benn has to be listened to to be believed. In his university days, John was a straight down the line authoritarian right winger. I believe he was even a member of the Monday Club. In his early years in Parliament he also gained a reputation as an attack dog, sitting for hours on the back benches alongside Eric Forth baiting every Labour MP in sight. They hated him, and yet only a few years later, it was Labour MPs, not his Tory colleagues who propelled him to the Speakership.

When I asked for this interview I half thought the request might be blocked. After all, on my blog I had been fairly critical of his bid to be Speaker. While I liked him, I had become very distrustful of the direction of his politics. Like many others, I had him marked down as the number one candidate likely to defect to Labour. But he never did, and after the conversation we had below I genuinely believe he never intended to. Perhaps I'm being gullible.

John Bercow is the most open, accessible and unstuffy Speaker the House of Commons has known. He wants to be known as a reforming Speaker, but he is still distrusted by virtually every Tory MP I know. They think he favours Labour MPs and is far harder on Tories than he is on their opponents. The level of vitriol poured in his direction is simply astounding. Frankly, I doubt if he can ever win around most of the malcontents, but it's safe to say that however long he remains in the Speaker's chair, we're unlikely to be bored.

So what's a nice boy from University of Essex doing in a place like this?
I enjoy it, I enjoy the role, I enjoy Speaker's House. It would be dishonest and misleading to pretend I don't. As Speaker you are the fortunate and temporary inhabitant both of a great office and of an exquisite building. There were 156 Speakers before me and there will be a great many after me. It is the office that is important not its incumbent, and I'm just going to make the very best fist of it for as long as I'm allowed and seems reasonable.

I suppose the point I was making, that twenty/thirty years ago when we were both students together, did it ever cross your mind that this would be the position that one day you would aspire to hold?
No! Absolutely not. I hadn't given it a thought before I came into Parliament and for a very long time afterwards. The first time the thought was planted in my mind was when it was put to me by Jonathan Aitken. It was in 2003. I'd left the front bench of my own volition and Jonathan, in his rather philosophical way, said 'Well of course you'll very likely return, if you want to do so, to the front bench. But you know John there are always other ways you can make a success of a political career and make your contribution.' He mentioned his Godfather Selwyn Lloyd who became Speaker. That was the first time the thought was even communicated to me as a possibility. It wasn't then and there I decided I'd like to do it, but, a couple of years later, towards the end of 2005 the idea did germinate in my mind.

Was there a point when you thought 'I'm not going to progress in the Conservative front bench and so I really do need to think about what I'm going to do?'
It's very difficult to date it precisely. But it was at about the time of the election of David Cameron as leader. In June 2005 I had got myself on

the chairman's panel. I thought I was unlikely to be asked to return to the frontbench and secondly I was extremely doubtful whether I would enjoy it. That, I may say, by the way is not and is not intended to be interpreted as a commentary on David Cameron or indeed on any other leadership contender. It was simply that when I was on the front bench, although I enjoyed parts of it, and it is a great privilege, I didn't enjoy enough of it, to be frank. And if I am really brutally candid about it: although I don't think I'm devoid of ability and some contribution to make, I think on the whole I was a pretty lousy frontbencher. I was lacking in self discipline. I was not willing to commit to a collective line. I was a poor team player. And it was neither in my interest nor in the Conservative Party's interest for me to be on the front bench. When I was on the front I wanted to be on the back. Periodically when I was on the back I wanted to be on the front. And I thought, this situation is a recipe for discontent and unhappiness and that's wrong because Parliament is a great privilege. So I thought come on, pull yourself together, you're now over forty. Make a judgement about what you think you should do and stick to it. And I made the judgement that I prefer to work away on the chairman's panel and if the chance came to stand as Speaker I would take it.

How does that qualify you to be Speaker? You said I don't like sticking to a line, you don't like rigidity. You don't have a huge amount of latitude as Speaker. You have various conventions and rules you are there to implement. How did you think this job would be different to the restrictions you have to endure on the front bench?
You're right that the Speaker doesn't have huge scope. The Speaker doesn't have huge powers, the Speaker doesn't have huge opportunities on a daily basis to make changes. But, the Speaker does have some opportunity to bring about change and the role of the Speaker, so far as I was concerned, was not something that should be considered to be set in concrete. In other words you could make some changes through exhortation and encouragement and working effectively with colleagues to bring about greater scrutiny. Secondly, you could improve and develop the Speakership to make it more outward facing. It was always in my mind that if I did stand for Speaker I would argue that the Speaker should not be a purely internal figure shrouded in mystique, dressed up in a fancy costume and largely inaccessible to the public. Of course, the chair comes first, but the Speaker should be out and about engaging with civic society and in my first five months that is what I've tried to do.

Did you ask Michael Martin for any advice? If so, what did he give you?
I didn't. And I don't mean that in any disrespectful way to him. I didn't. I

felt he'd done me a great turn in allowing me to sit on his panel. And, to be honest, Alan Haselhurst, who [also] did me a great turn in allowing me to sit on the panel. I felt really, in so far as I thought about it, that to ask the Speaker of the day for advice would be a bit in for a dig. What I did do was I told Michael Martin of my intention to stand shortly before declaring, if I remember rightly. I can't remember the exact chronology of events, but I indicated to him that I intended to stand.

So he didn't contact you to give you advice?
He didn't – no. Michael Martin took a very hands-off approach to the Speakership campaign which led to my election, or which was absolutely proper. I have considerable respect for him, he had a very rough time. Like every other Speaker he had his strengths and weaknesses; he's a human being. I'm sure at some point in the future we shall meet. I think he wants a bit of a distance; he wants to establish himself in his new role.

What's been the most surprising aspect of the job so far – the thing which you thought, well actually, I hadn't anticipated that?
It may sound rather naive. I hadn't fully anticipated that, I'm not in any way complaining about this for one moment, the extent to which the Speaker is said to be doing this or leading that or personally overseeing the other when very often it is not the case. You have to get used to the fact that the buck stops with you for all sorts of things. You've got to be thick skinned. You've got to have reasonably broad shoulders; you shouldn't take criticism personally or fret about it unduly. You should listen to advice and take note of valid criticism but you have to recognise that a lot of newspapers are tomorrow's fish and chip paper. You shouldn't be diverted from your strategic goals by day to day chatter.

What did you make of this apparent antipathy among many Conservative MPs towards you? You clearly didn't get that many votes from them and yet you are there to be in command of the whole House of Commons. You wouldn't be human if while sitting in the Speaker's Chair you didn't look at the Tory benches and think to yourself, 'well you bastards didn't vote for me…'
The Speaker has got a duty to be completely impartial and demonstrably fair. I said, Iain, in standing for election that that is how I'd go about the job and I meant it. It's probably human nature that people nevertheless speculate as to whether you'll lean a bit this way or a bit that way or whether your private preference is for this one or for that one. The truth is you do have a professional obligation to block that out and to make fair judgements. So if you say to me, do I sit there thinking this set of people or that set of people

is hostile and therefore either I'm going to be hostile back or alternatively I'm going to bend over backwards not to be, the honest answer is 'no'. If you ask me why there has been some Conservative hostility it would be coy and surreal of me to decline to answer and I would be quite happy to offer an answer. I think there are a number of factors. First of all I think there is a very natural Conservative disposition to favour someone for the role of Speaker who is somewhat older, who has perhaps served in Parliament for somewhat longer. If we can have prime ministers running the country in their forties why can't we have Speakers running the House in their forties? Secondly there is no denying that very significant numbers of Conservative Members felt that I hadn't been a team player and they didn't see why I should get the prize and the opportunity of being the Speaker. I can understand that point of view and even respect it but it doesn't mean I have to share it.

Wasn't the real reason for their antipathy the suspicion among many that you were considering defecting to Labour and you were being overtly friendly to Labour in some of the speeches you were making?
You've beaten me to it! I think there were people who felt that I had co-operated quite a lot with Labour and Liberal Democrat Members and, yes, 'he's one of our MPs' but only just. And my answer to that is to say that I never had at any time any intention of being other than a Conservative Member of Parliament or, eventually if I was fortunate enough, to be Speaker. I have no desire whatever to be a member of another political party and I don't say this with any resentment – I wouldn't be meeting you if I did – I don't say it with any resentment at all but I know you yourself have once or twice commented that you really felt I was the most likely suspect. In fact, I remember one point...

This is the bit I always hate... What did I say?
...somewhere in some piece you said something about there was rumour, I think it was about the time Gordon Brown took over, that there was much rumour, speculation about a possible Conservative defection and you said that you had a shortlist of one and I'm pretty sure you named me as the member and certainly somewhere you've said you really felt I was the most likely suspect.

Did I? I'll look back on that now...
I'm pretty sure that you did. I may be wrong, but I'm pretty sure. But anyway, I don't resent it. We have a free press, and that's a good thing, you're entitled to your views about everything, including me and I shouldn't be small about it and I hope I'm not small about it. I respect

you and I respect your right to your own views. The truth of the matter, which to be honest, only I know – and possibly Sally my wife – is I never had any intention whatsoever in joining another political party. Yes there has been much gossip and speculation over the years, but it was never my intention at any time. I received approaches before ever I thought about becoming Speaker. I received various approaches from various senior people in the Labour Party saying: 'Aw, you know, we'd love to have you on board, we think you're being discarded by the Conservatives, we think you'd be quite at home with us.' Senior people, not in a formal setting, but people sidling up to you, you know: ex-ministers, current ministers, backbenchers, whatever. And, I always said no, because I felt at heart that I was most comfortable being for a whole variety of philosophical and practical reasons. So yes, I'm sure there were people who thought, 'urgh, we don't want him he's been mooted to be someone who's going to defect, we don't want him he cooperates with the other side too much, he makes speeches that they like and so on'. All I can say on that, Iain, is that I had no desire to shift at any stage. I felt myself fundamentally to be a progressive Conservative.

You were caught up in the expenses scandal yourself and repaid some money. Do you find it more difficult to act as a spokesman for cleaning up the system when you were involved in the whole *Telegraph* saga in the first place?
I don't find it more difficult because I'm not in denial. I 'fessed up to the situation which confronted me. The issue that came up on me which I confess I had not been anticipating was the payment of capital gains tax on the sale of a property in 2003. I can tell you absolutely candidly, from the day I sold that property and for that year completed my tax return until the day I was approached by the *Daily Telegraph* about it, I hadn't considered the matter. I took professional advice at the time, and I did what I was told any citizen lawfully could do which was to take steps within the law to minimise my tax burden. However, if you say to me, is it actually right that a Member of Parliament should be expected to treat his or her property for tax purposes in the same way as for expenses purposes the honest answer is 'yes'. When therefore I checked, and I genuinely did not know, for I knew I'd sold my property for a very small profit, and I just didn't remember whether I paid tax on that or not. Do I complain about the fact that the *Daily Telegraph* highlighted that matter? No I don't complain at all. I think there are people who have some grounds for complaint. I think the *Daily Telegraph* sometimes is unfair to people. I don't complain about it, and it doesn't cramp my style as Speaker because we're not electing a saint we are electing someone who is going to chair effectively in the chamber, stand up for the rights of backbenchers, be an effective chair of the House of Commons commission,

which has got an important set of responsibilities, and be an effective and robust advocate of democratic politics on behalf of this place to civic society. I am not saying I am some sort of saint but I am certainly saying that I think it is possible for all of us to put the past behind us by accepting responsibility and committing to thorough going and immediate change.

Why haven't any senior officials in the Fees Office lost their jobs? It seems to me that they were the ones that failed in their duty, just as much as politicians. The Independent Parliamentary Standards Authority will in due course be up and running. Some staff from the Resources Department will join IPSA but by no means all, and I am not anticipating that the most senior staff from the House of Commons Resources Department will be joining IPSA. Repeat, I am not anticipating that the senior staff...

I got the hint... Why would anyone want to be an MP in the present climate? My family and my friends think I'm barking mad to even think about still wanting to do it. I found myself during this whole expenses thing doing radio phone-ins all the time and it was me trying to explain why MPs needed allowances and expenses, and I kept looking behind me thinking 'where are the MPs?' Why aren't they actually going out there and telling people what they do?
Well I think that is a huge responsibility. I do think that we've got to do that. Let me try and answer the direct question you asked. Why would anybody want to be an MP: because you are still passionate about politics, about principles you hold dear, policies you believe in, things that you'd like to make happen. And of course associated with that, perfectly properly, there can be an element of personal ambition. People feel: well I could make a difference, either as a local MP or as a Minister or, better still, both. And there are still plenty of capable, tough, ambitious people who are prepared to put up with an element of criticism and excoriation if they think they can do something worthwhile. Let me however, Iain, touch on the second point that is implicit in your question, in fact almost explicit, that Members of Parliament do have to have for the most part a second home. I think that is important because we do not want, in reforming the system and dynamiting past arrangements, to end up with a House of Commons comprised exclusively or even predominantly of people who have either inherited wealth, and fortunes, or external sponsorship. That would be a really bad thing, and it is a risk, and that's why it's important that we underline, to that section of the media and the electorate that doesn't think MPs should have any allowances, that some allowances are necessary. Where I think we went very badly wrong was first... for too long we continued with a system which allowed substantial personal profit in the form of capital gain on homes, and

I think that the public increasingly came to feel that that was really at the heart of the expenses scandal and could no longer be justified, and I agree. For what it is worth, I agree with Sir Christopher Kelly that we should end state-financed house purchase. However, that is a different matter from saying that it should be no housing allowance at all. I think the key point is that once that provision is in the form of rent, or the payment of hotel costs, then that element of personal profiteering is removed from the equation, but, just to go on the offensive for a moment, yes necessary costs – costs wholly necessary and exclusively incurred in the performance of parliamentary duties – should be met in relation to housing and also in relation to the running of an office, to the payment of staff, to the acquisition of equipment, and to travel to and from and within constituencies. Yes it should be strictly monitored, yes it shouldn't be excessively generous, but yes it is necessary, and you're right that we do have to make the case for a properly-funded politics.

Were you embarrassed by the coverage of the amount of money that's being spent on these apartments… because it wasn't anything to do with you, was it?
I was sorry that the coverage was what it was. I requested a number of adaptations to the apartment above these rooms, Iain, because I am the first speaker to live in the apartment with a young family at least for a hundred years, if not in recorded history, and there is a difference between a couple in their sixties living in a property and a couple with three very small children, and some changes did have to be made. I'm sorry that sometimes the point didn't get across that where changes are made, those are for the ongoing benefit of the property. For example – I give you an example – yes I can tell you I spent money on child blocks, public money on child blocks. I defend that; I don't want my kids falling on the terrace or into the River Thames. But it's true that we also acquired a new sofa suite. We did that, Iain, because the sofa suite there was massively uncomfortable, had been there for an unspecified number of years, the builders couldn't trace when it was purchased, it certainly hadn't been purchased in the past five or six years. And it was completely unsuitable for children. So we did say 'yes, we would like that to be replaced' if that was possible, and it certainly was possible and the Martins I think had acquired a new sofa when they entered, so we did. Iain, when we leave, the Speaker's suite, of course, stays. We don't cart it out and take it off to one of our properties. If we put in, I mean we haven't, if we acquire a new toaster, we put in a new toaster, it stays, it's for the permanent benefit… so I regretted that. And the rest I may say – there was a considerable amount of work done that was maintenance work which the house authorities expect to do it not at my say, so the

short answer is yes, I'm sorry that it was represented as being sort of an act of greed or selfishness on our part. It was nothing of the kind and I just wish that these papers were prepared to offer a fair characterisation of these things.

Does PMQs serve a purpose any longer? Does it not need to be drastically reformed? Not just changing the day but allowing you as Speaker to pick random MPs each week to ask the questions. Wouldn't that be a better way of doing it? It would virtually eliminate planted questions.
I do have some sympathy for that idea. I certainly think that the start of the next parliament is the time to make reforms. But such a major rethink is possible and desirable. I don't know if it will get rid of planted questions altogether because the whips will always want to be sure a certain message is percolated across their benches, and they'll have thought about that in advance. I don't think you can totally remove that possibility. But there is some merit in what you're suggesting, and we can certainly look at it. That isn't a 'I hear what you say' answer. I think it's a good idea.

I do think there's something to be said for the cut and thrust of exchanges between the Prime Minister and the Opposition. I still feel we could move to a model in which those exchanges were shorter and there could be more time for back benchers to take part. The time taken up by the exchanges between the Prime Minister and David Cameron and Nick Clegg is a very substantial part of Prime Minister's Questions. Certainly it's more than half. I am deeply discontented and inclined to look for any opportunity to foreshorten it. It's difficult to do anything more than that at the moment but if you ask me would I prefer that there should be less time for the front benches and more time for the back then the answer would be 'yes' and I would like to look at how we can achieve that in the early weeks and months of the next parliament.

You have in the past stopped Gordon Brown trying to turn it into Leader of the Opposition's Question Time. Is that difficult, because if you do it once, if you're going to be consistent, you need to do it every time? And yet, if you did it every time, frankly we wouldn't have a PMQs.
I take your point. There is a trade-off here between consistency and having the event of Prime Minister's Questions in any meaningfully recognisable form at all. So sometimes I'm afraid you have to work on the basis that you will intervene if you think there is a rather severe case of a minister or the Prime Minister going off piste and talking about opposition policy or trying to get the opposition. And other times you will tend to let it go. I don't actually accept that you have to intervene every time. Ministers have

to know that you might, and on the whole that will act as a brake. On the one occasion when I did have to intervene on the Prime Minister I didn't do it with any desire to score a point or to put him down, it was just that I felt it had been indicated in a very explicit way, it had been advertised, that the intention was to talk about Conservative health policy, and I felt it was not appropriate.

Can you let us in on the conversation between you and your wife, Sally, when she told you she wanted to be a Labour candidate?
[Laughs] I can't be an advocate of more women in Parliament, which I was consistently for a number of years, and then try to stop my wife exercising her democratic right. I know some people find this really hard to understand that you can possibly be married to, or partner with, somebody who's got a different party affiliation from you. Of course there are people who are going to find it odd, but I know Labour people who say oh they couldn't possibly be married to – in Parliament – a Tory. It just genuinely happens to be the case that my wife Sally and I have not argued much about politics over the years. We've disagreed about the Iraq War: I supported it, she was against it. We disagreed about hunting because I defended consistently – and I have no regrets about that – whereas she's anti-hunting. And those are two examples. We strongly disagreed on Europe, where I took a basically Eurosceptic position – I voted against all the treaties, and I was always opposed to joining the euro, whereas Sally's a very keen euro enthusiast. She has long been a Labour supporter and indeed since I think 1997 a Labour Party member, and I was, until 22 June of this year, a Conservative. So was I taken aback or shocked, or did I try to dissuade her? No, no, no.

The point I'm making is that it's going to inevitably bring press attention. We've already seen it with the *Mail on Sunday* coverage. That's a distraction for you, isn't it? An unwelcome distraction.
The way in which the media report these things can be an unwelcome distraction but an unwelcome distraction is not a good reason to try to stop somebody pursuing her democratic rights. So yes, if the way the press report it – you're asking me is the way the press report it a mild nuisance? Yes, it is but I'm not going to have my life dictated by it.

Look, I respect that people have got their own views about these things. One thing I do think is quite wrong and unfair is for somebody to say: 'Oh well, it's improper for the Speaker's wife to be engaged in acts of politics.' That's wrong. It may well add to the spice of life, it might well cause me some difficulties in terms of press coverage, but to suggest that it's somehow constitutionally improper is quite wrong. And the simple reason for that is that the obligation for impartiality applies to me. It does not apply to Sally, and deep down I ask you to consider this, and hope you might even agree. It's a deeply sexist view based on the idea that the wife is my chattel.

If Sally ever got into Parliament that would be no problem. I'll tell you something: if anything, Iain, it would be a problem for her because I would have to demonstrate very clearly that she wasn't getting preferential treatment. Julian Lewis is my best mate in the House. Julian never lobbies me to be called. He said to me on day one, 'I'll never do that John.' And on balance he probably loses out a bit because I'm very concerned not to call him particularly and be accused of favouring a friend, so Julian accepts that stoically.

You are facing a challenge at the next election. Isn't this convention that the Speaker isn't challenged a fundamentally undemocratic one?
I don't think it is fundamentally undemocratic because it isn't a rule, it's not a law. It is a convention and I think that you have to look at what the alternative would be. If you said, well, party candidates from the main parties will stand, it will be quite difficult to get anybody to stand for the role of Speaker. It would be very difficult to have more than a one-term Speaker because obviously a lot of people do vote, even now with declining party loyalties, on the basis of party allegiance

If we chose to reconfigure the Speakership in the way that it operates in many other countries where the Speaker does vote in all normal votes, not just where there's a tie as here, but in normal votes, and does campaign for a party, that would be a different situation. But I don't sense any enthusiasm on the part of the House to do that.

The second point is that now and again – I'll try and deal with it up front – it is suggested perhaps what should be done is that the Speaker should be given a separate constituency, usually known as St Stephen's, which represents a small area around Westminster, and that the local constituency he or she is taken from should be able to hold a normal party election. The House of Commons can always decide to do that if it wants; my attitude is that, as such a decision would affect me directly, it's not right for me to be either an advocate of it, or resistant to it. The only thing I would say is I do enjoy having constituents and believe that I'm still well and truly able, and demonstrate that I'm well and truly able effectively to represent the people of my constituency. I do just want to underline the fact that it is both possible and it would be necessary for the Speaker to continue to be a highly active constituency MP, but I won't face, I suspect, major party competition, but I will face opponents.

By raising that possibility of the Member for the St Stephen's, you do almost sound like you're advocating it.

No, I'm not advocating it at all. No, I'm not advocating it at all. No, I'm absolutely not advocating… No, Iain, I mentioned maybe in the spirit of Glasnost and mention it because it is now and again put. It was put, for example, by the *Sunday Times* recently. For the avoidance of doubt, I'm not actively seeking to resist it, but if you're asking if I'm personally in favour of it, my answer is 'no'. I love Buckingham, I love representing Buckingham, and I want to go on representing Buckingham.

Quickfire

Worst Christmas present you've ever given?
I once gave some lingerie to my wife that she regarded as naff, but I won't describe it further. And I have not repeated the exercise.

Favourite drink?
Lager.

Wig or breeches?
Neither.

The thing you wish you'd known at sixteen?
That short-term debt shouldn't have stopped me qualifying for the bar and practising at it. My only major regret is that I would have liked to have been a barrister. Partly because I have no private money and it was actually a bit beyond sixteen, I decided not to pursue it.

Best movie you've seen this year?
Changeling.

Favourite tennis player?
Unquestionably Roger Federer. In my view, and I've seen every Wimbledon final since 1972, Federer is the greatest player I've ever seen.

Speaker or Wimbledon finalist?
Speaker.

What book are you reading at the moment?
I've just started Sarah Waters' book *The Little Stranger*. I'm a huge fan of Sarah

Waters; I think she's a fantastic writer. I'd like to get her into the Speaker's House and do a reading.

What makes you cry?

Two things make me cry since I've become an MP: coming across really very hard-hit kids who are either unable to get the help they need or just suffer from a terrible disability, or the most excruciating poverty. And the other thing was when I went to the Thai/Burmese border I met people there who'd seen their parents shot dead in front of them, and then parents who'd seen their kids shot in front of them, and I remember meeting them. And it still brings tears to my eyes now.

Lord Pearson

Party affiliation: UK Independence Party (UKIP)

Born: 20 July 1942

Education: Educated at Eton College.

Family status: Married to Caroline St Vincent Rose, with three children from two previous marriages.

Pre-political career: Prior to becoming leader of UKIP, he had a career in international insurance.

Electoral history: He was made a life peer in June 1990 for services to the insurance industry, sitting as a Conservative. He was expelled from the Conservative Party in May 2004 after calling for voters to back the UK Independence Party. He eventually joined UKIP in January 2007 and later won the election to become the new leader of UKIP in November 2009, succeeding Nigel Farage. He officially resigned from this position in September 2010.

Career highlights: Being made a life peer and later becoming leader of the UK Independence Party.

Interesting fact: He is the co-founder of a pro-free-trade think tank website called 'Global Britain', which publishes research on the BBC's EU coverage and on the cost of UK membership.

Date of interview: January 2010
Extended version
Venue: Lord Pearson's house, Kennington
Total Politics Issue 20, February 2010

I can't think of anyone I know who dislikes Malcolm Pearson. He is a genuinely nice guy, who will go out of his way to be co-operative and helpful. But he must surely rate as the most unlikely political party leader ever to be elected. As leader of UKIP he was like a fish out of water. He struggled to cope with the media demands of the job and found it difficult to interest himself in the minute details of the policy formation process.

Just before this interview took place I remember driving late at night to the BBC in White City to do a paper review. I was listening to a discussion on private health on the Radio 5 Live Stephen Nolan programme. Nolan is one of the best interviewers on the BBC and when Lord Pearson came on the line, he smelt blood. 'Just before we talk about Europe,' he said, 'can I ask you about health, Lord Pearson?' Being a gent, Lord Pearson assented. And there then followed an absolute car crash of an interview. I was so appalled I rang his press spokeswoman, who I had got to know quite well. 'You really need to get him some media training,' I suggested. And when I met him a couple of weeks later he proudly told me that the media training was underway. Unfortunately it didn't really work and there followed some more absolutely cringeworthy interviews, none more so than during the election campaign where Lord Pearson admitted he had not read UKIP's manifesto and was not there to discuss the minutiae of policy. Oh dear.

The thing is, Pearson is so transparently decent that no one in the media or even within his own party held it against him that he just wasn't a media or platform performer. He actually said what he thought even if he knew it would prove unpopular in some quarters. I guess we need more politicians who are willing to do that. He had the self knowledge to know that leadership of a political party wasn't for him, but he held UKIP together after the surprise resignation of his predecessor, Nigel Farage, and for that his party should be grateful.

So what on earth made you decide to stand for leadership of UKIP?
There was quite a lot of arm twisting from a number of leading people within the party and from several of the major donors.

Because you haven't actually been in the party that long…
No, I have only been in the party a couple of years because before that I sat as an Independent Conservative after being sacked from the Conservative Party in great disgrace.

How much of a wrench was it to leave?
I was always a rebel. I said I would be loyal to Margaret Thatcher and I remained loyal to her, but that wasn't the same thing as being loyal to Mr Major. I'd been the most rebellious backbench peer in the Lords and when I was sacked for suggesting people should lend their vote to UKIP in the European elections it was actually a great relief. I have always been a bit of a maverick, so I'm afraid it didn't trouble me at all. I kept my personal friends in the party, not that there's very many of them.

It's slightly ironic though, isn't it, because the Conservative Party is more Eurosceptic now than it has ever been.
The Conservative Party leadership isn't nearly Eurosceptic enough. The

project of European integration, as originally envisaged by Monnet, is complete and I think everyone knows that Cameron is simply not telling the truth when he pretends a sovereignty act to prevent further losses of sovereignty to Brussels is meaningful. I think they know he's talking nonsense when he says he can reclaim various powers from Brussels.

But surely he would only be misleading people if there was no further sovereignty to secede to Brussels but there clearly is?
What further sovereignty?

Economics and taxation for example.
Well they've got that if they want it.

Well, they don't have the power to raise taxes.
I believe they do. You only have to look at their use of Article 308, which they have been using since the French and Dutch rejection of the original constitution, to do anything they wanted, in fact.

But if under that Article everything has to happen unanimously, a British prime minister can veto it.
He can, but the British government has not been vetoing it.

No, but a Conservative government could.
Yes, for anything new– not what's already been done. Don't forget our old friend the ratchet – the Aquis Communitaire. Our position is they don't need anything new now and even if they were to, they are already talking about raising tax and I'm not aware that either Cameron or any of the established parties have screamed about that.

So if all that is true then basically the game's up – what's the point of UKIP?
Because the only way out is the door and the point of UKIP in the next general election is to campaign try and inform the public more precisely about why we are in this position. The people have got the point about why this has gone seriously wrong. Even the lawyers and the accountants in the City of London have now got the point. They never cared about the fishermen or any other industries that have been damaged, sometimes to the point of extinction by our membership of the European Union, but they have now got the point because of the hedge fund directive. People are beginning to see clearly what this project has always been about.

Isn't part of the problem though that you can wax lyrical about Section 308 of the Treaty of Rome or the Hedge Fund Directive all you like, but you've actually

got to go to people's hearts and minds. Isn't the problem with UKIP that it looks less like the rest of the British people?
Well that's not what the latest opinion polls would tell you. A large majority of people wish to go back to free trade and friendly collaboration with the European Union. If you ask a slightly different question – do you want to come out? – then that's more frightening. In the general election campaign we are simply going to deliver two messages that are incredibly simple; one is that your democracy has removed your right to elect and dismiss those who make your laws. We are also going to run another idea which hasn't really been tested in the political world and it runs right alongside getting out of the European Union. The idea is direct democracy, power to the people, the Swiss system of referendums and the Daniel Hannan/Douglas Carswell plan. The British people are fed up with all the regulation that is coming at them from Brussels and to a certain extent Westminster.

Isn't it slightly ironic for someone who has never been elected to anything to talk about the wonders of direct democracy?
In our bill, which is a very brief debate, you only need to read two speeches, mine and David Willoughby de Broke's on the evening of the 6 July in the Lords. You don't even need to wade through the whole bill but the concept is very simple. We would reduce the House of Commons to only 250 members and we'd leave it with only the truly national issues of defence, foreign policy, the national Treasury and so on. Everything else goes local – really like the Daniel Hannan plan, and you have a trigger for referendums at the national level on the national issues and at local level for local tax powers and all the rest of it.

Actually, this takes a number of years to come in but at the end of the seven year period when we have had a bedding down system of a much reduced central government – very like Switzerland – staffed by real people, these people will have to have a real job, like the Swiss, an MP will be paid £30,000 a year and will have £170,000 allowance and that will be it and he will go up to Westminster when there is something to talk about and they won't go more than 100 days a year under our bill as everything else goes local.

Sorry, you're seriously suggesting an MP shouldn't be paid more than £30,000 a year?
Look at the bill, it's there as we want real people to do it and I'm not going to pretend it's only for the rich.

Well, you would only get the rich.
No, the trade unions could do it, the universities could do it.

Well I wouldn't do it for only £30,000 a year.
Well you won't be an MP.

I couldn't afford to do it.
That's why you need other support, you need a job in the real world as you would only have to go to the Commons 100 days a year as you are only going to be dealing with the national interest as everything else would have gone local.

But wouldn't that go totally against what the public mood is, they don't want their politician to have outside interests?
I'm not so sure as that's what the politicians say. You go to Switzerland, every MP you meet there has a real job, with this system of direct democracy, I mean quite frankly our system of representative parliamentary democracy has had its day, it made sense in the seventeenth to nineteenth centuries when the people couldn't read and people who could read and had position in life and so on went up to Westminster to take your decisions for you. Do the British people want their MPs to go on taking their decisions for them – the answer is no – it doesn't matter who you put in there, unless you have real people dealing with the national issues, everything else goes local where the people will have real hands on power.

And in our bill, actually after seven years, the future of the House of Lords, since you mention it, is up for grabs, it can either continue as it is, it can be abolished or there will be two other options and that will go to a referendum of the people. In committee we may amend the bill. To bring it back to Europe, if you think I, as an unelected toff, shouldn't be suggesting this wild eyed democratic ideas, let me put it to you – how would you feel if the House of Lords, unelected, had the monopoly of proposing all our legislation which it did in secret, if it then went to a committee of the House of Lords which negotiated it in secret and it then went to a council of the House of Lords, all of it unelected, about which it then passed in secret, now you wouldn't like that. But that is what is happening with 70 per cent of our law at least which is coming to us, imposed on us by Brussels.

So if it takes an unelected toff in the House of Lords to make these proposals and David Willoughby de Broke is a proper aristocrat, if it takes us to put this before the people then we will do it.

This is where I think you personally have a problem in that I could accept a lot of what you say, as could most people, if it came from Nigel, but people will have more difficulty taking it from an unelected member of the House of Lords.
I've been elected to the leadership, as far as the party is concerned I have

been elected and Nigel's one commitment to me is he will remain the chief party spokesman, he's going to be in charge of media relations and he is our front man with the media. Obviously he's a genius, he's a great man and a great politician and I don't pretend to be, he was a derby winner, UKIP have now got a sort of carthorse [laughs]. We know that and I accept that and I have said that all the way through the hustings.

But we all know that dual leaderships never work.
Nigel will be our spokeperson and obviously if I am called upon because I'm the leader then I will speak. I don't detect people are holding my background against me and if they are then there's nothing I can do about it. I'm not going to apologise, I'm not going to resign from White's Club, I'm not going to stop shooting and stalking and I'm going to carry on because I never wanted to be a politician. I have always said I'm not a politician and I'm not and I can't pretend otherwise. And so I make gaffes, I talk about the 'disband' word when what I meant was get together and fight. I've accused the Muslims of breeding ten times faster than us when what I really meant was their population is going up and so on. I've made mistakes and I will probably make more. I try and do better but that's where we are.

Do you not think though that you might be seen as the Ming Campbell of UKIP?
Possibly. I am sixty-seven years old. I have never been much involved in party politics. I've done a bit of canvassing but that's all, so therefore when I look at the structure of a political party I have to learn as I go along. The trouble with UKIP is that its success has outgrown its infrastructure and that needs putting right. Now that's not Nigel's scene, he's not an organisation chart man, he's a political genius and a brilliant man. Organisation charts are not his strong point and he's very happy to leave that to me.

The party itself historically has been a shambles hasn't it, organisationally?
I wouldn't dare to use that expression but it has certainly not been very well organised. Our communications have been bad. People have been learning things in the press that they ought to have known about in advance. A proper organisation chart and proper communication is not difficult and we are going to do that. We will have a more efficient fighting machine.

But isn't part of the problem that to do any of what you just said, which is obviously necessary you have to have money and UKIP has not got the money to do it, in fact it's got to pay back £360,000.

We have that covered already and I will try and raise more money for the rest of it. One of the reasons I stood for leadership was that I thought as leader I would be better able to raise money. As leader I would be able to raise the sort of money we need or would be more likely to be able to than if one of the other candidates had become leader. When I stood for leadership I didn't have a single enemy, but as leader of course one is bound to make a few. Those who find it an anathema that David Willoughby de Broke and I made the offer we did to the Conservatives which was give us a binding referendum on an agreed wording on our membership in the European Union and we will make sure you are in a position to deliver.

I thought the offer was on the Lisbon Treaty?
No, never! Lisbon Treaty was always a red herring really.

You couldn't have seriously expected the Conservatives to accept that. Wasn't that just a bit of trouble making?
No, not at all. Our position in the European Union is now so desperate the only way out is the door, it is unthinkable that Cameron will get anything worthwhile in any form of renegotiation.

Far enough but all I'm trying to understand is your thought process before you put that offer to Tom Strathclyde presumably and you hadn't cleared this with your party colleagues as such.
That is not so. This was, we thought, a settled policy from Nigel. He had the support of the National Policy Committee for it, he'd mentioned it at conference, he'd mentioned it live on the *Politics Show* and certainly to a large lunch I had attended. He was actually cross-examined at the lunch by Freddie Forsyth, who said 'Nigel did I get this right – what are you saying?' and Nigel said 'a binding referendum with wording we agree, free vote for the Conservative Party and we will...', Nigel did not say disband, I said disband at the end of the conversation with the lovely Alice Thomson and Rachel Sylvester. I should never have used that word. Tom's [Strathclyde] answer to us was 'are you sure you want this referendum because we will have the new Prime Minister, presumably we will be in a honeymoon period, you will have the whole Labour and the whole Liberal Democrat machine against you, Ok you will have the Conservative activists with you...' My reply was 'I couldn't imagine anything better'. Fighting an issue against the whole political class would be wonderful.

And then you heard nothing from them?
No not a squeak. I went back to Tom as Tom was seeing David two days

later on a one to one, and I asked Tom what had happened the next week and he had said 'oh it's all too bloody awful' and disappeared. I mean Tom's a lovely man, but he is part of the Conservative leadership apparatus in that sense.

Did you get the impression that Lord Strathclyde was in favour of it?
Well, he thought we might lose [laughs]. He actually said we might lose, and we said well we would have trusted the people. So then I asked someone else who sits on the front bench, who had better remain nameless, I said 'what's happened to this, we have given this offer and absolutely bloody silence?' and they said well the Norwich North by-election is coming up and the hope is you will fall back to 2 or 3 per cent and we can forget it. Well we got 13 per cent in Norwich North and in fact 43 per cent in some Cambridge council seats that day. But we have heard no more and since then we have got our answer because Cameron has ruled out any referendum for five years and thereby slapping in the face the whole of that part of the Conservative Party that actually wanted a referendum even just on Lisbon

Would you again now stand against every Conservative candidate including the Better Off Out people?
I hope not.

Well that's the logical thing to do now.
No it wouldn't, let's go back to square one. We must start to build in the House of Commons a genuine come out group of MPs so we will not be standing against Philip Davies, Richard Shepherd and Douglas Carswell, although I'm slightly talking out of turn as I haven't had time to clear this with the relevant constituency chairman and parties.

But this is an existing policy isn't it?
It is existing policy but it is resisted by some people who want to fight absolutely everything; but if we fail to get a referendum then all you can start doing is to start building [with] people in the Commons. . . If there's a seat where we don't think we can get in and there is someone who could get in with our support who will fight for it when they get in, and not be wishy washy Better Off Out of it.

Well what's wishy washy about that?
Well how energetic are these people in the Commons, what questions do they put down? Will they actually fight in the House of Commons for Britain to leave?

You're putting another hurdle in front of them, aren't you?
Yes I am. But each constituency is different, each individual is different, each UKIP political party is different and each individual case has to be looked at on its merits but it is madness if we put up a candidate against Philip Davies and he doesn't get back into the Commons.

What have you learnt from your first few weeks of being leader? Because you have had a bit of a baptism of fire; *The Telegraph* have had a go at you, was there a point when you thought what on earth have I done?
Oh yes, but I think I am over that now. The 'disband' word and 'breeding' weren't very clever, so I have learnt that one word out of place can cover the whole of the picture on a newspaper so I have to learn to do better and do less badly in future. I am having media training. What that will do I don't know because a lot of people say that I shouldn't be like 'them'.

You will inevitably be compared with Nigel Farage, won't you?
Yes and it's a great tragedy he's gone. I didn't want him to go. He was over worked with his job in the European Parliament. I tried to stop him going and I wish he had stayed on as leader, but he hasn't and he is now our spokesman. People will make of me what they make of me and I can't change that in any way and I'm not really going to apologise for it.

But do you think you are going to have to curb your predisposition to be completely honest about stuff?
I hope not.

How will you attract votes from the broader left, not just the white working-class left?
I think our policies do appeal to the broarder left. Nothing will appeal to the intellectual left and the crazy idiotic political class which have been running this country for far too long but the direct democracy definitely appeals and it isn't just Labour voters we have to make sense to but don't forget the 40 per cent who have given up voting.

As leader will you be inviting Geert Wilders back to this country?
Yeah, I hope he's coming back in early March.

Why – what purpose does that serve?
We want a conference in London attended by the black Christian community; some of the black African bishops who are really living through what violent Islam means, for instance the wonderful Bishop of Jos in Northern Nigeria whose wife was recently publicly raped and dragged through the streets,

these are people who can come and really warn what is in store from violent Islam. I want Geert there and I want the black African bishops there and I want the mild Islamic community there and I hope we will be producing a charter of Muslim understanding which will be an analysis of those verses in the Qur'an which uphold the disgraceful treatment of women and appeal to the Jihadists. I think our leading expression will be 'gender apartheid' and I think this country needs to address it. It needs to address it in cohesion with the vast majority of mild Muslims who at the moment are sitting there not doing very much.

Do you think there is a sort of apartheid operating in this country at the moment in some parts of our cities where you have essentially got areas that are entirely inhabited by immigrant communities who have not assimilated into our society at all – what do you do about that?
Surely the minority which isn't trying to assimilate is the Muslim community and Sharia law is gender apartheid. It is accepted by all the Muslims and sometimes it takes precedence over British law. We should be teaming up with Peter Tatchell and the gay lobby and the humanist lobby and so on. It's wrong for all of us.

What are you genuinely hoping for at the next election because there's all the speculation about what might happen to John Bercow with Nigel fighting him.
I think Nigel has a very good chance against him.

Is that what you will be throwing all your effort into?
No, at the moment I think we have about 500 candidates. We are going to fight across the board.

If we meet in a year's time what will you hope to achieve by then?
We have to go for a complete re-alignment in British politics and I think the first step towards that has to be a hung parliament. I am afraid and if we can help to achieve that I will feel we have done quite well. Now I know what they say against that, they say Dave needs a very large majority so he can cut public expenditure in a way to save the country, that's the counter argument – to which I say I see no sign of Dave even pretending that Dave's going to do that, he's backing the 50 per cent tax rate, he's backing the tax on bankers and so on and therefore helping to cripple some of the life blood in this country, part of the GDP that comes in through the City of London is oxygenated blood and it's madness to kill that and I don't see that he's talking of cutting anything like the amount that must be cut. So I think a hung parliament will be fine, it will be a first step.

But how would that benefit UKIP?
Well we would then be free to join up with decent real people, Liberal Democrats in the South West.

And then you will have a more Europhile government than you had before.
Not necessarily.

If there's a hung parliament, whoever it is will have to govern with the support of the Liberal Democrats who are the most Europhile party in British politics. If they are in a coalition it's possible Nick Clegg could be Foreign Secretary.
So what? The people will get angrier…

…oh so you will be troublemaking?
No it's not. It's answering what the people need. It's providing the only way out of all this. which is UKIP at the moment, Conservative activists will agree with you on that and quite a lot of Liberal Democrats in the south west will agree with you, quite a lot of Labour in the north and what else can we do, what else have they left us with. They have turned down an offer where we put our country before our party. They have done the opposite. The people know that, the people aren't stupid, the people are a bloody slight cleverer than the political class now, which is why they should have binding referendums.

Quickfire

What book are you reading at the moment?
Ten Years On: Britain without the European Union by Lee Rotherham.

What do you read for relaxation?
I don't read a lot of books for relaxation because I read very slowly and I am mildly dyslexic.

What's your favourite view?
Looking south on Rannoch Moor.

Favourite holiday destination?
Rannoch Moor or Davos.

What do you wish you had known at the age of sixteen?
I wish I had taken my studies much more seriously and not played quite so much football and squash. And possibly I should have gone to university which I didn't.

What makes you cry?

I think the triumph of good over evil and true love conquering the opposite

If you were holding a dinner party and you could invite four people living or dead who would you invite?

Churchill, Alexander Solzhenitsyn, Caroline Cox and I think Andrew Green, three of whom I am privileged to have known

What's your favourite food?

Fried potatoes and ice cream – separately.

David Owen

Party affiliation: Labour/Social Democratic Party

Born: 2 July 1938

Education: Educated at Mount House School in Tavistock and then Bradfield College in Berkshire before studying Medicine at Sidney Sussex College, Cambridge.

Family status: Married with three children.

Pre-political career: Began clinical training at St Thomas's Hospital in October 1959, later qualifying as a doctor in 1962.

Electoral history: Elected as Labour MP for Plymouth Sutton constituency in 1966 and in 1974 for the adjacent Plymouth Devonport constituency. He remained an MP for Plymouth Devonport until his elevation to peerage in 1992. On Labour's return to government in March 1974, he became Parliamentary Under-Secretary for Health and then Minister of State for Health. He later became Minister of State at the Foreign Office and then Foreign Secretary. He later split from the Labour Party to form the Social Democratic Party (SDP) with three others in a collective leadership. He became sole leader in 1983, but his involvement in the party finished in 1990 after it was merged to become the Social and Liberal Democrats (SLD).

Career highlights: Becoming the youngest Foreign Secretary for over forty years, being made a peer and creating his own party in the SDP.

Interesting fact: He has written extensively on the relationship between illness and politics, with particular emphasis on the 'hubris syndrome', a condition affecting those at the pinnacle of power.

Date of interview: February 2010
Extended version
Venue: House of Lords
Total Politics Issue 21, March 2010

David Owen, I think, would have made a very good prime minister. He has all the necessary qualities except one. He doesn't suffer fools gladly. He can be a very charming man, but finds it difficult to tolerate people he doesn't rate. I like a politician to display a certain arrogance, but Owen's problem has always been that people think that's all there is to him. They're wrong, but it explains why his career peaked in 1977 when he was appointed Foreign Secretary by James Callaghan.

I conduct these interviews in all sorts of locations, but this is the first time I have ever interviewed anyone in a broom cupboard. I jest not. We spoke for ninety minutes in a room which can't have been more than three feet across and ten feet long. The Germans would call it 'gemütlich'!

During the interview David was very keen to remain above party politics. He sees himself as an elder statesman but at the same time, is clearly searching for a new role. I'm not sure what that will be, but if I were on a negotiating team I'd definitely want him on my side. Beneath the surface charm, lies an inner certainty and strength of purpose. I wouldn't bet against David Cameron finding an international role for him.

What is your role in politics nowadays?
I am a voice. I very rarely vote in the House of Lords and I focus entirely on international affairs. It would be unwise to pretend you have very great influence. I don't consider myself part of the legislative process. I mainly vote on matters of conscience or moral issues.

Someone described you as a pro-European, Eurosceptic. Is that accurate?
I have never been a federalist. I accepted Gaitskell's assessment that if we were to reach a stage where we were heading for a federal state in which we were like California or New York – then that was not the sort of Europe I would wish to join. There is no doubt there is a continuing momentum towards ever greater unity and the aim of many of those is ever greater integration. I don't object to ever greater unity. Ever greater integration I do object to, because I think there are limits at many different aspects of community activity and I think we have to be much more aware of those limits.

I don't believe that is a Eurosceptic stance. I never accept that I'm a Euro-sceptic. I came back into politics with [the think tank] New Europe because I wanted to make sure that we didn't get rushed and pushed into the euro, and thank goodness we aren't in the euro. If we were dealing with our own economic problems today without being able to depreciate we'd be in a situation like Greece and Ireland and Spain, so thank goodness we're not in this vice.

You got involved in politics at quite a young age. Is there any part of you that regrets not being able to continue a medical career because of that?
I have never once ceased to be a doctor. When I was Foreign Secretary and issuing passports I still called myself medical practitioner and in the last five or six years I have been writing a book on illness and heads of governments. I really have gone back to medicine. Last May I wrote an article with Jonathan Davidson, a professor of psychiatry at Duke, in *Brain*

magazine, which is a very respectable international neurology journal, and we were submitted to peer review. It was actually an immensely interesting and enjoyable experience and there is no doubt they greatly improve the paper. And there was a great interchange of ideas about the 'hubris syndrome' and whether this is an acquired personality disorder, which I and Jonathan Davidson believe it is. It's been a wonderful thing for me in my seventies to be writing in learned journals, just like I did when I was twenty-four or twenty-five.

When you look at the three political parties and compare them to when you were at your height in politics, what do you think the differences are between now and the '70s and '80s?
I always believed that politics thrives on an ideological debate and I think that we've almost reached the point where having moved from too much ideology, which I think was the legacy really of the '60s and '70s, to too little ideology. I would not object if the debate became rather more ideological.

Couldn't you actually almost blame the SDP in part for that? The SDP was formed because the Labour Party had become very ideological, and indeed the Conservative Party also. That was the main selling point of the SDP – that it wasn't ideological.
I think that is a valid point. We certainly contributed to the death of ideology. But if you look at some of the SDP ideas – it was a social democratic party – there is a very definite ideological strand within it.

When you look at the Liberal Democrats now, do you think that the social democratic side triumphed in the end?
I think the jury's out. There is no doubt that the combination of Vince Cable, Chris Huhne and Nick Clegg has made the party seem much happier with social market economy. I used to have arguments both within the SDP and certainly with the Liberal Democrats about using the term. I feel it is still a problem for the modern Liberal Democrats. It is foolish for me to say that those people who took a different view from me and stayed with the idea of merging the parties haven't had an influence – people like Vince Cable and Chris Huhne. I do not want the death of ideology, I don't want too much ideology and I think a lot of the decisions you take in government are pragmatic. They are a matter of trying to weigh up facts and the evidence. But you go into politics and you become a minister rather than a civil servant, because you have a view about society. There are things you want to do and I think that must be a driving force about politics. And I think that the clash of ideas about how to control market forces is one which needs to be had.

How should the Lib Dems define themselves?
I think that in this election the jury is out on a lot of things, not least it's going to be very important for the Liberal Democrats how they define themselves in terms of the economic future. If they are seen to be principled but tough minded about the economy then I think people will be prepared to vote for them. They will be prepared to take the risk of not being exactly sure what sort of government will emerge. If they think that they haven't made that step to be an economic governing force, they will hold back. I think that Vince Cable, in personal terms, has done a lot for the Liberal Democrats but he's supported by others. Nick Clegg in his economic language is very Jo Grimond. I see more Jo Grimond in Nick Clegg than in almost all the previous leaders.

Peers don't have a vote but you sound as if, had you got a vote, you would vote for Nick Clegg.
I rather resent the fact you have to give up being able to vote as a peer. I have actually great confidence in the British electorate. I think they got every election right in my lifetime and that has kicked me out of government twice. It's quite a hard thing to say, but I think it was right we were kicked out in 1970 and I think it was right that we were kicked out in 1979. And I think that the British electorate have a pretty good sniff for this. It is pretty clear to me they're not decided which way to go. It's amazing that Labour can be in contention after what's happened to them. I think this is because the country has not yet made their mind up about the Conservatives but it's also the nature of the electoral system we have. The hurdle is absurdly high – grossly, unfairly high – for the Conservatives to pass. I think this is beginning to dawn on people. They understand this election is – when you begin to grapple the fact that the Tories could have a 10 per cent lead and still not win.

You sound as if you would prefer a hung parliament. Wouldn't that be a dangerous outcome in these economic circumstances, where you need a clear lead and a strong government?
I haven't actually not quite made up my own mind. I want to see more of the Liberal Democrats and I think we'll hear more about them and I welcome the fact that they again participate in these debates. I think that this could be the making of them. The mere fact that this is taking place is probably worth 1 or 2 per cent for them.

But now I am absolutely convinced that people must not be forced off voting for rather small parties, Liberal Democrats or others, by fear. There are no problems with a hung parliament. In any rational world it means that the electorate has taken one choice and the powers exist in British politics to take account of what the voters have said. But fact is they don't want to do it. They somehow have managed to convince themselves – I'm not sure if they have convinced the British people – that a hung parliament can only have one outcome, which is a minority government. And this whole absurdity of one is enough.

We cannot in 2010 go through what we did in the first in the first six months of 1974 – hang on for another election, not taking any unpopular decisions. Nor can we do what we then went on to do really with never having enough MPs to govern properly. We had the IMF coming in and making a discipline framework for decisions. So anyone who believes, any party leader who can go up and defend handling a hung parliament in the same way as we handled it in '74 is riding for a fall.

Haven't the Lib Dems got to decide at some point whether they want a formal coalition or, a bit like the Lib–Lab pact where they might allow a government to continue by individual votes?
Theoretically that option exists but the nature of the economic crisis, the nature of the economic choices that are going to be in front of us, are that unpopular choices are going to be in front of us for at least a year and probably two or three. And therefore it seems to me pretty clear that the more structured the relationship, the more reliable the relationship, the more long-lasting, the better it is in the national interest. We have a right to ask the particular candidates in this particular instance: do you accept a four-year term? I think there is an argument for whichever has won the election – combination of votes cast and MPs won, opening up to a possibility of a multiparty government even if they have got a majority of five, even ten, arguable even fifteen to twenty.

Which Blair had intended to do in '97…
Very few people realise how extensive a deal was envisaged by Blair and Ashdown. In fairness to Paddy Ashdown there was never any doubt he had abandoned equidistance and after the long period of Conservative rule he was undoubtedly clear that Liberals would go with the Labour Party. That was a perfectly legitimate choice. This time Nick Clegg seems to be saying 'I have gone back to equidistance' but he is obviously trying to strive for something a little bit more, a little bit more clarity, but not to be boxed in. These are issues for him

What did you make of the reports that Margaret Thatcher and John Major both wanted you in their cabinets? Were you horrified?
No, not at all. How could I have been?

What's the truth behind Gordon Brown asking you to become a GOAT?
He asked me to come to see him. As far as I was concerned, the conversation would have remained private. I saw him on the Wednesday, he saw Margaret Thatcher on the Thursday and I was in Chicago on the Friday. I was at a board meeting and I started getting rung up by people who had been briefed on the Sunday papers, saying 'I gather you are going to join the Labour Party.' I said no such thing. It then transpired that Number 10 had rather foolishly leaked the conversation. They should have rung me up and said 'this story we can't hold' and we would have reached a joint statement, because it was a perfectly amicable meeting. But I was obviously being asked to get involved in the health service.

You could see his reasoning before the meeting – David Owen is unsafe in terms of the Labour Party still on most issues but nobody in the Labour Party doubts his commitment to the health service, which was true. But this was in a period when, in 2007, I genuinely wanted Gordon Brown to be prime minister. I argued that Blair should have stepped down in an article in the *Sunday Times* in January 2004. So I had high hopes for Gordon Brown. But too many of my friends had told me he was not going to be a very successful prime minister. They talked about this indecision. But above all I wasn't really ready to come into the health service. I was out of date. If you go away for nearly three years in the Balkans you lose touch. So when I came back I never went on *Question Time* or *Any Questions* – I am not an instant pundit on every damn thing under the sun.

You say you will have no influence over the next election. Do you think if you had played things differently in '88, '89 you might have been still on the domestic political scene as a figure of influence?
I don't think so. I did my best to keep the SDP alive after '87 but my view was overridden by the parliamentary of only five MPs. I believe we had to have an amicable divorce. I knew that there were people in Social Democratic Party that genuinely wanted to merge. My agreement with David Steel was only up until '87. After the 1987 election I always knew that people would want to merge for perfectly reputable and legitimate reasons and I was never going to oppose that. But it wasn't for me. One of the reasons was I didn't think I would win my own seat as a Liberal Democrat.

There were some fairly bitter words spoken at that time, particularly against you personally. Have those wounds healed?
Yes, by and large. Certainly the original gang of three – Shirley, Bill and I – have resolved our problems.

Shirley Williams was quite kind about you in her autobiography.

It's not just for show. When I was Chancellor of Liverpool University it was a happy day when I gave an honorary degree to Shirley and Bill, both with their Liverpool connections. Shirley has been on holiday in my house in Greece. I am sure I was right. We should have had an amicable divorce. The majority probably would have merged but we would have kept a lot of people in politics if we had done it in a proper, civilised way. The party that believed in rationality ought to have been able to find an amicable divorce. We would have been smaller, the SDP would have continued, we wouldn't have had 50 per cent of the seats at the next election but had we stayed together as an SDP–Liberal alliance with a single leader, probably from the Liberal Democrats, we would have held the balance in 1992, and in my view John Major was someone you could have negotiated with.

But David Steel effectively bounced you didn't he?
Not really. I know it suited people to think that.

I always thought it was his revenge for the *Spitting Image* sketch! You must have smiled when you first saw that...
I did but I often said to myself it must be awful to have that. I know if it was being done to me I wouldn't have liked it. I think *Spitting Image* was a ghastly thing to happen for him and he handled it with great dignity.

David was always quite clear and democratically correct. His job was to look after the best interests of the Liberal Party. The best interests of the Liberal Party, as far as he could judge, was to merge. It was in the worst interests of the SDP to merge and that has been shown by history. We snuffed ourselves out. What was extraordinary was the method of merging was a legal merging, not allowing an amicable divorce but effectively saying we couldn't exist. Fortunately Parliament saved us because Parliament recognised us as SDP MPs and they couldn't do otherwise. But I never really believed that we could survive. We were a think tank really from '87 till 1990. We had some quite good ideas that have been absorbed by all political parties since but we were not going to survive, we weren't of critical mass.

I have had a thoroughly enjoyable and interesting life since I gave up the House of Commons in 1992. Yugoslavia was bloody awful penance really, but it was challenging and I have been in international business since then and thoroughly enjoyed it.

I was on your Wikipedia page earlier and apparently Jack Cunningham greeted your appointment in the Balkans saying that the 'Prime Minister's choice was regarded as somewhat eccentric by MPs and myself. David Owen is known for many qualities but not as a mediator. Indeed he has Balkanised a few political parties himself.'

I think it surprised people that I stayed on in the Balkans even when the Americans ditched the Vance–Owen Peace Plan. I could have resigned, and I nearly did. When you are in politics you do it for a purpose. All my resignations, and there have been quite a number of them, have been for a purpose. In those days the only people who would have been happy would have been in Washington. I was actually being supported pretty well by the European governments. So I stuck at it for nearly three years. I was happy to go at any time but the European governments wanted me to stay. In a way we held the ring until they made up their minds to use force. I never changed my mind. At various times I put to the European ministers that you will only get a negotiation when you allow us to enforce this particular settlement but they were never ready to do it. So it was a tough assignment, but challenging.

When you read profiles of you, particularly in the mid-80s and later, the one word that was always used was 'arrogant'. I have always thought that was a good thing for a politician to be, to a degree. Did that ever irritate you or do you recognise it as having an element of truth in it?
There is always an element of truth in pretty much all criticism. I think that people who just ignore criticism and say 'I never read newspapers', aren't being honest. I was impatient, I was in a hurry – you have to curb it as far as possible, but I was always quite good at listening to people and taking account of their views. Sometime people criticised me for being too much of a compromiser, surprisingly. But on fundamental issues I would fight my corner. And I used to enjoy the clash of opinions, I liked the House of Commons, I liked the debates. But underneath I knew you had to forge agreements, you had to work across political parties.

You have said you don't think Gordon Brown suffers from hubris but he suffers from self-doubt. How do you justify that?
Look at his nails, they are bitten down. He and Blair are very different. Blair sailed through with supreme confidence on reading one piece of paper. Brown reads everything and he's a hugely complicated man. He's a much better read, more knowledgeable person than Blair. They are just very different. Blair was always a classic case for hubris, and it took time to develop in him, as I don't think he had it in the early years. Brown I think is a tortured soul, in some respects in good ways. I think he agonises over issues but this has made him very indecisive. He finds decisions difficult. Not just calling elections – quite a lot of decisions he doesn't find easy to make. A prime minister has to have a certain amount of decisiveness in their nature. Things are comings at them fairly fast. They have to be able to make decisions and then move on and not be haunted by them.

The problem with the Blair/Brown presidency, as I call it, was that it completely distorted the structure of British government. Not only did the Cabinet matter very little, the civil service got used to funnelling domestic stuff through the Treasury and everything else through Number 10. These two would then argue between themselves, broadly speaking as friends. But Brown's biggest job was to stay in contention and not be sacked. The only way he managed to do that was by mastering his subject and sadly for all of us, Blair and Brown got into a competitive expenditure race. Expenditure went out of control after about 2000. That was largely because Brown was wanting to stay popular, ahead of Blair, so that Blair could never dare sack him! It's an extraordinary period. Let's hope we never have that again. It ought not to be possible and that is one of the other things we need to look at – what are the constitutional checks on personal power and two people in this case, not one, carving out the structures of government in a totally damaging manner?

What kind of prime minister would you have been?
I don't think you can really tell until you do the job.

You got on quite well with Margaret Thatcher didn't you?
I didn't personally get on very well with her, I didn't really know her in that sense. I believed that some of the things she was doing were absolutely essential to Britain's recovery, particularly economic recovery, and I supported them. I believed that the defeat of Arthur Scargill was an essential element – it wouldn't have been the same to have had the usual cobbled-up compromise any more, that had to be a defeat because he ignored the Pithead Ballot. But just say Kinnock had made a speech at the start of the miners' strike and said: 'I am the son of a miner, the issue here is the Pithead Ballot – that is the miners' democracy and no leader of the Labour Party can support a strike unless there has been a Pithead Ballot.' If he had said that and stuck to it he would have made his mark on British politics and I suspect the electoral cycle would have allowed him to be prime minister. You get one major thing like that wrong. The other things you change – he changed his mind on Europe, he changed his mind on nuclear. But what they really judge you on is a few big tests and he destroyed himself on the miners' strike. He had a perfectly legitimate position which is the Pithead Ballot and he did choose it for a while. He was knocked off it, he should never have allowed himself to be knocked off it. I think I would never have allowed myself to be knocked off some of the basic things which I held a view of. And I wasn't actually. They tried to knock me off it, when I was leader of the SDP, they tried to knock me off it on defence. They very nearly succeeded because they

had David Steel, Shirley Williams, Bill Rodgers and Roy Jenkins – which was a formidable combination. But I refused to let them – I wasn't going to go into the '87 election not having a proper defence policy. I hadn't left the Labour Party to be put in that position by anybody.

Do you feel any sense of unfulfilment in your political career?
No. My political career is over. My political career was over on the Sunday of the 1987 election. Once Roy Jenkins, Shirley Williams, Bill Rodgers and David Steel came out in favour of a merger I knew in my heart I couldn't block it. And in a way I knew it was quite illegitimate to try and block it. What I hoped was that we were adult enough to try and settle this dispute amicably and allow four parties. But by then they had become, quite wrongly in my view, fixated on the fact that a merger would solve all their problems. Well it didn't. Here we are, we are now discussing the Liberal Democrats as a serious force, possible, for the first time really. They have not been a serious force all this time, Labour dominated the scene. I do think that it would be silly for me to go to my grave thinking the Liberal Democrats are the same ones that I wouldn't join and possibly might have even been asked to lead in 1987. It's just silly. How long ago was that? Twenty-three years ago. I am out of politics and I have been firmly out of domestic politics ever since, really.

Nick Griffin

Party affiliation: British National Party (BNP)

Current position: Leader of the BNP

Born: 1 March 1959

Education: Educated at Woodbridge School and then St Felix School in Southwold. He studied history and then law at Downing College, Cambridge from 1977.

Family status: Married with four children.

Pre-political career: After graduating he worked at the National Front headquarters as a political worker (later leaving over disagreements about how the party was run) and at the same time launched the publication *Nationalism Today*.

Electoral history: He joined the BNP in 1995 and in 1999 became the party's leader. In the 2009 European Elections, he was elected as the MEP for North-West England.

Career highlights: Beating John Tyndall, the original founder of the BNP, to become the party's leader.

Interesting fact: He received a boxing Blue from Cambridge, having taken up the sport following a brawl in Lewisham with a member of an anti-fascist party.

Date of interview: March 2010
Extended version
Venue: Dagenham, East London
Total Politics Issue 22, April 2010

This is undoubtedly the most controversial of all the thirty 'In Conversation' interviews I have conducted for Total Politics. *I knew it would be. The very fact that I planned to interview Griffin resulted in two resignations from the editorial board of* Total Politics – *Denis MacShane and Caroline Lucas.*

I have never believed in no platforming politicians, no matter how much I might disagree with them or find their policies loathsome. No platforming can lead to martyrdom. And when a political party has elected representatives not only in several councils, but also in the European Parliament, they need to be scrutinised. To ignore them is to play into their hands.

I had already interviewed Nick Griffin once, on the night of the European elections in 2008 during an election night programme on the late, lamented

*Play Radio. It was quite an encounter, but Griffin proved more than a capable
match for my less than aggressive interviewing technique.*

*But I knew if I got this particular interview wrong, it could spell very bad
news for my reputation. However, I decided to approach the interview in exactly
the same way I would approach any other interview and that's what I did.*

*I was asked to meet Griffin's representatives outside a tube station in East
London. At the appointed time a car with blackened windows drew up. Two
middle-aged men emerged looking like stereotypical BNP supporters. We
drove for a couple of miles and ended up at the house of BNP Greater London
Assembly member, Richard Barnbrook, which doubled as their campaign
centre. Griffin hadn't arrived, so I chatted amiably enough to Barnbrook and
his colleagues. After about thirty minutes, Nick Griffin arrived. He's quite a
nervous man in some ways. He never appears comfortable in his own skin, so
I knew it would take some time to get him really talking.*

*In the end, this was the longest interview I have done. The transcribed
version amounted to some 23,000 words, only 5,000 of which could make it
into the magazine.*

*As you will see, this is by far the longest interview in the book. I decided
to include the 17,000-word version because I think it really allows the reader
to form their own judgement about Nick Griffin and I think it stands up to
scrutiny as an important piece of oral history.*

What did you feel like when David Cameron called you a 'nasty piece of filth'?
It scarcely registered. I suppose in a bizarre way I was pleased, because I
think it's so outrageous, unprofessional and childish that a lot of people,
especially Conservatives and Conservative voters, would have thought 'that's
unfair, that's wrong'. It reflects badly on him, and well on us.

Do you regard your appearance on *Question Time* as a triumph or a disaster?
Neither. I wasn't pleased with my performance – the first half particularly.
The problem was we'd taken an almost last-minute decision, that on the basis
that I couldn't possibly win against the panellists and Dimbleby, that rather
than getting into an aggressive fighting back/slagging match (which was the
only alternative), I would get beaten up on television. A couple of ladies said
'it doesn't matter, people will think it's unfair, you're going to get a hammering
anyway, so don't be too aggressive back'. I'm not good defensively, even when
I'm with journalists. I don't actually like soft interviews. If they ask 'what do
you want to talk about?' I waffle on, I ramble, I'm far better with a Paxman.
Fighting on the back foot doesn't suit me, so I wasn't particularly pleased.
Having said that, the response we've had since has been fantastic. It was a
disaster for the powers that be, and very beneficial for us.

So for those that say it was a propaganda coup for you, you'd actually agree with that?
Yes.

So are you putting pressure to go on again then?
We've been putting on pressure on the basis that they openly admit they changed the formula for the first time in thirty-five years.

That was a big mistake, wasn't it?
It was a big mistake, and I was a bit thrown by it.

Did they tell you they were going to do that?
They didn't. We looked into what happened when Gerry Adams was on first time, for instance. He wasn't picked up on 'how many people did he order killed' – he was allowed to talk about transport and other issues. We assumed there would perhaps be two or three legitimate questions about my presence and the BNP and so on because it was a news story, but then it should have moved on to cover other things.

Do you revel in being a hate figure?
I'd prefer not to be. I can't see why anyone would want to be hated, I'm quite happy to be hated by establishment figures and various people who I regard as thoroughly bad eggs, but to be presented as a hate figure for the ordinary public is unpleasant – it's unpleasant for your family, it's positively dangerous and it doesn't really appeal.

Do you fear for your lives?
Yes, sometimes,

What steps do you take to prevent anything untoward happening?
I don't travel to anything which is party related, or media and so on, without security. We try to avoid giving advance notice of being somewhere.

Do you believe in God?
Yes, in a sort of an agnostic post C of E sort of way. I certainly believe in fate. I think it's more likely that there's a greater power or things than we can't understand out there.

You are often described as far right but I always thought the BNP policy platform has more in common with the far left, particularly in economic policy. Where do you place the BNP?
You can't place us on the political spectrum. That's quite often been the case

with Nationalism. On traditional social things, we're on the old traditional right wing of the Conservative Party. On the other hand, on some economic things, on the railways, or natural monopolies, such as the post office, we think they should remain in the hands of the state, so that's put us well on the left. I think it'd be political ignorance to regard our economic position as leftist – it's fundamentally distributionist. We're certainly not state capitalists or Marxists.

It's socialism, if you nationalise a lot of things.
We want to nationalise genuine monopolies. I think when they're run by the state you should have incentives and disincentives for people not to skive. There should be profit sharing and so on. There should be an element of worker ownership where possible.

On social issues you say the BNP is on the authoritarian right…
I certainly didn't say authoritarian, I would say the traditional right. If you use the word 'authoritarian', I would take it to mean the state having a huge amount of control over what people can and can't do and so on and wanting a large state – wanting a giant police force and paramilitary police with guns walking around the place. We don't want that.

Most of your policies are arguing in favour of a larger state than we have at the moment. Nigel Farage says UKIP are the 'do what you like' party, and the BNP are the 'hang 'em and flog 'em party'. Would you accept any of that? Or if not, what's your opinion of the libertarian right?
Farage is a great snake oil salesman and great at soundbites and he gets an easy ride from the media, but they're the 'do as you like party'? Well, if he's talking about criminals, then if he wants to tell his basically right wing conservative type voters we're gonna let criminals do what they like and the BNP will hang 'em and whip 'em, then I'll be quite happy with that really. We believe that people should be free to do what they want unless the state, the government, the law of the land with a basis in tradition and democratic support forbids it. Unless it's specifically forbidden by the government for a damn good reason, you should be allowed to do it, and that would include things such as hunting, shooting, angling or having sex with a melon if you so desire. We wouldn't want to stop that.

Where do you think your support is coming from on the political spectrum, because the left always liked to say 'the BNP gets its support from the disillusioned Right' whereas I get the impression, particularly in areas like Barking, it's the disillusioned Labour voters?
Our voters can come from anywhere – our by-election victories are really hard won, because of the amount we get thrown against us, but we've taken

Lib Dem seats, Tory seats and Labour seats, the majority of them Labour. I put that down primarily to the fact that a Labour government is in power and the Labour Party has generally tended to dominate the local government of places where we've got particular support. So other things being equal they're easier to beat. Our support definitely comes from people who have voted Labour. A significant proportion of that has come to us via Maggie Thatcher. People in Barking who voted for Thatcherite Conservatism have now moved on to us, and we get a surprising amount of support from people who would vote or have voted Lib Dem – not the activists, we take Labour activists, we take Tory activists. I can only think of a couple of people who were Lib Dem activists, but in voting terms, Lib Dem voters are simply a plague on both our houses to Labour and Tory and because they've already switched they've already broken the old voter loyalty. So we can pick up their votes. Where we go head to head with the Labour Party we can whittle their vote away, lots of people who used to vote Labour will vote for us, but we reach a stage – around about 30 per cent, and we cannot get below that because they're people who have always voted Labour – you know, the 'my dad would turn in his grave' types. They simply won't change. There's an ethnic minority block vote for the Labour Party and there's a town hall parasite, leftist teacher type so there's enough of those that the Labour Party has a block vote. To take a Labour ward, we have to take away the Labour people available to us and we then also need some Tories. And probably the other thing we get that nobody else does, is the people who don't vote. When we're really contesting things hard the vote goes up, and there's a lot of people who previously have thought that 'all politicians are the same' so they know we're not the same, partly because of people like Cameron attacking me as filth and so on, so it gives them the idea that they can turn up and vote for us because we're something different. With the Labour Party we can only whittle their vote down so far. Where we've become, or can make ourselves, the credible winners in a seat where there's an unpopular Conservative and we take a Conservative seat, there's almost no limit to what we can take off the Tory vote. The Tory vote can collapse when we stand. It can go down to just 6 per cent. There's nothing left.

Do you see yourself on the modernising wing of the BNP, if there is such a thing?
Yes, the reason it doesn't seem like that is because the process is in large measure done. It was begun in fits and starts before I was even involved in it, but my winning the leadership election against John Tyndall and then carrying the changes through, that puts me down as a moderniser. I didn't start out life as a moderniser but that's how I ended up.

You present yourself as a moderniser, but you've still got people in your party who still hold to the old views. I was looking at a blog written by your legal officer Lee Barnes and it's virtually all about how ethnic minorities and the Jews are awful. He reckons 'Britain is controlled by Zionists and their media puppets'. You look through his blog and think, well, there's just no way that if he's a national officer of the BNP you can present the party as being anything other than obsessed by the usual issues.

Lee is a very strange and complex character, he's also regarded by all of Britain's Nazis as one of the leading treacherous liberal pro-Jewish . . . who's taken control of the BNP.

Well if he's liberal, I'd love to see someone who wasn't. . .

Lee is one of the people who believes that if you say that there's a Zionist influence in Britain, that does not make you anti-Semitic. It's a lunatic extrapolation, that. It simply is not the case and Lee was one of the ones who, over a number of years, has fought and argued on blogs and so on with the anti-Semitic crazies to draw a distinction between Zionists, which can include gentile politicians in any case, and ordinary Jews. We've got Jewish members, we've got a Jewish council group leader. Lee is one of the ones who has taken most flak from Britain's Nazis as he's taken the anti-Semitism out of the BNP, but he's still fiercely anti Zionist.

But if you say, 'Britain is controlled by Zionists and their media puppets', there is only one way to read that.

I would say that's a grotesque exaggeration.

So you don't share any of those views at all?

No.

But you've allowed someone who's obsessed by Jewish issues to hold national office in the BNP.

I do, yes. As I say, if you look at his blogs and his arguments with people in the round, you will see that he's one of the people who's taken the obsession with Jews out of the BNP. It was there, but he's one of the ones who've taken it out by putting it in context.

What do you make of organisations like Searchlight and Nothing British?

Searchlight, going back decades, has had its sloganising and it's 'oh we're going to expose them' but what it mainly does is harass people and get people sacked from their jobs. They phone and organise people to phone up landlords of venues at which we're meeting, and terrorise them. Searchlight is under the terms of the terrorist act, if it was applied properly, a terrorist organisation. Nothing British is slightly more political but still thoroughly dishonest in what it does, so they're one of the crosses we have to bear – people like that.

I read somewhere that years ago, you went on an all expenses paid trip to Libya. Has the BNP ever had money from Colonel Gadaffi?
No, we didn't at the time. We got a big crate of green books, which promptly disappeared in customs, so we didn't actually get any.

But at that time, he was funding the IRA, you didn't see anything wrong with going there then?
Yes, indeed, that's one of the things and probably one reason we got nothing other than a crate of green books. One of the first things we said was 'we're here to tell you on behalf of members of ours in Northern Ireland that we understand why you want to hit back against Thatcher for allowing airstrip one to be used to bomb Libya – an outrageous piece of aggression, so we understand why you want to hit back, but you should not be doing it backing what is not a group of heroic freedom fighters, but actually a Marxist/Irish imperialist organisation which kills working class people in East Belfast.

So don't give it to them, give it to us?
We weren't saying 'don't give it to them, give it to us'. We said you may be offended by this, but we're going to tell you right from the start that we want to tell you that you shouldn't be giving money to them and if that puts you off us we don't care, because we're here first of all to try and explain from the perspective of working class people in Belfast that the IRA is not a group of heroic freedom fighters.

You were asking them for money.
We were asking them for money if they were giving it, yes.

But you had no reservation about going to what virtually anyone in the world regarded as a terrorist government, or a government that supported terrorists, and asking them for financial support.
We looked at Gadaffi's ideas. A lot of what was said about Gadaffi in all probability is propaganda.

If the Equalities Commission hadn't forced you to accept black and asian members, do you think you would have got to that point yourselves?
There was a long running debate within the party whether this would have to be done, or should be done. It had the potential to be very divisive and by forcing the issue, they certainly brought it forward by several years, but

I think it would have happened anyway. Because it's been forced, it's united us. They've done us a favour.

How many black and asian people have applied or been accepted for membership so far?
We've had several West Indian members for years.

I thought it was against your constitution?
If someone sends in an application on behalf of Anjem Choudary it would be flagged up and it would be rejected. If someone's applied through the post as Tom Smith, they've been signed up, our organiser has then gone round to their door and found they're totally Anglicised West Indian and they've had a chat and explained their position and several of them can carry on being a member and won't come to meetings, and they have done. We've just told organisers to turn a blind eye, we don't want to upset the poor chaps, it's not fair, and so on. One of them had been in the army for years, he joined in good faith, it'd be cruel to kick him out. In terms of people wanting to join now, we have two Chinese ladies and a couple of long standing West Indians and the moment we're able to, we'll have them as members.

You've been at great pains over the past few years to say you're not a racist party, but that clause in your constitution proves the opposite.
It could be presented as proving the opposite, certainly. It's always been problematic in political terms, there's a bit of a debate, or rather a genuine question in everybody's heads. Superficially, it's a huge political albatross. I would say in effect, possibly, in public perception definitely, but in terms of its intention not. And it's intention really comes from three things. Firstly, in certain parts of the country, south London say with young, second and third generation West Indians, where they're a lawless menace to everyone around them – some of them – owing to our rotten school system, which has let them down thoroughly badly, the same as everyone else. Or in northern mill towns with Muslim gangs praying on white and Sikh girls and lads of other communities.

What a gross generalisation.
It's just a fact. You've got members of our community who want to sit and talk about these things and do something about these things. How can they talk openly and frankly about these issues if there are members of the community whose members who are doing these things in the same room with them.

Well why on earth not?
If you had a group of the women victims of rape, and the state comes along and says 'you must have men sitting in your discussion' that'd be outrageous.

That's a ridiculous point to make.
In northern towns, you're dealing with dozens of families with 13- and 14-year-old daughters, who have been and are being gang raped by Muslims, so it's precisely that. But this isn't a rape issue, this is a cultural issue.

Surely in that situation you do need to talk to leaders of that community to actually address the issue.
At some point you need to, or the police need to or someone does, yes. But in terms of people from the community who are victims coming together and concluding that this isn't happening because their daughters are 'slags' and because they've asked for it, this is actually a problem. It's a fundamental human right for those people to discuss this amongst themselves first.

But what you're doing is saying that an entire community should have collective guilt.
No I'm not, that clearly isn't the case. We said their community has been slow to condemn them. We believe that if the Imams said this was unacceptable, this is unIslamic, it would stop. Since it is not unIslamic, since it is very Islamic the buggers aren't going to say stop.

So you're saying gang rape is Islamic?
'These women are lawful to you, those who your right arm can own.' It's in the Koran time and time again.

Surely, you don't believe that moderate Muslims believe that?
Moderate Muslims don't interpret it like that, but there is a young street punk Islam that does believe precisely that, and that's what the ones who are funding most of the madrassas believe, and the Saudis believe that too. How else does a religion say 'you're entitled to four wives each' – all human societies have roughly speaking equal male/female ratios – how does any one community find four women for any one man?

Plenty of white people do that too though. Are you right to say this is all the fault of the Koran? Isn't it just plain human evil that does this?
There's always sex pests in every community, that's in every racial group and so on without a shadow of a doubt, yes. And actual paedophilia in terms of one male or a group of males grooming kids with sweets and so on, that tends to be a white community issue as a matter of fact, but what goes on in mainly the northern towns with mainly Pakistani communities, there's a repeated pattern to it. Though the Kurds are doing it in Liverpool right now, though there is a pattern to it, and it's always Islamic communities and young men doing it, and it's always other people's girls who are victims – they never do it to their own.

Everyone says you've got to celebrate diversity. It's a natural human instinct which most people have. The liberal upper classes just want to be amongst liberal upper class people, the rich want to be amongst rich people, but it's a natural instinct for most people to be with people like you, with your own culture and so on, and this is denied the white working class, not necessarily deliberately, but certainly in terms of its impact, why should people who are there, precisely because they see the traditions and identity of this country going down the tubes, why should they be forced, because it's PC, or because it's even good for votes, why should they be forced that even at meetings of people who feel like them, they have to have others who immediately remind them of the fact that their country has changed and they were never asked and they never gave consent? It's thoroughly unjust.

But surely we're dealing with the country as it is today. You're not going to get any form of community co-operation unless you involve all sorts of different groups in discussion. If you exclude a group you are paving the way for ill feeling.
There's certainly ill feeling now, and part of the ill feeling is that in most London boroughs as an example, every single ethnic cultural or religious group is encouraged to celebrate its own identity and its own day. But try having a St George's Day and the councils and the police, until very recently, are brutally against it, and that's changing, and why is that? Because we're here. If the white working class was silent and not prepared to turn anywhere, they'd be ignored and pissed on. It's only because there's now the possibility that they might get on their own back legs and start doing things for themselves.

There are plenty of people keen to celebrate St George's day other than the BNP.
Well there haven't been for a very, very long time. Until a few years ago, Labour councils, if you put your minicab in for its council MOT it would fail because it had a St George's sticker on the back bumper, because it's racist, and that's what's created hatred. There's no ordinary decent member of any ethnic minority in Barking and Dagenham that would actually have any concern about the English in particular celebrating their own thing. They wouldn't come to it, because it's not their thing.

A lot would.
I don't think they would.

There were plenty of Asians and Indians in Euro '96 flying the flag of St George.
That's a football thing, that's not a cultural thing. Here again it comes down

to 'are we authoritarian'; certainly the political elite says 'you've all got to mix' – now to me that's authoritarian. I think it's up to a group of individuals whether they mix or not, now we work very closely with Sikhs and I've got some good Sikh friends, but they don't particularly want me in their Gudwaras, and they certainly don't want my son chatting up their daughters. We work really together and we're very friendly together, but there's a certain community distance because I value them as Sikhs. If people want to have meetings to discuss and celebrate their own culture, their own heritage or problems, if they're discussing a problem of a hospital being closed, it'd be ridiculous to keep out members of ethnic minorities. If you're discussing a problem which specifically affects our community, such as the way that it no longer feels at home, then we will say to them, you can still have those closed meetings, but they can't be BNP meetings – they're indigenous forum meetings, so there will still be that element where we will support people's human right to associate with who they want.

So you effectively class them second class citizens, even if they are full British citizens.
No, because the second class citizens are the English because everyone else is allowed either to be part of the big group, or to hide themselves off and celebrate their own thing, and it's only the English denied that right. So I don't think we are making anyone second class citizens, we're re-establishing equality.

But if you're a first generation immigrant with a British passport and you've grown up in this country you have absolutely the same rights as you or I do. Why shouldn't that person be allowed into meetings and celebrate St George's day?
In the case, say, of a young second generation West Indian or mixed race fellow who plays football for the local pub and all the rest of it, of course they're going to come, and it's not going to bother anybody. But when you've got people like Simon Woolley, who's taxpayer funded and involved in 'Operation Black vote', that's a scandal. Simon Woolley is saying that we're going to get these people into the BNP to destroy it. Well, we're absolutely entitled to tell people 'no, you damn well can't join'.

Is there any truth to this rumour that you're going to create two types of member – a founder member who can decide policy and new people who won't have any say in policy?
The founder members have a very limited degree of blocking power on radical constitutional changes, including radical policy changes. That's nothing to do with race at all, and it's something I've been trying to do for

years and we've been moving towards little by little. When we get a Tory government in power and we get very large numbers of more right-wing Conservatives in, that then creates a tendency whereby 'oh we'll trim this policy, we'll trim that policy' particularly on economic policies.

The Labour Party didn't have any protection when Blair removed clause four. Now actually I think clause four was bad…

You want to do a lot of 'clause four'ing.
I want to do some 'clause four'ing, but only where it's necessary and the lesser of two evils. The Labour Party wanted it for the corner shop, they wanted it across the board. Blair castrated the party when he got rid of it and there was no defence for it. Having seen it in more recent historical terms, the National Front in 1977 and 1978–79 had a sudden influx of Conservatives. They simply swamped its Nationalist values and we don't want to see that happen again. So for a long time I've wanted to ensure there's a degree of stability ballast so that a sudden shift in the party's demographics doesn't suddenly change the direction it's going in. So what the founder members have is a veto power, but that is not racially or ethnically discriminatory in any way shape or form.

So when will that come in?
With the new constitution just passed

So you can see why people thought it was ethnically based, because you could have new members who are from ethnic minorities and they aren't going to have a say in policy.
It's designed to deal with the problem I've talked about, and also, quite openly, that since Simon Woolley, who is taxpayer funded, is saying 'we're going to get thousands of non-whites to join' why they didn't just do it with Marxist students I don't know, it would have been quite simple in those days. But whoever it is, it's an organised active and live threat by well funded people to take us over and swamp us and change what we stand for, so we can't stand up for communities who no one else will stand up for. So we have a duty and in modern PC terms, there's a health and safety duty to look after our own people, so therefore we put that in, but it's not racially discriminatory for this reason. 99.937 per cent of the white British public are not members of the BNP so to establish racial discrimination is has to be between two people in the same position and the two people in the same position must be you, who hasn't joined the BNP, and Mr Singh sat over there who hasn't. When you both join next week, both of you are in an equal position and neither of you will ever become a founding member. We've given a lot of extra power to voting members who are people that

have been in for two years and done various things. Both of you have an equal opportunity.

If Mr Singh has been a member for two years, does he get those powers?
If he is not just being a member, it's being a member, being an activist.

How do you define that?
Being an activist is turning out on average at least once a week for an activism session. Now if two years down the line, if we were to say to you, you can be a voting member, but say to him 'sorry, you missed one session because you had flu' and if you had missed three sessions that would be racially discriminatory. One it would be breaking the law, and two it would be showing extremely bad faith to Mr Singh who, once he is a member, if he's prepared to help us sort this country out, then he's as good as you are. In fact, because he's going to join in and you're not, he's actually better than you are.

But he can never get founding member voting.
No, of course he can't, but neither can you. It's only a slowing down and a veto thing, it's like the House of Lords, as when it actually used to work.

What happens when all the founder members are dead?
We're aware that's a longer term problem. We know that's something we'll have to look at. You could deal with it in several ways. You could make it something you bequeath, which would be thoroughly odd, though no odder than the House of Lords system was. You could perhaps have it that people who had been in for a certain period – people who had been in for fifteen years or whatever. You have to refresh it, but for now that's what it'll be, and it deals with Simon Woolley. But that is not racially discriminatory in law, nor is it racially discriminatory in effect.

What does it say about the BNP when violence is used to throw a reputable journalist out of a press conference?
Well, if I came to your house as your invited guest, or even worse, if I walked through your front door uninvited and just sat down, you would ask me to leave.

It was a press conference.
It wasn't a press conference.

Well what was it then?
It was an AGM and at the end of it, we allowed certain journalists to enter. But *The Times* has established quite recently such a shocking record of unfair

treatment of our events and our people and when reporting on us that we exercise the right to say to *The Times*, no, we don't want you there. He got in and then we found someone asked him to leave. He was asked to leave more than half a dozen times and he wouldn't go, so he was escorted out of the premises, which is unfortunate.

But all that achieved was pictures of BNP heavies throwing a journalist who has a national reputation out of a meeting. What benefit did that bring the BNP?
It didn't.

So why do it?
Because we'd already made a decision not to co-operate with *The Times*, because when you co-operate with a newspaper, with a journalist, the moment you start speaking about the issue, you give them more of a right and more credibility.

But on that basis, you can say 'I'm not co-operating with any newspaper' because you don't get any positive coverage.
We're not asking for positive coverage, we're asking for the truth. And if someone says 'we threw a *Times* journalist out because he was struggling, his nose was pulled, that was rather rough and that made the BNP look thugs', that's fact and opinion. That's fair, that's legitimate. But *The Times* has repeatedly lied in recent months about us to our people's detriment about what's going on so why should we allow a group of journalists and a newspaper who make money about lying.

I'll tell you why, because you're a national political party with elected representatives in the same way that the Conservative Party is. Should the Conservatives not allow *Times* journalists into their press conferences because of what they said about Lord Ashcroft?
They have the right, but as far as I know, what they're saying about Lord Ashcroft is true. But I know what they were saying about us were the most outrageous lies.

But every political party has that, and they don't go around banning journalists from press conferences.
They do, or they simply don't hold them. If you look at the Labour Party's spin machine, in terms of manipulating journalists, yeah, they're more sophisticated and more experienced, and if they had a journalist they wanted to throw out, they'd get the police to do it. We haven't got that.

The point I'm trying to make is that if you want to be treated as a mature political party looking to get more electoral representation, you collectively are behaving, in that instance, in a way that no other political party would.

But no other political party has journalists who work with Searchlight to put lies and smears out on the scale that try to get our members thrown out of their jobs.

Look at the *Daily Mirror*, every few months they try and infiltrate Conservative Central Office, but the Conservatives still allow Kevin Maguire to go to their press conferences, in the full knowledge he will never write anything positive about them.

Well that's rather up to them, it's not a matter of positive, it's a matter of the most outrageous lies. When they lie about the Conservative Party, it doesn't increase the chances of Conservative members having their houses petrol bombed and their children burned to death. For us it's much more serious, the lies are much worse and because of the climate this creates and all the rest of it, it actually puts our people at risk for their lives and their livelihoods.

If your son brought home an Asian girlfriend, what would your reaction be?

As I've always said, much the same reaction as I know many Sikhs and West Indians and so on would give, which is: 'I'm not comfortable with this and you need to both really think about it because you've both got two different bloodlines and two different cultures and when you mix them up you destroy both of them.'

Human emotion doesn't count in that?

Sure, absolutely. It's not the business of a political party to try to interfere in affairs of the heart, which is something we've enshrined as a definite statement in the new constitution. From a moral point of view, we believe that massive integration and mixing is bad because it's destructive of human cultures. According to ethnographers there's about 5,000 human cultures in the world at the moment and by the end of this century there'll be 800 left on the present trends. Which is an enormous part of human diversity. We actually believe in a bizarre way we are the only genuine multiculturalists. I understand why liberals can misunderstand what we think. People need to take a step back. Human diversity is being wiped out at a rate which is not happening with any other species. Every ecologist ought to be jumping up and down about it, saying this is wrong. Sting should be doing benefit gigs. Humanity as a whole has to come up with antidotes to the homogenising ideology of left-liberalism and the homogenising effects, cultural effects, of world capitalism. Because otherwise we are going to end up all the same, all mixed up, no history, no future, no separate cultures. I think that's bad.

How far you have delved back into your family history? I have got French blood in me. You and I have sort of similar skin tones.

I have Norman ancestry. It's shocking.

The Nick Griffin of the '70s and '80s would probably have found that you and I would probably not be fit to be English.

As a matter of fact I don't think so for one minute.

My point is that as a nation we have always been a bit of a mish-mash. It is very difficult to actually say what is pure English.

Of course, there is no such thing as racial purity. And it is bizarre when the left-liberals actually use the argument that the English are a mongrel race, or the British are a mongrel race.

But we are.

But that's then saying that there is such a thing as pure races. And there are not. Human populations mix.

If you say there is no such thing as a pure race, why on earth would you then have a problem with mixed relationships?

It's not just a matter of races. It's a matter of culture. It's a matter of all things. It's a matter again of human identity. And you can have a degree of integration of one community into another. So from community B into community A. You can have a degree of it. But there comes a point when the intermixture crosses a certain threshold and community A ceases to be community A, and becomes something different. And where that's going in present world trends is that there won't be any individual communities or cultures or identities left at all. We ideologically think that's a bad thing.

But look at America. America is the ultimate hotch-potch of nationalities. They all regard themselves as Americans, they pledge allegiance to the flag.

Well they don't. Look at the Mexicans. Sooner or later Mexico is going to end up taking back the south west states in the United States. The only reason they might not is 'cause that they won't get their welfare cheques.

Look at the Norwegians, the Scandinavians, the Germans, the Dutch immigrants, the Irish, they all have their own separate identities within America. But they all regard themselves as primarily Americans first. And isn't that what we have got to aim for here?

Well there are two ways of having a multicultural society. There is the American way, which actually isn't integrated. The different hyphenated European Americans basically get on and live in the same communities.

That's not a problem. But I have been over there a number of times, and it is an extraordinarily segregated society between white and black and Spanish and Chinese and so on. It's a complete melting pot.

Let's move on to something different. As far as I can see you have only got 120 selected candidates for the next election.
At present, yes.

Isn't that a bit of a failure, because I would have thought you should be aiming to stand someone at every single seat?
No. We considered standing in every single seat. One it would show we are a national party. Secondly, with the freepost it would allow us to put our literature in everybody's homes and that produces a lot of enquiries. We now have got the capacity to turn them into members far more effectively than we used. The third thing is that there is a possibility that state funding of political parties is inevitable.

We considered it, but we decided against it for several reasons. Firstly well we have been bled white by the Equality Commission to a serious degree, and that still hasn't finished. So we probably can't afford it. Secondly, we had, when we fought the European election, a catastrophic level of interference with our post coming back, and vast amounts of it disappearing. Meaning that people would write in, and they would then think we were ignorant buggers who hadn't responded to them, so we are not getting a chance to turn them into members. So for reasons of practicality and the fact that we don't necessarily get at the end of it what we really need, it is not worth our while, and there would be a tendency if we did that we would be stretching ourselves too thinly.

We have fewer activists than the Lib Dems. We are a smaller party. There is no point pretending that we are on the same scale as the other parties. And it is more sensible for us to apply a maximum amount of our political force on the enemy's weakest point, or points, a handful of them, rather than attacking on all fronts. Especially because it is quite likely that we will get a hung parliament, which means that we got another of those damn things six months down the line.

And if there was a hung parliament, and you had a couple of MPs and you did actually decide the fate of the next government... Just in your gut who would you feel closest to?
They'd be cutting bits of themselves with rusty razors before they accepted our support. In party terms to none of them... In party terms they wouldn't have us, and we wouldn't have them. Truly I don't feel any affinity or closer to one group or the other. At all. Individually there are a handful of MPs I regard as being better than the others, or not as bad as the others. Vince Cable and

Kate Hoey, about the only ones. Vince Cable because he comes across well on TV, and not slimey like the others. In terms of his criticism of the banks and generally when he is talking economics he is clearly actually thinking outside of dogmas, and what it's actually like for real people out there, which the others don't do. Kate Hoey, because she is really quite independently minded. From her Ulster background she has never completely turned her back on the Britishness of an element of Ulster in a Labour Party which is fanatically basically pro-Sinn Féin and. I think she is good and I know people in her constituency who say she is actually really good.

Do you expect to win in Barking?
We have got a serious chance of winning. We are not favourites. But there is a betting chance of winning this seat.

And what will that depend on?
What will it depend on? Whether the public are actually taken in by the wave of smears and haze that is going to come through their door, or if it actually backfires. The more they our hardcore voters get middle class students coming along and telling them how they should vote and how they are racist and stupid and bigoted, it actually confirms them in their opinion that yes they are going to vote for us, and fuck you. But on the other hand it does eat away, trip away, the floating vote, especially in a constituency where the Labour Party's majority of those votes are so huge. Then that could easily cost us the election. And we don't know how it is going to pan out.

Is it dependent on mobilising the ones who don't usually vote?
For us to win?

Yes, or does it depend on a low turn-out?
For us to win we would need the turn-out to go up, because we would need people who don't normally vote.

What is your second target seat?
Dagenham & Rainham, Stoke Central, Stoke South and we'll see what sort of fright we can give Hazel Blears in Salford. In the heart of the expenses scandal, there was a very unscientific express straw poll there and they said if the election was tomorrow the BNP would win Salford. We are not going to, but there is a number of places, what we are really after is coming second.

In a number of places you could actually let the Tories win. Because you could take enough votes off the Labour Party. Dagenham and Rainham is a good example.

Yes, the question there isn't as it appears or is there a counter intuitive thing? Do we take Labour votes that would otherwise vote Labour, or do we in fact take people who have already given up on the Labour, but think they can't really vote for Maggie Thatcher's party. But if we weren't here they would do. And not enough research has been done into that. There are whole books that have been written on the voting patterns of the three main parties, but not about our voters. Immediately after the election we are going to do a huge study of our members with people from a political science department of a university. Once that has been done, we'll get a far better understanding of our activists. The same will be done with the voters.

You refused to take part in the BBC *Politics Show* with your opponents in Barking, Margaret Hodge, Simon Marcus and Dominic Carman. Why was that?
Because these are the same people you see who organised the *Question Time* stitch up. And when they get a Cabinet minister to agree to break the Labour Party's no platform rule, something fishy is going on. And finally the key thing was when they said, it is going to be on local issues only...

That must be up your street? You are standing here primarily because of what goes on locally?
But it is still talking national issues, we are talking about immigration. And when they say if you are here we are talking about local issues that is shutting out key factors. First of all no general election has ever been decided on local issues, outside of a handful of extraordinary things like Kidderminster. It is utterly abnormal and is utterly false to say we are going to exclude national subjects...

Would you be standing here if it wasn't at least in part local...
Exactly. In part. And it's a combination.

In large part I would say.
Well no, it's what the Labour Party has done in terms of mass immigration, it is not just about how it has affected people directly here, in this street. It's about how it has affected jobs, the labour market, wage rates. It's the general complexion of the country in every sense of the word.

Well that's no reason not to take part in a televised debate.
It's because the BBC displays a huge amount of bias. It still hasn't even accepted it was wrong in what it did on *Question Time*. It has rejected our complaints out of hand. So it is institutionally biased against us. When it then comes up with something, they have given no attempts of guarantees to ensure this would be remotely fair. So I am quite happy to go on and

do something. We are trying to organise a hustings meeting with a local audience. There is another thing, there was no attempt to control in any way what the audience is going to be. We know what that means. Because in *Question Time* the audience was absolutely rigged. So we have a rigged audience, you have Dominic Carman who isn't even a genuine candidate, he is a spoiler just aimed at me and nothing else. The lies that man has told about me are outrageous, absolutely disgusting.

But wasn't that the real reason you didn't take part, you didn't want to be on with him?
No, no, no. I will be on with him somewhere or other. That's fair enough. But when it's the BBC saying 'we are going to control how this is done, we are controlling the audience, and we are controlling the questions'…

Well, there wasn't an audience on the *Politics Show*.
Well, right. But they are controlling everything, including an artificial blog, for instance on us, disgusting, about Afghanistan and PFI.

But frankly if you are on there and you start discussing them, and they are trying to stop you, then surely that is manna from heaven for you? In a sense that is what happened on *Question Time*, in that it was so appallingly rigged that even people who would never ever vote for you, actually started feeling a bit sorry for you. Surely, you could have used the same tactic, and I appreciate that wasn't your doing, but you could have used the same tactic on this programme.
Possibly. But in a meeting with a local audience, if the panel chairman tries to stop you, then the audience will come in and say well you won't be hearing this. To do it here in Barking, as we are trying to do, with a genuine local audience, it is Channel 4 trying to organise it, so as I said we need to work out between us and the Labour Party how we are going to ensure that it is a genuine local audience, but there are ways and means. Where you have a genuine local audience in a place, or any genuine audience, then the power of the chairman to simply bulldoze things through is extremely restricted. When you have either an audience which is handpicked or no audience, then the chairman, especially when he can even cut your microphone off, has enormous power over how the thing goes, which is the position Dimbleby was in. And the BBC made no effort whatsoever to provide any kind of say, even understanding of why it was wrong, let alone even an assurance of them not going to doing it again. And to have it here on local issues, again, the definition there is so broad. Now I can get briefed and hold my own on actual key local issues, there are things such as the Ford site, the hospitals, things like that. But when it is the BBC organising it, they are perfectly capably with those others, of coming

up with a local issue, which none of us would have ever heard about it. But in real life Dominic Carman would have been briefed, even though the Lib Dems have no presence in Barking and Dagenham. I wouldn't have been briefed. So the thing was designed without a shadow of a doubt to make me look out of touch and incompetent. That's what they would have been doing. And we are not going to give them that opportunity.

Let's talk about the BNP policies, seeing as no one else seems to. I was looking at a lot of your policy statements on your website, and there's a common theme about how globalisation is wicked, and how it is really damaging society, damaging the economy, and all the rest of it. Doesn't trying to resist globalisation make you look like King Canute?
No… I don't think so for a number of reasons. The key thing being actually, everyone is going to very soon find out that globalisation is going to go into a reverse in any case. Because globalisation is fundamentally based on almost free transport which is based on almost free energy. And because we have used up almost half the world's oil there is plenty left, but from here on it gets more expensive. The economic business model of China is making things with near slave labour, and shipping them here almost free, and undercutting Western industries is actually a badly flawed business model, because it ain't gonna get here free anymore, because fuel prices… are going to go through the roof the moment the world economy begins to recover. So it is not inevitable, it is going to go into a reverse. Nor is anything modern. The world in 1914 in trade terms was more globalised than the world is being now, until the last few years.

You sound like a member of the Green Party.
Well, maybe so.

Could I give you a bigger insult?
Well, no. I quite accept that. Equally I would say that in his critique of the inherent problems of capitalism Marx wasn't totally wrong. That doesn't make me a Marxist. His description was quite accurate in some ways, albeit his prescription of what to do about it was horrific. So I am not a Marxist, but you have got to say that some things that Marx said were correct…

That's a sentence I never thought I'd hear you say.
The Greens are correct in saying we are eating up the world. That is the biggest, long term problem with capitalism. It is not that it is inefficient or even corrupt. It is that it is so damned efficient that it is eating up the world far faster than anything else would.

I did have a good laugh when I read this sentence on your website. 'The British National Party is this Nation's only true Green Party'.

I would say that is very true. We would not put a motorway through the habitat of the spotted horned toads, whereas other people would. But equally we believe human diversity is worth preserving and the Greens don't.

We are the only true greens. The Greens are saying that they believe in preserving Britain's environment and all the rest of it, but they are still in favour of unrestricted immigration. And in one of the most overcrowded countries in the world, especially in southern England, it is self-evident you can either have people or nightingales and toads.

But what are we to make of a party whose first promise on the environmental page of their website is not about climate change, not about anything massive, but 'the removal of unsightly overhead power lines from beauty spots and their burial underground'. Well a very laudable aim maybe, but is that really the main thing which should be the number one policy?

Well no, it probably shouldn't be. But these things, the environmental section is overrun with volunteers, and we are not going to go in and stamp all over them and say you should do something else. I think it is fairly obvious to most people that the first point where the BNP connects with the Green or environmental position is immigration, so we don't necessarily need to hammer that. It doesn't hurt to mention something which would make people think 'ooh, I didn't think they would say that'.

Can you clarify something about climate change? Because again on your website it says 'the BNP accepts that climate change, of whatever origin, is a threat to Britain. Current evidence suggests that some of it may be man-made; even if this is not the case, then the principle of 'better safe than sorry' applies' and so on…

Good lord, I will just shoot someone for that. It's clearly dated. What climate change … one thing where it says climate change does happen, no doubt. But the climate is always changing. So that is the first thing. That is, I think that probably was written about three years ago, I would guess. And we have since…

Well you called it a hoax?

Well we have since then looked far more closely into it. And it clearly is a gigantic fraud. And I will, now that it has been drawn to my attention, make sure it will get changed, as it is off-message.

Nuclear power, yes or no?
Without a doubt, certainly, yes.

You have this quaint notion of going back to the nineteenth century and wanting to impose tariffs on lots of things, which would mean, for example, that iPhones would double in price and there would be a long waiting list for all sorts of vital products. Isn't that what we fondly remember from the Soviet Union?
No. What I fondly remember from the Soviet Union is that you would have one factory making a car. They would be turning out the most appalling junk. If you have several different companies competing, and making cars, then you get decent quality cars. So no, it is not Soviet at all.

But you do want to impose quotas and tariffs…
Well, let's take it the other way, because this election will be basically on the economy. We acknowledge quite simply that our broad brushstrokes picture of what we do economically really was inherited from John Tyndall from the National Front, from imperial preference. It's been pretty much what we had in the 1930s and hasn't changed since. That clearly has to change, for one thing if you say we have to have tariff barriers to protect British industry, that might have been feasible in the 1930s, it's not now because in huge areas we don't have home grown industry to protect. We've got to recreate it if we want it, so it's got to be more nuanced. There's some things we wouldn't bother to recreate. If you got to the other extreme – to the free trade extreme – say 'yes, it's fine, it's all efficient' and we can get everything so much cheaper then you have to accept that you will end up, logically, with no industries left.

No, you don't at all. You just accept that some countries can do some things better than you can.
Yes, but the Chinese can do everything better than we can. That's the problem. Adam Smith's comparative advantage theory, if you actually look in detail at what Smith was saying, it's got to be between countries which are vaguely similar, it's got to be a level playing field. There isn't a level playing field between us and the Chinese, and there never can be because they don't have environmental protection costs weighed on their industry, they don't pay their workers wages anything like you even need to survive in Britain and millions of them are literally slave labourers. We simply cannot compete with China. If you want to compete with China then you will end up with no industry. It's OK as a journalist to think 'we can compete with China', yes because most of them don't speak good enough English to compete with you but in any other industry you're going to be wiped out. In the end, to follow

it through logically, anything the Chinese can do cheaper than we can we should offshore to them, let them have it, then why don't we do away with the army and invite a detachment of the Chinese army to come in and do it for us.

Well, we're talking about products, I see no problem that if the Chinese can build better computers than we can at a cheaper price than we can, let them and we can import them.
There's a longer term problem which is, if you're reliant on another state, in particular a superpower for the technology with which you would if push came to shove fight a war...

Sure, but what you're saying is that the Chinese will effectively just make and produce and have the creative technology to do everything. That's just simply not the case.
Well we appear to be well through the line where that's going to be the case.

You could have made that argument about Japan twenty years ago. And no one would make that argument about Japan now.
No, but China is going to. Our generation has a fundamental clash problem now with Islam – we shouldn't have. But now, thanks to the war of civilisation and mass immigration our generation is going to have to decide whether Europe and the European nations are going to remain European, secular, post-Christian or whether they're in the end going to become Islamic. Our children's generation is going to have to decide whether there is only China dominating the world or if something is done so that China has its sphere of influence and it doesn't totally dominate ours. But that's not really for this generation.

You could have made the same argument about India.
I don't think so because India is not as advanced. China is a national socialist state, India isn't. China has a long term, historical and understandable aversion to and resentment against the West for what we did to China in imperial times. They're running an economic war against the West, in their own interest – and good luck to them.

But going back to the original point, you are not going to win votes if you tell people that mobile phones are going to double in price.
Sure, what we're looking at with the redrafting of this is to say it has to be far more nuanced, that it has to be done over a period of time. We have to be looking at industries which we really need to develop and in particular industries which are either strategically vital or which if we develop a lead

in a certain industry it'll create more jobs, more money, more tax revenue. No system is perfect, this is the problem and everyone involved in politics, with their own particular thing, their system is going to be perfect which of course is not the case. But you have to look at what the alternative is. Yes, if you have tariffs on anything, it is a tax on the consumer without a shadow of a doubt, so it has to be hypothecated. It can't be used just to have government spending on all sorts of things whatever particular ideologically driven nonsense this sort of government wants. It has to be for things which are genuinely worthwhile. The alternative isn't a win win because if you haven't got well paid jobs then whatever jobs there are you have to tax even more in order to do the things which well paid jobs would do. Places like Sheffield with a nightmare of hard drug abuse it's partly school problems, family problems but it's also because there aren't any proper jobs which give young men self-respect. So you can't say that my solution of putting tariffs on something is going to be hugely expensive and is going to cost people more without accepting that your solution which is no tariffs is forcing you as a fairly well paid presumably taxpayer to pay very large amounts of money to sort out the shambles which is post-industrial Sheffield.

Your core vote, I imagine, is the white working class, not necessarily very well-off. This is going to hit them.
That's why it has to be done in a very steady, slow and nuanced fashion. As long as it's creating proper jobs and helping in a rather more closed economy, it's helping to raise the tax base, it's helping families to help themselves not being forced to be a burden on the state, it's going to be a benefit.

What about another one which would hit the same group of people, increasing VAT?
We've never said we're increasing VAT.

I think you'll find you have.
We said that we believe the Labour Party and the Tories without a shadow of a doubt would increase VAT, and know they're going to increase VAT to 20 per cent after this election, and put it on food which is also a harmonisation with Europe so it's coming anyway, and that that's wrong. I'm sure we haven't said we'll increase VAT.

How would you cut the national debt?
By stopping bailing out the banks, because they've crippled themselves. They should all go to the wall. And we should simply pick up the pieces. So that would stop it getting that much worse.

But then the economy would've completely gone down the pan.
Well it's going to anyway. Now we've got enormous debts additionally . . . The fact is we're still going to go down that hole. But we've now got enormous debt.

So RBS, the Bank of Scotland, Lloyds, you'd have let them all go down the pan.
We'd have let them all go down the pan and we'd then have nationalised all the assets and turned it into a national reconstruction bank so that where people are still paying mortgages and all the rest there would be money coming in. We'd have looked after the share holders and written everybody else off.

But what about national debt?
We would get it down, it's safe to assume there'd be a great reluctance of the assorted financial institutions around the world to lend money to a BNP government, although generally they lend to everybody don't they?

Well, at a price.
Well there's a profit to be had, so they certainly would do. We would deal with the fact that we're getting into debt more and more by not being in the European Union which is a phenomenally expensive operation in direct payments and even worse in its indirect cost on business.

But I still haven't heard what you would do in the next year to two years to address the huge public sector borrowing requirement that we now have?
We would set about eliminating all the sectors of the politically correct servile state that we possibly could which goes well beyond translators and all the rest of it. We are in a terrible hole, so things have got to be fairly drastic to deal with it. So for instance, health and safety inspectors in restaurants, we pay a fortune for them!

Well that would save two million a year.
It isn't made up of a couple of huge sums this expenditure, it's across the board, it's an example.

There are some big picture things that you can do. What about Trident?
We believe Britain needs an independent nuclear deterrent, we would keep that. We would look for ways to develop it so that more of the work is actually in Britain.

What about Britain's role in the world?
We'd stop fighting any more of these stupid wars pretending we're a world

policeman. So, no Iran war, which is coming, all the last bits out of Iraq and end the Afghan war immediately. We're a bankrupt third rate nation now.

That's not very patriotic of you. I'd have thought that standing up to Iran would actually have been something you'd approve of.
No, the Saudi Arabians want us to stand up to Iran because they want to take out their rivals. The Saudi pressure on the old Iranian regime was enormous. No it's nothing to do with us.

If we withdrew from Afghanistan, wouldn't that be admitting defeat to Al Qaeda?
No, because we're not fighting Al Qaeda, we're fighting Afghan peasants and they've always beaten everyone. Of course we're going to lose. We can't win in Afghanistan. Even the Soviet Union couldn't win there. The only way you could win there is if you nuked it, which can't be done.

How can you fight Al Qaeda, then?
You can stop any more young Muslims pouring into Britain for a start because we weren't bombed by Afghan peasants on the 7 July.

You can't tar them with the same brush.
We were actually bombed by people who we, locally in the area, had pointed out to the police several years before as being radical and involved in paramilitary training in the woods. We weren't bombed by Afghan peasants.

But these Muslims who perpetrated the 7/7 bombings, they grew up in this country – they weren't immigrants. They actually were born here. So that rather defeats the argument of saying, don't allow any more Muslims in.
No, but that's a start. The ones who carried out attacks two weeks later – eighteen months before that happened I was put on trial for it and then it happened, it became very embarrassing for the prosecution – I said that sooner or later, we were going to be bombed – probably the London tube and bus services – by either second generation Pakistanis from Bradford or recently arrived asylum-seekers. And on the 7 July, we were bombed by second generation Pakistanis from the Leeds area – I was twelve miles out. And two weeks later we were nearly bombed by a group of recently arrived asylum seekers. Those are the people who are the problem. Radical and increasingly radicalised second generation/third generation Muslims, and every new generation and every few years they're more hard lines and extreme than the ones before. It's a cycle we can't get out of. Or by recently arrived asylum seekers. We're not going to be attacked by Afghan peasants. Does Al Qaeda as such even really exist as opposed to it being just an

ideological trend – it's a means on the internet more than anything else. These people don't need a guiding hand. It's a bit like the old anti-Semitic crazies with the elders of Zion. They never existed. And likewise – obviously Bin Laden existed – probably is still alive – but the young Muslims that probably make up ten per cent of Britain's immigrant population who are fanatically pro Al-Qaeda and Jihad – they don't need guidance from a man in a cave. They're going to destroy your society one way or another and they've got various ways to do it and they're going to do it.

One more thing on Afghanistan – in any case it doesn't help because our presence in Afghanistan is destabilising Pakistan and that's the real problem. So it is wholly counter-productive. Every time you and I see pictures of an air strike that has killed a group of villagers we think, subconsciously or consciously, well it's a war. It's very sad but it's collateral damage. These things happen. There's tens of thousands of young Muslims watching it, seething with hate, and they've decided to do something about it. We shouldn't be there at all.

But that's a total exaggeration. You say tens of thousands are seething with hate.
No that's not a total exaggeration. It's been shown by opinion polls – I think the last one showing 13 per cent to have sympathy with their aims. Every now and again, one of my mobile phone numbers gets put on left wing and Islamist websites and a few spotty students phone me up with abuse from the left wing and I quite often end up in quite deep conversations with young Muslims. And young Muslims recognise me in the street. It's a danger, it's a problem but I talk to them as well – more than, with respect – people like you do. I can tell you what the Muslim street thinks and it's increasingly radical. They consciously use drugs and the sexual grooming thing – it's a fun way of making Jihad and they're the problem for us. Not unfortunate Afghan peasants who just want to be left alone.

What about ID cards?
Absolutely not, that's a monstrous imposition. Even if they were going to make money we wouldn't have those. It isn't British and I don't mean that in a crude simplistic way. In terms of the British tradition of politics, the relationship between the state and the citizens, it's a monstrous thing – we certainly wouldn't have those.

What's your policy on Higher Education?
We would scrap the idea of telling any unfortunate child who's managed to get through school with a GCSE that they can go to university because we've devalued degrees and we've taken out a whole section of the

population who actually should've been and would've been really good plumbers and so on and so forth. We've kidded them that they can do things with their degree on 'the theme of incest in soap operas'. You know, it's got to go, all of that. And the kids who are actually academic and can get to university and do proper courses shouldn't have to pay. So we'd pay some more money there.

Do you believe in quantitative easing?
Quantitative easing is very interesting. We nationalists for decades have been saying the fundamental problem with the banks and the banking system is that they create credit out of nothing and then charge all of us interest for it. That should not be the prerogative of, in effect, private banks, public liability companies and so on. It always used to be the prerogative of the crown, not the state and we have got a problem with rolling up to the state the monstrous power of the banks that clearly isn't a good thing. But it's far worse that the creation of the nation's credit is in the hands of private corporations. What quantitative easing has proved is that yes, you do create credit at the stroke of a pen and that should then be sent into circulation on rebuilding British industry. Quantitative easing has established that nationalist economics is legitimate which is very interesting. It shouldn't have been done in order to prop up the financial system because the financial system has to crash. In the end the only way the world can get out of the appalling mess that finance capitalism has got us in is either going to be hyperinflation so the debts get paid over the kid's dinner money this week, in effect, or it simply all has to written off. It can never be repaid.

How would you reform the benefits system?
By recreating a proper hard industrial base in this country to create real decent well paid jobs. That would raise the overall wage rates up and make it worth people's while working so they could afford to work. There are people all around the country who genuinely can't afford to work. It's madness. Once there's work out there that is decently paid and people can take it, if they don't take it and they're fit to work they can starve.

And what about Israel? The BNP has always had this reputation of being anti-Jewish. What's your view on Israel and does it have the right to self determination?
Yes, we've changed the position very radically from being knee jerk support of the Palestinians, not solely from an anti-Semitic point of view, also sympathy – these are a people whose ancestral land has been taken away by recent arrivals.

Would you say in the past the BNP has been anti-Semitic?
Yes. Tyndall and others were extremely anti-Semitic. Part of that actually was in a way just a historical quirk. You've got to understand the people who created that movement and so on, you had a hugely disproportionate number of people serving the Palestine police. There were loads in the 1970s – you couldn't go to a branch meeting without finding someone that worked within the Palestine police. And they had a pretty rough time from the Sterngang and so forth, and that coloured everything. It's taken years to turn that around to a sensible position which is where I think we are now which is that all peoples have a right to self determination and a home land, that Israel is a fait accompli, and it really wasn't up to the Western powers to give large parts of someone else's country to the Zionists but it's done now. It's done and dusted; it's a fait accompli. Logically, there should be a two state solution because it's probably the best thing to give a chance of sorting the mess out but most of all it's not our business. So the West has got itself into a terrible bind. Israel is an irritant to the Middle East and Islam and while it's there that is something that the radicals, the Islamists and so on will use as a recruiter to great effect but if because of that you were to say remove it as an irritant, so we say close down the Jewish state, we'll have them all back here and that was it, that wouldn't put Islam to sleep, that would inflame it with success. So we're now in a position that actually, an Israel that once was an irritant causing problems now is a front line in a civilisational war which is a grotesque error and shouldn't have happened, between the West and Islam. So we believe that Israel should continue to be and we were the only serious party which, during the Gaza troubles, were saying, well it's probably not wise for Israel to be doing what it's doing, winding things up, but Israel is absolutely entitled to flatten the whole of Gaza if it won't stop shelling its schools and hospitals.

In the interview you did with Andrew Marr last year you said that you found *Mein Kampf* very dull but you enjoyed one chapter of it. Which chapter was that?
That was the chapter on propaganda – that was interesting.

In what way?
Because it's a long time since I read it, I can't remember it. The only thing I can remember is repetition. But I suppose perhaps the Nazis were ahead of their time in now standard advertising techniques … it's irrelevant really.

How do you react to being called a fascist? And what would you say are the three things that differentiate the BNP from being a fascist party? It's the word that is most often used to describe the BNP – that or racist.

We're not fascist. If fascism is defined in its proper sense, it's about worship of the state or of a man that personifies the state and our tradition is very much in the British tradition of limited government with checks and balances and so on.

You could have fooled me. Half your policy programme envisions a larger state.
We're not fascist in that regard. It's about a close, almost incestuous relationship, between the state and the corporations. It's corporate fascism. The Thatcherite, Blairite PFI – that's fascist. We believe in a mixed economy where the state or the big capitalist bits should only be there because economies of scale make it necessary, or control makes it necessary. Where possible it should be done by small businesses, family farms or workers' co-operatives. So completely unfascist.

The final defining factor of fascism is the use of political violence as a political weapon against your opponents. And we're the victims of a Marxist fascism – we do not either practise or want to practise violence against anyone else.

Apart from throwing journalists out of press conferences…
Apart from throwing out lying journalists when they're asked. He was breaking the law. He'd been asked to leave a private premises and he refused. He's breaking the law. So you're entitled to use the minimum force necessary to break the law. I've been instructed that the fellow that quite gleefully grabbed his nose and twisted it shouldn't be put on duties like that anymore because that was over the top. But he was still breaking the law and he was removed with the minimum force necessary.

In which year did you stop denying the Holocaust?
I've never actually denied the Holocaust. I've said some terribly rude things about it and the way it's exploited.

You said 'it's well known that chimneys from the buildings at Auschwitz are fake'.
Ah, but I also said in the piece that huge numbers of Jews were persecuted or murdered by the Nazis and their allies just because they were Jewish and it is one of the great crimes of the twentieth century. To deny the Holocaust is presumably to say that no one was killed, that the camps didn't exist. Obviously that would be nonsense.

Do you believe six million Jews were killed?
That's the same old problem. I genuinely cannot discuss it with you because European law forbids us to discuss it.

That's bollocks.
It's not bollocks. European Law…

What you're saying then is you don't believe six million were killed.
There are defence lawyers in Germany in prison now because they've explained in court what their client said.

It's a simple enough question. You either believe that six million Jews died in the Holocaust or you don't.
The Holocaust happened.

But you're not willing to say that six million Jews died?
Precisely six million?

Around six million – that's the accepted number by historians who are supposed to know about these things.
I don't think that there should be any restrictions on historical enquiry. Nor should it be an offence to be wrong. But since it is an offence to be wrong – it's an offence to discuss what I used to believe or even the extent to which I've changed my mind – and I have done, I really can't talk about it.

You can talk about it to the extent that you can say whether or not you believe that around six million Jews died.
I can tell you because it's – I've got tarred and I'm not going to be interrupted and left with something that I've said that I wasn't…

I won't edit this.
I suppose I can tell you that the reasons for my doubts were specifically with the six million figure. The problem was the way it was used as a moral club to prevent any sensible debate about immigration. That's the issue. It's nothing to do with anti-Semitism or anything and there's been people, including Jews and former concentration camp inmates, who've said that aspects of this history have been exaggerated and so on. So that's the base line. When I was at school, the figure of six million was made up of four million murdered at Auschwitz and two million murdered elsewhere. That's six million.

Well that's not true.
That was the fact as presented to people in the 1970s and then it emerged that the authorities of Auschwitz downgraded the scale of the murders there from four million to a still shattering and appalling 1.1 million. So you're 2.9 million short.

There were lots of other death camps not just Auschwitz.
No, but the figure of 6 million came from the idea that in all the other death camps and elsewhere 2 million died and in Auschwitz there were 4 million gassed and cremated – that's where the figure was made up from, if you forget and take the noughts off, if you have six and take away 2.9 do you still have six?

No one would say where they came from, all they would do is anyone who said 6 take away 2.9 does not equal 6 was persecuted but in prison, beaten, had their houses firebombed, driven from their jobs and that greatly offended me and made me take up the issue of their behalf. But what I will say now is that I believe that the evidence that came from British intelligence of German operations behind the lines on the Eastern front make it quite possible to believe that a million people were shot to death on anti-partisan warfare, mainly as hostages and that the Germans naturally enough didn't pick white Russian or Belarussian peasants who were quite often on their side, they picked the local Jewish community because most of the partisans were Jewish which again you can't really be surprised about as its one of these cycles of horror. So therefore, you are no longer missing the 2.9, you are missing nearly 2 million. That's all. So it would be interesting to be told where they come from, but because the powers that be are so convinced that it's true and have passed laws to say that it's true and because it is irrelevant and because it's deliberately misunderstood, anyone who questions this is held up as anti-Semitic whereas it's nothing to do with anti-Semitism at all, it's about the rights of free speech or the right of the states and powerful vested interest groups to prevent free speech – that's what it's actually about. But because everyone's misunderstood or it leads one to jail I have no doubt whatsoever that the others, the missing ones, must have been there so clearly the 6 million figure is correct.

You have used the image of Churchill a lot in your recent publicity, but a guy called Mark Collett, who I gather is your head of publicity, said that Churchill was a f**** c***...**
He said that as a silly ignorant 19-year-old. I sacked him. At the time he was the head of the young BNP and he was actually very good at it. It was at its best under him, lots of great stuff going on with the kids. He didn't get a position for the best part of two years which when you're nineteen/twenty when you think back all those years ago, two years is an awful long time. So he was punished for that as was warranted.

Can you think of one positive aspect of immigration?
Well a wide range of curries is a plus, but there again I've got the recipes.

The reason I ask that is when you look across the range of policies you outline on your website almost whichever one you look at – and you demonstrated it earlier with the environmental stuff – leads back to immigration and it seems to me as a party you are desperate to be trying to say 'well we have lots of other policies, it's not just all about immigration' and yet they kind of all lead back to that – is that a fair summary?
It's a fair summary of the situation, as all things are interconnected and secondly of a failing of ours and a failing of quite a lot of our writers as they are all virtually untrained and virtually all volunteers. They write about things with their own glasses and perspectives on. We'd be better as a propaganda machine if we did have it separated out and even where you could see a connection we didn't point to it. But we're not a spin party.

Even though you like the spin chapter in *Mein Kampf* so much. In your 2005 manifesto you said 'we will end immigration to the UK and reduce our land's population burden by creating firm but voluntary incentives for immigrants and their descendants to return home'– question, what does 'firm' mean and what does 'home' mean because they are quite difficult to define?
Firm would mean that certainly in the case of serious criminals and illegals and people whose right to work was removed, for instance, when we left the European Union, there wouldn't be a choice about it. They would have to go.

Where?
If we are talking about the Eastern Europeans, who have got the right to come here, it is obvious where home is. With most people it is clear where they have come from. If people have entered this country and torn their documents up, then even if they have been granted asylum, they shouldn't have been, and we would reverse that.

But if you don't know where they have come from, you can't return them there.
If you want to, you can virtually find out which village they come from in Africa with DNA tests, if you are particularly fussed. Someone has got to take them. But their presence here isn't fair. And it is not legal.

But the state doesn't have to agree to take somebody… Just because you want to send them somewhere, doesn't mean that the state you want to send them to has to accept them. What do you do if they say, 'no'?
Well… we'll find some silly European liberal state which will happily take them. Someone will take them.

You reckon?
Yes, someone will take them. India said years ago and maintains the case,

that they would take back any of their nationals who were expelled from anywhere. We are not looking to expel Indians who came here legitimately. But if there were any that had to go back…

What about people who aren't criminals and haven't been convicted of offences?
But if they are legally here, they have to stay unless they want to go.

'Firm but voluntary incentives for immigrants and their descendants to return home…' Is that policy still your policy now?
Yes, broadly so. Let's reword the bit in the case of ones who have no right to be here. It would be firm. It wouldn't be brutal, it would be firm.

But you would quite like Dame Kelly Holmes to bugger off?
In the case of people who have come here legally and so on, who are integrated into our society, we would say, 'Look it is on the table, if you want to take it, you can take it.' The direct parallel is that for a few years after the police agreement in Northern Ireland, the British government here was paying Northern Irish businessmen £40,000 quid to relocate back in Northern Ireland. There was no force involved. No one thought that this was discrimination against an English businessman who might want to move to Northern Ireland. It was just clearly practical but because in order to bed things down over there and provide jobs and so on, it would be sensible to get people back there for various reasons. It would also be sensible for the West Indies for us to say, 'Right, we will buy as much sugar and soft fruit off you, at 10 per cent above world rates, as we can buy for the next twenty years. If you'll take some of your people back.' Youngsters often go with their grandparents because they know that if they are growing up in London schools, they are growing up to be scumbags. If they are going back to the West Indies, they can grow up in a proper, Christian school and get caned if they do something wrong. They grow up properly decent kids. So having more money involved than there is at present on that, it would make it more likely. Which would reduce the appalling problems both environmental and social and so on and economic which mass immigration has brought to London.

There are about 5.5 million British people who have emigrated or are working abroad. Do you think that the countries in which they live should encourage them to return here?
That is up to them. That's their right. It is the democratic right of their peoples if they choose to decide that. In many cases, it would help Britain because we have suffered a brain drain. They have only left here because

this isn't the Britain they feel at home in. They'd feel more at home in our Britain, and where they are skilled, we want them back. One final thing on immigration policy, because it is always put against us. It is put into a moral perspective that we are the ones that are bad. We have African leaders all over Southern Africa begging Britain to stop poaching our NHS staff. They use them as cheap labour, they often aren't up to the skill levels that are the best that we can produce. Once they have been here, if we could say to those countries: 'Here is money for infrastructure and so on. We will help you with foreign aid because you will have a larger population.' We would use it partly to undo some of the damage that mass immigration has caused.

It says on your website that you would abolish foreign aid.
We would abolish foreign aid as foreign aid. But we would use a large part of it to say instead of scattering it all around the world to use by various crazed dictators to put into their Swiss bank accounts, we'd say to specific countries, 'Because we have a significant number of your nationals, who with these incentives, will actually want to go home. And it is good for you, and it is good for us, we recognise as a practicality for you…' There is no point doctors and nurses coming back. You haven't got hospitals. So we'll help you build hospitals. It is a one-off deal. It is not out of guilt. Which is the foreign aid thing, it is basically a liberal guilt. They take taxes off ordinary poor people and they need it to assuage their guilt. It is not that at all. It is just a practical deal that will help these countries to establish their infrastructure so that they can take some of these people back, if they want to go.

Isn't there a part of you that thinks: 'I really would quite like a quiet life now.' How long have you been leader?
I have been leader for… eleven years. It is a long old time. Yes, the same with virtually everybody. Certainly, of the serious activists and people we have would all far rather be doing other things. So why do you do it? It is an idealism. Because somebody should do it. Why did people in the last war and the First World War go off to fight, it is not in their personal interest. It is altruistic. It is in the interest of the greater good. So it is that. I suppose that is the rationalisation. Underneath that, the human being, especially the male is interested in food, sex and status. So I suppose that is probably there.

So you get all of those three. You are turning into Nigel Farage.
I was thinking of the food and the sex is private and at home, but the status I suppose there is an element of that. I would far rather go out anywhere with Jackie, my wife, and the family as well. You go out anywhere and people want to come up and shake my hand and have my photograph taken. So you can't go to a country pub quietly because it ends up a photograph opportunity.

It is good and it is heartening and so on but it is extraordinarily intrusive. I understand… We haven't for some years criticised, it was jumped on the *Sun/Mail/Express*-type position, criticising Gordon Brown for having a holiday abroad. Or Cameron for that matter. It's only human to go away somewhere where you are not constantly recognised and either loved, loathed or an item of curiosity and I'd rather not have that.

Why is the BNP so anti gay?
We're not drastically anti gay. We were, but it was just a reflection of white working-class culture of the '70s and so on. It's unfamiliar, it's odd and I'm afraid it is creepy. Grown men kissing in public is creepy to most people. You don't often see it but if you do see it, it's not a matter of homophobia, it's odd and you have to explain it to little kids and so on – that's strange. We're not anti gay. I took over a party which had a total ban on homosexual members. We've got gay members now and people know who they are, but it's don't ask don't tell.

Why should it affect anything?
Because it does affect because of the actions of the militant gay lobby.

Who are about as insignificant as the number of terrorist Muslims…
All Muslims are not terrorists but all terrorists are Muslims and as for gays, not all gays are militant and want to shove it down everyone's throats…

…so to speak…
Indeed. And force sex education on young children, and of course it isn't just a gay thing, it's a leftist break up of the family. It's Marxist in origin, but it's the rainbow alliance of Marxists and gay activists and so on. There is a hetrophobia amongst some of those people when they refer to us as 'breeders' and so on.

Amongst about a quarter of a per cent.
I know it's a very small number.

You are generalising…
…but you were asking where it came from and that's where it came from. The simple fact is that the party that I took over had a policy of persecuting gays in the party, and was homophobic and also had a policy of re-imposing the 1968 ban on homosexuality. The position we have moved to which has taken some doing because there are people who didn't like it, wouldn't change the old reactionaries, the gays in denial. Different people fought it tooth and nail and accused me of all sorts of selling out and wondered: 'is he a fag himself?'

We are now in a position where we simply say what people do in private amongst consenting adults is their affair and their affair only and that the state has no right to either have a window into men's souls.

Would you reverse civil partnership legislation?
Yes, but that's not to do with wanting to persecute homosexuals. Marriage is between a man and a woman and rearing their own children is not perfect but it's the best model and basis for a society. So therefore, the civil partnership between a faithful stable and gay couple is just as a civil partnership perhaps between two elderly sisters in terms of inheritance and so on. They have to, regrettably, be collateral damage, because you have to put the family above everything in order to say: this is what our society aspires to. Marriage is only between a man and a women and ideally with kids.

But a civil partnership isn't a marriage.
I know it's not but it's part of the left's war against marriage and the family. I find it hard to grasp people who are essentially conservative with a small c who can't get the point that most of what's been done to our society been deliberately done by a hard core Marxist left who have infiltrated their ideas into all aspects of our society.

I accept that could be the case with some things but to normal people who just think stable relationships, whatever kind they are, are a good thing for society.
I agree it's better if two gay men are in a stable relationship rather than cottaging all over the place.

So why can't society recognise that?
Well perhaps you can recognise it in some way, but not by creating this bogus leftist alternative to marriage whose purpose is to help to break up the family. That's the cause of the left.

It genuinely isn't.
That's where I believe it has come from and it has that effect.

If you believe that homosexuality was quote 'curable' I would accept your argument but if you believe that people are either born gay or they're not then why should that group of people – and we are talking about who knows what the percentage is, say somewhere between 5 and 10 per cent of the population – why should those people be disadvantaged by society from actually being recognised in stable relationships.
Because the effects of that are to devalue marriage.

No, you're wrong. If you have a choice between a child being brought up in a children's home or between two people of the same sex in a stable loving relationship then I would argue I would rather that child was brought up in the latter. Because I think they are more likely to emerge as a normal member of society than in a children's home.

Yes. But it is not necessary to do that because there's a huge number of straight couples who want to adopt kids who can't or aren't allowed to. There is a shortage. So therefore, if we reach the stage where there are so many children in children's homes that you run out of would-be adopted ideal families, then I would be inclined to agree. But we are not at that stage. It is regrettable that it is collateral damage of the family.

I am now going to ask you a question in which you are either not going to answer or hit me. I have seen videos on YouTube of Martin Webster, the former leader of the National Front, alleging that you and he had had some kind of affair which involved gay sex.

It is bullshit. It was an old trick.

I have to say, it looked fairly convincing.

Yeah, but it is balls.

So you are not going to give me a Michael Portillo moment?

No, indeed I am not. It was an old trick. It's to say: 'Oh, that person I had an affair with them.' It embarrasses or used to embarrass more straight people. It was quite often done. When I and several other members of the National Front ousted him from his utterly dominant position, we did so partly because it was creepy, when he would come and put his arm around you in the office and so on. And when you are twenty-two and straight, you don't really like that. And you had no choice because he had all this power and so on. But that was a tiny fraction of it. Basically, he was a bully and not politically on message. He really was a racist bigot and so on, and a really crazed anti-Semite. So we got shot of him for organisational reasons. But when we got shot of him we thought actually he was very old and we were very grown up. We were actually in our early twenties and he was about thirty-five at the peak of his powers and so on. He was ousted by a group of kids. We used to say the balls had just dropped. So he would never ever forgive those of us who ousted him from that position. So it is a good way to hit back. That's where that came from.

You didn't hit me.

No, it doesn't bother me. I know what I am. I am perfectly comfortable.

Did that whole sort of thing colour your views on the subject of homosexuality anyway?
Did it? I don't know really.

A lot of people think any gay man basically fancies anything in trousers. And he probably was one of those.
To say that people are condemned to hell because of the way that nature or God made them, that's actually grotesque. That's not right. But still I think the homosexuality thing is overplayed. I do think that, well, as a male, although obviously females can be wonderfully promiscuous and great fun. Nevertheless, wanton, rampant promiscuity is more of a male thing than a female thing. Therefore it is entirely logical that homosexuals tend to be more promiscuous but only because of the opportunities.

Have you actually been to a concentration camp?
No, I haven't. I think, no.

Adam Boulton

Current job: Political Editor of Sky News

Born: 15 February 1959

Education: He has a Masters degrees from the University of Oxford and John Hopkins University.

Family status: Married with five children.

Broadcasting career: Before joining Sky News, he worked as a journalist in the parliamentary 'lobby' and then became political editor for TV-AM. He has written for various newspapers and magazines, including *The Times*, *Sunday Times*, *Guardian*, *Spectator*, *New Statesman* and *Independent*.

Some Career highlights: Moderating the first ever Sky News UK 2010 Leaders' Debate between Gordon Brown, David Cameron and Nick Clegg. Gained a UK exclusive broadcast interview during the US President Barack Obama's historic visit to Ghana. Became the first British television reporter to conduct a joint interview of US President George W. Bush and his wife, Laura.

Date of interview: March 2010
Extended version
Venue: Sky News Studios, Millbank
Total Politics Issue 23, May 2010

Adam Boulton is a legend and I have huge respect for him. He probably spends more hours live on air than any other political journalist. He has an incredible knack of explaining complex political issues to the Sky News viewers, he can be combative and is also increasingly opinionated. He's been at Sky News since its launch in 1989 yet shows no sign of being bored or complacent. It was he who was the driving force between the Sky News campaign for prime ministerial debates and he is a constant source of innovation on the channel.

One of the most striking TV scenes of the post-election period was the moment when Adam Boulton completely lost his rag, live on air with Alastair Campbell. Having conducted this interview with him only a few weeks prior to that, it didn't especially surprise me. There's clearly little love lost between them.

His interviewing style is the opposite of that of Jeremy Paxman, but he arguably gets more out of his interviewees by allowing them to speak without being interrupted every two seconds. Boulton clearly loves politics but carefully maintains his independence from the politicians he mixes with.

I'm a fan, as you can tell.

How did you get into politics and journalism in the first place? What sparked your interest?
I realised when I was in my late teenage years that I wanted to be a journalist. It was largely because, looking at my general interests, I thought analysis, précis and having a wide range of subjects you could deal with was good for my talents. What really made me do it was that one of my best friends' fathers was a *Sunday Times* Insight team journalist and to be honest, it sounds like a terrible thing to say, I'd not really thought about people who went to university, who were educated, becoming journalists. I suppose I had a rather sleazy image of a bloke in a dirty mac bothering people.

Hey, that's you!
I suddenly realised it would be consistent with going to university and studying things so I did English at Oxford and then I did a degree in America in international relations. And by that stage, I decided I wanted to go into broadcasting rather than print, because I wasn't interested in doing partisan journalism.

I was lucky that I came at the '80s from America at the time when the new television channels were starting out – Channel 4, TVam and others. So I didn't have a political grounding but the '83 election came along pretty soon and I got involved in that, so after that I tended to be asked to do politics.

So you didn't actually go into it saying 'I want to do politics'?
No, or news strangely enough. I think if you'd asked me, I'd have seen myself as a kind of a *Panorama* producer or something like that – doing detailed reporting. But what I realised very quickly was that that the technology was rapidly undercutting current affairs. When things like *Channel 4 News* and *Newsnight* came along you could do fairly detailed work on the day. I was also interested, having been in America, in what you could do live.

In 1983 when Greg Dyke was running breakfast television, I worked on the election with people like Diane Abbott, Mark Damazar and Jackie Ashley. Immediately after that, simply because I'd done some work with live outside broadcasts, I ended up doing *By the Seaside* with Chris Tarrant. So it was a fairly mixed if chaotic learning on the job type apprenticeship.

Have you ever thought about going to the other side, because a lot of journalists do drift into politics? Has that ever crossed your mind?
No, it hasn't. Genuinely it has not crossed my mind. I do see what I'm doing

as analogous a bit to being a sport commentator. There aren't many sport commentators who qualify for a premiership side. Something dies inside me when I see a journalist becoming a candidate.

Do you think the Westminster lobby is an outdated institution?
I don't really. I've been chairman of the lobby, and I've defended the lobby on occasions. We've had to fight continuously for access to the Commons and elsewhere and I feel if one said 'OK, well the lobby's a terrible idea, let's try something else' we'd be worse off. I think it's certainly the case that the whole process has got a bit debauched during the New Labour years. There are some people who say that dated back to Bernard Ingham, although I would say he was a straighter operator compared to what came afterwards. There's also a question about who is admitted to the lobby, because you've now got new media appearing. Since I've been in the lobby, it's always been a fairly organic institution and people or organisations who were big figures in the lobby have faded away and new ones have come in.

I know we're just starting to see some of the online people come in, but I think the principle of having right of access on behalf of your news organisations to Parliament is a good one, because a lot of people often think it's a deal between the government and the lobby. It's not. The lobby is a parliamentary institution, it's not a governmental institution. I personally think that is quite important, and I'll be honest with you, I am one of those journalists who thinks that in a lot of areas that we can afford to lift our game. By which I mean that I would say there's quite a significant chunk of my colleagues who I think are not primarily interested in politics, the decisions which Parliament is taking, how it's going to affect individuals. They're interested in Westminster as a source of gossip and secondary stories. Sometimes I think we do need to think 'why are we doing this?'

You said you thought that print media was more to blame for this than broadcasting. Couldn't you also argue that 24-hour news channels are to blame because they've got so much time to fill?
Sometimes I think you get bushfires, but I do think if they're not very significant they tend to burn themselves out quite quickly. I think what we can do on 24/7 media is do things in more depth. Likewise we can show twenty minutes or half an hour of a news conference or a statement to parliament. That is how we fill the time.

You've been at Sky News since the beginning. How has your job changed in the years you've been doing it?
Over time, the nature of television news has changed. The formal two or three or minute package has become rarer. You do more stuff on the hoof so

over time on air I've really evolved to doing almost exclusively live stuff, live interviews, presenting programmes and live commentary and building this machine. We've gone up from four people working in Westminster when we started, and we've now got about thirty. It's always changing, we're now going to completely revamp and rebuild our offices for HD and change again, so I think it's almost the restless nature of it that's kept me in the same place.

The other thing that happened is that we've gone online. There was a period in the middle of my period at Sky, where I was practically illiterate. I didn't write anything down. But obviously with the growth of online I'm now writing much more really than I ever have done before in my career, in various forms. So that's been a rediscovery of a lost art.

How do you see 24-hour news developing in this country? There are one or two people at Sky who would like to see it develop into a Fox News operation – much more opinion than straight reporting. Is that a route you'd like to see Sky go down?
I think there are big questions about television as a whole because the bar to entry has been lowered so much by digital technology. There's a lot of competition coming. If you're going to continue to be influential in the cacophonous marketplace, you need to have a very strong relationship with your audience. You can go in different ways on that. In America, Fox News has identified a section of the audience, a section of the electorate and it caters to their needs and because there isn't one dominant broadcaster providing its signal for free, you can make a great deal of money that way.

While people want greater choice, they do want to look to their news providers for authority. Opinion polls show they trust broadcasters. I think if you just became another voice in this news market, in this news culture, I think you would rapidly disappear. It's noticeable that – not at Sky – when other people have tried to do very strong opinionated news, they haven't taken root to the extent that in other cultures talk radio has.

I certainly think that you and Jon Craig in particular have become slightly more opinionated. I don't mean in the party political sense at all. I just mean that you do give your own opinions more than you did ten years ago, or am I imagining that?
I think there's an element of truth in that, and I think that's partly presuming on the relationship of trust you've built up with the audience, that they can take it. But one of the problems in political broadcasting is that we've grown up in a culture where balance is a bit from Labour, a bit from the Conservatives, a bit from the Liberals.

I'm very conscious of trying to be fair, but sometimes the nature of the debate does involve being more explicit, and I think there are some areas where you can take a different position. Jon Craig is of the old school of 'snouts-in-the-trough, how can MPs behave like this, let's expose them, they deserve what they get' and that's fine. But when I've been doing commentary I'm more concerned to try to explain to people how this had happened and almost to relate to it as human beings, how would you behave if you'd been in those circumstances.

Would you agree that the media often operate as a herd? We've all seen examples of Nick Robinson, you, Gary Gibbon and Tom Bradby expressing views and the print media falling in behind you all. Do you think that's healthy?
I had a very bumpy relationship with Alastair Campbell, but he did say to me once that the difference about you – i.e. me – is that if you express an opinion you try and attribute it. I do see that as being quite important. I wouldn't go on air and say 'that David Davis speech, I was falling asleep'. I would go on and say: 'That David Davis speech, I saw quite a lot of people in the audience falling asleep.' They amount to actually pretty much the same thing, but I do think there's a difference. Nick and Gary and Tom and I, we do work in isolation and we don't actually see that much of each other because television tends to take you away a bit from the pack a lot of the time. But there are certainly occasions when big things are afoot where we do just in the margins in either side of going live at Downing Street, just say 'what do you think, how soon do you think this is?'

So it's like the sketch writers' cartel where they basically sit together and decide how to carve it up!
No, we don't do that and actually quite often, we might bump into each other and we might say 'how are you doing it' which is a kind of reality check. It doesn't mean we just sit down and say 'right, definitely take this line'. And I think it's been noticeable at the moment as elections come on that the BBC does have this quite strong balance tendency. It's been pretty clear that ITN for quite a long time or ITV News has wanted to be very vigorous or very characterful in what its saying. And I would say, we're somewhere in the middle precisely because in 24-hour news you are always a marketplace.

What's the competition like between you? Because ten years ago, Sky and all the BBC felt they had won if they got a story on the screen quicker than another. Whereas I get the feeling that now that's changed and the competition is a bit more subtle than that?
I would say that we've always wanted to get things on first, but we've always wanted to get them on right, in the sense that we would break a story, but we wanted to qualify it with saying 'this is the best information we have at the moment' or 'more on that story'. I think there was a period when Roger

Mosey very much wanted to just compete on that basis as to who is doing things first. And I think it got a bit slack with people just rushing to break things all the time and getting things wrong. I would say the BBC got it wrong more than we did. I think the BBC News Channel is probably less of a priority for the BBC than it was a few years ago and that, therefore, has given us a bit more space

How much influence does Rupert Murdoch have in what you do? How often do you see him or speak to him? Does he ever ring you up?
No, I've never been rung up by Rupert Murdoch. I'll now be dropped from *The Guardian*'s 100 most influential people in the media! The truth is that I think in more than twenty years at Sky, I've probably been in the same room as Rupert Murdoch about half a dozen times. And I'd say I've probably had three conversations with him.

Do you ever feel used by politicians?
I do think that's part of the deal, at one level. John Lloyd said that journalism has three functions: it has reporting, it has analysing and it has commenting, and a lot of 24-hour news, a lot of the news business is reporting. It's getting to people, finding out what they want to say, pushing them that bit further to say what they really mean and getting that across. So you know, politicians don't have a right to get on the airwaves, but part of our job, I think, is to facilitate them and to say what they're doing. But if politicians lie to me I do remember it.

Give me an example.
Well, I always resented the fact that Nick Raynsford lied to me about running for London mayor. I had asked him in an interview: 'If Frank Dobson comes into the race, you'll pull out in his favour, won't you?' He flatly denied it and then I think eight days later he opened the Frank Dobson campaign with the words 'everyone's always known I would always support Frank if he came into the race'. I just feel that kind of thing is unnecessary. If someone flatly denies something and says 'that's not true' and subsequently you read in their memoirs or somewhere 'tough interview but I think I managed to brush him off' that annoys me.

You must get that every day though. What about Alastair Campbell's briefings? You only need to read his diaries to see how many times he would mislead the lobby.
While I have admiration for a lot of Alastair Campbell's professionalism, I think the problem was that he introduced a culture where it was OK to lie. There were occasions when he actually said to me, while he was still in the

job, 'Oh, sorry about that Adam, but you know why I did it' and I just think there are some lines you shouldn't cross. And I think that became a culture which is satirised brilliantly in *The Thick of It*. It's not just Labour but there are some people who think the job of press officers or spin doctors or special advisors is to lie. Call me naive, I don't think that is the job and I think it's corrosive.

The Sky campaign to get the party leaders to debate each other was a massive success for Sky. How did it come about?
Well, we also did the BBC and ITV a favour as well. Had there not been the Sky campaign concentrating minds on all sides, I personally don't think the debates would have happened. That's me beating Sky's chest but I think you can ask other people and they might well agree with that. It was quite simple. John Ryley, the head of Sky News, is a thinker and he sent round a paper saying that he was concerned about the lack of political engagement which we can see in the decline in our audiences for elections and obviously you can see it in voter turnout and all the rest of it. He canvassed ideas for what we should do about it and I think we concluded that it wasn't our place to campaign for turnout or to run celebrities saying 'use your vote' or whatever because that would be a kind of intrusion in the market place.

We ended up with a campaign which basically was us saying 'listen, we think there should be a debate, we're going to stage it. Be there or be square' and of course Cameron and Clegg said very quickly they would take part.

Will the debates dominate the whole campaign? Each debate will probably take up three days' news agenda – so it's nine days out of the campaign which will be dominated by them.
I don't know. I think we'll have to see. But the print boys are quite sulky about the whole thing. I've been surprised talking to the parties how little they are varying their timetable of battle buses and news conferences.

Are you surprised the two main parties agreed to let Nick Clegg in on all of them? Because I've been told by someone on the Liberal Democrats negotiating team that they didn't expect to be let in on all three of them and that they would have been happy with two, but the other parties didn't even mention the possibility.
I was surprised that it wasn't such an issue. As you said it wasn't basically discussed and I give credit frankly to the other parties on that. What I think happened was that separately, everybody looked at what the possibilities were and basically concluded that realistically within the bounds of possibility on the basis of number of seats contested, shares of votes, credible shares of votes, that there were only three people who could be prime minister after

the next election and everyone seemed to have reached that same conclusion, therefore there wasn't that much discussion of it.

Do you think it's a shame that the format is so rigid and there are so many rules? Would it not have been better, at least in one of them, just to plonk the three of them on the stage, have no moderator at all and let them have a dialogue with each other and the audience?
Listen, it's taken us fifty years to get here! Certainly for Gordon Brown and David Cameron, it has involved conceding quite a lot of ground or potential advantages certainly passed in the direction of Nick Clegg. Therefore, I think it's only right that there should be a bit of a softly, softly approach this time round. Secondly, as I've said, just to get it done and to get it done away from the election campaign there was a strong desire to negotiate with the broadcasters as a block. Therefore I think it's understandable that this time around people have gone for similar formats. What I think will happen is that the debates will look and feel very different. ITV, BBC and Sky have very different styles in the way they do things. I think that will come through. I think once people become more familiar with what's going on there will be developments in what goes on. The big issue that we've had this time around has been the issue of the audience. People are used to BBC *Question Time* and regional shows which basically end up pitting the audience against the panel and I do think it's a different concept this time around. You don't want them forming a panel against an angry public. So I think that's a new dynamic which we've got to explore.

You're moderating the Sky debate. Do you still get nervous about these things like that or do you take them in your stride?
Oh yeah. It certainly gets the adrenaline going. It's a big gig. You always wonder when you first open your mouth if there's going to be a dreadful croak which is going to come out. And for me personally, because it's been a Sky campaign and I've been very invested in trying to get debates going, I desperately, desperately want the debates to succeed and to be successful and useful and informative, and all those things are things which are going to be on your mind.

What kind of campaign do you thing we're going to have this time? Do you think it's going to be a very dirty campaign?
I think we're going to have a personalised campaign partly because there is big convergence between the parties in a lot of areas and almost where they are most different is in the personal contrasts of David Cameron and George Osborne, Gordon Brown and Alistair Darling. So I think there's going to be a lot of that. What I hope is going to happen is that it's going to be less gimmicky because there is a sort of yawn yawn factor now when there is another poster

launch or even another clever internet viral, or whatever, and what I hope the debates will do is just engender a culture of people and politicians actually trying to sit down and tell people how it is and what the consequences are going to be. I'm not sure that that is necessarily going to happen.

Where do you stand on paid for political advertising? If parties can buy slots in cinema why shouldn't they be able to buy slots on Sky News?
Well I think Sky has a position on this which is that we're not opposed to it, so that is where I stand. I do think that money is a big issue and if you allow a total free for all then I don't think you necessarily improve politics, particularly in a system where we've got such a strong party structure. Would the world be a better place if instead of spending 20 million pounds each party spent half a billion pounds? I just think there might be better things to do with the money overall.

You've got a problem though after the next election though whoever wins because there's going to be between probably 250 and 300 new MPs. How on earth a) will that effect what you do and b) what kind of parliament do you think it's going to be?
Well we thrive on change and actually where I think Sky has been good and where hopefully I've been good as well is actually trying to make sense of what's going on rather than going by any preconceived notions of who matters and who doesn't matter, so in that sense it's going to be a bit of free-for-all – I'm looking forward to that. I think we do need fresh blood and different types of people. And one thing that we've been doing at Sky is meeting quite a lot of the PPCs from all the parties. I do think they are different types of people who are coming into politics and that's a good thing. The era of the special advisor becoming a Cabinet minister is drawing to a close and I think that's probably a good thing. In the end I do think that all politicians would be well advised to work towards a system where Parliament and the government are slightly more separate from each other and Parliament has slightly more of a scrutinising role. I detect that a lot of the new people coming in just won't accept as many three line whips.

How many hours a week do you work when parliament is sitting?
I've not quite worked it out. I don't know, sixty? Something like that.

Whenever a big job at the BBC comes up, your name is always in the mix. I've always thought that you'd hate to work at the BBC because you wouldn't have the opportunity to do what you do at Sky.
Yes there's a lot of truth in that. I'm not at the BBC am I? I would say that there are three people, all men I regret to say, that have jobs as good as me,

in the totality of what they do. And that would be Jon Snow, David Dimbleby and Jeremy Paxman. This job is as good as that, but it obviously means that there are a lot of people who might say 'why don't you go and do that' but I'm just not really that interested.

Do you prefer reporting presenting or interviewing? At the moment you're doing all three, but which do you get the most kick out of?
Well presenting and interviewing, they go together. I like all three. To me what is good about what I do in whatever form I do it is that it's raw and it's first hand. I think there's been a slight problem, it doesn't bother me, but perhaps in people assessing me, in as much as we've tended to have this hierarchy that you know you're a reporter and then you graduate and you become a presenter and an interviewer and so its seen as a step up, whereas I've managed more in the American style to mix the two and therefore I don't really have that strong a preference. Probably the television skill I'm least good at is reading the autocue.

I've always thought it's really weird on your Sunday show when you're not there they don't actually have another one of the political team doing it. They seem to pick random people to do it. Or in fact they don't even do a proper programme they just make it into a news programme – I've never quite understood the logic of that.
Well it's always good knowing that you haven't got a great substitute.

When you married Anji Hunter did you find that you had a bit of a problem with Conservatives at that point, because they felt that maybe that was a signal that you were closer to the other side?
Not to my face. No I never had any problems. When I met Anji I think I did have an independent track record doing what I'm doing. In fact the day that all the gory details were all over the front page of the *Mail on Sunday*, I was interviewing Iain Duncan Smith, then the Tory leader and you know before we went in I said, 'you might want to see this'. And he said: 'It doesn't make any difference to me. I know you, I know what you do, and I hope it works itself out.'

Some people, and you read this a lot on blogs, think that Sky News is a New Labour dominated institution and there are other people that think it's completely right wing. The lazy answer is to say that you must be doing something right to have offended both sides...
Yes, that is the lazy answer. Or another answer is that everyone knows that New Labour was very right wing. Look I think that I would have two answers to that. One is the standard sticks and stones answer. But the other

one is when people make criticism of you, at least to entertain it. As I've tried to explain, I don't really think in party political terms personally. My view about New Labour, as I said in the book I wrote about Blair, is that so far it's been the political story of my lifetime. I've known these people all the way from before they were Cabinet ministers and before they were in Parliament all the way through to when they've become ex-Cabinet ministers. And so inevitably I've known a lot of people in that world, I've known a lot of New Labour people. Likewise, in terms of my background in public school and Oxford and all that, it's not as if Tories are an unknown species to me, or Liberals either. So I just think that you have to take it on. I think it would have been a bit different if I'd married Alastair Campbell.

Completely different. For all of us.
I think Anji has an independent record of her own and she's been out of politics since 2001.

What does she make of your book? I remember going to the launch and she said that she point blank refused to talk about the book while you were doing it. I assume she's read it.
I'm not sure she's read it cover to cover. She respects the book. I said to her right at the beginning that it might be difficult for us and I could not do it. She said 'no, I think you should do it'. A lot of the things in it she got quite cross about. She was very unimpressed when the paperback serialisation went to the *Mail on Sunday*. And I told her on the Saturday before the Sunday.

I can imagine her being unimpressed by that.
So she generally supports me in my work as I support her in her work, but people find it hard to believe, but she doesn't have much influence beyond that.

Is it an issue do you think sometimes when journalists can get too close to the political set? I don't know whether you have or not. I know some journalists have spent the night at Chequers for example…
I've spent the night outside Chequers.

You can be drawn in. Journalists are only human beings and I think you can be drawn in to something and I think that New Labour was that kind of entity. It was quite intoxicating at one stage. People did get … I'm not saying you did, but I think some journalists did get drawn in too much.
I think there is a fact that you could want to be … you get so close to people that you want to be a cheerleader for them and all that. You have to be aware of that.

That's enough about Kevin Maguire...
One of the things I've noticed as the election has got closer is that, without blowing smoke up your arse, I would exempt your site, but actually a lot of the Tory sites, or Tory leaning sites I think have become a lot less worth reading. I think Guido has been poor, Coffee House has been poor. I think ConservativeHome has become poorer than they were eighteen months or two years ago. Because clearly they have an investment in this outcome.

What did you get out of your time in America last year? To me, you did something very different in that period where you were doing mini documentaries. I thought they were absolutely first class. Did you gain an appetite to do more of that sort of thing?
Well I know people won't believe this. It wasn't my idea to go to America. It basically came from the editorial people at Sky who just said that Obama was a big story and they wanted some way of marking it. They asked me if I thought that we would have an election at the beginning of 2009 and I said no chance and so I was very happy to be asked to go there for four months and it happened to coincide with Anji being between jobs so she was able to come too. I always relish doing things which take you out of your comfort zone and which develop new skills. It's one of the reasons why I enjoy doing sport and entertainment interviews on my Sunday show. Would I like to do more of that? Yes. I think varying the pace of what you do if you have the opportunity is always exciting. But you have to remember that this is a competitive environment and you don't want to give up the day job. A special project is normally one stop from the door.

When you had that blow up interview with Gordon Brown last year, when he stomped off in a huff, what went through your mind at the time?
What you want to do when you interview someone, particularly politicians, is to make a connection. Because politicians are interviewed all the time and the last thing you want to see is them walking out with their advisors and saying 'that went well... there was nothing in it'. What you're trying to do is to make a connection which involves pushing them away from the line to take at a certain time and getting under their skin and within that you have your own style. What I want to do is to ask them a question that makes them think and to give me a reply that isn't premeditated. Therefore, with Gordon you could see I'd made a connection and so I was pleased by that. When he said I'd become a campaigner I was also quite interested in that as well but there is a certain kind of way in which journalists are conniving little bastards. If you're interviewing someone and they're making a fool of themselves, it's not your job to stop them. If they're given the opportunity to express themselves or they're losing their temper, again, it's probably not

good if you lose your temper as well. It's best to keep them calm. In that sense, I just felt that it was an interesting interview. I was sure that there was some outside thing not to do with me but to do with the fact that this was the morning after *The Sun* had switched its allegiance. If I get a response from someone, I don't blame them for it necessarily.

Did you think 'we're never going to get an interview with him again'?
No. I didn't think that. I didn't think he'd think that either. The only person who won't do interviews with me is Prescott. But in Prescott's case it seems to be more to do with the fact that we broke the story of the punch. I still think that a deputy prime minister shouldn't go around belting the electorate. It still seems to annoy him.

Who do you find the most difficult to interview?
The most difficult class to interview are people who don't want to engage. People who just basically turn up and say 'I've got my message I want to get out'. Consistently the most difficult class of people to interview are actors, because in their own right a lot of actors don't actually think a great deal for themselves. They've waited for someone to write the script.

When there's been some awful disaster or awful tragedy, it's actually not that difficult to interview people. Bizarrely, people do want to talk about it. I hope I'm a professional interviewer, I don't find it extraordinarily hard to interview people. Just occasionally you might be doing an interview with someone and you just realise that you're basically on completely different planets, that they are worried about their next meal, the roof over their head or they don't really know who Gordon Brown is.

What's the worst moment you can remember live on screen when something went wrong or someone said something that...
I love live television and I think that when things go wrong, the autocue goes down, the lights go out all of that pumps the adrenaline. It's never a good moment when you get someone's name wrong, or you say 'Mr Johnson' and he says 'no, actually it's Robinson' or when you're interviewing someone and you've just got to the key question, so you say to her 'are you going to resign' and they give you an answer but you don't hear it because someone says in your ear 'one minute to go Adam' and then you have to recover from that.

One disaster was interviewing Sarah Myles and asking her if her memoirs were true and she started crying. This was a moment where you felt that perhaps this has not been a triumph.

Quickfire

What book are you reading at the moment?
Game Change – about the American 2008 campaign.

Your favourite view?
Probably somewhere in north-west Norfolk, on Brancaster beach or something like that.

Favourite food?
Peanut Butter.

Favourite holiday destination?
I want to go back to Sicily.

Best friend in journalism?
This is a chance to offend millions of people. Probably Michael Brunson.

What is the music that makes you dance?
I'm not a great dancer. Usually those things that it's compulsory to dance, like Scottish reels. Agadoo, I've always liked Agadoo.

Last film you cried at?
I know people think it's terrible, but the *Burning Issue,* the Sandra Bullock film, has its moments.

Ever thrown a Nokia?
Yes, by accident. I was doing a 'quick draw' on my phone out of my pocket and sent it flying. So yeah. I've gone through a few Nokias in my time, but more in sorrow than in anger.

Favourite interviewer?
I do think Melvyn Bragg is a very good interviewer.

Journalistic hero?
Sam Donaldson.

Favourite hate figure?
There's a classics don called Mary Beard. I think she's the worst of kind of modern liberal. Or you could widen it to the London Review of Books.

And finally, guilty pleasure?
Strip cartoons.

Andrew Neil

Current position: Presenter of BBC's *Daily Politics*

Born: 21 May 1949

Education: Educated at Paisley Grammar School and the University of Glasgow, from where he graduated with an MA (Hons) in Political Economy and Political Science.

Career overview: After working for the Conservative Party for a short while, he joined *The Economist*. Neil was the editor of the *Sunday Times* from 1983 until 1994 and in 1988 also became founding chairman of Sky TV. He eventually parted company with Newscorp executive Rupert Murdoch and became a writer for the *Daily Mail* and later editor-in-chief of the Barclay brothers' Press Holdings group of newspapers.

Some career highlights: Creating Sky TV, bringing *The Simpsons* to UK television and becoming editor of the *Sunday Times*.

Interesting facts: During his time studying for his MA in political economy and political science, he was tutored by Vince Cable. *Private Eye* nicknamed him 'Brillo' after his wiry hair, which is perceived to bear resemblance to a form of kitchen scouring pad.

Date of interview: May 2010
Extended version
Venue: The Spectator office, Westminster
Total Politics Issue 24, June 2010

When we first started publishing Total Politics, *back in July 2008, Andrew Neil declined an interview with us. I couldn't blame him. We were a brand new magazine and he probably couldn't see what was in it for him. In early 2010 I decided to ask again. Andrew replied saying how much he enjoyed my interviews and said he'd love to do one.*

I have always found Andrew Neil to be a delight to deal with. I've been interviewed by him on both 5 Live and the Daily Politics *and have found him to be a courteous and knowledgeable interviewer. He has a transparent love of politics and an inquisitive nature which means you always learn something from his interviews. He is also unfailingly pleasant and he remembers you, even if he hasn't encountered you for a couple of years.*

I met Andrew on the Monday after the general election. In many ways it was the worst possible time to interview him as were both glued to the TV screen trying to keep up with developments. In fact, Gordon Brown announced his resignation just as we finished.

I loved the fact that in the interview Andrew made it clear he was desperate to present the BBC's election night coverage next time. If truth be known I had expected him to give a less categoric answer. He would be brilliant at it but I really wonder if the BBC head honchos really 'get' Andrew Neil in the way that his audience so clearly does.

I read on Wikipedia that you were tutored by Vince Cable at university.
Only briefly. In my final year at university when I was doing political economy and political science at the University of Glasgow. Vince arrived from Oxford to do his PHD at the department of political economy and he did handle some of the tutorials that I had to go to.

Does that explain your aggressive nature at interviewing him? Because you're the only interviewer that's ever actually properly questioned him. Everyone else regards him as a God.
He wasn't the most exciting of tutors I do have to admit that. He was very Labour in those days. Those were the days when he went on to become a Labour councillor in Glasgow. I thought it was time, since the Liberals were playing for the big time, to treat them seriously and treat them the way we do everybody else. And no more so than Vince Cable who so often had been treated by the media not as a politician seeking power but as a pundit. No one ever asked Vince 'why are you arguing that?' They always said 'what do you think of that?' We treated him like one of us, we treated him like a journalist and that helped his stature to grow. So I decided it was time to treat him as a politician seeking power like any other and not as an impartial pundit. I think all of the media has been culpable in treating him too much like an impartial pundit. When he's treated in the same way as we would treat Alistair Darling or George Osborne I do think you see a different Vince Cable.

How would you characterise your interviewing style?
Some have said it's aggressive. I don't think it's aggressive so much as desperately trying to get them to answer the question. The questions I ask are quite straightforward and they're not long winded and most of them can be answered by yes or no. Sometimes people criticise me for being rude or interrupting too much.

When you have a particular politician on the programme and you've interviewed them before, do you automatically change your interviewing style because you know what you're going to get from that politician?

Yes. You try to cut them off at the pass. By now you know what the stock answers are going to be to difficult questions so you try to frame the question in a way that allows for that. I have to say it still doesn't result in getting very clear answers. It's really frustrating to try and get clear answers from politicians. I came close to losing it with Douglas Alexander. The idea that Peter Hain and Ed Balls were not sending a massive neon sign saying 'look, if you can beat a Tory by voting Lib Dem do that'. For him to come on to the programme and deny they were saying that I think was, for me, a low point of honesty in the campaign.

Are there any points – I mean particularly in an interview like that – where because you're on the BBC you feel you have to slightly pull your punches, are there guidelines of interviewing that you think you have to adhere to?
I think you cannot – unless it is so demonstrably true – say 'why are you lying to me?' I think that's probably unacceptable for the BBC. In the Alexander case, by the technical letter of the law, of what they had said, in a sense he was right. But we all knew, in a grown-up world what they were really saying.

And I think that's probably right. I think to accuse someone of lying is a pretty big step. But I have no doubt that Mr Alexander knew that day he was being less than honest with me, which is not the important thing, but he was being less than honest with the viewers. Viewers were as angry as I was with him.

You've got the best of both worlds as far as I can see with interviewing. You've got *Straight Talk* [update: the BBC cancelled Straight Talk a few months after this interview] which is about the only programme now on television where somebody comes in for a question for more than ten minutes, but what do you think the reason is why we don't have programmes like *Weekend World* or *On the Record*, the Sunday lunchtime programmes where one politician would come under inquisition for up to forty-five minutes sometimes? Is it because TV people think viewers now have the attention span of a flea?
Correct. I think it is. It baffles me why *Straight Talk* isn't run on BBC 2 rather than just on the News Channel. We think we're now dealing with the MTV generation, the generation that's been brought up on the two and a half minute pop video. And they don't think we have the attention to stick with anything, so everything on TV has to have pace and constant movement and constant changes. And of course that's true if you're talking about something where you want to get a mega-audience. But if you want something that gets a decent audience and a serious discourse I still think there's an audience for that. And there are so many platforms that the BBC has now. And it's cheap television too.

Even with your fee.

Haha. Even with my fee it's still pretty cheap television. I just think they should do more of it now. They've got four channels, four television channels that you can get through television and Sky. They've got the iPlayer and online. I think we should do more of it. I saw the general director recently saying that we had lost that long form interview and I felt like emailing him and saying 'have you not seen *Straight Talk*?' And the other one, *Hard Talk* where you get that long form interview. And it's interesting, on American television they still have that. They have the long form interview on the *Meet the Press* programme on a Sunday morning, and of course the *Charlie Rose Show* on PBS which is on every night and it's very like *Straight Talk*. There's just two people in the studio and a black curtain background. It runs on PBS every night.

I used to do the hour-long interview when I was doing 18 Doughty Street. People absolutely loved it. Which of the three programmes do you get most out of?
I enjoy *This Week*. It's fun. *This Week* has to be different because we come off the back of the network news and then an hour of *Question Time*, which therefore means we've had an hour and a half of traditional mainstream current affairs. John Lloyd from the *Financial Times* complains that *This Week* is too cheeky and irreverent and gets politicians to do silly things. But after ninety minutes of current affairs you can't then give people another hour of mainstream current affairs. You have to think of a different way of doing it and that's what we've tried to do. *The Daily Politics* is the one that I enjoy most because it's straightforward interviewing, it's straightforward politics. We've imported some of the irreverence and humour from *This Week* into *The Daily Politics* and that's just happened over time.

Do you think that sometimes on *This Week*, the production team have their meeting and think how can we top having Timmy Mallett on?
I think sometimes, when you're trying to get different names onto a show, like a different kind of person who aren't the mainstream politicians then sometimes you just get the wrong person. She didn't appear in the end, but I don't think Lady Sovereign was our finest hour.

I went to bed five minutes before she was due to be on, so I missed that.
Well I wished I'd gone to bed. Actually it turned out OK in the end, I forget what we were talking about but we had a much more sensible conversation with me, Diane and Michael than we would have if Lady Sovereign was there.

Why would anyone be interested in Timmy Mallett, Jade Goody or whatever they think about anything?

We have quite a younger audience compared to most political shows and we use that kind of celebrity name really just to keep you through to the end. Not you, because you're already gone!

Have you ever gone into the office and they've said 'Guess who we've got this week?' and you've just said, 'That's gone too far'?
I've come close. And there's been a couple of times when I've said I really don't want to talk to that person, as I don't care. The 'Lady Sovereign slot' is the final five minutes of the show and its twenty past twelve by then. We have a lot of students who switch on then after coming back from the pub. When you push the boat out you don't always get it right. Sometimes we do, sometimes we don't.

Would you say that your time as editor of the *Sunday Times* was your happiest time in journalism?
No, I would say that now is my happiest time.

Really? Joking aside you do actually always seem to be revelling in whatever you're doing at the moment, but it must have been fantastic to have been editor of the *Sunday Times* at that time.
Being editor of the *Sunday Times* for eleven years in the 1980s with the politics as it was then, very different from today, and with Wapping to do as well, was huge. I wouldn't have missed a minute of it. It was fantastic. We were doing things I think that really mattered. I'm very proud of what we achieved with the *Sunday Times* and what it stood for in those days, but it quite often wasn't enjoyable because there was so much stress. For thirteen months I had two bodyguards with me wherever I went and a special forces trained driver. Also I had [Rupert] Murdoch in my life. Although overall Murdoch and I got on pretty well and there were very few times when we had harsh words he was always an omnipresent figure in your life. When the phone rang, was it him? And if you had a big decision to take, you had to ask yourself what would Rupert do? Second guessing Rupert is still the biggest industry in News International. The joy of that is that someone like that can make you editor of the *Sunday Times* or ask you to go and start Sky television. But it's also a huge presence in your life, which it's not healthy to have for too long and I had it for eleven years. I should have gone after ten actually. We parted on good terms, though. The falling out came after my book came out and he hasn't spoken to me since. I just wrote how I saw all the plus sides and the warts as well.

Being editor of the *Sunday Times* now I imagine is not such an interesting job.
Well you're still running the flagship Sunday newspaper. You are running the paper that sells more than any other, than I think the next three combined.

But is it as relevant?
Is the press as a whole as relevant? It doesn't have quite the same impact. I think the *Sunday Times* is more accepted now across a wider spectrum because the ideological divisions have gone and you don't need to stand, take a tough stance on issues which anger people who don't share your views. I mean the *Sunday Times* when I ran it… We were pretty divisive; we took tough positions on cruise missiles, on reforming the British economy, on taking on the miners.

That's kind of what I meant, because now I couldn't tell you what the *Sunday Times* stands for in the same way that I could when you edited it.
Look, every editor's different and I had very strong views about things in those days, about what needed to be done. But secondly the issues were much starker. I mean we've just had an election where we've been arguing about £6bn in a £1.5trn economy. You know, when I was doing it, when I was editor we were arguing about the future of the country, about the cold war, about the deployment of cruise missiles, about whether we were going to reverse our decline, about whether we were going to be a market economy or a wholly state-supported economy. These were huge issues. They're not the same. Partly because on most of these battles we seem to have won.

And to people going into journalism now, again it's very different to going in in the 1980s. Is it a career that you would really recommend people to go into now?
I would recommend it but it's very hit and miss and needs a lot of luck.

Because it still seems to be based on who you know.
I think it's a combination of who you know and as I say, luck. And being in the right place at the right time. It's not a profession. It's not like being a doctor or a lawyer or an engineer. There's not a clear career path. It's much more like being a plumber. It's much more a trade or a craft. Unlike being a plumber it doesn't' have a city and guilds. It does depend on being in the right place at the right time and in getting the breaks. I had two huge breaks in my career which were just luck. One was that Alastair Burnet was editor of *The Economist* when I applied to join. *The Economist* was a complete Oxbridge fiefdom but Alastair took a shine to me because we were from the same part of Scotland and we really hit it off. I think if it had been anybody else I wouldn't have been offered the job. It's as simple as that.

And on such decisions your whole life depends.
And the second was Murdoch was looking for a new editor and a couple of people including Irwin Stelzer and, funnily enough, Peter Walker as well.

Alastair Burnet pressed on him that I should be the new editor. Now, never mind that I'd never edited a paper before, I'd never worked on a national newspaper before. My life before that had been ten years at *The Economist*. And I was just lucky that Murdoch was the kind of person who would take a risk. And when we met we hit it off. He was looking for a new way of doing things. He was looking for someone who was more in tune with the zeitgeist of the politics, that was moving that way, getting rid of the old collectivist 1970s attitude that dominated then, and he took a risk. Frankly if I had been him I wouldn't have taken the risk.

Do you think the BBC took a risk with you?
No, I don't think the BBC has taken a risk at all. I think the BBC has been very careful to use me in an episodic and cumulative way.

I suppose by that I mean you are quite opinionated, you have your own opinions, you're not frightened to voice them on the programmes, which most other political interviewers do not do.
Yes, I had a history. Most BBC presenters have done nothing but the BBC. And they have no hinterland. They all have strong views of their own but quite rightly they keep them quiet because that's what we should do. I had a history before the BBC and people know what my views are on a number of issues.

But it's quite rare that they take on people who've got a history.
I think they found it advantageous to take on someone who is outside the normal BBC culture and they also know that wherever my own views are it doesn't matter whether you're Labour, Liberal or Conservative I don't take any prisoners. And the biggest rows we've had has been with interviewing Conservative politicians who think they've been treated unfairly. So I'm quite comfortable and I think the BBC is pretty comfortable too that we're an equal opportunities kicker.

You were there at the start of Sky News, what effect do you think Sky has had on the BBC and BBC journalism?
The first thing Sky proved, which no one believed at the time was that there was a market for 24-hour news. People didn't think it would work in Britain and I think we showed it did work and the politicians liked it and the other journalists liked it as well. It gave Sky an entreé into political elite which hadn't really wanted Sky to exist in the first place. I think if Sky News was to close down now there'd be an outcry among the politicians and the political elite. And the BBC then had to follow suit. Twenty-four hour news is here to stay.

Do you think though that it's been a wholly good thing because you could argue that it has led to, or at least it's contributed to the rise in spin?
Well the real rise of spin came with Mandelson and Campbell in the mid-90s and I don't think that had anything to do with 24-hour news. That was in their DNA and they knew above all that New Labour had to be a marketing message. I don't think that had anything to do with 24-hour news. It's the bear that needs to be fed. Feed the bear, feed the bear. Though sometimes I don't understand why politicians do it. Why don't they just step back? Why do they keep on having to feed it all the time? I don't understand why they do that.

Do you ever wonder why politicians just take it in interviews when you or John Humphrys or Paxman are having a real go at them? They never hit back do they?
No. I do sometimes wonder. I try not to do this but if you ask them a question and they've barely got two words out before you've interrupted them I sometimes wonder why they're not tougher on that. Cameron did it within the month of becoming Conservative leader and then he seemed to drop it.

The worst thing you can do to an interviewer is to say 'explain that, what do you mean by that?' Because they're not expecting it and yet politicians never do it.
If you're an important minister or chancellor or prime minister sometimes I'm surprised that they don't say, well, do you want to argue with me? Or do your viewers want to understand where I'm coming from, why I'm doing this? They don't have to agree with it but I just want them to understand. Or do you just want to have an argument with me? Is this a conversation or is it a question and answer? What's more important, your questions or my answers? And I think sometimes they lack confidence, partly because when we are interrupting and hectoring, having a go at them, they're on the back foot and they're so worried about their own position and not saying something wrong that they forget these rather simple ways of getting out of a sticky situation.

Do you think OFCOM rules should be relaxed and we should have Fox News or a left-wing version of Fox News in this country because at the moment you can do it on the internet but you can't do it on mainstream television. Although Fox News is allowed because it's on the Sky television.
Yes it is.

I've always wondered why it says it fair and balanced when we all know it isn't balanced.
What makes it so entertaining is that it's unfair and unbalanced.

If I got the money together now to launch British Fox News they wouldn't allow it would they?

No, they wouldn't. You'd have more chance of doing a *Guardian* Fox News. That would be probably be regarded as more acceptable.

What about *Channel 4 News*?

This is what possibly I had in mind. Though I'm a great fan of *Channel 4 News*. I love it and I'll always watch it and I know where it's coming from and I don't care because I can allow for that and it still has in depth reporting and form reporting and Jon Snow just presides over it magnificently. I'm not sure I would want that, though I can see there's a market. We are a less ideological country than America and I think people may not want [it]... And I think one of the problems in America is that it pretends to be conversations of like-minded people taking to themselves in these shows. All I can say is that it may, I'm not sure it would be against the interests of the BBC for that to happen. Because the one thing that the BBC would have to be is a purely impartial non-partisan news. And I think in times of national crisis, of really important stories, most people would rather hear the news from someone who's at least attempting to be impartial and not partisan, and doesn't have an axe to grind than to turn to those journalists who have axes to grind all the time. And in a sense it would give the BBC even more purpose because as a national public service broadcaster it could not go down this road. It could not be a *Channel 4 News* and it could not be a Fox News. So it could help to differentiate the BBC.

How on earth do you fit in all the things that you do and I'm sure you get asked this. You do all the TV stuff, you have *The Spectator*, PFD, God knows what else. You must be the most brilliant time manager in history.

Brilliant may be too strong a word but I'm good at time management and I run my own diary. I tell my PA what's in my diary not the other way round. I book all the appointments myself and I carve it out and I've got good at it over time.

It's a good job being your PA then...

Well, actually, don't mock it, it is. Compared to working for a Chief Executive of a big company it is. Because I do all my own letters.

You are very sensible. I think whenever I've emailed you, you've answered it within about three minutes. Peter Mandelson's the same.

Is that right? I haven't got Peter Mandelson's email address. If I had I would try it out. I put together a portfolio of work after leaving the *Sunday Times* in 1995 so I've got used to doing it over fifteen years. I do it myself and the other thing is I'm single. I haven't got a family to worry about, I haven't got a family to give quality time to, I haven't got a wife who's sitting at home nursing her ire saying 'where is he, he's not home, yet again?'

Do you regret that?

Yes I do regret it. But you know you can't have everything, and one of the minuses is not having children and not having had a wife. The plus is that I'm in control of my diary and all the time is for me. It's quite a selfish existence.

Did you actually make a decision to live that way?

No, it just happened. If this had been even ten, certainly fifteen years ago I'd have said I would have got married and had a family life but that's just how it is. I didn't set out not to have a family. It's just the way it's been and that's why I've always taken more interest in my godchildren because if you haven't got children and you are very fond of kids. I get on well with kids. I'm invariably the one that the baby gets passed to quieten it down. This weekend I'm off to Dubai for a board meeting and some other meetings with a magazine company in Dubai. If I was a family man that would be more a difficult thing to do. I think my partner would be saying 'Come on, do you have to go to Dubai now? We've not seen you for four weeks' whereas the only person that cares is my housekeeper and she's pretty glad to see the back of me. Sadly the dog doesn't get to see me at all because he's in France.

What have you brought to *The Spectator*?

I think we've brought it into the twenty-first century for a start. It's now a well-run business and it is a proper business. I inherited something that was already on the way to becoming a better business because Conrad Black had begun to do that and we built that process. It's now an independent stand alone company and of course we share the same owners as *The Telegraph* but this is a magazine company now in its own right which is looking to grow and is a magazine that makes profits and that protects our independence. I learnt a long while ago at *The Economist*, from Alastair Burnet, that if you make money you are independent. And I think with Fraser [Nelson] we've modernised it and made it very much part of the centre right debate.

Can you say what happened with Matthew D'Ancona?

No. I mean Matthew was doing a lot of other things and had a lot of other things to do and you know editors are like football managers. Here today, gone tomorrow. As a former editor myself I know what it's like.

Do you? Talking about the election, do you think it was a good thing the fact that the whole campaign was dominated by the debates?

In retrospect, no. Because the debates turned out not to have the seminal influence we thought they had and one of the surprises – I know you're just as surprised as me – the one thing that made me doubt the BBC, well it wasn't the BBC, but the broadcaster's exit poll on the night was the number of seats they gave the Lib Dems. It just didn't gel.

You didn't say you would streak down Whitehall…
I think they didn't have quite the… I mean the whole campaign built up to them, and then came down from them, build up to the next then down, up, down. And sometimes the campaign went dead other than for the debates.

But they are here to stay. How do you think they should be reformed for next time?
They have to free them up more. They've got to be freer. I mean like the *Daily Politics* afternoon debates we had. They were probably too free for a prime ministerial debate but something in between how we did it with a minimum rules and the overruled ones of the prime ministerial debates. I think the anchorman has to have a role. Not to assert himself or herself too much into it but I think that they have to have more power to do a follow-up a question, or to ask for clarification or say 'I'm sorry Mrs Smith didn't ask about that, she asked about this, could you answer the question?' And then they would be fine.

Do you think it would be better if they were all much earlier in the campaign so the last bit could concentrate on all the other things?
Well I think there should be a look at that to see whether they dominated. It may be a five, ten day period in the run-up to the election period where it's not the debates. But we got it wrong. We thought the debates were – by 'we' I mean all the journalists – we thought the debates were the defining events and it turned out not be. And the one thing we didn't get, you could see that Clegg was being deflated by the time we got to polling day but we didn't know it had gone flat. We didn't know it had been completely deflated. We could see them falling from 27 or 28 per cent. And then of course you have this liberal mantra which says they always do a couple of percentage points better than the polls, but actually it turned out that won't happen again. What none of us saw, in a way as no one saw with Kinnock in '92, was this 24-, 36-hour move away altogether from it. The problem for the Conservatives, which I don't know quite what the answer is, was we all said all along that it's the Clegg bounce that's going to make it very difficult for the Conservatives to get an overall majority, but in the end there was no Clegg bounce and they still couldn't get an overall majority, and I don't quite know the answer to that.

Do you think the minor parties got too much prominence in this election? Every day had some sort of nutter party on your programme?
We certainly had an eclectic mix. The head of the Libertarian Party had to resign after I interviewed him, though I think he's been reinstated by his six members or whatever he has. Look we give them three or four minutes. We had an hour long show every day and there was room for that. The Scottish and Welsh Nationalists feel very aggrieved that they weren't in the national debates but frankly, how could you accommodate them in the national debates? Mr Salmond was not standing for prime minister and they had their own debates for Scotland and Wales. The intriguing thing for me was that on three occasions the BNP refused to be interviewed by me.

Is that right?
I chaired the London debate for BBC London and they pulled out of that. Then we had them as part of our minor parties debates. We had the BNP down to do an interview with me and they pulled out of that and then we asked them again and they said they'd do it as long as it's not me. The BBC quite rightly said, you don't get to choose who interviews you and they pulled out of that. It's interesting, something happened in the BNP. They used to be desperate to get on television and indeed said that we were ignoring them and keeping them off and then they decided that television wasn't good for them. Didn't do them much good though, since they've lost everything.

It was a terrible campaign for them. I interviewed Nick Griffin on LBC and asked him if his position as leader was now in danger. 'Oh no, I don't think so,' he said.
Well they lost every councillor in Barking.

Yeah, I was astonished. I thought they would put on councillors there.
It shows you that even though immigration is an issue it's just that people want to have a moderate discussion about it.

Well the other thing is, and this story hasn't been told yet, Labour threw so much money at Dagenham and Barking, not in terms of political campaigning, in terms of the council who have done huge amounts there. There's a story to be written there.
Well, maybe Labour got something right during the election campaign.

Maybe it was worth it
Exactly.

I haven't seen the BBC coverage because I was presenting LBC's programme but there's been a lot of comment about your boat…
Well, it wasn't my boat.

You know what I mean.
I wish it was my boat.

Did it work?
I think it worked. David was anchoring the television centre coverage from ten at night to at least six in the morning, so you needed a bit of light and shade. The people who've criticised this have mainly been newspapers that have an anti-BBC agenda in the first place, so any excuse to give them a kicking. Also, the same newspapers who complained we had some celebrities on the boat are the papers who live by celebrities. The *Daily Mail* has endless celebrities every day. It was quite an eclectic mix that we had.

Even I was invited…
I know you were, and you didn't turn up!

I couldn't! I was presenting LBC's election night programme! I suppose the point is this: do we need to hear Bruce Forsyth's thoughts on politics during election night?
First of all you need a break. Every media that's on for that length of time, or whether it's a newspaper with lots of sections needs light and shade. It cannot all just be relentless 'here's another result'. The people on television themselves need a bit of a break, just even three or four minutes, because the BBC doesn't have commercial breaks, just to draw breath and say 'right while Andrew is interviewing Bruce Forsyth or whoever, what are we doing next? What's going on here?' Of course the papers all concentrated on Bruce Forsyth and Joan Collins and so on. Let's not forget that on the night we had the first interview with Alastair Campbell as well. We had Simon Schama and David Starkey, I interviewed Andrew Rawnsley, the editor of the *Financial Times* Lionel Barber, Will Hutton on the situation in the markets and at ten past five Lord Ashcroft, so it's interesting the papers have done 'oh we don't want to hear from all these celebrity non-entities and so on'. The fact is we had an enormous mix of people.

Would you like to be the main presenter on the BBC's election night coverage next time?
Absolutely!

Well that's categoric. I thought you might duck that one.
Sure. I mean I'd love to do it. I don't think it's going to happen but I'd love that. You know the first time I did television was as Alastair Burnet's researcher in February 1974 election which he anchored. If you see the opening shot, because they did aerial shot when Alastair comes out, you see a young fresh-faced lad sitting a few feet sunken behind him and that was me. My job was to write little notes and pass up to him about Newcastle Central's coming up, the Labour candidate's called Pickup and he's a lorry driver. I always liked the way Alastair did that. And yeah, I'd always love to do that but I feel that there are many more ahead of me.

I would have thought there were only a couple – Huw Edwards and Paxman. They are the only serious ones. Do you care what politicians think of you. In fact do you care what anyone thinks of you?
I don't know what politicians think of me because they never say, and if you have had as much bad publicity as I've had from the newspapers then life wouldn't be worth living if you cared what they thought, but in some sense you care. You know sometimes it can be annoying or even hurtful. You can't dwell on it too much. There's no point. It used to matter a lot more but it would be false to say that it's now just water off a duck's back, but if you have the kind of profile I have you just have to take it.

Producers at the BBC tell me about the huge amount of preparation you do for your programmes. How much do you actually do to get on top of a subject, particularly on *Straight Talk*? What's the process for that?
Rod Shepherd and Amy, his assistant, produce fantastic briefs. I then work through them and whittle them down and add in things. In a sense my whole life is a research project. I am across nearly all the major issues and I do a lot of research for myself. I make my own folders, I make endless notes and keep the folders up to date. I just genuinely absorb information myself and so I try to be as well prepared as possible and then on top of that I have the brightest people on the BBC preparing their notes and their background for me as well and if I take what I've done and then add in what they've done when I go to do a major interview I'm pretty well informed. I see quite a lot of interviewers struggling when they deal with economics, and economics is the lifeblood of politics, no more so than now. It was really a sensible decision of mine to do political economy at university. It really was. Particularly at Glasgow which has such a wonderful economics department that really set me up. It gave me a competitive advantage over nearly everybody else. To have an economic background, to be economically literate just gives you confidence. Even interviewing the Chancellor you know that obviously he sees the secret papers and so on but there's nothing he can tell you that can baffle you.

Why do you cycle around Westminster?

As a way for getting some exercise because I have a really busy life and it's sometimes quite hard to get exercise. It's a way of getting from A to B and getting exercise at the same time, and it clears the head and I quite enjoy it.

Does your nickname of 'Brillo' annoy you?

It's in with the woodwork now. It's just, to complain about that, what was it that Enoch Powell said? It would be like a sailor who complains about the sea.

How much do you hate *Private Eye*?

I don't hate *Private Eye*.

They do seem to have a thing about you don't they?

Yeah but that's a bit… I mean I get on very well with Ian Hislop. They always think there's bad blood between us so they put me with Paul Merton but there's no bad blood. Last time I was on his team, not Paul Merton's. *Private Eye* is strange. I used to read it religiously when I was at the *Sunday Times*, now I just see it every now and then.

It's a bit like a paper blog now

Sometimes when you are in it you think 'oh I wish they hadn't said that' and then you're not in it and you think 'oh, don't I matter anymore?' The one thing that they get completely wrong is the picture in *Private Eye* of me and 'Pamela Bordes'. Except it's not Miss Bordes.

Isn't it?

It never has been Miss Bordes. That was a picture of a woman from New York that I was going out with in 1995. She worked at Fox and she is an Afro-American. She's not Asian, she's not Indian, she's not British. She's an Afro-American. The picture was taken as we came off the beach in Barbados by Terry O'Neill and it's been presented now as if a) it's Miss Bordes and b) that we were in some kind of nightclub and I'm there in this stupid shirt in a night club. It was a beach we'd come off hence the baseball cap and the beachwear. And this woman, this lovely, lovely – I've not seen or heard from her for fifteen years – she's no idea she's the most famous face in *Private Eye*. But it's not Miss Bordes. Anyone slightly looking at her would see these are the features of an Afro-Caribbean lady, but sometimes these public schoolboys are not very good.

Quickfire

Favourite Book

The Glory and the Dream. A Narrative History of America 1932-1972, by William Manchester.

Favourite view?

Anywhere on Loch Fyne.

Best friend in politics

The late Peter Walker.

Political hate figure?

Too many to mention.

Most memorable quotation?

'There goes another elegant theory mugged by a vicious gang of facts.'

Favourite holiday destination?

The Cote d'azur.

What makes you cry?

Just about everything these days.

Which period in history would you most like to have lived through?

The Roaring Twenties.

Alastair Campbell

Party affiliation: Labour

Current position: Journalist and broadcaster

Born: 25 May 1957

Education: Educated at the City of Leicester School and Gonville and Caius College, Cambridge, where he studied modern languages, French and German.

Family status: Married with three children.

Career overview: After starting his career as a sports reporter on the *Tavistock Times*, he moved to the London office of the *Daily Mirror*, where he later became political editor. He then became political editor of *Today*, which he later left to become a spokesman for Tony Blair. He moved into government in May 1997 and later resigned from his position in August 2003.

Career highlights: Becoming Press Secretary and later Director of Communications and Strategy to the Prime Minister of the United Kingdom at the time, Tony Blair.

Interesting fact: It has been suggested that the character of Malcolm Tucker in the BBC's *The Thick Of It* is based on his reputation for having a short fuse and tendency for using very strong language.

Date of interview: May 2010
Extended version
Venue: Random House publishers, Pimlico
Total Politics Issue 25, July 2010

Of all the people I have interviewed for Total Politics, *Alastair Campbell was the one I was most pleased to have landed, mainly because he had been avoiding my invitations for eighteen months. Before the interview I had never met him, but we had struck up a rather bizarre 'friendship' via Facebook and Twitter.*

Back in 2008 he had contacted me to ask my advice on blogging, as he wanted to set up his own blog site. 'Everyone tells me you're the one who knows most about blogging,' he wrote. Flattery gets him everywhere. And so it was that we emailed, Facebooked and tweeted each other over a number of months. Every now and then I'd float the idea of an interview but he'd sidestep in the way that only professional spin doctors can manage. The closest I got to actually meeting him was when I was in the middle of a Radio 4 interview on College Green the day after the election. He walked past and winked – very disconcerting when you're addressing the nation.

But when his diaries came out I seized my opportunity. We met in a rather austere meeting room at his publishers. I like to do my interviews in more relaxed surroundings as people tend to open up more, but in the end it didn't seem to matter.

I still remain fascinated by Alastair's 'mind' issues. How was it that he managed to cope with the rigours of a decade working for Tony Blair without cracking up completely, given his history? He's done more than anyone to address the issue of mental health in politics and deserves full credit for that.

He still remains a bit of an enigma. He's hated by so many people, but in reality he can charm the birds off the trees. There is a vulnerability about him which is somehow indefinable yet completely obvious. This will sound a bizarre thing to say but at a couple of points in this interview, what he said made my eyes moisten. That may say more about my own vulnerability than his.

But you sense that there is a profound sense of unfulfillment within him. He's not 'in the arena' any longer. That was why he went back to help Gordon Brown – he missed being at the centre of things. But the question is: what now for Alastair Campbell?

You've just published the first volume of your diaries, but about a quarter of this book has already appeared, hasn't it?
No. Seventy-five per cent is new.

So a quarter isn't. When did you start writing your diary?
I've always done a diary, I started when I was a kid when my dad was in hospital and I used to write him daily digests. As Tony was preparing to leave I was getting so inundated with ideas, other people's ideas, about how I might say something, do something about it and I just thought sod it, I'll do it. I'll give my own version based on the diaries but it would be just be a single volume which was just extracts. Obviously a lot of focus has been put on the fact that I took out stuff that people thought might be damaging to Gordon but actually what I was trying to do was do a book about Tony. It's very much the key episodes for Tony really. So that was what *The Blair Years* was largely about, and then this just follows on from it.

But how unexpurgated is it because presumably you can only ever publish a fraction of the material that you've got.
It's pretty much unexpurgated because I've kept out a lot of stuff that people would not be remotely interested in. You know, how your kids are doing at school and holidays. Some judgements you had to make legally. But by and large in terms of the key moments and the big stuff,

it's unexpurgated. Bear in mind most days I didn't have more than ten, fifteen, twenty minutes to write. So where some days are a couple of sentences, that's all I did. Other days where it's ream and reams and reams, that's what I did.

How difficult do you find the judgement about leaving stuff in that you know is actually quite hurtful to someone?
I did think a lot about that. And some stuff, where I felt… you know, I did make a lot of judgements in *The Blair Years* and I veered towards leaving out. This time I probably veered towards leaving in. Partly because we're talking about a long, relatively long time ago. Also to be absolutely honest every single one of us who's a big player as it were within the New Labour, it's not as if we're not used to people saying part true critical things. Now I suppose the difference is that it's us saying it. I sometimes left things out if they were in the mouth of others and I felt actually it was unfair to them. But when I say unexpurgated, it's 'unexpurgated'. There's nothing there I've taken out. Sometimes taste, sometimes law, you know, libel sometimes just because you think it's too harsh or it's something that is so rooted in that moment that you think it's unfair, either unfair on the person saying it or about the person about whom it's said.

And who do you think will feel most uncomfortable reading them?
I don't know. I think of all of us. When *The Blair Years* came out Jonathan Powell came up with this really great line. He said, 'well no one can say this is a self-serving memoir because you come across as a complete lunatic.' So I think all of us at points will think ooh, maybe I would have rather not have seen that in print.

How can you go on about change when you've been in power for thirteen years and Gordon Brown as Prime Minister then brings Mandelson back, brings you back and one or two others. It completely goes against that message doesn't it?
I can see that. I think the change, from Gordon's perspective was that he had to represent both continuity and change. I felt he could do both. Continuity is a good thing, it gives him experience, it gives him the record, it gives him a sense of he knows what he's for and what he's on about. I think change was about the way the world had changed and the change challenges. If you were talking about the economy, or public services or foreign policy or the constitution or climate change the challenges had changed and that was what would give you the policy agenda going forward.

But wasn't his problem right from the start that there was no plan? You just kept waiting for this vision and it never really came. He had thirteen years to

decide what to do, for goodness sake! This was illustrated in Peter Watt's book when he said come the election that there wasn't even a draft manifesto ready and Harriet Harman ended up writing it!

I think he needed the continuity. The change bit was more difficult because Tony and Gordon were politically not that far apart. Tony may have been more on the outer edges of modernisation and the public services end and so forth, but actually, certainly, going back to where this book starts, the differences in so far as they existed were deciding who's going to do the job and whether they can stand against each other. So I think it was the loss of the sense of continuity that gave him that problem that you defined. People were saying hold on a minute where is all this new stuff? I mean there was a plan.

My view is that if Tony Blair had been leader at this election he would still be in Downing Street now. What do you think?

Well it's an interesting hypothetical. Tony used to say that no one in a top job should stay more than eight years. Now, I don't know if that's right or wrong. I certainly think that Tony, if he had been able to get through and fight this election, he was certainly the sort of opponent David Cameron would have found very, very difficult.

Did he ever contemplate actually carrying on that long?

No, I don't think so. He was always of the view that eight years was about as long as you could go. And he went ten. Now that being said I mean who knows? Who knows? Who knows whether the party would have allowed it?

Why did you go back into Downing Street after it nearly ate you up the first time around?

John Harris in *The Guardian* said it's perfectly obvious to him Gordon Brown was the source of my depression. And I said, oh no, I used to get depression before Gordon. But people like him were saying how can you put up with all this angst and grief he's causing you and then go back and help him in 2010. Now part of it is tribalism...

And that's what people who aren't involved in politics never get.

Yeah, I think that's right. They just see the 'how can you put up with it?' But part of it is also a residual understanding of his strengths and so I found at every stage, there were points at which I said to Tony 'this is just terrible, I can't go on like this'.

Did you actually ever come close to snapping?

Well there are points at which you think, there is another way here. But the point is Tony was the boss and Tony was always of the view, certainly for the bulk of the time he was always of the view that the problems were way outweighed by the strengths and the brilliance that Gordon brought to it. One, he was the boss and you had to go along with that, but secondly, he had a point. And so before the last election where there were lots of people saying that Gordon should be replaced kicked off, I was never 100 per cent of that view because you just don't know what's going to happen, you don't know that we might've ended up in a worst position. You just don't know.

But if Blair knew Brown was going to succeed him, it would have been good for him to be Foreign Secretary for a few years rather than just be Chancellor.
I think Gordon would have found it very hard to be anything other than Chancellor. Not that he couldn't have done those jobs, but you know how they would have been perceived. But looking back, and I mean I haven't talked to him about this, but would it have been sensible to have some sort of competition, some sort of leadership election? There is a view that the party would have found it very difficult for Gordon not to have been Tony's successor.

But Gordon Brown appeared to think that the leadership was an entitlement, his by right and I think that was the root of the reason why he ultimately failed...
Possibly.

Because a normal politician would have had to fight for it and he just didn't. He fought for it in the sense that there was a continual undermining of Blair but that was it.
No, I can see that and I think it would have been better had there been a fairly broad field. When you look now and see David and Ed Miliband in competition you do ask yourselves whether it might have been better back then. Prescott said so at the time.

Prescott comes out of your diaries as a bit of a hero.
Tony had a lot of doubts about John from the start but I think at the end he would say he had a great deputy leader. Really great.

He was sort of Heineken deputy leader – he could reach parts that Tony couldn't.
But he was also somebody whose political judgement and expertise is not to be underestimated. John's always been somebody who, because of his rather curious relationship with the English language, has always been underestimated. People by and large do wear their hearts on their sleeves. I do, Gordon, whether he was saying what he thought or not you could always

tell. Tony was probably the most able to just hide a little bit, what he was thinking. Peter maybe a bit as well. But basically we were all pretty open people and John Prescott is somebody who, you know when he's in a good mood, you know when he's in a bad mood, you know when he's serious, you know when he's not. And I was the person who dealt with a lot of that.

And Peter Mandelson doesn't come out of the book so well.
There was a problem there with me and Peter in that I never felt I could be totally open with Peter and I think funnily enough in this recent campaign Peter and I worked really well together. Total openness, close. Back then I was never quite sure what he was up to but that's part of who Peter is. The other thing I've learnt over time is that we've all got strengths and weaknesses and you have to appreciate all them. Sometimes the weakness is just the flip of the strength. It's the other side of the coin and so you don't necessarily get one without the other.

Is there part of you that would have liked to have been an elected politician but you had enough self knowledge to know that you were psychologically unsuited?
No, I don't think so. The answer to the first part is yes. The answer to the second part is no I think I would be quite unsuited to it but it's just the way the thing has worked out. In 1994 I was getting bored with journalism. In my mind I was thinking about moving into politics in some way. John Smith dies, Tony asks me to work for him and I do. Now actually there's a passage towards the end of this volume which I'd totally forgotten about until I transcribed the diaries where Tony starts sounding me out about whether I should stand. By then I felt I was doing what I needed to do for him and for the Labour Party in that position. By 2001 I'm thinking as David Miliband Pat McFadden, James Purnell, you know these guys they're all starting to get seats and I'm thinking maybe I should do that, but actually by then I'm kind of a round peg in a round hole. But then by 2003, when I left, I just wanted out of the thing. By 2005 when I go back it's very much to go back and that's it. In 2010 I go back again and I sort of feel if I was going to stand I should have done it when David [Miliband] did.

Surely when Kitty Ussher decided to go in Burnley, you must have thought, maybe now's the time.
I did think that in 2005, and I thought it again this time. And actually when the results came in from Burnley and we lost it I felt quite bad about that because I think I could have won that. But you just have to make judgements and I did make a judgement about it when I left in 2003.

You will never escape the so-called dodgy dossier, however much you try and explain what it was or what it was not. That will hang around your neck for the rest of your life.

Well that's for you to say. I get asked about it in interviews but when I go about the place talking to people very rarely does it come up.

You will always be associated with David Kelly. Whatever the rights and wrongs of it are, you will still always be associated with that.

If you put your head above the parapet and you do the sort of job that I did in the way that I did it there'll be lots and lots and lots of things. I was thinking the other day, 'bog-standard comprehensive', 'People's princess'… But every time I get into a cab in London if the driver is from Kosovo, I promise you I never pay. The driver will say 'what you guys did in Kosovo, we'll never forget it'. Going to Northern Ireland and it's different. Yes, I accept the premise of the question and it's a very, very odd situation because David Kelly, I never met him. I never met him. And yet we became inextricably linked. But all you can do, as you say, is keep explaining. That would never have happened if it had not been for what Gilligan broadcast.

When you learnt of David Kelly's death you must have felt like jumping off a cliff.

I felt a juggernaut coming my way. That was exactly what I felt. I felt an absolute juggernaut. And the truth is, you think about it. You do think about something like that. I don't want to be pompous about it but they [the diaries] are, I think, quite an important historical document because they show politics and politicians in all their guises. And it shows how hard it is. It was hard enough for me but what it's like too for Tony Blair, Gordon Brown, David Cameron? I mean it is such a difficult job. And it's why although I will continue to work against the Tories and so forth I will always try and step back because I know how hard it is. And the other day for example when the David Laws thing was breaking and I did a blog about it, Fiona said why are you so sympathetic? I said look, you've got to step back a bit and try and imagine you're in their shoes. I don't know them. I don't know these guys as well as I knew our own guys. I've got very little time for Cameron in relation to this because of the way he exploited it in our campaign. But I did feel some sympathy for Laws.

Is there part of you that thinks you don't want to push someone like that too far because you've always got David Kelly in the background? I'm not saying you pushed David Kelly to that, but I've always thought over this expenses thing that at some point someone could top themselves.

No, funnily enough.

I mean Laws, I'm really worried about him.
Really?

I've been there. I've had to come out to my parents at his age, I know what it was like.
Well I can remember the Nick Brown thing. When Nick Brown was being done over by the *News of the World*. I remember that, I very quickly sensed that eventually he said that was the thing he was most worried about. I don't really want to go there. Look, some MPs did terrible things but the general sense being given is that they are all at it but they are not. Most MPs have to subsidise their own existence. You know that, I know that, most journalists know that.

What do you admire about Adam Boulton?
I suppose the way he's been there for a long time but I think that's part of his problem to be honest with you.

Have you spoken to him since your incident?
No.

But what happened when you went off air? Did it continue?
Oh yeah he just carried on ranting. 'You're a fucking liar, Mandelson's a fucking liar, you're all fucking liars.' Poor old Jeremy Thompson was trying to carry on his broadcast.

And what provoked that? Just the fact that he was tired after the election?
I think it's that, I really don't know. Look, he really doesn't like me, there is no going back. I think a lot of these journalists who see other journalists actually going over the other side of the fence have an issue with it. If you think about Adam Boulton's life, he stands in Downing Street and talks about what's happening inside but he's not there. I think over the years he has really come to resent people like me. And he's got this thing you know. I love the way he is describing me as unelected. Most people in politics are unelected, let's be honest about it. Civil servants, defence chiefs, the people who run the quangos, journalists, people like Adam Boulton. The reason I was there is because Gordon Brown, in this very odd constitutional situation, had asked me to go back and help him, and then asked me to go and do some interviews because the Cabinet were meeting. So Boulton says he resented this unelected person telling him what the government was doing. Well that's what he does 24-hours a day.

Did you actually think he was going to hit you at one point?

I thought he might headbutt me at one point. He came so close into my space. I remember thinking what happens if somebody headbutts you live on TV. Are you entitled, a la John Prescott, to go and hit back or do you have to stand there? I really was thinking about that. I thought he totally completely lost it. Now I don't know if it's true, I heard that Murdoch phoned him the next day and said well done. What Sky love is being talked about so they were being talked about. The really funny thing is when, if you are involved in something like that, you're so conscious, I mean I was very conscious I've got a bit of a temper, so I was saying to myself 'keep calm', so when I was saying 'calm, calm' I was probably talking to myself! I went back to Number 10 and I walked into what is my old office, you know the suite of offices at Number 12, and they all stood up and clapped. I had no idea it had become this instant big thing.

But didn't he do just what you did with Jon Snow after the Hutton Report was published?

No I don't think so. To this day, I think I did the right thing there. Don't get Fiona going on it! That was one of our biggest rows, of the many we have had. It reached that point where the media wasn't listening on that story, and I just thought sod it, I'm going to have to do something about this. Now did I get a bit aggressive? People say they want candour and passion in politics and I was very candid. I've not seen that interview since – I'm not someone who goes and looks at how you did on the telly – but I read the transcript when I was appearing for the Chilcot enquiry, and I stand by every word. I stand by every word.

It wasn't the words, it was the demeanour.

Yeah but sometimes you have to go just a little bit over the top for people to notice, and I'm not saying that was planned, but nobody could say I wasn't saying what I thought.

And do you think it was right in retrospect to do the presidential thing after the Hutton Inquiry, the podium at the bottom of the stairs?

Well look, I felt I was entitled after all that we'd been through to say what I thought and, you know, I think that as to the venue, somebody else found that for me. It wouldn't have mattered to me where it was. But I think I was entitled, after all the shit that was thrown at me over such a long period, you know with war protestors outside the house and all the rest of it. I was entitled to have my say.

How often does depression strike you, and how do you know what's triggering it?
That is a hard one. I don't record all my kind of depressive moments in my diary.

Reading the last book, correct me if I'm wrong, I just got the impression you could tell when something's really building up, but you can't actually stop it.
I can tell but you can't stop it, no. Some people can. Now as it happens I had quite a bad episode just before Easter. It doesn't take a rocket scientist to work out, that was probably all the angst of going back. I'd promised Gordon, Gordon had been trying to get me to go back for a long time. I knew I could help him in some ways…

In your former position?
Or any other position. Lots of different positions but certainly that would have been one of them. And I just knew that it wasn't right, for me, and it therefore wasn't going to be right. I had a pretty bad episode. Funnily enough, it's just amazing how sometimes other people can see things for you. We were in Scotland on holiday at Easter and met up with Charles Kennedy and his wife Sarah, as we usually do. I don't think she's even aware of this but Sarah basically persuaded me in my own arguments about how the Tories were stoppable. I'd been saying that Cameron had a problem with the public, that the people were beginning to resent the money and the posters and the negativity about Gordon and so forth. So I actually came back early from my holiday. I came back the next day. And the point I was making is that I neither saw that one coming, nor did I see it going. You always tend always to get a depressive episode after you've been through a big thing. I've had a bit of a wobble since.

Is depression also largely the reason why you haven't gone into elected politics?
No I don't think that's the reason. I honestly think that I would have done had events worked out differently. I still might, but if this thing lasts five years I'd be fifty-seven at the next election. I was fifty-three last week. Back in the old days that was fine.

Well I've already decided that I'm done with it now.
Have you?

Because I'd be fifty-two at the next election. Who do you know that gets selected in the Tory party over the age of fifty?
I've probably made that decision too but I just don't know it now. Depression is interesting because it's really hard to describe, because it's like childbirth. I've seen Fiona having a baby three times now, and you just think, how do

you ever want to go through that again? Answer: because you forget the pain, and it's the same with depression. When I'm not depressed I find it very hard to explain what it's like and one of the reasons I wrote the novel was because I wanted to give some sense of it. I used to have to wait until I was depressed to get in the right mood to write. But if I waited too long and became genuinely depressed I couldn't write. The thing that really helps is having a sense of purpose. What must it be like for people who are depressed and unemployed? I can't even begin to think. Tony, to be fair, he didn't know how bad it was until he read the diary. I used to tell him but he said he never realised I was actually that bad.

Is it something that unless someone suffers from it they can never really understand? It's very hard for me to understand because I've never ever had any kind of depression whatsoever.
Fiona finds it hard as she has to live with it so she sees what it's like when it's really bad. I find for example with the kids even though they can see when I'm depressed, I'm not quite as bad with them as I am just with Fiona because with Fiona I can feel that I can let myself go. Likewise if I'm out and about. I mean you know, I remember periods when things were really, really intense at work, when I was actually in a state of clinical depression. You've just got to keep going. It's very hard.

How bad does it get in those circumstances? Have you ever come close to thinking 'I'm going to top myself'?
No, but you understand why people do. Where I've got to now is, depression at its worst is feeling dead and alive at the same time. You feel you're alive, there's a glass of water there, you know you've got to drink it, you've got to eat but you feel completely dead inside and where I've got to is an understanding that it passes. One of the first lessons of crisis management is to understand it will end, and that's the same with depression. It will end. It may end in medications, it may end in you going to hospital but it will end.

When you had that incident on the *Andrew Marr Show* were you in the middle of it then?
Possibly. That was just a moment of absolute frustration. I'd been through the whole inquiry. I'd really prepared for that inquiry. I'm self-employed and I literally blanked out a month to prepare because I knew there were a lot of people gagging for me to screw up, desperate for it. So I prepared very very hard and I answered all the questions fully, honestly, fairly. I took it seriously. As I came out there were hundreds of journalists hanging around and I could sense their disappointment. There's a guy [Andrew Marr] who has made a very good living out of being part of this media culture, and

when he threw in that question about the figures – by the way the BBC have apologised on this about getting the figures wrong, they won't do it on air but they have apologised. He got it wrong. He said they were UN figures about casualties – I think it was just a combination of things. The thing that was going through my mind was like you said earlier, that, it didn't matter what I said to him, it didn't matter what I said to him. And they like to say that, like Adam Boulton, they've got no agenda, they're totally impartial. Bollocks.

And what about this role you have now as a sort of ambassador for people with depression? Are you comfortable in that role, is it something you like doing?
Yeah, I've got, I mean the only problem it gives me is that leukaemia, lymphoma research, they think I'm theirs…

They've done quite well from you haven't they?
Cathy Gilmore is the chief executive, she's brilliant. She started off as a volunteer eight years ago and she's now chief exec, and whenever I pop up on the radio or television talking about mental health she sends me this text and she says 'tart'. I do, because if one in four people in the public get mental health problem in their life, why should politics be any different?

There are a lot of politicians, past and present who have suffered from depression aren't there?
The Norwegian Prime Minister told his cabinet he had to resign because of his depression and they insisted he stayed. He took a sabbatical, his ratings went stratospheric. I do feel comfortable with it because I've never felt ashamed of it. It is like some people get cancer, some people break their leg, some people get depression. And I think it's important that we understand it in politics because I suspect it attracts more people of a mentally ill bent than other areas. We should be open about it. I won't say who it was but there were a couple of candidates at the last election who came to me and said 'look I've got problems' and I said look I think it's great that you're open about it but I don't want to be prescriptive. And neither of them were. I feel it's never harmed me. I feel I get a pretty unfair press. I'm not moaning about it, it's just a fact. On this issue I don't. I feel actually the press have been pretty fair on this and I think that's in part because within journalism you'll find there are more people getting this then you'd realise, so I don't mind that.

Is it true, as Lance Price told me, that it was actually Tony Blair who made the psychologically flawed comment?
You'll have to wait for future volumes of the diaries.

Oh come on.

No I'm not saying.

You took the rap for it. Did you, in the final days of the Brown bunker, take the loaded pistol to Gordon Brown and say 'it's time to go'?

No. It was a fascinating few days. We were conscious about what was happening with the Liberals. I wasn't aware of what was going on in the Tory party at all. There was certainly a point at which I wrote Gordon a note, saying in addition to pursing this track with the Lib Dems, we do need to start planning as it were, you know, an exit and it will be an important moment. These are really important moments. You've got to think about them and so I certainly wouldn't say that was his lack of involvement, just saying you've really got to think about this, assuming this [the Lib–Lab coalition] wouldn't work.

Why did Gordon Brown surround himself with thugs like Whelan, Balls and McBride?

I don't know. There's quite a lot about Charlie in this volume. I didn't know McBride at all well. Ed Balls, he does have a lot of strengths. Charlie Whelan had some but I think Gordon would have done himself a service if he'd not had people like that too close to the operation.

What was the truth of the meeting that was helped with the Lib Dems on the Monday afternoon?

I was getting text messages from Liberal Democrats who were not at the meeting saying this is all going very badly. So I sent a message back saying why, what do you mean? Oh, Balls really rude, duh duh duh. So I sent a message to Peter [Mandelson] saying 'don't know what's going on but I'm getting messages from Liberals saying this is going terribly and people are being really rude to them'. Peter sent me a message straight back saying 'I don't understand where that's coming from, it's going perfectly well'. You know what Peter's like, he's a very good judge of mood and that sort of thing. Afterwards when I talked to Peter and Andrew [Adonis] about it they said Ed Balls had been polite and Ed Miliband had behaved perfectly well. What that said to me was actually that the Liberals had already decided, that they'd already made their choice.

I think I wrote at the time that they were doing this to get cover with the left wing of their party.

Absolutely right, I'm sure that's right. Vince [Cable] was the one that was talking most of all from a let's try and keep it going viewpoint. Paddy [Ashdown], Ming Campbell, Charlie Kennedy, David Steel were all pushing towards us.

Which hurt more, Labour losing the election or Burnley being relegated?
Well I'd prepared myself mentally for Burnley over a long period, but it was a bad week though wasn't it?

Quickfire

What book are you reading?
A Tale of Two Cities (Charles Dickens).

Favourite view?
From the place where we go on holiday in France looking at Mont Ventoux.

Favourite food?
I'm not a big food person but we go to an Italian restaurant in South End Green that does this amazing pappardelle with prawns.

Best football moment?
Promotion at Wembley against Stockport, bizarrely.

Worst football moment?
Having to come to terms with the fact that I'm not in Sport Aid this year because of this book.

Favourite music?
Jacques Brel or bagpipes.

Jack Bauer or James Bond?
James Bond.

Owen Coyle [former Burnley manager] or Alex Ferguson
Alex by a stratosphere.

Do you view Coyle as a traitor?
Yes.

Most inspiring speech you've heard, other than ones you've written...
Neil Kinnock domestically – the Militant speech, and Clinton at Blackpool about why always go for progressive politics and why compassionate conservatism is a myth.

Malcolm Tucker or Toby Ziegler?
I've never ever seen the West Wing so I have to say Malcolm Tucker.

Political hero?
Nelson Mandela

Villain?
Paul Dacre

***Britain's Got Talent* or *The X Factor*?**
The X Factor. Piers Morgan's not on it.

Eric Pickles

Party affiliation: Conservative

Current position: Communities and Local Government Secretary

Born: 20 April 1952

Education: Attended Greenhead Grammar School and later Leeds Polytechnic.

Family status: Married.

Pre-political career: Consultant in Employment Practice and Local Government Editor for Conservative Newsline.

Electoral history: He has been Member of Parliament for Brentwood and Ongar since April 1992. He became Parliamentary Private Secretary to Tim Salisbury, Minister for Industry before being appointed vice-chairman of the Conservative Party in May 1993. He then held a variety of roles, including shadow Minister for Transport and for London, deputy chairman of the Conservative Party and chairman of the Conservative Party from January 2009. In May 2010 he became Communities and Local Government Secretary, a position he had shadowed before the election.

Career highlights: Assuming his current position as Communities and Local Government Secretary in the Conservative–Liberal Democrat coalition government.

Interesting fact: The Brentwood Gazette printed a verdict on their MP in the midst of the expenses scandal, which was titled 'Our MP is squeaky clean on expenses'.

Date of interview: July 2010
Extended version
Venue: Secretary of State's office, Department of Communities & Local Government
Total Politics Issue 26, August 2010

I have no hesitation in saying that Eric Pickles was the absolute star performer in the first six months of the coalition government. He gripped his department like a vice and imposed his will at every opportunity. Quangos were axed, savings were made, power was devolved. He was the political equivalent of a whirling dervish. I think part of the reason for his apparent success was that he had previously run a big metropolitan council and knew how to manage and lead a big organisation. And he had a clear agenda for the first three months. The question is: can he keep it up?

There's always been a suspicion that the Cameron inner circle don't really

'get' Eric Pickles. He appears to be treated with some contempt by them, especially when they feel he's getting above himself. As party chairman, there was a feeling at Cameron Central that he took a little too much credit for the stunning victory in the Crewe & Nantwich by-election. It was rubbish, of course, but these things matter.

I met Eric in the same office in which I had interviewed Hazel Blears eighteen months earlier. The decor hadn't changed much, apart from the addition of a bust of Che Guevera. 'It's there to remind me that if we let the system take over before we stop in any way, then the cigar-chomping Commies take over again. The cigar-chomping Commies are not going to take over on my watch.'

And it's because of comments like that, that he's one of my favourite politicians. What a man. What a chum.

You hit the ground running when you first got here. How long is it now? Six, seven weeks?

Something likes that, yeah. These are precious times. If you don't set things out now, it's just not going to happen. I've taken over an organisation before and I know that to get things going, there's got to be a certain rhythm. There's got to be a combination of stopping things – and there are some pretty obvious things that need to be stopped – but also you need to set in trend the kind of things you've got to be announcing. I've got a whole raft of announcements, right the way through virtually until Christmas Day. I've done nothing that hasn't been part of the plan in terms of what I wanted and to fit it in. Even those rather unfortunate remarks about the uselessness of chief executives have all been part of the process of trying to get authorities to move together and recognise that they needed to do something, other than an alternative source of power to the leader of council. I discovered a new word, which is my new favourite word on that, which is German. I hope I'm pronouncing this right. *Doppelsplit*, like *doppelgang*. *Doppelsplit*, meaning to be competing. The idea that a chief executive in a small district has any real prospect in the modern world of surviving without being part of a movement to merge neighbouring authorities in terms of administration or be involved with other organisations is well over.

Were you given any hints that this was the job you'd be given after the election?

No, I read you tipped me for it, so I thought it was a done deal.

Unfortunately David Cameron didn't follow all my other recommendations.

Well, he can't look like your puppet, can he?

What happened when you walked through the door to Number 10?

It was a nice moment. Andrew Griffiths, who's now the MP for Burton and my former chief of staff, came to sit with me, which I thought was quite sweet – waiting for the call or the non-call. We walked across to Number 10 and it was like having my mum take me to the school gates. I'd not been to Number 10 for thirteen years and it had changed a bit so I couldn't work out how to get in at all. Actually a very nice camera crew from Channel 4 showed me how to get in. I went in and got appointed. It was a nice moment. I worked with David really quite closely for a year and a bit. I'd seen him walk out to the Palace and all of that kind of thing. It was quite emotional really in its own way. I'd seen various folks and asked, what happens now? 'Someone will ring you.' So I went to have some lunch and sat there waiting and the telephone rings. 'It's Nick. Is that the Secretary of State, Eric Pickles?' I thought, 'Yes it is!' He said 'I'll meet you outside. The department would very much like to meet you.' I thought, well that's very nice. I said 'It's at the end of Victoria Street. I'll wander down.' He said 'Don't worry, we'll send a car for you. I'll meet you outside in ten minutes.' I went outside into New Palace Yard, but I couldn't see anybody. So I thought, what if he meant St Stephen's? So I went and had a look there and I couldn't see anything. By now I'd forgotten his name, so I had to ring Central Office, to ring his department and it turned out he was waiting for me in Downing Street. He comes round. I sit in the cab and off we go. We arrive at the front and there is Peter Housden, then the Permanent Secretary, waiting for me and I shake hands. I walk out and I arrive at this North Korean moment. The entire building is out there, right up into the atriums, politely applauding me. You can see them saying: 'Is it the fat guy? Is it the fat guy that's been appointed?' Then I made a little speech saying I normally only get applauded when I go round Tesco in my constituency. Then I came up here and just started.

After that the various ministers arrived, we divvied up what we were going to do and tried to work out a protocol in terms of the coalition. It was massively important that nobody could ever play games inside here, in terms of playing both ends against the middle. We have a meeting at 8.30am on a Tuesday for forty-five minutes then a political meeting for fifteen minutes with my Liberal colleagues, which kind of sets out the rhythm of the week. Andrew [Stunnell, Lib Dem DCLG parliamentary under-secretary] has just been saying that we have been keeping them informed.

It must be odd though sitting down at a political meeting with a Liberal Democrat there?

Funnily enough, the way in which I think Oliver [Letwin], George [Osborne] and William [Hague] did the negotiations was unusual. The way these things usually work is almost on issue by issue. But, by and large, they had spent some time on the four big issues. They'd put together a position paper and they'd worked out where the areas of dissent were well in advance. So we're actually working on agreed policy more than we probably would've have done had it just been us.

Do you find that because you've got a political opponent there, that actually policy is tested more than it might have been otherwise?
The last thing you want, the last thing you'd need, the last thing that would screw everybody up, is if you marched folk up the hill and somebody 'coughs' and you have to march down again. I would lose authority, this place would lose authority and suddenly it would be absolute anarchy. It would be like it was under Labour, where you have competing ministers fighting each other for authority within this building. This building was the Balkans until I arrived. I don't say this with any disrespect for John Denham or to John Healey but they were two competing positions in the way that [Caroline] Flint and Hazel [Blears] were. Ruth [Kelly] never really had much authority anyway. I needed to be absolutely certain that when I said something it was never going to be contradicted.

Effectively you've come in to be a 'change agent' in management speak. Parts of the civil service are there to resist big change. Probably in this department, you've got to institute some of the biggest changes of all.
Yeah, you are acutely aware that you are saying to people, who spent most of their professional life building it up into a particular model: 'Thank you very much for doing that. But I'm afraid it's got to be different and we don't want to do that.' I want to put this politely, but occasionally you do things that surprise them. For example when we got rid of the Comprehensive Area Assessment (CAA), we were just talking about it. They said 'You want to replace it with what?' Nothing. 'Yes, okay. But what things do we want local authorities to be judged on. What's the regime?' Nothing. 'So just to be clear Secretary of State, when you say nothing, what do you mean?' Nothing. I mean nothing, absolutely nothing. It's pointless. It doesn't do anything. It doesn't get a bin emptied. No sure, of course, we are going to inspect children's services but it's going to be in terms of life threatening right through to personal liberty. Of course those kinds of things are going to be dealt with. But some of the stuff was pointless. You just became quite good at filling the tick boxes. Nothing actually happened.

I've always thought 'community' was an intrinsic left-wing word when used by government. Are you tempted to rename the department?
I'm not going to change the letterhead. I suppose I feel a little bit like Scrooge and Marley. Community is going to stay on. I do think it's about

neighbourliness. I want to make neighbourhoods, long-term, the residue of finance in local government, and short term, the residue of service delivery. You're not going to find anything restyled here. I don't know if they've cleaned the settees since John [Denham] left but he always looked to me like a pretty neat sort of guy. I can't imagine it was ever needed. The paintings... I've put my Che Guevara portrait up there.

I've noticed that. What is the point of that? Very unsound...
Che is there to remind me that if we let the system take over before we stop in any way, then the cigar-chomping Commies take over again. The cigar-chomping Commies are not going to take over on my watch.

There are a fair few of them in this department.
Bless their hearts. I don't mind what they do in their private lives. There is a default mechanism that exists and its intention, which is big state, this is how we're going to do it. We've had quiet tussles. I've tried to do a number of things. Basically, I'm not mad keen on reports longer than two pages because after that most things are just word processing. I do think it helps to refine the argument and to try to get the argument out. We've done a number of things: going for shorter reports – I try to reply to letters on one side of A4, again because you just need to. We now have a terrific record of replying to MPs. You will find the odd one will sometimes drift on to about three or four weeks, but that's mostly because we don't like the draft. For most MPs, we get a turnaround well within a fortnight which is quicker than most departments do.

Would you like to stay in this job for the whole of parliament?
That's up to the Prime Minister.

If you're constantly reshuffled every eighteen months, what can you achieve in that time?
Nothing is forever. I stay at the Prime Minister's pleasure. It is as simple as that. I am in a terrific hurry to make sure that we get things out that I think are very important. I've spent a long time in opposition. I can tell you that opposition is no fun at all. You can achieve absolutely nothing. It was a wonderful thing for me to sign that HIPS notice to get rid of that great big pile of usefulness. Anything symbolising the state, it was HIPS. A package that was of no help, that did nothing and was a drag anchor. We are using primary legislation and if I can deal with secondary legislation, I'll deal with it. But a whole load of stuff we're going to get rid of, we'll do through statements to the House through changes of play. I will confess, I got my cheap Bic when I signed the order to do that. I was humming to myself, I was so happy.

Localism is a buzzword that everybody seems to subscribe to nowadays. You have, in the first few weeks of your tenure made some decisions which people have criticised because you're issuing edits to local authorities...

I've exulted. I've urged. We've asked them to do the transparency and, by and large, they've responded to that. But localism doesn't mean you go along and do what you like and never hear anything from me. I'm an opinionated so and so. Yes, folks have not been terribly happy with the things I've said about chief executives and pay. But it needed to be said. Have I introduced a pay scale for chief executives? No, that's none of my business. But that doesn't mean to say I don't have an opinion. Authorities need to know if they're coming and talking about a lack of resources, and they're a little district and they're paying £180k for their chief executive, or if they're a county with a chief exec on over £200k, I am not going to take them seriously. There's been a rush of increases in members' allowances. I'm not going to introduce a national scale. I'm not going to cap them. But I have to say to them, I don't take it terribly seriously at all. Don't tell me that some independent people agreed to this. You are the politicians, you've got to see the political climate is such where you've got to set an example. You've got to be reducing what you do. You're going to be asking your staff to take a pay freeze. How can you look them in the eye when you've taken an increase?

How much does it help having run a large council yourself?

I haven't had too many whinges so far, I have to say. I think the nature of local government has changed quite a bit since I was last doing it. I suppose it is helpful to have run a largish council [Bradford Metropolitan]. At that time, it was the fourth largest council in the country. So you do get a kind of perspective. The perspective you probably get is how long it takes to do something, which is why again I'm in such a hurry. It's like the old poem: 'For the sake of a horse and the battle was lost.'

What about local government structures? Labour wanted to have this regional agenda and elected mayors. Have you got any plans in that direction?

We want to see this in our larger cities. But, by and large, I'm not very interested in a restructure. Every single mistake people make is usually tied up with restructuring. I can't afford for local authorities to take two years out while someone decides who the new chief executive is, where they're going to have their headquarters, what does their paper look like, going back to the rebranding and all that kind of thing. I'm much more interested in the formal power structures. Now, I think it makes a lot of sense at a managerial level to merge functions at lower tier authorities.

Are you at all attracted by the idea of saving money by stopping annual elections in councils?

I've been thinking about that a lot. I think that's your unique contribution to the day. By and large, my stance is that people came to a decision when authorities were created. I am attracted to the idea of an all-out election because you can actually have real change created there. But it is something that I think might get wound up in the constitutional reform that the coalition is considering. But I don't think it's a bad idea.

The cabinet system in local authorities is very unpopular with a lot of people. If local authorities wanted to change that and go back to the committee system, what would your reaction be?
Fine. We will be putting something into the local government bill to let them do that. I don't care how things are organised. They can have it on the basis of a committee system, on a cabinet basis, on the mayoral system. If they want to introduce it on a choral system with various members of the council singing sea shanties I don't mind, providing it's accountable, transparent and open. That's all I need to know.

With regard to local government finance, successive governments have really ducked out of revaluations. Any views on entering that bear pit?
We are going to have a review of local government finance. We're not really ruling anything in or out. But, I have to say, revaluation in many ways is a red herring. What is immensely important in revaluation is keeping the property value between the north and south on roughly the same kilter. They are almost exactly what they were when they were first introduced. We certainly won't be getting in a spotter plane and saying: 'I see No. 27 has got themselves one more gnome than they are entitled to.' We're not going to do any of that.

Have you made use of the relaxation room yet?
Harriet [Harman's] green monument to tranquillity. I haven't. I just don't think I've got the karma to be there. I haven't even sat on those lovely couches. What are they called? Contemplation suites. It's funny I was looking around the office on my first day. I saw these and asked how much they cost. Two grand a pop!

What's the most shocking thing you've discovered?
We've stopped a lot of things. There were all kinds of things that we were going to do in terms of meeting staff, costing hundreds of thousands of pounds when I could just walk around the office instead to meet them. Press cuttings were costing ten grand a month! My papers are the only papers now because I think I'm the only person that reads them. They come up and they're covered in ketchup and God knows what. There are other things but I really don't think I can go into that kind of detail here because we're in the process…

What do you think the good Lord Ashcroft is going to say about you in his book, which he is apparently writing?

I've got enormous respect for the good Lord. Bless his heart. I don't think I'd be sat here without him. But the guy is caustic and jolly and, whatever he has to say, I'm sure I'll enjoy it. We would not be here without him. I know he's very controversial. But ultimately we're here because of what he did.

Did you enjoy the election campaign?

Yes, I did. The ups and downs I did enjoy.

Do you think it was a problem though that there wasn't one person in charge. There wasn't a Lynton Crosby figure?

I thought George [Osborne] was very focused throughout the whole campaign. He knew exactly what he wanted to do, exactly the mountain we had to climb and I think he played a pretty good hand. He was the guy that was in charge. Right from the beginning people were saying: 'Oh it's going to be dreadful with Ashcroft doing this and George is doing that' but I always took the view that my role was to get the best out of them, to try to smooth any channels of communications, to be someone they could come to. I have to say it was a pleasure working with them all.

What was the worst moment of the campaign?

There is not a chance I'm going to answer that.

You clearly just thought of something.

I'm not going to lie to you, there were moments.

Are you happy with your public image? And what do you think it is?

Sort of fat, kind of… I think because of the job I did, being the party chairman, you cannot have a view other than the leader's view. You cannot see things in shades of grey. Labour is wrong, the Lib Dems are wrong, we are right. I've always been more consensual than my image has been – a kind of hard man that pushes things through. But that's largely because of the jobs I've had to do. I just had that thing on Radio 4, a profile, which I thought was pretty accurate. I don't think I know what my image is. Sometimes you see things on Twitter and you think, these people have no comprehension of what I'm actually like. But I don't care.

After Crewe and Nantwich, you got a lot of flack supposedly from people around Cameron. They were saying you had got too big for his boots. It wasn't all down to you. How did that affect you?

I didn't mind it. There might have been some truth in it. I don't think you could ever point to a single interview I did at Crewe and Nantwich where I didn't talk about the team and I didn't praise Stephen Gilbert [campaign director] and I didn't praise the people around us. I think I've consistently done that. You can never entirely predict how things… because I know who was responsible for the victory in Crewe and Nantwich; me or Stephen? Stephen by a mile. But I was working very closely with him. He asked me to take the weight of the press off and he asked me to be the campaign spokesman. Some people may have been unhappy that I did that very well but there was never any intention to be anything other than part of that team.

Doesn't it slightly irritate you when you see yourself written up as basically David Cameron's bit of northern rough?
I see myself as a diamond geezer.

Was *Question Time* the worst experience of your political life?
No not by a mile, not by a country mile.

It's one of those occasions where you could see the shovel, but you couldn't quite resist picking it up.
We rehearsed what I was going to say as well, that was the worst thing. I was as out of touch as other MPs. I was so irritated by it, I didn't actually tell the audience that I stopped claiming some time ago before the controversy arrived. It was just, you know… I was just as out of touch as anybody.

Can instances like that be a good thing in some ways because you do loads of interviews which you think are really good and then there's one that's an absolute disaster?
I've still got the disc and if I do something really well I always make sure to play it late at night just to remind myself. I can virtually recite it. We had rehearsed it. It wasn't that I was caught unaware. But I was unaware in the sense as I was unaware as most MPs. My claims were tiny but that didn't matter.

Do you think it's possible to make real friends in politics?
Yeah, you've got to understand that nothing is forever. If you sit at a table and plan out your career, a bit like telling God your plans, it's not going to work. Life is not a rehearsal for something else that's coming. I've seen too many people just eaten up by unfulfilled ambition that then destroyed their political career, their family life, without leaving any trace of a human being you'd like to have a drink with or a chat with. So yes, it is possible to have people you can actually trust.

Why have you given up twittering?

I haven't given up twittering. I'm still doing it, just not as much as I did. I twittered at the weekend. I just know too much now. I know too much. I can't be taking lumps out of Labour; they're broken and horrid. I'd feel like I'm mocking them. And certainly can't with my colleagues, the Lib Dems, which I did specialise in. It would be dreadful if I just did the 'rah, rah, rah'. I've done the odd bit of commentary.

Quickfire

Favourite food?

Bouillabaisse. French fish stew. Yeah, I like curry too but my absolute favourite is French.

What food do you hate?

I don't like chicken at all. I will have it but I don't like it with skin on it or with bones.

Tell me something that few people know about you.

I really like opera.

Your favourite view?

My favourite view would be Bay of Naples.

Favourite music?

Bach.

Favourite holiday destination?

North Norfolk coast. I just love that stretch from Titchwell, all the way through Wells, to Sheringham.

What would Mrs Pickles like to change about her man?

My weight, I'm sure.

What book are you currently reading?

Wolf Hall by Hilary Mantel.

Favourite film?

The Searchers.

One thing you wished you had known at sixteen.

That you aren't always going to be sixteen.

The worst gift you've ever given someone?
I was once given a musical farting Santa Christmas by my staff.

What makes you cry?
Anything, opera, anything. Never take me to a chick flick. I just go. I must have seen *The Searchers* hundreds of times. There's a moment when John Wayne picks up the young Debbie. 'Let's go home Debbie.' Every time, hit the button. Boomf.

Political hero?
De Gaulle.

Villain?
Stalin.

Matthew Parris

Party affiliation: Conservative

Born: 7 August 1949

Education: Educated at Waterford Kamhlaba United World College of Southern Africa in Mbabane, followed by Clare College, Cambridge, from which he gained a First Class degree in Law, then winning a Paul Mellon scholarship to study International Relations at Yale University.

Family status: In a civil partnership with Julian Glover, a political journalist for *The Guardian*.

Electoral history: He served as the Conservative MP for West Derbyshire from 1979 until 1986, being selected over Peter Lilley and, later, Conservative leader Michael Howard. He retired from politics to pursue a career in journalism.

Career overview: Began working in the Foreign and Commonwealth Office for two years, eventually joining the Conservative Research Department and becoming correspondence secretary to Margaret Thatcher. He left Parliament to take over as host of the ITV current-affairs series *Weekend World* in 1986. In 1991, a compilation of his pieces in *The Times* was published, entitled *So Far, So Good*, and has since had further books published, including *Scorn* and *Great Parliamentary Scandals*.

Career highlights: He has received many awards for his work as a journalist, including Writer of the Year in Granada Television's 2004 'What The Papers Say' Awards, Columnist of the Year in the 1991 and 1993 British Press Awards. Also, the London Press Club's Edgar Wallace Outstanding Reporter of the Year Award was given to him in 1990.

Interesting facts: His career may have been dramatically different had London Transport accepted his application to become a diesel-fitter. With a time of two hours, thirty-two minutes and fifty-seven seconds, he holds the fastest London Marathon time ever run by a UK MP. If he'd run that time in 2009 rather than 1985 he would have finished in seventy-ninth place.

Date of interview: July 2010
Extended version
Venue: Matthew Parris's flat, Limehouse
Total Politics Issue 27, September 2010

If you poll any group of politicians, journalists or newspaper readers and ask them who their top rated political columnist is, chances are that Matthew

Parris's name will emerge at the top. I don't read many newspaper columns.
I buy newspapers for news, rather than opinion, but I find Matthew Parris's
columns unmissable. He writes in a uniquely personal style and provides an
insight which is unrivalled by his competitors. Even though he left Parliament
twenty-five years ago, he manages to display an empathy with politicians his
rival columnists find impossible to emulate. He doesn't necessarily defend the
parliamentary classes but he explains what lies behind a lot of their actions
and utterances. And he uses humour to absolutely devastating effect.

We conducted our interview on the riverside balcony of his docklands flat.
As we were finishing he told me that the following night he and a friend were
going to go to the other side of the river and then swim across. 'You're mad,'
I said. 'You could die. The tide will carry you down river.' 'No, we've checked,
it'll be fine,' he reassured me. I thought no more about it and assumed he
wouldn't actually go through with it. But he did, and I read all about it in
the Evening Standard *a few days later. I was right, to the extent that the tide*
did indeed carry them a mile. Unfortunately Matthew had calculated the
time wrongly, having forgotten to allow for the fact that we were on British
Summer Time rather than GMT. Or was it the other way around? Anyway,
the two of them found themselves in Wapping rather than Limehouse,
dripping wet in their underpants at 3am. They had no choice but to run
home, hoping that no one would see them. What an adventure!

How has turning sixty affected you, if it all?
I've got a bit of a limp which comes from literally tens of thousands of miles
training for marathons. I did my last London marathon in 1985 when I
was thirty-five and achieved a very good time. I've given up long distance
running since then. I think running is bad for you.

**I definitely agree with that. Did you get reflective about where you're going
now?**
There does come a point, and I guess in my case it has comes about now,
when you think you probably aren't going to do anything else big career-
wise. I am now definitely not going to be Prime Minister, Foreign Secretary
or a minister, or write a great book.

You've written several great books.
Well they've been fun to do. My agent Ed Victor, tactfully not associating it
with me, his client, said that there was a kind of writer who happily accepted
that God had given him a minor talent and wasn't expecting anything more
and at the age of sixty, I see that God has given me a minor talent and that's
all really.

In terms of writing, do you prefer the 1,000/1,500 word article to actually writing something really substantially lengthy?
I don't think it's a matter of prefer. It's a matter of habit and I think anybody, any columnist would tell you this, that when you've spent your life writing things in 1,000 word chunks, a little bell begins to ring in your brain automatically when you've reached 1,000 words – you just know you have. After that you find you haven't anything else to say because your brain has ordered things into something that lasts 1,000 words and it's hard to get out of the habit. But as I have a funny butterfly mind, I've probably chosen the right career.

Have you got a big project in mind you never got round to starting?
No. Were I serious historian, I'd like to have done a history of the road and the path, a history of the tracks and trails that human beings make to transport themselves terrestrially. I don't think any world history has ever been written and I'd like to do that. I've never had any ambition to write a novel, ever since I read George Eliot's *Middlemarch*; I never saw the point of trying to compete in that market. The political stuff I have done has been minor but I'm quite happy with it. So no, no big project. I am at the moment, for this autumn, putting together a book which I'm having a lot of fun with, called *Parting Shots*. I did a radio series, collecting ambassadors' valedictory dispatches, the final sort of parting shot, a polite and gentle version of the office leaving do where they say everything they've always wanted to. Some of these dispatches you can get out of Freedom of Information are fantastic and we are getting a book out of them. I may do a few more things like that.

Is it writing that gives you the most pleasure?
The two things I like are writing and radio. I love radio, I love writing. I really don't like television very much. It's partly that I don't approve of television very much because I think it is an inherently stupid medium.

Why?
Because if you must accompany every thought and piece of information with a picture, you enormously slow down and shallow-ify what you can communicate. So much can be communicated in words that can't be communicated in pictures which is why human beings, unlike other animals, speak. It's partly because I'm not very good at it. I enjoy reading my own stuff and some of it is quite alright. I like listening to myself, I sound like a sort of cross between Little Noddy and a pussycat. I don't mind the sound of my own voice but I don't like looking at myself. I'm a huge disappointment to myself visually. They talk about people being comfortable in their own skin. The minute I'm in vision, I feel a little uncomfortable. I can't walk for

television, I begin to mince. I can't do natural movements for television, they begin to look stagey.

You have to do exaggerated movements, don't you? They look natural on screen but don't feel natural when you do them.
Yes. There are people who do this second-nature and I don't. The other lovely thing about radio is that it's communicator-led rather than technician-led. It's the presenter and, to a degree, the producer. At the very most a two-person team and quite often a one-person team who are making the programme as they go along. Television has so many people involved and usually technical people telling you what you can and can't do and 'would you please do that again'. Something gets lost.

How do you feel your writing has changed since you first started writing for *The Times*?
Hardly at all. There's hardly been any development in my writing. I read some of the early stuff I wrote. I got more practised at it. I can't say I see any sort of enlargement in my style or deepening in my talents. I think that people have got used to my voice as a writer and so think I've got better as a writer. I haven't actually. I started writing sketches and very much thirteen years later I stopped writing sketches. I developed a bit of a judgement that most columnists develop about how to set about tricky or sensitive tasks.

The thing with your columns is you develop an argument better than anyone else. When I was writing a column for *The Telegraph*, every time I pressed the send button I thought they'd send it back saying 'this is crap, start again'. Have you ever had that feeling?
Yes I do have it but I can usually see what is wrong and I do start again. John Birt is quite out of fashion now but Birtism at the BBC, for all its slightly caricaturable side, had one big central truth. John Birt always used to say when he was at LWT and I was presenting *Weekend World*, 'but what is your argument?' If you just keep, as a columnist, putting that to yourself, you'll be OK. Were I a great observer of human behaviour, were I an evocative re-creator of landscapes or situations, or had I any talent to reproduce conversation, then I might be a different kind of writer but with me it's 'what's your argument?' It is always the first question and if you hold onto that like you hold onto the mast of a ship in a storm, you'll always get through as long as you have an argument.

You mention *Weekend World* there. You're quite critical of yourself in your autobiography on that. Was it something that you felt instantly uncomfortable with?

Yeah. I felt instantly uncomfortable with it when I started. I thought, and I suppose everyone does, that after a while you'd get better at it but I found after two years I still wasn't getting better at it and our ratings were dropping. I don't think I was a flop. What I failed to be was the new Brian Walden. The programme itself was probably out of date. The concept was arthritic and old-fashioned. I think a really sensational presenter could have given it a new life and I just wasn't doing that. I just wasn't sensational.

Don't you think nowadays there ought to be something like that on television? There is no longer any inquisitive interview that lasts longer than ten minutes.
But would anybody watch it? If you want a presentation about something that develops an argument carefully and thoughtfully, is television the best medium in which to do it? No, I think people watch things like *Weekend World* because there wasn't anything else to watch. They learned to appreciate its strengths and they developed the patience you need, but modern viewers don't have that patience and why should they?

What frustrates you about the way the modern media behaves, if anything?
I like the modern media. I thoroughly approve of it. I think a good deal of it is absolute nonsense but that doesn't matter. A lot of people want to read and see absolute nonsense. Most of it is dross but most of any age's media and art will be dross. Amidst all the dross, there is as much good stuff now than there has ever been.

But isn't it quite shallow? Look at the 24-hour news channels, you and I go on and give our views, but what can you say in two minutes on Sky News that's of any benefit?
Ask Adam Boulton. I think Adam Boulton, as a commentator, or Nick Robinson on the BBC, are as good as any equivalent that you could name from thirty, fifty, 150 years ago. Plainly there wasn't rolling television then but were the commentators in the eighteenth and nineteenth century better? I get the impression when you listen to Nick and Adam that you have two people who do really understand it, they sum it up beautifully; they lead your thoughts in the right direction. I have no problem about it. I think rolling news may be a bit old fashioned because you can go quickly and unerringly towards the report that you want to hear about – you don't have to sit and wait until something rolls around.

What do you think it says about politicians and politics in general that the likes of you and I are invited to give our views? We're not elected to anything and yet twenty or thirty years ago, the newspaper would have gone to a backbench MP about something rather than an independent pundit.

Well, they get a better comment from us than they would have from a backbench MP twenty or thirty years ago.

Correct answer (both laugh). I always remember when the Hutton enquiry was going on, I did half an hour straight off on Sky News live on College Green when nobody else was about. I thought 'why am I doing this? It should be someone from the security committee'.
No, but then you look at the membership of the security committee and you see very well why you're doing it and not them.

Do you think there's any hope for backbench MPs now in a new political environment? Is there going to be change? Are they going to break the shackles?
Yes, I do feel a little bit hopeful about the new parliament. I think backbenchers could do a lot better than they have done over the last twenty or thirty years. Looking at the backbenchers we have now, I think there'll be all kinds of ideas and movements and campaigns that are going to add a lot to national life.

You seem quite comfortable about the coalition. In one of your columns you wrote 'Lib Dems bring to government a distinct and healthy slant on politics. There is a reactionary component in the Tory make-up; I often share it, but it must always be kept in check'. That almost seems to buy the Lib Dem line that it's their main job in the coalition to keep the Tories in check...
Yes, but not just as a brake. You do need a brake on some of the hot-headed reactionary instincts you find in the Conservative Party, but as an accelerator too for ideas of their own. Michael Gove's education policy is not at all unlike David Laws's education policy was or indeed Tony Blair's theoretical education policy was. In all parties you have people who are dynamic. What I like about the Lib Dems is they do combine creativity and dynamism with a belief in the individual, and you don't get that in the Labour Party. That is what I hate about the Labour Party and is the reason I could never have joined the Labour Party. The Labour Party in the end and in its very core is distrustful about the individual.

The Lib Dems tend to be quite a 'big state' party...
Some of them are. Some may not in the end feel that they are natural members of the coalition like this. I can see the coalition not splitting, not fragmenting but being shaved at the edges, at the right and the left, of people who don't feel it's for them. I find it hard to reconcile some of the things Tim Farron says with what the coalition stands for. Simon Hughes, it's sometimes hard to know what he thinks and he may feel uncomfortable too. I can think of

plenty of people on the Tory right who are really not for this sort of thing at all. The coalition may lose a few at each end but I think the centre is strong.

Do you think the media coverage of the coalition is slightly behind the curve with everybody trying to find evidence of a split here, a crack there, without actually thinking of the bigger picture that in coalitions there are inevitably going to be differences and it doesn't mean that in a year's time there aren't going to be differences?
Yes but that is the media's job. When two parties that have been part of the warring tribes in Westminster for as long as anyone can remember suddenly join to form a government, it's right for the media to push and probe and ask how far they really are apart. The media will notice, the newspapers will notice and are noticing, that the public quite like this thing. It's for the coalition to prove that the centre is strong and the ideas are real. I think it is for the media to probe, I don't think David Cameron or Nick Clegg would expect anything else.

If you were a coalition MP, what would be your biggest difficulty?
It sounds slavishly adoring but I'm completely on board with the whole idea and for what they're trying to do. I as a Conservative think we should make the positive case for cuts rather than just wringing our hands and saying 'I hate it, but I do it and it's hurting us more than it hurts you' because it's not hurting me. Some will hurt me but the idea of reducing the size of the state seems to be an idea that will stand on its own – should stand on its own, and it is simply convenient that the impending bankruptcy is forcing the idea in the country. I want it anyway but I can see why from the point of view of the coalition, that case can't be made.

Has a part of you ever thought 'I'd quite like to be an MP again in this government'?
No, because I really wasn't very good at that either. Certainly not a backbencher. No. I'd still like to be Secretary of State for Transport but I'm not going to be.

Really? Because I've always wanted to be Transport Secretary too!
I'm sorry Iain, but I'm older than, you so it's my turn first.

I've always said that if any ministerial job was to come my way, Transport Minister would be it. You actually do things as Transport Minister.
Of course you can! Where is there a better case for big government than in providing roads and railways, it's just obvious. I really disapprove of the way the Conservative Party has never thought that transport mattered.

Have you ever, since you left Parliament in 1986, thought 'actually I shouldn't have done that'?
Not for a moment. But that was only because I wasn't going anywhere. There have been times when prime ministers have been appointing junior ministers when I thought 'if only I had been doing well as a backbencher, I might now be being made that appointment' . . . John Major told me he would have made me a junior minister if only I had had a bit more patience, and that he was fairly confident I would have made a hash of it.

That's a very nice thing to say.
He said he'd give me a try.

Rail privatisation! That would have been you!
Absolutely! Or I would have said something to Edwina Currie that a good winter cuts through the bed blockers in the elderly population like a knife through butter. John Major said he would have defended me on my first gaffe but perhaps when it came to the second he would have let me go, and I think he's spot on.

How did your political views form originally? You don't sit in any particular Conservative camp.
Two things form my political views. One is being brought up in Southern Africa and my mother being involved in the fight against white supremacy in what was then Southern Rhodesia. So I then became very interested in human rights, although I don't really believe in human rights. But I became very interested in equalities between people and opposing discrimination, that's the liberal side. At university, when I began to follow British politics, I became seized with a conviction that collectivism as seen through the prism of a Labour government would be the downfall of Britain and the state and the gradual extension of the state was slowly taking us to destruction. So I didn't join the Conservative Party out of any enthusiasm for the Conservative Party but out of a feeling that socialism, even the weak milk and water variety of socialism that we got from Harold Wilson's Labour Party, had to be stopped. When it came to Margaret Thatcher, she did seem a person who would do that. I had already become a Conservative, but then I became enthusiastic about it.

How did you get to work for her?
I was sent over by Chris Patten. I was working for the Conservative Research Department. Chris sent me over to what was considered in the CRD, who were a bit sniffy about Mrs Thatcher in the early days, a very unpleasant job which was answering her letters from the general public. I was her

correspondence clerk for her last two years in opposition, which I also cocked up.

There's a theme developing.
Yes, it makes a good after dinner speech, I can tell you.

Her image is so different from that which anyone who has ever worked with her would tell you.
Loyal to her staff, but not always to her colleagues. I think she was a very tricky person to work with. Certainly loyal to her staff. There are bits of Mrs Thatcher's public image that are right and bits that are wrong, the bits that are wrong you're right – she was loyal to her staff and it's also true that she was much better at compromising. Although she raged against contrary advice, she often took it. There was, is, a sort of coldness about her. I never felt that she especially loved human beings. She had great faith in the qualities of the human animal but a love and a warmth towards particular human beings, apart from Denis, didn't, I think, characterise her. She treated people well, I think, because she had been brought up to treat her staff well. But not because in her heart she really cared.

Do you think politics is very much a young person's game now in this country?
I was the chairman of a number of selection meetings, constituency associations, Tory ones, choosing their candidates. The last that I did was for Stratford on Avon which Nadhim Zahawi won. One of the people who didn't win was a woman called Georgina Butler, who had been an ambassador in her career, just recently retired from the Foreign Office. I thought what a good person she would have been, on the backbenches or as a junior minister, and I felt sorry that there is this prejudice now. I think these things go in cycles. There'll be a fashion for youth, then we'll find out what youth lacks, then there'll be a fashion for grey hair and then we'll find out what grey hair lacks. It is just swings and roundabouts.

Is it healthy for politics when you have all the leaders look, to the public, the same?
No they're not the same, even though they may look the same. They are all about the same age. The similarities between Cameron and Clegg are quite striking although the differences are quite striking too. Certainly in backgrounds, the similarities of the two Eds and David Miliband, but in outlook they are very different, very different indeed. I think it is just something of a coincidence there that they are all the same age. In the selection panels I chaired, there is quite an appetite now for candidates who have done something else in their life – like Dr Sarah Wollaston in Totnes, I

chaired that one. It definitely was the fact that she was a doctor that helped her and the fact that she had only relatively recently joined the Conservative Party didn't help her at all – so again these things swing backwards and forwards.

Do you think some of the new MPs might become disillusioned with their existence fairly quickly? You talk to some of them and they are not happy people.

Disillusion is not quite the right word with IPSA. It's just a sort of rage. I don't think they're disillusioned with the House of Commons, they're not disillusioned so far with their roles and their constituents and that side of things. But IPSA is just a disgrace, and I'm completely on the side of Members of Parliament here and I don't know what we do except wait for the wave of public indignation to die down and then just double all their salaries. I don't think increasing all their allowances again in a slightly surreptitious way is the right way to do it. I'd double all their salaries and then abolish their allowances. But now is not quite the right time to double MPs' salaries. I'm not sure the individuals who staff IPSA are the problem, it was the circumstances in which it was born and the expectations placed on it and the rules it has to implement. I don't think the *Daily Telegraph* played an entirely glorious role in all of this. They were probably right to publish once they had the disks. I think it could have been done in a more balanced way. They have done quite a lot to discredit the whole profession of politics. MPs themselves have done something, but so has the *Daily Telegraph*.

Do you recognise that you have become a bit of a role model for younger gay men in politics, or more generally?

I do hope not. I'm a completely crap gay.

But you've been completely open for years at a time that many weren't … when I wasn't. I think you underestimate that.

Yes, but I judge these things as everybody does, there were years until which I wasn't open because I judged I would never get into politics and I wouldn't have and I wouldn't have been selected.

I wasn't!

I wish now that I had come out when I was a Conservative MP. I think I could have got away with it in retrospect, but I think it would have been a close run thing. I had the nicest constituency and the nicest association and it would have given them an awful shock. A lot of them, I'm sure, had their doubts already and I think I could have ridden the storm. I so much admire Chris Smith for taking the risk.

He came out when you were an MP, didn't he?
No, it was some years later. Nobody did in that parliament. I think it was in the next parliament. It's true he was a Labour MP in a metropolitan constituency. I can rehearse and believe me in my mind a million times I have rehearsed all the reasons why he could do it and I couldn't have. But I still wish I had.

Did Mrs Thatcher know you were gay?
Yes because I went to see her.

She was always quite tolerant of things out of the ordinary…
I think she quite liked gossip. I think she thought that the things human beings do are really very strange and unknowable. I told her I was gay when I went to say goodbye to her and she put an arm on my wrist and said 'Matthew that must have been very difficult for you to say'. She meant it kindly.

Do you think in this country we are a little bit obsessed with anybody who might be gay? The David Laws issue wouldn't have been such a big story had there not been a gay element to it.
What gay men who are not really out need to beware of, and Peter Mandelson notwithstanding, this is a warning not a threat, is the status of being a little bit gay and kind of suspected of being gay but not having admitted that you are gay, because it really whets the media's appetite. Either you stay right in the closet, or if you've edged a little way out, for God's sake come all the way out quickly. There is no status, although Peter Mandelson hoped there would be, in your homosexuality, as Peter puts it, being 'private but not secret'. It's public or it's nothing.

Has he forgiven you for outing him on *Newsnight*?
He may have forgiven me, he's perfectly kind about me in his autobiography and I've nearly forgiven him. I do think he made the most tremendous hoo-ha about it and I don't think the BBC would have been so silly unless they thought Peter wanted them to.

Just to put it on the record, you thought genuinely that he was out in the open?
He was. He may not have thought he was out in the open, but as he says in his book you'll see that he points out, as I pointed out endlessly at the time without anybody being remotely interested in hearing it, that he had been comprehensively outed by the *News of the World* ten years before. I read that and I had read the other articles in the *Evening Standard* which had described him as gay. It was the media who decided to use the rather high profile glancing reference as their peg. Peter got quite unnecessarily cross, the BBC

took huge fright, I was sacked as a columnist from *The Sun*. I don't suppose Peter spoke to Elizabeth Murdoch or anyone else. Plainly somebody did what they thought he would think was appropriate, so I've nearly forgiven him. After his memoirs which were quite kind, I've almost completely forgiven him.

Do you think politics is sleazier now than twenty or thirty years ago?
It's definitely not sleazier now. It probably was sleazier twenty or thirty years ago. It has been getting steadily less sleazy for about two centuries. The next big sleaze story is lobbying. They don't call themselves lobbying companies now; they call themselves public relations and all that sort of stuff. Strategic consultants. It has wrapped its tentacles around the American political system in the most throttling way; it is just beginning to do that here. We could well do with a new wave of sleaze busting whose target is not the politicians but the commercial interests who attach themselves limpet-like to the political process. If I was advising a young man or woman thinking of going into political communications, I'd say 'watch out' as the industry could be the next big car-crash.

Back in 1990, I turned down a job with Ian Greer.
So did I. He wanted me to be a director of his company. What were you going to be?

I don't know but when a poodle walked into the office during my third interview I decided it wasn't the job for me. I also turned down a job to manage Shirley Porter's re-election campaign. I regard those as two of my better decisions in life.
Ian Greer got a rather raw deal because he was a bit extravagant and colourful in the way he went about the schmoozing. He became the lightning rod for the whole industry and the media decided that it was just Ian Greer Associates. All Ian Greer did was in a more flamboyant way the things that a lot of other companies were doing and that crash has still to come. It's not enough to send Ian Greer off into exile as some kind of scapegoat. He was in many ways a nice and generous man.

Lobbying is a perfectly legitimate activity, if you want legal advice you go to a lawyer, why shouldn't a company go to a professional firm of political consultants for advice on how to get their message across?
Because if you want legal advice, you need to understand the law. If you haven't followed the law and learnt the law, you won't understand it so you have to ask somebody who does. A democracy, if it is to work, has to be something that anybody with an argument to make or evidence to give can feel they can go directly to the people whom they've represented. They shouldn't need intermediaries. Once you begin to establish intermediaries,

the intermediaries begin to establish a convenient working relationship with the politicians and begin to exclude the public from coming to them or interest groups from coming to them in any other way than via the intermediaries – and it's a very malign process.

You're very rude about Gordon Brown in a few of your columns
Yes, I'm proud to be.

Do you think he was bonkers?
I think he was unhinged. That's the same word Tony Blair used of Margaret Thatcher. I think Tony Blair was a bit unhinged too. I think Margaret Thatcher had her unhinged moments. I think there was something very odd about Gordon Brown. It wasn't an oddness that made him unfit for any useful role in public life but it certainly made him unfit for any central role as a communicator or explainer but more than that as a listener. He wasn't a good listener, he wasn't good at being honest about what the problems were. He seemed to have a difficulty with bad news that was more than the difficulty Tony Blair had, which was he didn't want people to know it. Gordon didn't seem to want to hear it himself.

Have you read Alastair Campbell's diaries?
Yes, now! I hadn't read them when Alastair Campbell put me as a quote on the back cover saying 'these diaries are brilliant and future historians will read them gasp and come to rely on them'.

How did he come to do that?
I wrote that about something else. Other diaries that he wrote that I had read, but not the latest.

Didn't you feel having read the Campbell book 'how on earth did the rest of the Cabinet allow this man [Gordon Brown] to become prime minister'? The whole book is a catalogue of incidents that show him to be demonic in some ways and totally irrational.
When you've finished Peter Mandelson's book, you'll feel that three times over. From Peter Mandelson's book, an even more weird character emerges. It isn't just the demonic nature of Gordon Brown. It isn't just the fact that he was impossible to deal with, the rages and the refusals to listen to the truth and accept bad news and all the rest. Some very great men and women have had those traits. It was that in the end he had nothing to say. There was no treasure trove of new political ideas. The cupboard of his philosophical mind was completely bare and anyone who had followed him as I had, and the things he had said and written and listened to him answering questions

would have realised that from the start. I have a real problem with his senior colleagues who knew what he was like and did nothing. I also have a bit of a problem with the media and the lobby who decided that he was a great man because he told them he was a great man and started writing he was a great man, when it became apparent that he wasn't emerging as a great man, started writing that he was a great man but his greatness had not yet emerged, which was really by way of an explanation of why they had said he was a great man in the first place. The truth was he was never a great man, he wasn't a great man, there were never any hidden depths and none of us should have been conned into thinking there were.

In one of your more generous moments to Gordon Brown, what would you advise him to do now?
Quit the House of Commons as there is no way he could creep back as a backbencher. I think he will quit the House of Commons before the end of this year and write, and perhaps teach. I think he could be an interesting lecturer to an audience that knew what he was talking about. I don't think he's a good explainer to the uninitiated, I could see him at an American university. I could see him writing about the subjects that he knows a lot about. I don't think his memoirs would be very interesting unless he suddenly discovers an element of self examination in his character which has not yet been displayed. I know people say he should go to the IMF or the World Bank or all that but I'm not sure.

Since you've been active in politics, who are the three most impressive figures you've encountered?
Keith Joseph, who really drew me into politics not long after I left university because he seemed to say the things that I was thinking that no one else dared to say and the Conservative Party wasn't then daring to say. Nick Ridley, who was Secretary of State for Transport when I was still hopeful of becoming a junior transport minister. I loved his honesty; I loved his uncompromising right wing views. I loved his liberalism in the economic sense. Who I would choose as a third person whom I admire? I'm afraid it would be David Cameron who has seen what the Conservative Party needs to do and needs to be and has had enough steel to bend the party to his will and I believe is going to be a great prime minister.

I think in party terms he is the most powerful Conservative leader since Churchill. I'm not even sure Churchill had complete control over his party. Margaret Thatcher certainly didn't but I think he does.
Yeah which is partly judgement, partly luck. The coalition and this is something that never occurred to me, didn't really occur to many

commentators before the election, the coalition has left us with a stronger government, not a weaker one. I never wrote a more mistaken column than the one in which I say that England doesn't like coalitions and if we have a coalition government, it'll just stumble onto another election in a year. Looking back as I did. I don't know why it didn't occur to me.

You had your three most impressive, what about three people that you've just thought 'why have they bothered?'
If someone was completely unimpressive, one wouldn't want to knock them. I think there are a few people who have really significantly increased the amount of evil there is in the world. Alastair Campbell is one of them. I believe he has made a personal contribution to lowering the terms of politics and the media in Britain. I think Tony Blair has actually done more evil, much more evil than Gordon Brown, who is simply incompetent. Tony Blair was a confidence trickster of the worst kind. I'm not going to cast around for a third person!

You spend a lot of time in Spain, what does Spain give you?
It's family really. Wherever my family were, my father until he died recently, my mother and my five brothers and sisters, three of whom live in Spain, there I would be. We have this great house that my sister and her husband and I have been restoring in the Pyrenees. I love that project although it's nearly complete now. I love mountains and where my families are is the Pyrenees but really if it were the Andes, if it were the Pyrenees, if it were the Drachensburg Mountains in South Africa, I love mountains.

Do you ever go back to Africa?
Yes. I haven't been back to Zimbabwe because until recently I have thought I might be persona non grata because of the things I have written. I think I might now. I've been back to Swaziland where I was educated, back to South Africa. I go a lot to East Africa. I've got to like Ethiopia a great deal and I love Algeria.

Quickfire

Favourite food?
Bread and butter pudding.

Tell me something that few people know about you.
I have a rudimentary third testicle.

I wasn't expecting that! What does rudimentary mean?
It never completely formed. Apparently it's not uncommon!

Ok... pity we don't have a cameraman here.
You're blushing Iain!

What's your favourite view? Don't say 'my third testicle'!
It's the view of the City of London from Waterloo Bridge.

Favourite music?
Richard Strauss

Favourite holiday destination?
The Andes.

One thing you'd change about yourself?
I'd like to be astonishingly good looking.

What book are you currently reading?
I'm just finishing Peter Mandelson's autobiography.

Favourite film?
Whistle Down the Wind.

One thing you wish you'd known at sixteen.
That if you pull the paper hand towel from the dispenser in the public lavatory before you wash your hands, it won't come to bits in the way that it does if you try to pull it from the dispenser when your hands are wet.

What makes you cry?
Other people's misfortune.

Hero?
Peter Wildblood. The journalist convicted in the Montagu trials who wrote the first book about being gay that has ever been written in the English language.

Finally, villain?
(Laughs) Tony Blair.

I thought you may say that.

Shirley Williams

Party affiliation: Liberal Democrat

Born: 27 July 1930

Education: Attended Somerville College, Oxford.

Family status: She has a daughter, a stepdaughter and two grandchildren.

Pre-political career: Journalist at the *Daily Mirror* and *Financial Times* and then General Secretary of the Fabian Society in 1960.

Electoral history: Elected as Labour MP for Hitchin in 1964, a seat which she held until 1979. In 1974 she joined the Labour Cabinet as Secretary of State for Consumer Protection, moving two years later to Education and Science. After losing her parliamentary seat, she remained on the Labour Party National Executive before resigning in January 1981 to form the Social Democratic Party (SDP), which she became President of throughout the party's independent existence. She became a Liberal Democrat peer in 1993, taking the title Baroness Williams of Crosby, and the party's spokesman on foreign affairs in the Lords in 1997. From 2001 to 2004 she was the Liberal Democrat leader in the House of Lords.

Career highlights: Forming an independent political party, becoming a peer and, in 1981, turning a Conservative majority of 19,272 in an SDP majority of 5,289 in the Crosby by-election.

Interesting fact: She was named after the argumentative heroine of Charlotte Brontë's novel *Shirley*.

Date of interview: July 2010
Extended version
Venue: Little College Street, Westminster
Total Politics Issue 28, October 2010

Shirley Williams was the first politician I ever met. She came to address my school, Saffron Walden County High, back in the halcyon days of 1978 when I was fifteen and the country hadn't yet experienced the winter of discontent. When I met her three decades later I joked with her that it was she who had turned me into a raving Thatcherite. She smiled. I think.

Shirley Williams has become everyone's favourite political grandmother. Her appearances on Question Time *light up the programme. And yet she is still seen on the right as an incredibly divisive figure because of her role in the comprehensivisation of secondary education.*

I was approached last year by Lib Dem MEP Andrew Duff who asked if I would be interested in publishing a book on Shirley to mark the occasion of her eightieth birthday in July 2010. He was adamant she wouldn't want a so-called 'festschrift', so instead he got together a collection of high-powered politicians, journalists and academics to write essays on issues close to her heart. The book, Making the Difference: Essays in Honour of Shirley Williams, *is now available and I was honoured to speak at its formal launch in September.*

I really do wonder if Shirley Williams now feels totally comfortable in the coalition supporting Liberal Democrats. She denies it, but there must have been times during the Blair years when she wondered whether she should return to her spiritual home. And I suspect if she had been fifteen years younger she may well have done.

Do you enjoy *Question Time*?
Mostly I do. I've had a couple of experiences that I didn't enjoy at all. I think almost entirely with the Hitchens brothers. I can tell you from personal experience that if you have both Hitchens, it is devastating! One thing, they don't like each other at all. I went into the green room and there was a Hitchens at each end of the green room and they had no conversation, and no reason to have to pretend to have one. Once the programme began, they began by ripping each other to bits then they turned on me. It was like living with several fox hunts simultaneously, very unpleasant.

You have just turned eighty. Is that a real milestone in your mind?
My friends and acquaintances have been really sweet in insisting I recognise it. I've had four birthday parties. Everyone loves celebrating someone else's eightieth birthday. The actual person who has the birthday isn't so sure. I've noticed several of my friends are very keen indeed on my eightieth birthday. Whether it means I won't be there that much longer or they genuinely love parties, I'm not sure. Certainly they seem to be enthused about it.

I'm reading Peter Mandelson's book at the moment. Reading that, together with Alastair Campbell's, you wonder how that government survived so long.
First of all they are extraordinarily gifted people. So in a way, other people would put up with a lot more from them than they would in most cases. In most cases you have to bang people's heads together and say 'what the bloody hell do you think you are doing?' When Peter Mandelson became a peer and answered a question in the Lords, I was terribly impressed and I sent him a note saying 'I know when I can see a class act'. Not that Peter

Mandelson is someone I feel terribly close to. But I was just impressed by the sheer professionalism of the man. I think you could say the same about Tony Blair, an extraordinarily professional performance. Possibly less so Gordon. Gordon had more solidity than the others. I think he was a man of huge intellectual power. You wouldn't send a note to Gordon saying 'this is a class act'; it would be an odd thing to do. I think that was one element of it. The second element of it was that in the key periods Alastair Campbell was quite good at balancing it out to some extent. I think he coped with some of the confrontations quite well. In a funny way I think that Gordon was slightly haunted by a feeling of having been cheated – which everyone talks about. He was also haunted by a very powerful non-conformist conscience which nobody talks about because nobody remembers what it is. It was something very real, very strong. And that non-conformist conscience partly affected him when he felt that he had not conducted his policies according to what a powerful non-conformist preacher would expect. The second bit was when he thought he behaved badly towards people. He could behave very badly towards people but I didn't think he did it without cost.

So you think he recognised that he had behaved badly?
I think he did to some extent. I think he felt, retrospectively, rather bad about it.

In the Campbell book, Blair comes out the worst, very weak and unable to make the confrontations that he should have made...
I don't think 'weak' is the right word. First of all he was a man who hated confrontation. Don't forget for a lot of his life, his father was very ill. If you are a child, whose parents are ill, you spend a lot of time being told not to shout and don't kick a football around the house and that sort of thing. You develop a great adversity to being engaged in conflicts and rows. In his relationship with his colleagues and with Cherie, you always see him playing a conciliatory figure. I think it has a fair amount to do with his childhood, actually.

If you had been in Blair's situation, I can't imagine you would have done the same thing. You would have knocked their heads together surely?
I think I would have gone and had it out with them, yes.

Wasn't that part of Blair's lack of overwhelming success in his political career that he didn't? There was always this running sore of Gordon in the background. It was the same the other way around with Gordon.
First of all I think there was the fact that Gordon felt he had been cheated. It

doesn't really matter if they did or didn't have that famous dinner. Gordon had laid down this solid step-by-step ascent up the stairs of the Labour structure. Not only going through all the motions you go through, student politics, youth politics, Scottish politics, parliamentary politics, ministerial politics etc. – starting very young and being very predictable. We've got Blair still running around being a pop star at the point at which Gordon has already become rector of Glasgow University. There must have been a deep sense

There was a sense of entitlement from Gordon. He was prepared to not push that entitlement while John Smith was alive. Gordon deferred to him, although I think John Smith wasn't that much older than him. When it came to Tony, parachuting in from nowhere much, in Gordon's view, I think Gordon must have felt both revulsion and anger, so I think he clearly felt cheated. It was feeling cheated more than being overtaken that really rankled with him. I think, Gordon is a difficult man by any standards, but also in some ways a very impressive man. I always felt with Tony he was brilliant. He was a brilliant communicator, a brilliant actor. I always thought he was more actor than politician. Incredible, he could play Coriolanus at the drop of a hat, or Henry V part 2. A lot of him was like that, he was chameleon like in a way. He could slightly change his colour as he went around, according to what the scene was. He also, I think, became very seduced by two things. The first thing was being seduced by America to an extraordinary extent. Having spent a lot of my life in America, I like a lot of things about it and I find lots of things very attractive, but I'm not seduced. I can see what's wrong too. I'm always interested by the way in which one British politician or another is just swept off their stupid feet. Geoff Hoon is another one.

Do you think Gordon Brown was undone by his own ambition?
No, not by his ambition, by his bitterness. The ambition was, in a way, defused by the extreme difficulty in becoming Prime Minister and the fact that it had ceased to be enjoyable. I think the ambition had been defused in the long years between. I think it was two things really. I think one was a slight feeling of déjà vu, 'I mean here I am, all the things that I've wanted to have either been done or can't be done'. It was like getting the fag end of an administration. Already the Labour administration had become relatively unpopular. Secondly he had inherited what was beginning to be quite a split party. Not split over him but split between Old Labour and New Labour, with quite a lot of restlessness about New Labour.

Gordon's great opportunity came in the economic crisis because he was suddenly able to project himself as being a world statesman and onto the stage of the G20. He was one of the people who had a solution and a solution that with a lot of hard work he had won the G20 over to. All of that buoyed him up. I think the real disappointment came shortly after that when we first of all learned that we had a new crisis over the deficit and so forth, and even the global response couldn't get us completely out of that. Then you have a fairly sharp decline. A lot of the Labour Party didn't really understand what he had done as it was quite technical stuff. Perhaps more significantly by that time a lot of the media had just got it in for him. They never liked him, they didn't like the fact that he didn't have press conferences and he didn't schmooze them as Tony did. They really had it in for him. They decided he was going to be an ogre. I don't think he had a clue how to handle that.

I think we underestimate his status in other countries. They really did respect him, didn't they?
With ICNND [Internal Commission on Nuclear Non-proliferation and Disarmament], I spent the last year and a half travelling extensively around the world. Not all the time but probably a third of my time has been going to Cairo, Tokyo, Santiago and God knows where not. It gave me the opportunity, in most places, to talk to some of the leading figures. The ICNND is a very small commission, only fifteen people altogether. I was very impressed by the number of people who said to me 'I cannot say how grateful I am to your Prime Minister, he has been immensely helpful to me, and he has given me support all the way along the line', particularly from developing countries. An example was Michelle Bachelet, President of Chile, who said he [Gordon Brown] had been wonderfully supportive and had assisted her with economic ideas and so forth. I talked to the Indonesians who felt he had been very helpful, a couple of African leaders. His standing in the world is such that it makes the assessment of him in the UK look bizarre, to say the least of it.

By this time, Tony had, if not left the stage, had done himself so much damage in Iraq that most of these third world leaders were not going to be particularly nice about him. Some may say he was a charming man but there was no substantial serious appreciation of him. He had thrown that away by the Iraq thing. Gordon was untouched by Iraq, really, and you remember he said almost nothing during the period. He was thought to be supportive because he couldn't say he wasn't. He did have this astonishing following which came mostly from his economic capacity but mostly from his evidently very honourable commitment to economic development. He always ring-fenced that, put it first and cared about it. It was a funny mixture of socialism and imperialism. I think therefore I would say that Gordon was badly underestimated in the country, seriously underestimated. I think that is quite souring. If you know people love you somewhere else and in your own country you're treated as a joke, an ogre, a bad tempered-bear or whatever it was that our friend the cartoonist did.

It's not unusual as Thatcher had a higher reputation outside this country than she did here, as did Gorbachev in Russia.

Perfectly true. Slight difference is Mrs T was vastly admired in those countries that went her way. She wasn't much admired in Europe, very little really. Eastern Europe, hugely, non-EU Europe hugely. EU Europe, hardly at all.

Was there any time in the New Labour years when you thought 'Actually I could go back now'?
Never. I was asked more than once, by people like Peter Mandelson. The reason was quite straight forward. It was actually to do with the liberal core about civil liberties. They were bad about civil liberties; there was no doubt about that. I was outraged by how they dealt with terrorism for example. I was outraged by how they pressed on and on for further detention without trial. I was pretty outraged by the unquestioning willingness to see the prison population go up and up and up, without asking whether it was a sensible way to deal with a falling crime rate. I know some people would say it was a falling crime rate because they were all locked up. It doesn't work in America where they are all locked up as well. When it came to almost all the Home office stuff it was terribly disappointing. No I couldn't have gone back. I could have gone back on social welfare grounds and also on constitutional grounds. On constitutional grounds it was terribly disappointing as when Tony smiled kindly on people like the Maclennan committee... when you actually look at what happened once the Liberal Democrats stopped being a potential party of government, which brought us devolution, human rights etc, by 1999/2001, it had almost all gone. Almost all enthusiasm for constitutional change had simply left. Parliament was increasingly being treated as a rubber stamp, MPs were increasingly treated with contempt. There was no attempt to try and avoid select committees simply being imposed on MPs by the whips. Labour simply treated Parliament as a sort of machine. Mrs Thatcher began that way but Labour took it further and at no point really seriously... individuals like Anthony Wright were brilliant but the government, no.

How did Mandelson try to tempt you?
He just rang me and we had lunch. A nice lunch.

[Laughs] A way to a woman's heart?
I think he thought the time had come to try. I think I was just a trophy wife.

This was in the early days?
Yes quite early on. Must have been 2002 I think, when Tony had been re-elected. About then.

Let's talk about the coalition. I can imagine you weren't enthusiastic...

I began by thinking we should try for a Labour coalition. I realised after a while that a) they didn't even want it and b) they were clearly quite contemptuous of the whole idea.

Which they deny!
But they were though. Also the attention had shifted over who was going to be a new leader. Once Gordon was going to go, a lot of the energy of the Milibands and so on went over to who will be following, not 'let's have a coalition'. I think a lot of them were scared that if you were seen to be cosying up to the Liberal Democrats then they would burn their boats with the unions and the left wing. So it wasn't a very attractive suggestion from their point of view. I'm satisfied they didn't want it. Then I thought 'how about a minority Conservative government' with what they call a support and supply, which is probably what I'd have gone for myself. But reflecting back I'm not sure I was right. What is true is, I didn't like the idea of a coalition with the Conservatives and I still find elements of it very hard to live with.

Isn't that endemic in any coalition? Particularly with the junior partner in any coalition. There will always be parts that are difficult to stomach with whichever party it would be.
There are some things from my point of view that are peculiarly difficult. Education is one of them. Probably education and then, luckily the Conservatives as you know have avoided a great conflict over the EU. Those two are the most neuralgic for me. I wouldn't have left the Labour Party in order to join a party that was going to do the same thing all over again.

I think in the end, two things persuaded me. For the whole month of April, I travelled from the top to bottom of England, Newcastle to Penzance and Land's End. I didn't just do meetings, I spoke to thousands of people on the streets and pavements and because I've been a lot on television, particularly *Questoin Time* and *Any Questions*. Probably about one person in ten knows who I am. I'd get scores of people coming up and talking to me. What I got from them was a very strong sense of outrage about MPs expenses, disproportionate outrage really because the level of anger was even greater than the level of misbehaviour. Some of these were a shock to the core, some things were, you know, almost ludicrously exaggerated like the issue of the rocking chair and things like that, or the dolphin or whatever. It was very silly of the MP but not wicked, just very silly. There were wicked things like the switching around of one's house to get capital gains, etc. I was quite surprised by the fury of the public which was very very powerful. I got exempted by being a 'national treasure'. I say that in quotation marks. But because I was a 'national treasure', they were all the angrier not with me but with what was happening. That was the first thing;

the second thing was this very intense sense of a 'plague on all your houses', a 'we don't want any of you in government'. The Liberal Democrats were not so morally accused as the two [bigger] parties, but there was a sense that you're all up to it, you're evil. So we got a plague on all your parties, on all your houses. Therefore, when the electorate voted in fairly substantial numbers, it was an improvement on earlier elections, not a drop. What you got was this very strong feeling that we're going to give you another chance, we're going to stick to the mainstream parties. There wasn't a huge upsurge for UKIP, as you know, or the Greens. What they wanted was, I think, the parties to work together. I don't think they worried explicitly about which party they wanted to work together but they wanted to see politicians working together. There are lots of places that I went to, what we got was people saying 'you've bloody well got to work together'. They said so very explicitly so I think the message was people wanted a coalition.

I have a very strong sense, partly affected by Greece, that because we have such a serious economic problem that we would need more than just one party to get it through and we would have to have something resembling a consensus on the way the reductions should be made and so forth. Therefore, I know this sounds awfully corny, we had a semi-patriotic duty to be part of this really tough story. In this really tough story, I hope, and it remains to be seen, that the emphasis on social justice would be real. So, I'm a fairly outright critic of the banks. I've been pushing really hard recently for the argument for the proposals that came from America about splitting the retail banks and the gambling banks. I'm a strong believer in having limits on what could be paid for bonuses. I feel very disappointed that we do not have a more effective policy for affordable housing which I think is becoming a really big issue, especially in the towns. So, on quite a lot of things, there are clear benchmarks for me on whether we have had an impact. I think we have had a good impact on civil liberties areas. For example the decision to not proceed further on detention without trial and to look into the torture issue and to move from locking up everybody who you could possibly lock up.

They were existing Conservative policies, surely?

Some were, mainly due to David Davis. I do respect the man. We have got extreme luck in having Clarke as minister of Justice. So we're going to get a lot further than when we had people like Straw there. So things like that have been rather good. Some of them come out of expenditure. For example, education, and I am strongly in agreement with stripping off these endless bureaucratic orders all over the shop. I know this isn't specifically Conservative... but they're quite right about that. I think it goes, quite rightly, to back away from the tremendously restrictive attempt to try and hem teachers in in every possible direction. I'm very surprised by the degree of, perhaps the only word is detestation, for local government. I'm a believer in it. I've seen how countries like Spain and France have been regenerated by regional autonomy. By tapping into the good ideas and thoughts of people at a regional level. If you go somewhere like the Rhône in France or parts of Spain, you see the amazing differences that have been made. Both the old parties seem to be united in their total contempt for local government and kicking them out of any area of responsibility that they have.

I never understood why local government has to run schools.
It doesn't have to be, but it is. It's where you start from. You start from a situation where it has the biggest single responsibility and biggest single source of funding. You can't take that away without a) wondering whether it is good or bad for education itself and secondly without recognising that if you take it away without replacing it with something else, you are going to have a very emasulated local government, which is what we have got.

Isn't it more important for schools to be able to run themselves rather than local government?
Primary schools can't. They just haven't got the means to do it. You could argue that some big secondary schools can. I suggested to Michael Gove that we ought to delay the primaries to see how it went before we leapt into this…

Has he ever talked to you as a former secretary of state?
Oh yes, I'm in the coalition aren't I?

Well I know, but you're…
A long way apart?

Well no, I just thought as a former secretary of state, I hopefully thought that he would consult you…
Oh he did, greatly to his credit. I think Michael and even possibly more Jonathan [Hill]. There has been a real attempt for minds to meet. They've been extremely good that way. They've been open to talking to us. I know how busy it is being a minister. Both of them find the time somehow. I think they probably think that because I'm a former Secretary of State that they want to persuade me that this is the right thing to do.

I do think primary schools are the building blocks of community really. They are not quite the same as secondary schools. At their best they're embedded in the community. If you close a primary down in a village or a small part of town, you gradually kill the community, it dies. In a small village it dies completely. There is nothing else that's there. In the towns and urban areas, it isn't quite so difficult. But even there it is quite difficult as a lot of cases in primary school, the teachers and head are an alternative to a family for kids who don't have a family, who come from very deprived social backgrounds or very deprived emotional backgrounds. The amount that teachers do there is just incredible. To actually then drive them out into the private sector which is much more expensive, is not very clever actually. In a big secondary school you may have a head and a team who can handle it and decide 'do we go to a local authority or do we go to the private sector' but in a small primary school, maybe a couple of hundred kids, it's just not there. That really worries me. I think we may have run ourselves into deep trouble.

Do you think one of the reasons the coalition has worked so far is because of the interpersonal relationships between the different personalities and that they're all learning together at the same pace?
I think that's a perfectly fair point. Most of the Conservatives ministers have not been there before. What I don't really know is quite where Iain Duncan Smith and Frank Field fit in. Clearly there is quite a lot of innovative thinking going on about welfare and so forth. What I can't really see is what the positive incentives are to people who for example live on disability benefit and so forth.

I think in ministerial terms, that department [the DWP] has the strongest team of the whole government.
It is a strong department. I think the problems are more likely to rise either in the Home Office, which at the moment doesn't seem to be doing too badly, or Defence. Liam Fox has got his wheels off the rails once or twice already. There is a big issue with Trident. That one is hard to walk away from having to make a decision one way or another. You can delay the decision. Personally I'm strongly in favour of delaying it, having been involved in all the nuclear proliferation stuff for a year and a half, this seems a very bad time to make a decision of like for like because you are going to have forty years of sitting on top of a deterrent which may prove to be totally pointless. It is a lot of money to be totally pointless.

The Lib Dem leader of Liverpool City Council thinks that the coalition will result in the obliteration of the Liberal Democrats at the next election.
A lot depends on how the thing plays out. If the coalition is directly associated with the economic crisis and how that is dealt with and it's dealt with in a way that although painful, most people accept it was fair, then I think it'll go the other way. I think the Liberal Democrats will be seen as serious people who have the experience of government. Our problems have always been being seen as the ones who are ineffective or unlikely to win or

so improbable that you wouldn't vote for them – that is largely got over by having come into a coalition because we'll be able to say here are half a dozen people with considerable experience of government as Liberal Democrats. That, in turn, will turn on whether the public does see the final approach to fiscal problems as good and influenced by the Liberal Democrats or bad and influenced by the Liberal Democrats. I think that will be the key issue.

The historical precedents aren't great, are they?
There aren't many. There was a very successful coalition during the war which we all pretend wasn't a coalition, but it was. It was a five-year long extremely successful coalition which among other things threw up the origins of the welfare state. It was probably the most impressive government we have ever had. People all go back to the '30s, which would have been a depressing time whoever was in government. They all neatly forget the war. I think the parallel is closer to the war than it was to the '30s because it was about taking very tough decisions which are painful decisions for a lot of people, but somehow holding them to feeling that was the right thing to do and therefore being closer to government rather than further away from it – which was what happened in the '30s, a sense of people moving away from the government, but not in the war, not at all!

When you go around the country and talk to Liberal Democrat members in your role as 'national treasure' [laughs], do they ever take you aside and say 'Oh Shirley, it's terrible, I can't believe we're in this awful coalition…'
No, actually, not. Most recently I've been doing quite a lot of book festivals. I'm well aware that the people that come are Liberal Democrats or Liberal Democrat sympathisers, and they come out in very large numbers. They pack the hall out every time. Quite a lot of people ask me in the book signing what I think about the coalition. So far, I've said to them what I say to you. In almost every case, I would say probably two out of every 100 would disagree. They say 'Oh good, yes I think it's a good idea, we have to make it work, etc.' They are still in love with it. A lot of people say to me 'It's such a wonderful change that we can have new ideas and new thoughts, we've lost that endless bickering of the Labour Party and Cameron is a decent Conservative and is keeping his right wing under control.' That is very much more the reaction.

How do you judge David Cameron?
I only know him as a member of the public. I've never even met him. I don't know him at all. He hasn't asked to see me either. I would say he is a good deal more impressive than I thought he was. I thought that he was a lightweight charmer, a kind of Cecil Parkinson type – able to charm the birds off the trees but with not that much to offer. I don't think that now. I

think he has been quite impressive. He has been quite brave. On a number of things he has taken a strong line. I have to agree with my dear friend Nick Clegg that he is actually an impressive fellow. They seem to get along like a house on fire.

Do you think women who go into politics have it easy compared to when you started out?

No. not really. In some ways they have it harder. They don't have it harder in the sense of running into a tremendous amount of patronage from men, which I certainly did. I had a permanent secretary who wouldn't speak to me about things at all. He was the permanent secretary during the seamen's strike when my minister was in hospital. It was rather difficult. I ran into a huge amount of patronising. I also ran into people who thought a woman minister was waiting for their charms to become obvious to her, particularly when I was Prices Minister. They all fancied themselves as people who could get me to agree that an increase in profits was badly needed for investment purposes. The way they thought they could do that was by taking me out to expensive lunches. They got that completely wrong. I ran into a lot of that too. I think the reason I think it was in some ways easier was first we were seen as exceptional. Just being a woman was being remarkable. You didn't need to be much of a woman to get started. We had quite a lot of solidarity amongst ourselves, feeling that we were a minority so had to work together. Finally I would say that the absolutely devastating business was Blair's babes. I always remember when I saw that photograph, being reminded of those Italian paints when you had God's face surrounded by cherubs with lovely pink wings and pretty rosy bodies. The Blair picture with all the women around him, with identical haircuts and suits ineluctably reminded me of Renaissance gods. In the way they were background, they weren't foreground. All of that, I think. Finally one big difference, if I go back to when I was very young, you either had women like Lady Astor who had total staffing, so the domestic burden wasn't there for example. They were grand, they had nannies and all the rest of it. There were a few women subsequently, they might be like Mrs T and have the good luck to marry a wealthy man but had staff, as it were. Most current women politicians are terribly distracted by having two jobs to do. They don't find it easy to balance them up. Normally they're married and have children whereas they used to be single or widows. So in that sense I see more women I know struggling with the two lives as they try to keep them both up in the air. There are some remarkable women coming up, I think. There are some very good ones in the new crop. I think the Blair crop was foreshortened by being seen as background upholstery or decoration.

Would you like to have been prime minister?
No, not really. I never thought I was good enough.

Oh really?
Really.

You really surprise me as that isn't what comes through in your book at all in many ways.
I think I say it, but actually it's absolutely true. First of all my father brought me up to be excessively admiring of the great men of politics. Rather like you might feel about Mr Gladstone. You are a fairly tall tree but he was a pine that was twice your size. I was brought up particularly by my father to see people like Cripps and Bevan and so on as remarkably great men, not in terms of them being rich or aristocratic but in terms of them holding political office. I was slightly overawed by political men, both men and women actually but obviously many more were men. Secondly I always thought of myself as not quite good enough. That is very characteristic of women. Almost all the women I know underestimate themselves and all the men overestimate themselves.

Is it a case of not being good or ruthless enough? Not actually wanting to be involved in what Harold Wilson engaged in...
Poor Harold! [laughs] He wasn't really ruthless. He was manipulative.

Everyone always says about you 'she's so nice'.
It's rather damning.

I think it's a good thing.
It's also damning. I suppose I might say I've survived in politics for a long time and held some fairly important offices and don't like to be too horrible about it. I think men swallow the Alan Sugar picture of leadership. I won't bore you by going into too much philosophy but for the first time we may be seeing a different kind of leadership emerge, mostly from women but not entirely from women. This leadership is much more consensual, much more reasonable and much less tribal. It's not emerging very much in Britain, though. Cameron may turn out to be an example. When you go to places like Michelle Bachelet in Chile and Dr Sirleaf in Liberia, you come across this different kind of leadership which is basically about healing broken societies. I don't think our society is broken, I think it is cracked in places. A truly broken society like Liberia or Chile in the past is one where this kind of consensual healing leadership is crucial and works and the very typical ruthless managerial view of politics you get in Britain and the

United States simply disregards the fact that this kind of leadership is often more successful. It isn't sentimental, it is necessary. I think that is what is beginning to happen. People are beginning to recognise there is more than one type of leadership.

I read your book and I remember thinking at the time that you haven't used the book to settle scores, which is what many use their memoirs for. It's a very human book and I think it does sum up your career. I think it demonstrates why people say 'she is nice, she didn't really set out to do what most politicians do'.
I don't think I have many scores to settle. Well, not many…

Not many! [laughs]
No, not now. I'm not inhuman. I'm certainly not God. I've had some scores to settle where people have leaked to the press. I got one or two really difficult bits in my life, Grunwick, which lead me to have endless libel cases and so on. I had a very difficult time with *The Sun* when they announced I had never taken up, what was the phrase? 'A single challenge to beat the left.' I did think that was a bit hard. I've had my fair share of libel cases and all the rest of it. Maybe I am mellowing in old age, I don't know, but I don't really have a strong sense of scores to settle, no.

Final question, Enoch Powell said all political careers end in failure, how would you sum up your career?
No, certainly not true. I think I end up with a sense of huge pleasure with the life I've lead. Huge excitement brought to me by the life of politics and a patchy sense of achievement – some achievement, some not – some being highly controversial, comprehensive schools and so on. I don't regret any of them actually. None.

Quickfire

What is your favourite food?
Spare-ribs.

What food do you hate?
Beetroot.

Tell me one thing few people know about you.
That I'm eighty!

What's your favourite view?

The south end of Windermere Lake.

Favourite music?

The Beethoven Quartets.

One thing you'd change about yourself?

Looks. Hair particularly. Not looks, hair, I hate my hair. Nothing I can do about it except pull it out.

What book are you reading at the moment?

At this moment, the *White Tiger*.

One thing you wish you'd known at sixteen?

How to dress.

The worst gift you had ever given someone?

Oh dreadful. I once gave somebody a jar of marmalade that they had given me two years before. That was dreadful [laughs].

What makes you cry?

Actually very little. Onions.

Political hero?

Gladstone or Mandela.

Villain?

I'll get shot for this. I suppose I have to say Enoch Powell. Entirely because of race.

Iain Duncan Smith

Party affiliation: Conservative

Current position: Secretary of State for Work and Pensions

Born: 9 April 1954

Education: Attended HMS Conway School, Anglesey, and later the Royal Military Academy, Sandhurst.

Family status: Married with four children.

Pre-political career: Served in the military with the Scots Guards before leaving to join General Electric.

Electoral history: First elected as MP for Chingford and Woodford Green in 1992, a position he holds to this day, he went on to become shadow Social Security Secretary before taking up the role of shadow Secretary of State for Defence. Between September 2001 and October 2003 he was the leader of the Conservative Party. He recently, in May 2010, acquired the role of Secretary of State for Work and Pensions in the UK's coalition government.

Career highlights: Fighting off big-name candidates Ken Clarke and Michael Portillo to become the Conservative Party's eighth leader since Winston Churchill and later returning from the backbenches to become Secretary of State for Work and Pensions.

Interesting fact: His mother was a ballet dancer.

Date of interview: October 2010
Extended version
Venue: IDS's House of Commons office
Total Politics Issue 29, November 2010

Iain Duncan Smith is a man to be admired. Why? Because after he was ousted as Tory leader in 2003, he picked himself up off the political floor, dusted himself down, didn't feel sorry for himself and he set out to do some good. He formed the Centre for Social Justice and never looked back.

Some say IDS has got religion over the issue of social justice, and I think they have a point. He's become almost obsessive about an issue which had been the traditional preserve of the left. And he's made a real difference, not just on Conservative policy, but on the lives of so many who the CSJ have helped over the years. If he never achieves anything else in politics, he can look back with pride at that.

As Secretary of State for Work & Pensions, Duncan Smith is in a very strong position. He has no ultimate political ambition and is unbiddable. That means he stands more of a chance than most of driving through some serious welfare reform. And if that is his main political legacy, he ought to be very satisfied with that.

Iain Duncan Smith was in his final two months as party leader when I became a Conservative Party general election candidate in North Norfolk back in October 2003. He was very supportive and came to spend a day with me campaigning a year later. He didn't need to, but he was happy to, and I have never forgotten that. Whatever his failings as a party leader may have been, he is someone who now commands huge respect right across the party spectrum. And rightly so.

You've got a better than average office here, haven't you?
This office was originally the ex-leaders' or ex-prime ministers' office, and I got it when I finished being leader. Michael Howard had it before me. He'd managed to engineer it because William didn't want it. Gordon Brown could have had it because he's ex-Prime Minister, but he didn't want it. What little time he spends here he spends in Portcullis House. I didn't want to go behind the Speaker's chair, so I stayed here. This used to be the Clerk of Works office – they didn't stint themselves and there are false cupboards [gets up to open one of them] and they contain real Pugin wallpaper samples! Every now and again an official comes in and opens the cupboard door and looks through them.

When did Cameron first talk to you about doing your current job.
I'll tell you when it was – it was the day he was announcing out the Cabinet positions.

Because he announced at the conference last year you'd be taking on a senior role…
He announced that he wanted me to head up a committee, and I said to him at the time – fine, that's as far as I want to get. I didn't really want to commit at that stage, because Betsy wasn't well and I didn't really know where I'd be. I said look, I'm happy to help and assist in any way I can but you should understand that I'm not putting a pitch in for a job, I'm just simply saying that I don't really know so I'd rather not discuss anything further. He was quite happy with that, so we never really talked about anything until the day he rang me up, I said 'Can I get back to you?'

What persuaded you to do it? It must have been quite a big decision?

It was actually, yes. Most people say 'oh of course you'll have jumped to that and gone straight in' but I didn't actually, I'll be honest with you. I needed to figure out where we were with Betsy's treatment because that was a priority and still remains a priority, because she's still in recovery. So I needed to figure out whether I'd need to be with her as much as I had been and whether I could cope. She'd just finished the radiotherapy and was still pretty knackered. The energy levels are really appalling. She's had the chemo and the radiotherapy and the operations. So I wasn't sure about that, needed to balance that, needed to talk to her as priority number one. Two, I needed to balance in my mind whether I thought that what I was trying to do through the Centre for Social Justice (CSJ) was better served by me continuing to do it that way or whether being in government focused in one department, whether this was going to be a positive, or whether it was going to be a way of me disappearing into a department and not achieving very much. So I needed to balance that, which I duly did, and on balance I thought: well, first of all there are big things that I want to drive through on welfare reform, pensions reform, which we have talked about. That's one chunk of it. But because he also wanted me to chair the social justice cabinet committee, which was a new one, this would allow me to range a bit wider and to talk about the issue in other departments and encourage them onto the social justice agenda. That balanced off some of the other items.

So, with that combination I thought 'well, probably the best thing is to do it rather than not do it'. It does sound a bit mealy mouthed when I put it like that doesn't it? But it's not meant to be, but I did look at it as a sort of balance of decision.

Did you ask for any guarantees?

Well, that was the social justice committee really. Yes, the point that you're making is pretty much that and I asked him how determined he was to make reforms. Because I said that I'm not interested in coming in just to function. I said there are lots of people out there younger than me, keener than me to get on, to make their name, that's great, that's fine. But if you want someone to reform I'll do the reform, definitely, because that's what has to happen.

And was the key that reform has to be for the long term and not for short term political headlines?

What I want to do is succeed in this and wider. I don't just want to succeed in this, although this is big enough. The welfare reform stuff is enormous. But I also want to make sure the government sets itself in the right direction from the word go, which is very important to me. So I'm engaged in a lot of discussions wider than this about other things that impact. You know, I've talked to Ken Clarke about his justice reforms, which I initiated via the CSJ. And I'm fully behind him and helping him as far as I can. I'm looking at drugs policy, alcohol policy, across health, home affairs and our area. Driving stuff, driving lots of change in the agenda to see if we can't help. Education's got stuff that the CSJ wanted, free schools is part of that, we're very keen to support early years – that's really important to me and a number one priority.

How do you find dealing with other departments? Because Tony Blair went on about joined up government, and this is what you've got to achieve if the social justice agenda is to get anywhere, isn't it?
That's what the new Social Justice Cabinet committee has to do. If it's going to be effective, it has to drive new ideas through government. We have to make sure that drugs and alcohol policy doesn't just become a criminal affair. That actually it's hugely locked into health and rehab, and we make sure rehab and everything else is part of that. So at last we begin to square that up. And it's not going to be easy, because you know what departments are like. They'd love their secretary of state to say 'Get away, this is my island and you only come here when I invite your ship in'. We have to change that, and that's a culture that we're all engaged with trying to sort out.

Have you come across difficulties in that area so far, and how do you get over them?
I think the best way at this stage is character. I think you have to negotiate your way through so that people don't get the chance to stand on *amour propre*. We don't just take what the civil servants say to us about our status. That we become statusless, in the sense that we see ourselves not as secretaries of state, but as politicians trying to get a job done. And don't let the civil service package us off into silos. It's easier said than done. Some departments are past masters at capturing their ministers and their secretaries of state. I think most of my colleagues seem to be aware of the fact.

Interestingly, I was talking to a couple of civil servants and they said what's nice to see is that the cabinet committees are functioning again. The system pretty well died under the last government. It was so much sofa government that decisions were being made without going through proper procedure. And at last that's reignited. Hopefully we can drive through various cabinet committees, particularly mine.

What's been the reaction in your own department? I always think civil servants like the firm lead. There are some departments which have been given clear

leads – Eric Pickles has really shaken up his department. When you went in is that something you were conscious of, that you needed to provide that firm lead?
Yes. It's about management and how you do it. The first thing is that I thought that I'd have a lot of resistance. In fact, I was astonished that I had no resistance from all the key players. The first thing they said was 'we know what you've been wanting to do, we've been watching it for ages, we agree completely with what you're trying to do, we here think this benefits system is broken, we're sick and tired of trying to pick up the pieces every day trying to make it work. Everybody knows that it's got to be changed, what do you want?' So from the word go I was able to set down the parameters of where we were going to try and drive. What we needed was universal credit, which of course I hadn't got agreement for at that stage. We had to get that through, we had to work on the modelling work programme. We had to drive hard. So in other words we've pretty much had our foot to the floor and pressure on everybody to get from a to b. And the interesting thing about it has been that they've joined in with that. The vast majority of people in the department, as I said in my conference speech, I only have praise for. This is exactly how it should work. They've taken their political direction, they've taken – I hope – a sense of urgency and for the most part they've pretty well stuck to it. Obviously they've got little bits and pieces in there that aren't right. In terms of managing the department I feel it is much easier now because we have a sense of direction. Because I came and said 'bang, this is where we're going over the next eight or nine years, here's the reform, here are the time schedules, all I want from you is yes – this is how we're going to do it, here are the problems and let's sort them out'. And pretty much that's exactly what we did. And every one of them has done just that. And in the midst of that we've found savings. So I think that I haven't any problems at all with that. So strong leadership is right, but it needs to be strong leadership not because you're kicking them, it's strong leadership because you've given them a sense of direction and get them to sign up to that. That's the key.

Did you have any say in who your ministers were? Because I think you've got probably the strongest ministerial team in the whole government…
I agree with you. Interestingly I did, but I didn't have to say very much. There were a couple of potential adjustments but by and large these are the decisions that I would have made. If you'd asked me who I really wanted, I'd pretty much pick this team I think, particularly at minister of state level. On the one hand Steve Webb, on the other hand Chris Grayling. I think Steve coming in as a Liberal Democrat has been fantastic. They've all been great, but Steve because especially, because he's had the furthest to travel to join us.

He's always been traditionally seen as on the left of the Liberal Democrats, hasn't he? Are there any sort of creative tensions with some of the things you want to do?

None at all! The good thing about it is we just basically said 'Look, we're in here we've got to achieve some things. What do we want to achieve?' So we set out and discussed it. What do we want to achieve in pensions? Proper reforms, re-linking, changing the retirement age, looking at a proper pension reform which will knock people's socks off when it comes out in a few weeks' time. I'll say for Steve categorically, yes, people will always write that his reputation is that, but what I actually find is that he's said 'look, how often is a Liberal Democrat ever going to get into government? I've been moaning and complaining about the pensions system, this is my one shot changing it with you'. I recognise we have to compromise to do that, and that's been great really. So I think you're right, I do have the strongest ministerial team.

How do you avoid becoming bogged down by the sheer complexity of the whole system, and the size of the challenge? Because it's sort of like a Schleswig-Holstein question, isn't it? Three people completely understand it and two of them are dead.

Yes. The answer is don't stand still. If you're running over soft ground, run over it, don't walk. You have to get to the other side. The point is that we just have to keep the pace going. Getting bogged down is when you lose sight of what the far horizon is about. You just get locked into the nitty-gritty. And I say to everybody, let's keep constantly knowing where that flag is on the horizon, that that's where we're steering to. We may meander a bit while we're getting there, but we need to make sure our goal is still there. If for one moment we think otherwise then we need to consider what we're doing right now. So in all of this we've set the flags out up ahead of this. Whether it's the work programme, pensions reform, or massive universal credit reform. This is where we have to be by the end of this parliament. Can we make it? That's all I want to know. The rest is detail. We have to get it right. But if we have a doubt about that we have to make that clear. Keeping the process moving along the right track is what I think I have to do.

How do you avoid being Frank Field Mark Two?

Well, I love Frank to bits and I think he's great. He's a good friend and he's a very good politician. The difference I think between us is that I set up a structure while I was out of power – the Centre for Social Justice – that then worked in detail on programmes, particularly on this universal credit. We built a model that modelled the benefits system and we thought it through. The DWP, unbeknownst to me, was paralleling that work – unbeknownst to the government at the time as well – because they were convinced that this is the area they'd like to move on. So when I came in we knew how we'd achieve it: in other words we know what we've got to do. And the DWP have signed up to that straight away. So the real difference is that we've got a real, genuine structured work programme now. Frank hadn't quite reached that point, I think, because there was no sign-up at the highest level. I spent my first four months, as you may have read in some of the papers, getting sign-up. Now that process can be robust at times, but it is what I'm a politician for. I know what my bottom line is. I have to get myself to my bottom line through. And that does mean that some of these engagements will be reasonably robust. But we're all politicians and we know what the terms of the deal are, and that is that nobody respects somebody who doesn't know where their bottom line is. And I do. So with that, getting sign-up early on, which is what we've succeeded in doing, means the rest then is the matter of how do we achieve what we've agreed to sign up to.

The problem I think for Frank was that although the Prime Minister said he was on-side, the PM never squared Gordon Brown. Brown was never on-side. Frank then proceeded as though the PM would intervene, and he never intervened, and Gordon Brown won the day. So to be fair to Frank the deal was never on. For me, the deal has always been on from the word go and I've simply said number one, we're not going to repeat this. There's the line, that's where you sign, once we've all signed on that, now we know, no questions, the rest is getting it done. And that seems to me the way we have to be. I don't say we won't get things wrong, I won't say there won't be problems – these are huge changes we've been going through. But as long as we have sign-up to the principles of what we're doing, and to a greater extent the overarching detail, then the rest is a case of managing the process.

The Treasury has always been a great block to reform on this kind of issue because they are always watching the bottom line on a year to year basis. How robust did the exchanges get?

We're all friends, let me just say that. We're all friends. It's what politics is about. If you look back to the old Thatcher cabinet, people always had engagements, and debates and rows and arguments. The trick is can you walk away from it afterwards and say 'Let's go and have a drink.' I think the difference between us and the last government is that they seemed to hate each other personally. Strangely, they often agreed on political things, but hated each other personally. I think it's the other way around here – we all get on pretty well, we'll agree, disagree. But even the disagreements, and this is the important one, these disagreements are only about how to do things, they're not disagreements about the principles. For example the Chancellor signed up for reform, the Prime Minister signed up for reform, pretty much on the line of what we wanted. The question was how quickly can we deliver it, how much money does it take to deliver it? And if I was the Chancellor I'd have been in exactly the same place. I'd have asked the same two questions which he kept on asking me which is 'Are you certain that this will work? Show me, prove to me, let me become a believer that this process works. Secondly, are we also certain in the course of this we will ultimately save money?' Those two questions are critical and I believe that we've got the answers to them. And because of that very exhaustive process, which is very good for me and very good for him, we'd both sign-up for something which we'd be both believe we've actually gone to because we've been convinced by the arguments, rather than saying I have to do this because I've been bullied by somebody else. Not like that, we've actually agreed this.

Which of the two of you turned up the volume the most?
I would think it was at a collective calm and reasonable level really. What can I say? Amenable.

How much do your benefits reforms actually rely on there being jobs for people to go into in the end? Because you can't have an economic recovery without a lot of extra jobs being created. George Osborne is pinning a lot on the fact that the private sector is going to create huge numbers of new jobs. What if that doesn't happen?
You can't always predict where the economy will go. Our general belief is from the IMF right through to the OBR to the OECD, they all believe that we're taking the right action. They all predict growth of between two and two and a half per cent. Which is not startling, but for a developed economy at the moment is not bad, it's pretty good. That level of growth would deliver a big increase in private sector jobs. First of all I do actually believe we will see a greater level of jobs. People tend to just look at this period of the recession and say that it's all doom and gloom. Not it's not! First of all, there are millions of people still in work. They're still working, and their prospects are good. The second fact that we have is that the job centres have significant number of jobs vacant. And they're not all skilled jobs. I think it's about 450,000 or 460,000. So straight away there are jobs available even in the height of the recession. And second of all we all know that there are lots of jobs that aren't listed at the jobcentre and that are outside in the casual workforce. The last point is that even in the last quarter we saw the biggest jump in employment – 280,000 went back to work in one quarter. Which is the biggest jump since 1989 which is when these figures were first collated.

So the signs are... they're not great, but they're good. And they show there's activity. The important thing to know is that there is turn-around, there are jobs being created, there are people going in to work, yes it's not enough, we need more. But the point I make is that these reforms aren't just about there being more jobs. These reforms are about saying that throughout the growth of the last ten years, we have parked between 4 and 5 million people of working age, who didn't do any work at all. We had 20 per cent of all of our households doing no work at all. So that's the bit that you have to break into, that's what our reforms are really aimed at. Breaking into that resistant, residual unemployed group.

Where you've had a family for two or three generations where nobody's worked, how do you get the work ethic back into people who are in that situation without being unacceptably brutal in cutting benefits?
There are two or three ways that you do it. The first is that we don't have to cut the unemployed benefits as they stand. The key thing is to get the juxtaposition between being in work and not being in work as positive in financial terms. The way I describe that is by saying look, if you're out of work in such a household it's no good a politician saying, as they always do, and even commentators, it's no use lecturing about moral purpose to a family that doesn't really have a lot of work or no work at all. The problem is that's fine for you and me and others who've been in work or who have come from families who work even if we haven't got work, you've sort of sensed that work is just bigger than the idea of earning money.

So, accepting that we get the finger wagging and lecturing out of the way, we have to look at the nature of the family that we're talking about and then say what are the things that stand in the way, why somebody wouldn't take a job? And that's really what this reform is all about. And there are two or three things.

The first is that when they look at getting back to work they recognise that on the margins they don't think it pays.

Even if you marginally say that it pays – then you take your travel to work costs. Quite a lot of these jobs will be a little way away from where they work, so then they assume that it's too expensive. The aim of universal credit is to make work pay. That's critical. Because that's the big bit that says actually I'm better off in work. So that starts the process that says 'well I will look for this work, I will look for this job.'

The second thing is dealing with the family that surrounds them. So how you deal with that is that you set out what we call this big work programme. What this does is that in private and local sector voluntary organisations you tie a work programme around people to change their culture. That is to say, you get them work ready, you work to get rid of their difficulties, their problems, their addictions, their misunderstandings. You stay with them and mentor them, so they stay in work three, six, nine months, a year.

And the final bit is that you make sure that if they have particular disabilities you deal with that.

So those two go together. The work programme and the universal credit together actually allow you to knock out the things that stand in their way and allow them to progress naturally to work. Once they've been in work for a while they get what I call the work habit. At that point they're always going to want to stay in work so they'll have that impetus, they'll understand the whole idea of 'the purpose of my life'. That becomes clear to them in terms of work. But the bit you have to fill in is the bit before that. And that's the bit that you're talking about when we want to break down these workless households. And many of them can't go home and say to mum and dad 'I've got a problem at work, what do I do about it?' because their mums and dads have never worked – so what do they say? 'Why do you bother?' So what do we do? We need to replace that person with a mentor. They can turn to them when they have difficulty in the early period until they're settled. Once you start that flow of breaking those families down it allows you then to narrow and target in, and our early intervention work then follows in, which we're working with Michael Gove on, to then start targeting the difficult, difficult core families that we get after and that we start to break down on a much more structured basis.

Frank Field said he would rather see benefits cut for poorer families than see children's centres suffer because he thinks that they are so crucial to the development of kids in the early years. What are you doing to ensure that kids at that age don't suffer from the inevitable cuts that there are going to be?
There are certain priorities that a government must remember, that we were about when we were elected. I think early intervention is one of those areas. Now it's not my area directly, but it's an area I wrote a book on, and it's an area incorporated into the social justice cabinet committee. I discuss it constantly with Michael Gove and Sarah Teather. I think we're all passionate about it and heading in the same direction. I know David Cameron shares that sense, as does Steve Hilton, that this is the big life changer for those difficult families – early intervention. So all of that tells me that we will do our level best to make sure that these key high priority issues such as dealing with troublesome, difficult families, kids from difficult backgrounds, are informed by intervention.

The child benefit announcement slightly dominated the party conference. How did that come about?
Well, these matters have been discussed. I confess I had had discussions with the Chancellor about this for weeks, actually probably months, going back to when we first got elected, so I know all about them and know all about the ramifications and permutations of where do you find money, how do you share the load. The two principles of this are 1) I am desperate that

the changes taken from the start of the budget process to the end of the spending review are not seen as regressive but they are progressive. What does that mean? That means that we take a share of the burden so that it isn't all falling on the shoulders of those who are in the lowest economic deciles. That's very important. For me, it's an absolute matter of 'doability'. In other words, if we can't say that, we'll have difficulty getting these measures through.That means basically you're looking to see how do you get people higher up on the income scale to make some contribution to this deficit reduction programme? So that's the principle that lies behind it. We have a major deficit, we have to take a share of the burden. On child benefit Labour says it's all about getting the middle class to buy into it, which is why you give them benefits. That is absurd. That is a complete nonsense which has been concocted by them to justify why they've done nothing to it. The real reason for universal benefits such as child benefit was that it was the only way in the early days of making sure poorer kids got the money, because they didn't have to make any claims for it in the sense that they didn't get means tested. So every family could legitimately claim and not worry about getting the money.

If the middle class have to buy into benefits by being part of the benefit system then this is an absurdity, and why stop there? Why don't we go everywhere with this? Which is why Labour, with their child tax credits, ended up giving money to people earning more than £50,000. So it is long overdue that we look at this and ask ourselves the question: what is child benefit really for? It's for supporting children, particularly children who come from difficult backgrounds where money is really really tight and where that little bit of extra money really makes a disproportionate difference to their lives. And to do that sometimes you need to take some tough decisions about that. And the answer for us if you want to reward people further up the income scale for working hard and for doing the right thing then that's where tax changes are relevant. That's what you do. What you don't do is take money off them, siphon it off two departments and pop a little bit back to them as though this is a little gift you're giving. It's not a gift to take large sums of money and take a little bit back. It's bribery really.

But what about the unfairness of the double income family on £80,000 getting it and a single income parent on £44,000 losing out? That smacks to me as a policy that might be right in principle but actually in implementation wasn't thought through before it was announced.
The biggest problem we've got in the short-term is the nature of the tax system. For thirteen years the Labour Party were in government, and I don't recall once they talked about reforming the tax system to make it less unfair. Right

now the tax system does exactly that, to families that have a single earner, they get taxed at the higher rate, if they go above £43,000. It does not find that two earners who break £43,000 get to the higher rate. So, before we get too caught up with the child benefit being unfair, right now the tax system according to Ed Miliband is deeply unfair, but he never proposed to reform it. So he's happy to have unfairness in the system. What we're trying to do is use the tax system to do the child benefit so that inherent unfairness, that he calls it, is already in the system working it through. Now, I happen to believe there are ways that we will ameliorate that later on, and get rid of that unfairness, and those are matters that are for discussion further down the road. But my point is, right now, we have the system that we inherited. To make any changes, we have to use that system, and that's the point, so if Ed Miliband can quietly show me exactly which point in the last ten years he campaigned to change the tax system so that we could take account of dual incomes and households, I'd be very happy to hear from him.

You say you have been having discussions over many months with George Osborne about the child benefit system, but I understand you didn't know until quite late in the day that this announcement was going to be made.
I, probably most of all, of all of the Cabinet ministers knew all about this announcement. It's not an issue for me. I'm not going to pre-comment about what the others knew or didn't know at the time. But for me I've always been aware of this and I was prepared for it.

Isn't it strange that it wasn't discussed in Cabinet before it was announced? It was a pretty major thing to do.
Yes. It's difficult to know with these things because we are running towards a spending review, and the spending review is quite complex, pretty detailed, each department pretty much knows where they are. Some departments like mine and me know where others are, because it's the nature of what I do, so I know where the Treasury is, I know where I am, so all of that, so to that extent, it's difficult sometimes to get people completely lined up about these things.

It seemed to me that it was something that was announced, just before the conference, well at the conference, for a political reason whereas actually wouldn't it have been better to announce it in the CSR, because it's really a part of it isn't it?
It could certainly be argued that, but politicians take decisions and stand by the decisions they take, and it was deemed that this was the right thing to do and so collegiately I think that's a good position. Collegiately, what am I talking about, that's a terrible word. God, I'm beginning to sound like New Labour. Sorry.

Do you think there's any argument for having regional variations of the minimum wage?
There is certainly a reasonable argument to be had for all of that, including collective pay bargaining. To what degree does it help parts of Britain outside London, and London itself? I can understand that a big debate is to be had about that. That's not something which is going to come through in the comprehensive spending review and over this spending review period that I'm aware of. But I know there are difficulties, I talked to a businessman about three months ago, who has a factory up in the north-east and he simply told me that he found difficulty getting people to work there, even though he had spare jobs. I was astonished. I said we've got a recession on, why's that, and he said, because I can't compete with the public sector, what they pay up here. I've got the minimum wage but I can't compete with what I put over the top of that because it's very difficult. So people wait for the public sector jobs in this area because they know they pay better, and they can wait. I can see that there are disparities and you know, we'll have to look at all that, but there isn't a policy from the government on that. There is certainly a legitimate debate and if people want to debate it they should press hard on it.

You talked a bit about Betsy at the beginning, can you take me through what's happened to her?
I won't go into detail about it because she doesn't want me to say very much about it and I can understand why. All I will tell you is that in July last year, out of the blue, she discovered that she had breast cancer. There will be lots of people who read this whose wives, girlfriends or themselves as women have had this same problem. It's shocking. Then you discover that one in eight women in Britain get breast cancer, one of the highest rates in the Western world. Betsy went through what lots of women have done. She's had a huge amount of chemo. She's had a whole shed load of radiotherapy. Three operations. We now think she's recovering. It's very slow. The thing is that all that treatment takes the stuffing out of you. She's not a huge person so she doesn't have huge reserves of energy. She finds she gets tired very easily. But, you know, we're getting there really. It's a slow process. Maybe another operation to come.

And how has that affected you because I know before the election and the years before that you spent a lot of time caring for her. That must have been very difficult.
When she told me, I packed my bags here and I went home and I said look, I'm going to be here. Somebody said, that's all very well for him, he can do that, but to be honest, I did all my work that I had to do. I didn't stop working. I did as much work as I could from home. I came up here to the Commons when I had to, when I was needed for votes. What I didn't do

was spend my days here doing my work. I transported it back home so that I could be close to her and help her and you know, there were times when you needed to be there really, a lot of times. It's a difficult process and I feel sorry for somebody who doesn't have somebody else with them because it's a mental process as much as it's a physical process.

Because she took a lot of flack when you were leader, didn't she?
Well at the end, unfairly too. She was used by some people as a way of getting to me. I don't mind. I'm broad shouldered. I'm a politician. I expect what comes with it. You know, you live in a goldfish bowl, you get attacked. I never used my family so they were always out of bounds, and I didn't really use Betsy either. The fact was, she was wrongly accused of something, which was that she had not been working for me when we were able to show she did. She's an expert in doing what she did for me, and she did it properly. It was all properly above board. Life's too short. But I do say that was unfair. And actually, interestingly, a lot of Labour politicians came up to me and said to me this is not in the rules. We don't take out each other's wives.

This is seven years on from all that. Can you forgive people who did that to her?
Yes. My job is not to sit here with vendettas.

Forgive but *not forget, maybe*?
Forgetting is a different matter as well but I just get on. I'm not going to spend my whole time saying I wish or I'm going to get even. No point. You know, you pick up things, you learn stuff about yourself when you go through difficulty. It helps, strangely enough. I had an objective which was that I had promised that we were going to focus on social justice. I gave that my word and I tried to stick to it.

Have you ever thought about quitting politics completely and do something completely different?
Yes, the whole time really. You know, when you sit here frustrated, you think to yourself, God, why am I doing this all in the last seven years. Of course I did. I'd be a liar if I told you there aren't times when you think to yourself, you know, I could be doing something different. But my wife often tells me, the problem is that you're driven and you'd never give this up without wanting to come back into it again.

What do you think you might have done?
That's the sixty million dollar question. I don't know, business? I love how business works and I was always involved in that. I was on a board of a company

before and I've always taken a fascinating interest in how entrepreneurs work. How do you make an idea take from nothing to making a business success.

Do you think true friendship is possible in politics?
It is, it is difficult but it is possible. And the trouble, with politics is, you're always left with a dilemma of the final moment when it's either your friendship or the decision you have to take about what comes first, national interest or friendship? And these are the really difficult decisions which have broken friendships. You go down through the ages. People come in, they're close to each other. I mean look at the Brown and Blair friendship. It's pretty much like that all the way through.

Have you ever had to do anything in your political life, like when David Cameron fired Hugo Swire from his shadow Cabinet? Hugo had been with him right from the beginning and I did think that displayed a certain ruthlessness. Have there been occasions like that when you've really had to wrestle with something you know you should do but friendship has sort of got in the way?
Not in a direct sense but the decisions you often take which you feel are not quite what people would have expected of you who are your friends. That's always a difficult moment. Being Prime Minster or even Leader of the Opposition is a pretty lonely place. Having done Leader of the Opposition I just know what it's like when you're alone with your thoughts at night and things aren't going right and you've got problems. There is nobody you can turn to really. You have only yourself. It's a lonely, lonely place. It's different from any other job. It's very difficult to explain to people who are not in politics or, actually even politicians who have never been leader, what being leader is really like. It's not like doing what I do, being Secretary of State. That has responsibilities, it has difficulties, it has problems. But having done Leader of the Opposition and now I'm doing this, I can tell you that the Leader of the Opposition's job is tougher by a country mile than this because there is no rest for you. It's a seven-day-a-week job. You know, suddenly somebody does something stupid in Cabinet and suddenly bang, it's 2 o'clock in the morning on Sunday when you thought you had Sunday off, you don't have Sunday off. You're back up, you're on Prime Minister's Questions every week, there's no escape for you if you make a mistake. The ground doesn't open up, you have to stand there and take it. These are the things that happen to Prime Ministers and to Leaders of the Opposition because you are on your own and they are unique, and until you've experienced them, you cannot describe them to anybody.

Is it easy to develop a bunker mentality, where you think that everyone's sort of out to get you but actually maybe they're not?
It's too easy to do that. As Prime Minister you have patronage. As Prime

Minister you have real power, as Prime Minister the world is prepared to listen to you. As Leader of the Opposition everyone assumes that you have power, you have none. You have absolutely no patronage to persuade your colleagues to toe the line or to do something. You ask them to do jobs that they aren't being paid for. And you live off a shoe-string, and often with support that may not really be the top quality support. So if you're in trouble it's quite easy to split into a bunker because there's nowhere else for you to go. As PM it should take you a lot longer to get to the bunker. Gordon Brown made it to the bunker in the end and he never really emerged. It is easy, because you're on your own at the end of the day and bunkers are designed ultimately around you.

Margaret Thatcher said her overthrow was treachery with a smile on its face. How would you describe what happened to you?
Politics. Politics is a rough trade, I know that. I think we did some great things as Leader of the Opposition, I think many of them still stand. Just one which no one ever remembers going back is the fact that we're not saddled with the euro at the time of the recession is because had I not been elected we might have actually divided, split, except on the euro we didn't. Little things like that which you can do and we influence what happens nationally. You can make mistakes... sometimes you get things right, sometimes you don't. It's tough like that. But I just don't even look back and think about it in any way at all. Some people didn't want me there. Some of it was get-even for the fact that I was quite rebellious in my first parliament over Maastricht. So there's mixtures of stuff, but, hey, I've moved on and that's what you do.

Do you sometimes have a little wry smile on your face when you see what's happened now with female candidates for example? That actually was started under you but no one remembers that now.
Yeah, occasionally I look at things and say 'I think we started that process'. We started opening up the party to the gay community. I was there. It was a tough struggle trying to manage the processes. Getting [section] 28 out. We took some strides towards that, we didn't complete it. Cameron completed it. No problem with that. Managing the party so it didn't break up on stuff was a key consideration for me, because we had to be at the other end with our meagre resources to still be there as a party. Andrew Marr summed it up when I went I think. I remember seeing something on the news there was a clip that said 'these are the things that happened under him, that he had taken the party from A to B but no one's gonna thank him for it'. And I accept that. But the key thing was that I came in to try and get the Conservative Party in the right direction. I hope we made some good changes. Lots of them were stuck to. There were other things we've since changed. I mean

the social justice agenda was embedded in. I like to think it's embedded in. If you want to know what I'm most proud of, it's that my party has moved to recapture the ground that says we're decent, reasonable people who care about society regardless of whether they vote for us and we're here for the poorest as well. Now that to my mind is a big shift from where we were by the time we hit 1997. And getting that back is enormously important, so for that I'm enormously pleased.

What's it like being in a Cabinet run by the two people who used to brief you for PMQs? You must at times think: 'That should be me.'
I honestly do not. I sit there and I accept that it's like policemen – am I getting old or are prime ministers starting to look younger?

I can't believe all the three party leaders are younger than me now so…
[Laughs] I get on well with David. Much of his programme, as you know, I support. A lot of it was stuff that I initiated so I'm very pleased. He was a great help during Prime Minister's Questions preparation because we shifted our system. We changed the style.

Boris used to do help as well, didn't he?
Yeah, Boris would come in and read the paper and say a couple of things and then he would leave! Boris was always late. He'd say 'it's all going wonderfully!' and then up and leave. I love Boris to bits but he'd be the first to admit that he didn't really produce that many one-liners. George and David were very good on the one-liners. Sorry, Boris will kill me for that now, saying 'no, no, I was really influential!'

People always try to keep religion out of politics, do you think that's a good thing, or do you think actually religion ought to matter more in our political system?
First of all I think we've tended to look at religion from the standpoint of where we are now, and I don't think it's always been like that and I don't think it'll always be like that. I think these things are cyclical. I think politics is a living breathing animal and it doesn't stay the same at any stage. If you go back to the middle of the nineteenth century religion was absolutely part of politics. You know, Shaftsbury driven by his religious beliefs to make the factory changes, the change to chimney sweeps. He was driven by that evangelical determination. Then there was Wilberforce. After that period in the nineteenth century, then we come into a period that becomes much more secular. America has those cycles very clearly identifiable. The constitution was written in a secular period. Had it been written fifty years later, when Lincoln and co were around, you would have had much greater references to

religion and schools. So first I think it's cyclical. We've been in what I think is a very strongly secular period in a sense that we don't 'do' God, we don't talk about it. It's very much a part of the last government. I think that will shift and change simply because it changes with the characters who occupy the posts.

I think in the UK it's a slightly more balanced approach. You'll go through periods where it's very secular and periods where religion takes a strong role.

The Republican Party in the States has almost become a quasi-religious sect rather than a political party.
Well, there are elements of it… I remember talking at length about this but there are large swathes of the Republican Party that are not. You tend to only hear from the bit that is. Having said that, the Democrats are also just as involved. Theirs tends to not be so dominant in the way that it shapes politics, but it's very strong. You will never get an American politician saying that he absolutely does not care about religion in the way that you can get a UK politician saying that.

If Nick Clegg had been in America he could not have admitted to being an atheist, could he?
Absolutely not. If he did he'd have known very well that he could not be making it to top office, that's a fact of life. And certainly he might just have got away with it in the states in the north east but you would not get away with it anywhere else, and even there it's debatable.

How did you find your relationship with Tony Blair when you were leader? Did you think that he was someone who was genuinely motivated by trying to do the right thing, or did you see that messianic zeal in his eye that made him go off course on one or two things?
I don't really know. I think there are two Blairs. I think there's the Blair that got elected and governed for the first four or five years, maybe six at a push. And then there's the Blair that occupied the office for the next six years. And the reason I say they're different is the first Blair that came in was conscious of always one thing, which was his place in history, being re-elected, being the first Labour politician to be Prime Minister through two terms. And I think that was drummed into his head. Campbell was aware of it, everyone. So their first parliament was really risk averse and there were things they should have done – things like we're trying to do at the moment. Welfare reform was dumped. There are a lot of things they didn't do. They really didn't do the health service at all. And that was at a good time for them. He was scared stiff of the Tory party. He felt that if he gave us an inch we'd be back straight away. I think he completely overestimated our capacity for

recovery and underestimated the damage that we had taken in the last four years of the Major government. History relates that quite clearly now, but I think they were just obsessed by it. So the first four or five years were wasted years for Blair. Most of his politics was presentational. My general feeling was that Brown ran domestic policy.

Then I think something changed once Blair got re-elected. I think his place in history was now assured, and it was the war on terror I think that changed him. It was almost as if Blair said 'now I'm gonna show everybody what I'm really worth and I'm going to step up the plate, make these decisions and make the tough ones' and from that point onwards I don't think he really cared whether they were re-elected or not. Having been obsessed with re-election he ceased to care. And when he ceased to care, that's when the gleam came and he said 'this is it, my real place in history is making these decisions like Mrs Thatcher, taking the tough decisions, taking people on, doing it' and I think that's how he saw it. Now, it's not to say that he was wrong. People will decide whether the war in Iraq was right or wrong. I still believe ultimately it was the right thing to do, but the post-war in Iraq was a disaster. That was the bit we should have got right. We didn't. Nonetheless people will argue with me, I accept that. But he drove on that hard and that was the real issue so that from that moment onwards there was a different Blair in the office. It was the not the Blair that they elected in 1997. It was a new Blair and he got more strident, much more forceful, much more determined, far less willing to listen to any counter-arguments and more and more determined that somehow he had right on his side. So there were really two different Blairs completely. And my dealings with him were really more with the second Blair than with the first.

Looking back do you think he misled you at all on Iraq?

No, I never really… I mean the point was as the opposition you cannot get locked too deeply into information. Because things that we would want to disagree with, I would not have been able to raise in the chamber. So I never asked to see clear and detailed papers. What I was shown once was the report nine days before it appeared. There was stuff missing from it which then later on came out. I don't think that was them hiding it from me. I think they put stuff in at the last moment, the 45-minute stuff. I don't think was even in there when I saw it. So no, I don't think he was deliberately withholding stuff. I do think that the mistake they made was to be so narrow on the reasons for going to war. The WMD was *a* reason for going to war. It was not *the* reason. The reason was Saddam Hussein, and the reason was that country was in a total disaster and a shambles. After the Kuwait invasion we should have taken a decision about whether Saddam was tolerable there any longer. I think we should have acted, we should have taken him out, and we could have then managed Iraq into a safer place. Instead of which we put sanctions on, we then allowed him to fly his helicopters south, to beat up the Shiites. It is disgusting what happened there – the million that died there were all our fault as an alliance. We turned our backs on them. So I think that there were lots of good reasons [to oust him]. If they were explained to the British people they would have realised that this was unique because a lot of it was of our making. Not all of it, but we left it like that. Sanctions weren't working, they were being abused, we were still at war with him because we were bombing his sites, how long did you want that to go on for? Could you have him back in the UN? Was it tolerable, building his weapons of mass destruction again, even if he didn't have them? So they got very narrow and the reason they got very narrow was because Labour would never have bought the wider argument. The truth was America wanted the wider argument and we stopped that case being made and that was the tragedy. The tragedy was that the British people and everyone else were never allowed to engage with the much wider argument of why we really dealt with Saddam Hussein. And it was regime change. And the question was, that in these isolated circumstances, is it acceptable?

Quickfire

Favourite book?
To Kill a Mockingbird but I also love War and Peace.

Favourite view?
Without question it's from the top of a highland mountain just over the rest of Scotland.

Your best friend in politics?
That's a difficult one. I guess the person that I know best and am closest to is Bernard Jenkin.

Political hate figure?
I don't really have hate figures. I can't think of anybody that I absolutely loathe.

Favourite film?
It's a Wonderful Life.

Political hero?
I think Peel is probably my main political hero, although I have others. Wilberforce would be the other. I'll have two if you don't mind.

What food do you most like?
Anything that I've cooked, because I like cooking.

Is there a quotation that you've found particularly inspirational over the years?
The one that I constantly think of is 'All that is required for the triumph of evil is that the good men should do nothing'. That's the one I think that guides me most.

What makes you cry?
I don't know really. I get soppy over commitment, I suppose. People who commit everything to something makes me emotional.

If you were to invite four people to a dinner party, living or dead who would you choose?
Can't we have a few more? Well I'd have to have Mrs T, certainly I'd have Churchill. I'd love to have Ghandi and Nelson Mandela.

Which period of history would you most liked to have lived through?
I think without question the Second World War.

Opposition politician you most respect?
I actually get on quite well with a number of them … I'm just casting around in my head here which ones. Jack Straw. I like Jack. I get on well with him. I think he's a survivor. And in politics sometimes you have to respect the survivors. He's consummate about it. And he makes people laugh while he survives.

Peter Mandelson

Party affiliation: Labour

Born: 21 October 1953

Education: Educated at Hendon County Grammar School and St Catherine's College, Oxford, where he studied Politics, Philosophy and Economics.

Family status: Lives with partner Reinaldo Avila da Silva.

Pre-political career: After graduating he joined the staff of the Trades Union Congress.

Electoral history: Elected to be a councillor for Stockwell on Lambeth Council in 1979, he left to become a producer on the LWT current affairs strand 'Weekend World'. However, in 1989 he returned to politics, and in 1992 was elected MP for Hartlepool. After playing an essential role in Labour's successful election campaign in May 1997, he later acquired the role of Secretary of State for Trade and Industry in July 1998. He has had a number of roles since then, including Secretary of State for Northern Ireland, EU Trade Commissioner before, in October 2008, being made Business Secretary by Gordon Brown and being made a life peer. He lost his cabinet position after the general election in May 2010.

Career highlights: Being made a life peer and holding numerous prestigious positions in the Labour Cabinet.

Interesting fact: After being promoted in June 2009, he gained one of the longest titles in political history: Baron Mandelson of Foy in the County of Herefordshire and Hartlepool in the County of Durham, First Secretary of State, Secretary of State for Business, Innovation and Skills, Lord President of the Council.

Date of interview: October 2010
Extended version
Venue: Policy Network office, London
Total Politics Issue 30, December 2010

Quite a few years ago I published Peter Mandelson's book The Blair Revolution Revisited. *At that point he was between jobs, having resigned for the second time from the Blair government. He was a fish looking for water. What impressed me about him then was his complete understanding of what was expected of him as an author. I thought he was a class act then, and I still do.*

Ever since then I remained in email contact with him, as I had his private
email address. From time to time we'd exchange pleasantries, but one thing I
noted was that each time I sent him an email he would reply within minutes.
Andrew Neil is another one with the same admirable habit. But our paths
didn't cross again in person until the autumn of 2008, shortly after his
surprise return to the cabinet for his third incarnation.

I was in the House of Commons walking up the wide staircase to the
committee room corridor when I spied Peter Mandelson coming the other
way. I didn't expect him to remember me, so I affected not to notice him. But
he immediately stopped and said hello. 'How's the blog doing,' he asked. 'All
the better when you feature,' I responded. 'As it should be, Iain, as it should
be...' And he then glided away. It was a typical Mandelsonian performance.
Right, I thought. I'm going to get an interview with you if it's the last thing I
do. And two years later, I eventually succeeded.

There's no doubt about it, as you will shortly read, Peter Mandelson gives good
interview. I haven't quite worked out yet if he realises what he is saying or whether
he does it deliberately, but there were more stories to come out of this interview than
any other I have ever done. I don't think Peter Mandelson has ever knowingly given
an uncontroversial interview in his life. And long may it remain so.

So how has the experience been of doing the book because you aren't writing
as much as the sort of aftermath of the publication.
The book has been in the process of being written and produced over many
years. It didn't start after the election, nor was I writing it during the election
campaign at all. It had two false starts when I embarked on it but something
happened to divert me, either to Brussels or back to government here. But
the construction of it, the conception of it, took place over many years and I
worked on it on long intercontinental flights. I researched it. I had somebody
go through thirty-six box files of papers. I worked out what I wanted to
say and then the real intensive writing and production of it came after the
election. I went off and hid with two of my closest advisors and two people
from HarperCollins who were absolutely indispensible. It's not something I
could go through again in a hurry.

It was interesting because it was kept quite a good secret until very shortly
before publication. Was that planned?
The reason for that was I wasn't sure that I could do it. I didn't sign the
contract with HarperCollins until end of May, beginning of June. It was
published in the middle of July. And the reason for that was I just did not
know physically whether I could pull it off in the timescale, and I didn't want
to announce that I was doing it, wind everyone up, send all the alarm bells
clanging and then suddenly it didn't appear.

Why the rush? To beat Tony Blair?
Because I wanted to move on in my life. And I did not want to have such a book come out at the end of this year or beginning of next, when the Labour Party wants to move on. And I wanted to move on too. I wanted to draw a line. But these things have to capture a moment and I felt the moment was then, as did the publishers.

Well I think the fact that it was number one in the bestseller charts has proved you right on that.
Well it was number one for five or six weeks.

Were you expecting that?
No. I was told that a political biography or ministerial memoir doesn't sell anymore. If you're not Thatcher, Major or Blair, and they had their own particular market, you would be lucky if you sold more than forty or fifty thousand.

Most politicians are lucky if they sell more than five thousand nowadays.
But that was forty or fifty thousand if it was a real cracking read and the timing was right. And it was honest. It was an authentic thing and I didn't want to do a sort of Michael Heseltine or Norman Fowler type memoir in which I told everyone which committees I attended, where I made my speeches. No. It would have been ridiculous for me to do that and it wouldn't have been published, it wouldn't have sold, it would have reflected poorly on me. But there were a whole series of difficult judgement calls about what to include. In the end I decided that I couldn't tell the real story unless I told broadly speaking, the whole story. I couldn't leave certain events or exchanges or episodes out because I wouldn't be able to explain what happened later. So, having approached it in the first place in a rather sort of cautious, judicious, discreet way, I found that I had to put in more than I originally intended because that was the only way to tell the story and to have it make sense for people. But not in a nasty way, and I think that people reading it will feel that it's balanced, it's rounded. It *is* honest about people, but it's not nasty about people and the only thing that I regretted about some of the newspaper coverage of it, was that the book was presented as me settling scores or getting my own back on people or whatever, and that was simply not how I felt, not how I wrote it, but I guess that's the only way in which newspapers know how to write stories about such books.

I said in the review I wrote: 'He's painfully honest about his relationship with Gordon Brown and completely up front about his political and personal weaknesses – almost completely. Yet in the chapters on his return to

government you sense that he would like to say more, but he doesn't want to hurt his old political friend (and foe) anymore than he has to.' I can hear his editor saying, 'but Peter, we need just a little bit more here', on more than one occasion, but I don't blame him for not complying.

That is absolutely right. There was an editor who will remain nameless…

…Well I know because I've done it myself…

…who said, you know, 'I think you've got to be more explicit here. I think you've got to lay it out more fully. I think you've got to be tougher here'. And I said 'I will be tough in my own way'. People will know what I'm saying without me laying into an individual and even now I, with the documentary that was premiered on Sunday, some of the newspaper reporting is me being nasty or catty or bitchy about Gordon. That's their take on it. If you look at how I talk about Gordon it's with affection. When I talk about him being a combination of a snowplough and a combine harvester, that's a compliment. I mean Gordon had, as I described in the book, a certain *force majeure*. A determination not to allow anything or anyone to stand in his way when he was doing what he thought was right. Now that's a vital ingredient that I believe a prime minister needs. In some respects, I wish Tony had had more of the *force majeure*. Similarly, I wished Gordon had had a little bit more of Tony's sort of feline charm.

Do you think if you actually combined Gordon Brown and Tony Blair into one politician you'd almost have the perfect politician?

Yes, and I nearly said it in the book. Did I say that in the book?

I don't know.

I can't remember, but I nearly said it in the book and I was told that it would sound just a bit clichéd. But if you had Gordon's intellect, his grasp of the big picture, that sort of forcefulness that a prime minster needs, you know, a determination not to let anything get in his way, plus Tony's charm and tact and communication skills and ability to pull together a team and the leadership skills he had, you would, I think, have the perfect prime minister.

Do you think you overplayed at all in the book your own role because obviously in any autobiography it is the chance to…

…difficult not to in an autobiography…

Indeed, and that's kind of my point. The title, *The Third Man*, almost says it all. You considered yourself the third piece of the jigsaw in the creation of New Labour.

That's how we started out in the '80s. People could be forgiven for thinking only of the present, but this is a relationship that has gone on, stretches back, over twenty years and more. It's difficult. On the one hand what's the point of writing a book like this without casting yourself in a fairly central role, but without appearing vain? On the other hand, I was very clear about how when I left government, I was operating in the shadows. I wasn't a front rank minister. I wasn't able to influence vital decisions like that over Iraq for example.

But that's the running theme through the book. There was a growing frustration, particularly in the run-up to '97, that you were always operating in the shadows.
It was convenient for Tony but damaging for me. But you can only understand me, and what happened to me, by realising how difficult a role it was. Tony was very conflicted on this. On the one hand he regarded me as a good minister – somebody who could take on a department and a portfolio and deliver. On the other hand, he was affected by people whispering in his ear, and saying, 'Peter's too controversial', or 'Peter attracts too much media attention', or 'Peter's too manipulative', or 'Peter's a problem between you and Gordon', and he had a lot of that going on in his own circle. None of it designed to help me. And I had to cope with that, whilst at the same time facing Gordon's hostility from outside the Blair circle. So I got it from both directions, both within the circle and outside it.

I think it's fascinating going through the book to see the development of your relationship with Alastair Campbell. Having read his diaries as well it's clear you're quite good friends and yet you can have blazing rows. You'll then go round to his house that evening and have a perfectly amicable dinner with him and Fiona.
Well I've known him for such a long time. As I describe in the book, I knew Fiona, his partner, first and her parents and the Labour Party circle in Marylebone. I remember when Alastair first appeared with Fiona. In the 1980s I looked to Alastair as a real help and support when I started to work in Walworth Road in 1985. He was always there, with his advice or ability to rewrite things, or to ghost write articles, or name party policy documents. But when he came to work with Tony in 1994, the other side of Alastair came out. Very competitive, rather domineering, and a huge but fragile ego. It wasn't easy.

He might say the same about you.
He might do. Except that what I was trying to do was to get out from my role as Blair's spin doctor. What I wanted to do was to be a Labour Member of Parliament and would-be minister. I didn't like Tony constantly sort of using me as a sounding board, as an advisor or concierge when it undermined my

independence in the political career which I was trying to construct for myself. But I couldn't do anything about that because of the roots of our relationship in the 1980s and the fact that the three of us and then, after 1994, the two of us, looked to each other as friends, as allies, as constant supports.

What I think people outside politics don't get is that every political leader, particularly the party leader or prime minster, has to have someone in that role, who they can trust 100 per cent, who they can bounce things off. It's like Margaret Thatcher said, 'every prime minister needs a Willie'. Well Tony Blair could have equally said 'every prime minister needs a Peter'.
Yes. But I was completely un-self-interested and that's what I think some people didn't realise at the time. I was working for the success of Tony Blair because I believed we'd only be elected as New Labour and that we had to govern as New Labour as well. It was the Party's success that mattered to me more than my personal ambition. If I had put myself first I would have done things quite differently. Quite differently.

What would you have done differently?
Not been as so much at the cutting edge of change in the Labour Party. I would have been less outspoken, less forceful. I would have spent much more time in the Parliamentary Labour Party, in the tearoom, in the smoking room, making friends, agreeing with everyone, rather than contesting…

…You're almost describing Ed Miliband…
…contesting a lot of their views. You know, the problem is, as I explain candidly in the book, that I not only have very strong views about what the Labour Party had to become and change in to to be elected, I was forceful in expressing those views and I didn't really take hostages when people were trying to oppose or derail us. Now, that is not the recipe for a successful political career. Politics requires you to be a bit more amenable, a bit more accommodating, nice to everyone's face, whatever you say behind their back, just altogether more oleaginous. And I didn't do oleaginous.

But I would say that when you came back in 2008 we saw a different Peter Mandelson from the Peter Mandelson that we'd seen before. The general public saw it, and maybe your colleagues as well.
My colleagues as well, very importantly. I mean I came back as a sort of elder statesman. Somebody who had gained considerable experience and status as a European Commissioner. I returned as a fireman, as a safe pair of hands to help the government and the party in what was a crisis. And I want to continue as a trusted and respected grandee or great uncle. What's happened since the election is that we've all made up now. I felt hurt, I felt denigrated by

some of Ed Miliband's remarks. I mean talking about me in terms of 'dignity in retirement', I felt as if I was being unfairly treated and packed off rather prematurely to an old folk's home. I also thought to define himself against New Labour, as opposed to being a development of New Labour, was electorally unwise. But again, we've all moved on. What I've got to do now is remain a candid friend but also constructive and always loyal. I was always loyal.

I started at the beginning of my career, my full-time career in politics, as very loyal to Neil Kinnock, even though I didn't agree with everything he was saying and doing, but I nonetheless thought he was tremendously courageous and bold in the leadership he gave to the party. I ended up equally as loyal to Gordon Brown who I didn't agree with entirely either and I will be loyal to Ed Miliband because that's how I am. I don't want to become a sort of irritant or a backseat driver. I want to continue as I began when I returned in 2008.

But if you had been advising Ed Miliband on his campaign, you can see, and I don't know whether you would have done this or not, but the fact is, he knew his electorate. He wasn't playing to the country, he was playing to the people who were voting for him. And he was very successful in doing that.
Well, he has a very strong character and personality, as his brother discovered. He has strong personal qualities and something that people don't realise is that when I came back in 2008, the colleague with whom I spent most time in the Cabinet was Ed Miliband. Partly because he was a neighbour in north London and partly because he went out of his way to befriend me. He really wanted to bury the hatchet and to put all that he did for Gordon against Tony and all that he did amongst the Brownites against the Blairites.

People tend to forget him in that. Everyone thinks it was all Ed Balls.
He played his part, but he also wanted to put it behind him, and by befriending me and by spending so much time with me, I think he succeeded in that. I didn't realise he had such strong leadership ambition. For me, the sort of default candidate and next leader was David. To be honest I didn't really think that seriously about Ed as a would-be leader, and I missed that. And as I said I spent much more time with Ed, and Ed was going out of his way to be more friendly towards me when I came back in 2008 than David did. But that again I think shows some of Ed's cleverness.

Or deviousness. But it's interesting that you didn't identify him as a leader. Do you think he actually has what it takes to be a leader?
Well I think the fact that he came forward and challenged his brother, and conducted such a strong campaign, shows that he does have what is needed in politics to be the number one person. I mean, the one piece of advice I gave at the beginning of the leadership contest, was that he shouldn't say

anything to win the vote of the party that might make it subsequently more difficult to win the votes of the country.

But he ignored that advice didn't he?
He ignored that advice but he's made up for it since.

But Iain Duncan Smith, and he ought to know, said that a new leader has got ninety days to define themselves. Now that was back in 2003, today you've probably got less than ninety days...
That was the example of Tony. When Tony was elected in '94, he did some things on policy, on education, on family and a number of other areas, not the least of which was Clause Four, which were breathtaking.

But Ed has had a month in the post. Now ok you can't rush your judgement after a month. He's been ruthless with one or two things in appointing his team, getting rid of Nick Brown for example, he put in a reasonable performance in his first outing at PMQs, but the second one was a disaster. Appointing Alan Johnson, most people think is a bit of an odd thing to do. What else has he done in his first thirty days?
I think appointing Alan was smart because what Ed has done is construct an economically sensible third way on the deficit. He's avoided both extremes.

But you've been criticising him for the deficit strategy, according to the *Daily Mail* today. It says here, 'praising the coalition for tackling the deficit head on'.
No, no, no, I'm sorry Iain. I was very clear in what I said. I said, in terms, that he has been economically sensible in avoiding both extremes – the deficit deniers on the one hand, and those who are only focused on the deficit and are conducting policy like one club, on the other. Couldn't be clearer. And what I said about the coalition... This is the *Daily Mail* for goodness sake. What am I doing commenting on something in the *Daily Mail*? What I said about the coalition is of course they were confronting issues, very, very difficult public-spending issues which we would have had to confront if we had been re-elected, even if some of our judgements about specific cuts, their scale and their timing would have been different.

But doesn't this...
We fought the election, Iain, committed to halving the deficit in four years.

Well to my mind you fought the election on virtually identical policies to what the coalition are carrying out anyway...
And what Ed has done very wisely is stick to Alistair Darling's approach, and that's what I congratulated him on, on his approach.

But in a way you could say that George Osborne isn't doing it that much different, he's doing it slightly more, slightly quicker but it's only slightly.
Well I think he would take issue with that. He's made a virtue of going hell for leather.

No, but the PR and the reality are rather different things, and if you look at what he's doing it's 5 per cent more over one year fewer. Now, most people would describe that as a minor difference.
I'm sorry I don't know whether it's 5 per cent more, I don't know what you've based that on and it's not a figure I accept because I haven't worked it out for myself.

He's trying to say it's actually 1 per cent less, that thing that he came out with at the end of the CSR statement was actually classic Gordon Brown wasn't it – pull a rabbit out of the hat right at the end to keep your backbenchers happy.
This is game play by the government. They can't have it both ways.

Isn't the reporting of what you said in this *Mail* article illustrative of the fact that you have to be so careful? Anything you say will be misinterpreted – either your motives or your words. You're one of the few people in politics who is listened to. Everything you say people are interested in, and I wrote a couple of months ago that I thought that you've got similarities to Norman Tebbit in this in that you both have an ability to get media coverage when you don't need to.
And that's why I have to use my interventions sparingly and judiciously. And I will. Look, I want to offer counsel to the new generation of Labour leaders and activists. I want to pass on my experience and my wisdom – not to interfere, not to try to rock the boat or drive the car from the backseat. That's why I say that having coming back as a safe pair of hands I want to continue as such. It won't stop me being candid in how I engage in Labour Party debates. But when you're in a position like mine you have to weigh your words. I want to be trusted and respected for what I am and what I say, not regarded as somebody who just can't bare to move on.

But isn't the key there 'trusted and respected by whom'? Your former, current, Labour colleagues or the political classes generally?
By the new generation of Labour leaders and activists. I'm not going to say things I don't agree with. Take another example from yesterday. When I was being interviewed at lunchtime, somebody asked me if I agreed with David Cameron's Big Society idea. I said look back to the Progress lecture that I delivered in September 2009 and you will see the argument I made then that we have to maintain the quality and performance of our public services within new spending constraints. That their productivity, their

efficiency, their accountability, tailoring them to the needs of individuals now had to be achieved not by simply spending more money on these services but by reforming them. And the last thing I said was that you will find many of the ways in which we seek to change public services coming from within the communities and the people who depend on these public services. And that requires, I said in September 2009, a new path between those who deliver public services and those who use them, and depend on them.

I said that long before David Cameron came up with his 'Big Society' concept. The way that was reported in one newspaper was 'Peter Mandelson praises David Cameron' but that's politics. That's creating a story but I think I can live with that. I think it is better than being ignored altogether.

I guess the difference is if you're a Norman Tebbit or a Simon Hughes you can say a lot in public but have absolutely zero influence. Norman Tebbit has no influence over the Conservative Party. Simon Hughes does with a section of the Liberal Democrats, but not beyond that section.
But that's the difference here. I know that I have to be trusted and respected to have influence. And it is an influence. It's not a control, it's not a power. You know, I will move on and do other things in my life.

Have you decided what?
I'm not quite sure what, but amongst other things I have to earn a living. I don't have an income any more.

I've always imagined that you might well become chairman of some big company, but would that excite you as much as politics does?
Have you seen the Hannah documentary?

No.
You need to see it, because you can see the sort of pressure I was operating under in the last two years as a minister in my department or the industrial policies and the interventions that I was trying to make – the time I spent in Number 10. What I was trying to do was support Gordon and help to manage different aspects of our communications and then our election campaign itself. And I hear myself saying in that documentary 'how will I ever live without that pressure?'

Well it's an adrenaline rush, a constant adrenaline rush?
Well I'm not sure that rush is the word. It's more like an ever flowing river. And I will find it difficult.

Have you found it difficult in the last six months?
Yes, I have, the truth is… Look, I know I should say to you that I've adjusted, I've moved on, I'm happy, I'm looking to the future with confidence. But the truth is that I feel a sense of bereavement for our government. Personally I feel like a rather displaced individual and I'm not coping perfectly. But my word, I would have been in a much, much worse position if I hadn't written a book and had that to talk about and present and do events about. It is a bit of therapy, but I also thought that it was an interesting story and a historical account that needed to be given. I had not just a ring-side seat but I was in the ring for a lot of the time and if you're going to read the sort of book I've published on somebody like me, without being vain about it, I think that politics and how we've seen how we can understand the past and see the future would have been the poorer.

You use the phrase called 'in the ring' I don't know if you've ever read a book by Richard Nixon called *In The Arena* but this book explains how you do actually have to be in the arena to actually achieve anything. You can't just stand on the sidelines and commentate, like I do, you have to actually sort of be there. But can you get that back?
You have to be a Member of Parliament. In reality in the House of Commons rather than the Lords. That is the essential platform and qualification for anyone who wants to be influential in British politics.

Is that true nowadays, in this media age? Do you think that you actually have to be?
Governments are drawn from Parliament. The executive is made up of members, chiefly of the Commons but in some cases of the Lords. You don't have a system as in the United States or almost all the European countries where you can be brought into a government because of your personal qualities or your knowledge. We don't have that system in this country.

Gordon Brown did bring some people in, but it didn't really work, did it?
I think it certainly did work. It worked in the case…

Well it did in Ali Darzi's case but the others didn't last very long.
Absolutely wrong, I totally disagree with that. It worked in Darzi's case, Alan West's case, Mark Malloch Brown…

Well it didn't work in his case…
No it actually did work. I actually think that Mark actually had bigger potential and could have been used more.

They all buggered off after a year
But in my case, in the case of my department both Shriti Vadera and Mervyn Davis made really important policy contributions.

I would loved to have been a fly on the wall in meetings with you and Shriti…
We got on well.

Really? She has a certain reputation.
She certainly does. And it is well deserved. I respected her and she respected me.

Have you ruled out a fourth comeback in terms of being in the frontline of things in politics.
I tend not to rule out of anything in politics, given my career, given my roller coaster career. Would you predict anything? I don't think so. But I'm not going to sit by the telephone. I'm not going to hang around in expectation or with some sort of entitlement. I will find other things to do in my life. Things that I enjoy, things which I think are stimulating or important but also enable me to earn a living. If you were to ask me though, whether fundamentally I'd rather be in public service or the private sector… I'm a public service man. I was brought up in that way and that set of values and motives will never leave me.

If there was a vacancy, would you be interested in the job of EU Higher Representative? Would you consider it?
I wanted to do the job. I couldn't because I was a member of the government who had been called back. To be called back and then to leave a year early would have been impossible. I'm honest about what I say about it in my book. I think in the circumstances, with David Miliband not taking it, we would have been better to have an economic portfolio on the Commission. But I don't expect it to become vacant so it's a hypothetical question which is left hanging in the air.

Let's talk about the election. There was a time when a lot of people in the Conservative Party feared that you might have pulled it off.
Iain, we didn't nearly pull it off. We got the worst result in electoral share.

But there was a time at the beginning of the year when it looked as if it could be possible, the Tories were really in the doldrums. The polls were tightening, and a lot of us thought at the time that it could happen.
First of all, the Tories were never in 'the doldrums'. Secondly, they were making the mistakes that arrogant people often make in politics. They just thought they had to sit tight and allow their opponents to lose the election.

When the spotlight fell on them, people found them wanting. There wasn't enough there, there wasn't enough substance, there wasn't enough policy, too few ideas, but also people felt that for all his brave words David Cameron had not actually changed, let alone transformed the Conservative Party and they didn't want the old Conservative Party back.

I believe that we could have taken advantage of that if we had had a more credible and acceptable position on the deficit. Gordon got the economics broadly right in the financial crisis but I think he got some of the politics wrong. He seemed to be the guy who was good for the war but not so good for the peace. I said to him on one occasion – you're likely to become the Churchill of this. The guy whose strengths the public recognised in fighting the crisis but they didn't think was the right person for the next leap forward.

I bet that went down well…
You don't understand the relationship I had with Gordon. I can say these things to Gordon. You don't have to sound nasty or spiteful when you say these things. You can have a perfectly good conservation with somebody who you've known for twenty-five or thirty years.

But I don't think anybody understands your relationship with Gordon Brown…
They understand it a darn sight better having read my book.

But when you read in your book, and indeed Alastair's book, the things that went on between '94 and your second resignation, you clearly thought the man wasn't fit for the job and you advised Tony Blair to get rid of him at one point.
I didn't advise him to get rid of him. I advised him to reshuffle him.

You know what I mean.
No I don't know what you mean, could you please be a little bit more specific.

In Alastair's book, and I thought in yours, but I might be wrong…
Alastair's is not a book, it's a diary. And what you are reading is night after night, the world according to Alastair's mind and head as it was then. Mine is a more reflective and analytical book. Drawing yes, on my experiences and what happened, but I hope giving a balanced account and that's why I include in the book Gordon's own words on how he saw the situation, why he found it so frustrating, why it was driving him so mad. Just as it was totally aggravating for Tony as well. You see it from both sides.

You do, I accept that. But there are so many instances which you catalogue, and so does Alastair and you don't really disagree on them.
But they happened.

The interesting thing about both your books is they're on the same hymn sheet. Often two people can attend the same meeting and they have entirely different recollections. That hasn't happened here.
It was quite clear what had happened. It was also clear what Tony was doing during this time.

Being very weak...
No, not being very weak. Managing a situation which he was unable completely to cure.

He could have cured it by being stronger, surely. Every time he seemed to give in to Gordon Brown.
Look, it's very easy for an outsider to say of a PM that he should have done this or that. He had to trade off or balance the frustrations of having a difficult Chancellor, but also a good and effective one in many respects. And on the other hand, the risk of disruption, destabilisation of his government and the party if he had shuffled Gordon out of the Treasury. Now, that is a judgement call that only a PM can make and it's easy for an outsider – and we are all outsiders if we're not the PM – to say that he should have done this or could have done that. True, there were options. But his judgement had to be about what was in the broader interests of the government. How was he going to sustain it? And if you contrast Blair with Thatcher, Thatcher's Cabinet fell apart at the end of the 1980s. She drove very senior members to resignation. They walked out and finally got rid of her. That didn't happen in Blair's case.

It did in Brown's.
Well, one person resigned.

Hazel Blears, James Purnell, others.
Fine, but I'm talking about Tony Blair now. You asked me a question about Tony Blair. Was he right or wrong? And I'm saying it's very easy for us to say he should have done this, he should have done that. But if he had shuffled Gordon he might have created the same circumstances which saw Thatcher's Cabinet breaking up at the end of the '80s.

You talked about the broader interest of the government. What about the broader interests of the country, because I can't understand how you, Alastair, Tony Blair – you experienced these deeply unbalanced rages from time to time – how could you have allowed...
Politics is about passion.

Yes, passion sure. But this went beyond that. The way that Alastair writes it up, the way that you write it up, it's not just about passion. There was something deeply, fundamentally wrong about the way that he would react to situations. And yet he was unopposed as party leader.

In a lot of cases Gordon was right. Gordon came into government in '97 with a clearer gameplan and a set of policies about what he was going to achieve than Tony did for the government as a whole.

I agree with that. He had a brilliant side to him, and no doubt still does. But I would argue that he wasn't fit to be PM and yet he was elected unopposed. Every single Labour MP knew what he was like, they all knew, and yet none of them had the guts to do anything about it.

Who's the person who called for a contest rather than a coronation. Me! I was the only person who did. I went on the *Andrew Marr Show* when I was being interviewed from Brussels and said that in my view the interests of the party, the government and the country would be served by a contest, not a coronation. And I was right. Because Gordon suffered more than anyone from the shoe-in.

What was your biggest frustration in the election campaign? That you didn't have the resources that you were used to?

We certainly had zero resources. It was shocking. We couldn't even use our ad-agency. We had no bought media. That wasn't the case in 1987, let alone '97. My second frustration was that we had failed to hammer out an electoral strategy and only the leader can make sure that happens. As I describe in my book, that process hadn't happened. Look, what I wanted was to get the best possible result in the circumstances but above all to see the Labour Party united and with its dignity intact whatever the outcome. And keeping that campaign together, keeping it on track, making sure that we didn't either fall out or fall apart was quite an achievement, given the pressures.

I was the guy in overall charge. I wasn't organising the campaign itself, others were meant to be doing that. But if I made any contribution it was to ensure that we emerged with dignity and much to people's surprise we even emerged having robbed Cameron of an overall majority.

That was a surprise to you? You thought that he was going to win...

Of course it was a surprise, because it's not happened in British politics. It hadn't happened since 1974 and even that was a real flash in the pan.

So had you not planned at all for a hung parliament?

The polls did not indicate that that would be the outcome. In my view we could and should have started paving the way for that eventuality not weeks before, but years before, because we needed a good relationship with the Liberal Democrats of the sort that Cameron and Clegg were able to create. We hadn't put in that spadework.

In his book on the coalition, David Laws contrasts what your negotiating team were able to do and the Tories. And believe me, there was a great contrast.
Do you know the difference? The Tories had a head start. They had very good personal chemistry between their two leaders.

But they hadn't beforehand. They barely knew each other.
No, no, no, no please. They did. I know a little bit more about this. Thirdly, and most importantly, that was the outcome they wanted.

I shall send you a copy of the book, because I think you'll find it very interesting. Obviously he's writing it from a Liberal Democrat perspective.
I'm sorry Iain, but with the number of seats that we won, we were not in a good second place. We lost that election and to put together such a coalition and stay in power on the back of it would have been a very hard if not an impossible thing for us to achieve. Secondly, I stand by my view. It's not a criticism, it's an observation. Chemistry between Cameron and Clegg was good.

You heard the conversation initially between Brown and Clegg didn't you? You were there.
I heard all the conversations and indeed, was in the key meeting...

...and it was sort of a one-way conversation...
...no it wasn't. No it wasn't a one-way conversation, I'm sorry. Read my book.

I have read it.
It's not a one-way conversation. Iain please don't introduce your views and prejudices...

I'm not. I'm just saying...well I'm not introducing mine I'm introducing David Laws'...
It was not a one-way conversation. It was a perfectly good conversation between Gordon and Nick. But it wasn't one in my view that was going to deliver a Labour–Liberal Democrat coalition. The personalities were wrong. The politics didn't stack up.

I agree with that. I said that right at the beginning and on the election night.
But don't blame me or the Labour Party. It would have helped and made a difference if we'd won just twenty or twenty-five more seats. But we didn't.

Quickfire

What book are you reading at the moment?
Niall Ferguson's biography of Siegmund Warburg.

What's your favourite view?
The view from Anacapri towards Naples.

Best friend in politics?
Roger Liddle.

What food do you most enjoy? Apart from mushy peas obviously.
Unfattening Italian.

What do you do to relax?
Read, run and cycle, and look at DVDs, but very infrequently.

What makes you cry?
Emotion.

Invite four people to a dinner party, living or dead.
In politics they would be people like Hugh Gaitskell, Harold Macmillan, Jack or Bobby Kennedy. What women would I invite? Difficult. Oh, Barbara Castle.

Which period in history would you most liked to have lived through?
The Second World War and the Labour government that followed.

If the producers of *Strictly Come Dancing* come knocking at your door, what might you say?
They had their opportunity and now they can get lost.

The Milibands – a GQ feature

Ed Miliband

Party affiliation: Labour

Current position: Leader of the Labour Party

Born: 24 December 1969

Education: Attended Haverstock Comprehensive School and Oxford University, studying Politics, Philosophy and Economics, and then the London School of Economics, where he obtained a Master of Science degree in Economics.

Family status: Lives with partner Justine Thornton and two children.

Pre-political career: Had a brief stint as a television researcher before working for Harriet Harman, then shadow Chief Secretary to the Treasury, and Gordon Brown, then shadow Chancellor.

Electoral history: Elected Member of Parliament for Doncaster North in 2005 and within a year was made Parliamentary Secretary to the Cabinet Office. In 2007 he rose to Minister for the Cabinet Office and was promoted to the Cabinet before becoming Secretary of State for the Department of Energy and Climate Change. In May 2010 he announced his intention to stand for leader of the Labour party to succeed Gordon Brown and in September 2010 he was declared the winner, defeating his brother David Miliband by 1.3 per cent.

Career highlights: Being elected leader of the Labour Party, the first Jewish person to rise to the position. At the age of forty, he is also the youngest of Labour's ten leaders since the Second World War.

Interesting fact: According to the diaries of Tony Benn, Ed Miliband once worked for him as an intern.

David Miliband

Party affiliation: Labour

Born: 15 July 1965

Education: Attended Haverstock Comprehensive School in London before studying Politics, Philosophy and Economics at Corpus Christi College, Oxford. He later won a Kennedy Scholarship to study for a Masters' Degree at the Massachusetts Institute of Technology.

Family status: Married with two children.

Pre-political career: Worked for the National Council for Voluntary Organisations and then as a Research Fellow at the Institute for Public Policy Research. He became Tony Blair's Head of Policy in 1994 and was a major contributor for Labour's manifesto for the 1997 general election.

Electoral history: First elected as MP for South Shields in 2001 and after only a year was appointed as Schools Minister. He then replaced Ruth Kelly as Cabinet Office Minister in December 2004 before becoming Minister of State for Communities, Local Government in May 2005 and Secretary of State for Environment, Food and Rural Affairs, and then Foreign Secretary in June 2007. He was shadow Foreign Secretary from May 2010 until October 2010, when he resigned from front-line politics after losing a battle for the Labour leadership to his brother, Ed, by 1.3 per cent.

Career highlights: Becoming Secretary of State for Foreign and Commonwealth Affairs in Gordon Brown's first Cabinet.

Interesting facts: His first career ambition was to be a bus conductor. His wife, Louise Shackleton, plays the violin for the London Symphony Orchestra.

Back in June 2008 I got a call from Dylan Jones, the editor of GQ. *Would I like to have lunch at The Ivy, he asked. I tried not to sound too keen, but of course I would. I was a big fan of Dylan and a subscriber to his magazine. 'I wonder what he wants,' I thought. The reason I became a subscriber to* GQ *was simple: Piers Morgan's interviews. Indeed, it was those interviews which gave me the inspiration to conduct my own 'In Conversation' interviews for* Total Politics. *Piers, I felt, got far more out of his interviewees than most interviewers because he simply had a chat with them, rather than give them a grilling. And once people became comfortable, they opened up and said things they hadn't intended. It's exactly the style I now adopt both in my* Total Politics *interviews and on LBC Radio. If people become defensive you get nothing out of them. If they're relaxed and comfortable, they spill.*

Anyway, to cut a long story short, Dylan asked if I would like to write a profile of the Miliband brothers. To say I was surprised would be an understatement. Why me, a right of centre pundit? Why did he think I would be the right person to write this? I just managed to stop myself saying 'but couldn't I do one of a Conservative instead?'

So I spent the next three months researching the piece and speaking to those close to both the Miliband brothers. I had never met Ed or David personally but had formed a reasonably positive view of both of them. So I asked for a meeting – not an interview. All I wanted to do was to have an hour long chat so I could form my own judgement of them as men, rather than politicians.

As time went on I began to form a distinct view that Ed Miliband was the more likely one to reach the top – not because of any personal failings on the part of his brother, but because he had the ability to appeal right across the Labour Party. His enemies were fewer, and if you look at the system Labour uses to elect its leader, you will understand how important that is. Second preferences really count. As we found out.

I've included this piece partly as an indulgence but mainly because it's a piece of writing I am proud of and which I think has stood the test of time. It's not often I get a prediction right, but I reckon I was the first to spot Ed Miliband's potential as a successor to Gordon Brown. It's only a shame I didn't put my money where my mouth is and put a bet on it.

It's every politician's dream. Imagine it. You appear on BBC's *Question Time*, get mercilessly harangued by a beautiful young woman who is so impressed by your erudite answer that she sends a note to your office the next day asking you out on a date. This sort of thing doesn't happen in real political life … unless you happen to be called Ed Miliband.

While brother David hogs the headlines and is touted as a prime minister in waiting, Ed has hunkered down, got on with his job, made many friends in all sections of the Labour Party and just as importantly avoided making too many enemies.

It is seventy years since two brothers served in Cabinet together, when Edward and Oliver Stanley were appointed to Neville Chamberlain's pre-war government. It is not a propitious precedent as Edward died only a few months after being appointed. But the Milibands are the very opposite of latter day Cains and Abels. Siblings they may be, but rivals they are not – at least in their own minds, and not yet. They shrink from the comparison, but many Labour Party insiders are talking about them in the same way US Democrats used to talk about the Kennedy brothers. The Labour Party needs a saviour and many believe he will answer to the name Miliband.

David Miliband is not in any way a young man in a hurry, but he often comes across as impatient. He's frustrated at the clunkingly slow pace of public service reform and baffled by the inability of his colleagues to see clearly what needs to be done to get the Labour Party on track for a fourth election victory.

His article in *The Guardian* in July, which nearly provoked Gordon Brown to sack him for disloyalty was aimed fair and square at the Labour Party. His aim may have been slightly askew – most interpreted it as the start of a leadership bid – but he was trying to encourage the Party to turn its fire on David Cameron rather than itself. The article's spectacular consequences left Brownites appalled and his cheerleaders delighted. Their man had displayed the very kind of *cojones* he had appeared to be lacking only sixteen months earlier, when he ducked out of fighting Gordon Brown for the post-Blair inheritance. At the time, many Blairite Labour MPs pleaded with him to stand even though he would have undoubtedly lost to the Great Clunking Fist. One MP is adamant that if he flunks it again, it's game over. 'If he doesn't wield the knife this time, it's two strikes and you're out,' says a junior Labour Minister frustrated at the Prime Minister's failings.

Few realise how close David Miliband came to making Gordon Brown fight for his job in May 2007, when Tony Blair announced he would be stepping down less than two months later. Brown's henchmen had issued dire warnings – anonymously, of course – about the consequences of Miliband challenging Brown for what they regarded as his job by right. Miliband desperately wanted to ignore these threats and stand, but there was one thing holding him back – his young family. At the very same time as nominations for the Labour leadership opened, the Milibands were about to adopt their second child, Jacob, in the United States. At any time, the birth parents could have withdrawn from the process, possibly horrified by the publicity giving their son to the potential British prime minister would no doubt have attracted. Miliband decided the risk was not worth taking, telling friends: 'The one thing I was never going to compromise on was Jacob.'

Miliband and his violinist wife Louise Shackleton had already adopted one child, Isaac, in 2004. They chose to go to America to do so in order to avoid the intrusion of the British tabloid press and because adopting new born babies in this country is notoriously difficult. Nevertheless, the tabloids made every effort to seek out the baby's birth mother, something which rankles with Miliband even now. He gives the distinct impression to friends that it wouldn't take much to give up politics if the intrusion into his family life became too wearing. All fathers are devoted to their children, but with David Miliband this devotion borders on an obsession – something not uncommon in the fathers of adopted children. There's that subconscious need to try just that little bit harder than normal fathers. He knows the toll his career may take on his kids, and older son Isaac has already started to notice his father's long absences brought on by the demands of his job. 'Daddy stay, Daddy stay!' he implored his father recently, as David Miliband was about to leave his South Shields home to travel down to London on a Monday morning. 'Give Daddy a kiss goodbye,' said the doting Dad. 'No. Daddy stay, Daddy stay,' pleaded Isaac. It was all David Miliband could do to tear himself away and walk out the door.

Such dilemmas have yet to trouble younger brother Ed, who has to rank as one of the most eligible bachelors in politics. He has a long term girlfriend, a feisty environmental lawyer called Justine, who is fiercely protective of him, but far from the stereotypical political partner. 'She's a still waters run deep kind of woman,' says a friend of the couple.

The same friend tells how she met Ed at a party during the painful breakup of long-term relationship. 'I'd only ever exchanged a few words with him but at a party he bounded up to me and said: "Justine tells me you're having a rough time, are you OK?" Not many men would have done that. It showed empathy and a willingness to discuss personal stuff. He's good at putting people at their ease.'

Despite their reputation for making friends easily, it is easy to dismiss the Miliband brothers as political geeks, reared on a diet of politics, Marxist history and lefty doctrine.

It's true they both studied politics at Oxford (and both emerged with Firsts). It's also true that neither of them has ever worked outside politics and the media. They belong to a new political class which believes it can run the country without ever having experienced life in the real world. Their contemporaries in the Labour Party like Andy Burnham, James Purnell, Liam Byrne, Douglas Alexander and Ruth Kelly all hail from a similar background. So do George Osborne, David Cameron and Nick Clegg, for that matter. It's almost as if they were born to rule.

While David Miliband can indeed appear a little intellectual, if not geeky, his brother has more of the common touch. Perhaps it is because Ed is more ambivalent about politics. He has told friends that his happiest year was spent teaching at Harvard. Some friends feel that because politics is not his be all and end all, he is better at it than most.

Ed Miliband has it in him to be inspirational. He was giving off the cuff speeches before David Cameron had even thought of it. Indeed, it is a rarity for Ed Miliband to ever deliver a speech from a prepared text. He believes that the era when a politician can turn up, read out a pre-prepared speech and then leave is over. He maintains he hasn't delivered a speech from a written text in more than two years. He's learnt the art of conversational speaking – talking to an audience at its own level, without any appearance of pretention. And it is for this reason that many in the Labour Party think he has it in him to go right to the top. He's brilliant at hustings, loves Q&A sessions and can tickle an audience's G-Spot without appearing to try. He doesn't speak in soundbites and despite the constraints of collective responsibility he usually appears to at least attempt to answer a question honestly. His brother tries the same approach but sometimes appears to struggle to find the right words.

While they may differ in their approach to public speaking, their politics are almost indistinguishable. It was for this reason that they were the oil which managed to smooth the wheels of the very spiky relationship between Gordon Brown and Tony Blair. Ed Miliband spent a decade working as an advisor to Gordon Brown, while his brother was ensconced in Downing Street as Tony Blair's chief policy wonk. Whenever misunderstandings occurred between the two Labour titans (which they frequently did), a crisis brewed, the brothers attempted to avert it, sometimes successfully, sometimes not. Both remain loyal to their masters. Tony Blair once called David Miliband 'my Wayne Rooney', while Gordon Brown demonstrated his hopes for Ed by promoting him to his Cabinet only two years after first becoming an MP – a stratospheric rise in anyone's book.

But the 'geek' label is a difficult one to shake off, especially for the older Miliband. One Labour MP told me: 'David has got the worst of all worlds. He's too geeky for the Home Counties Labour people but also too geeky for the Labour heartlands.' His haircut and dress sense add weight to a slight sense of otherworldliness. He's not quite on Planet Redwood but he needs to ditch the striped ties and add a bit of colour to what some perceive – unfairly – as a slightly monochrome personality. When David Miliband first joined the Cabinet Office under John Prescott's tutelage, Prescott introduced him to the Department's staff with the words: 'The Mekon has landed.'

The importance of their upbringing and family background is crucial in understanding what makes the Miliband brothers tick. Their father Ralph, one of the last Jews to escape Nazi-ruled Belgium when he fled to Britain in 1940, was perhaps the pre-eminent Marxist historian of his time. The Miliband parents insisted their young offspring attend their intellectual-filled dinner parties from a very early age. A friend of the family says: 'Theirs was an equal voice in the conversation even when they were quite small. It was a fantastic example of how to treat children.'

Ralph Miliband's brand of socialism is today considered almost quaint. In essence he believed that if socialism compromised with capitalist structures it could never achieve its objectives, and that the Labour Party exemplified all that was wrong with that compromise. Quite what he would make of the Labour Party today is anybody's guess. It's easy to believe he would be horrified by most aspects of New Labour and his sons' crucial role in its development. But despite his ideological predispositions, Ralph Miliband would, according to both his sons, be proud of the fact that they have reached the political heights.

So how did the Miliband brothers become Labour? According to a family friend, the jury's out. 'For a reason I have never really understood, they just became Labour. Maybe it's generational or about the politics of Oxford. Or maybe it's about ambition. What's intriguing is that they not only rejected the old Trot politics, they also rejected the left of the Labour Party.'

A friend of Ed Milband's from Oxford, Marc Stears, is more categoric: 'Back in 1989 few of us saw New Labour coming, but Ed was already there. He knew what had to be done for the left to get power.' Of course, Ed was following in his brother's footsteps, and by all accounts had a hard act to follow. It was a pattern which would repeat itself time and again in later life.

During his time at Oxford David Miliband had been President of the Junior Common Room and led a student campaign against the apartheid regime in South Africa. When Ed arrived at Oxford he just got on with it. There was no resentment, no feeling of something to live up to. He did things his own way, although was irritated by being known as Ted, rather than Ed. Marc Stears paints a glowing picture of the student Miliband. 'Everyone knew Ed. He had instant low level popularity and he was disarming, principled and non tribal. We all knew about his father's work but Ed had his own distinct social and political agenda.'

While their father was an idealist and a benign ideologue, the sons decided that they would rather put theory into practice. There was only one vehicle for that – the Labour Party. Labour historian Brian Brivati thinks it goes further, and that the notion that we all need to find a way of rejecting our parents or at least superceding them, is at least subconsciously at play here. 'They were rejecting the route of transformatory Trotskyite politics and accepted the parliamentary road and gradualism' he says. 'In a way that was a rebellion in their own family, a rebellion against the parental millieu.'

Rebellion or not, former Labour leader Michael Foot, now 95-year-old, says: 'Ralph was incredibly proud of who they were and what they have done, but would like them to have been a little more left wing.' When you ask the Milibands what their father, who died in 1994, would have of their Cabinet careers, both look wistful, as if their main regret in life is that their father died before he could share in their success.

One Labour MP thinks their background gave them the intellectual rigour to succeed. 'Marxism is a bit like Christianity. It gives you the intellectual discipline which sets you up for any kind of politics. What it doesn't give you is an emotional link to the Labour Party,' he says, hinting that the Milibands, like Tony Blair before them, have a slightly detached and unemotional view of their own party. To them it's a vehicle, rather than a way of life.

Despite that, their involvement with the Party goes way back. After taking his 'O' Levels in 1986, Ed got a summer job as a researcher for Tony Benn, not for the first time following in the footsteps of brother David, who had already done voluntary work for Ken Livingstone. Later on, David worked for Patricia Hewitt at the IPPR, a leading left of centre think tank, and Ed became Harriet Harman's researcher. They both got sucked into Labour Party politics at a time when the left was in decline. They hitched themselves to the right, who were in the ascendant and never looked back. A friend of David's says: 'They were always left progressive but it was always with that New Labour careerist shine. They were going places and they wanted to achieve concrete things.'

Ed Miliband is the kind of politician who inspires loyalty both from his own political coterie of friends, but also his civil servants. He operates with a degree of informality which the more stuffy civil servants find difficult to get used to but eventually come to like. He's 'Ed' and corrects anyone who addresses him as 'Minister'. Brother David prefers informality too, but in the Foreign Office it's more difficult to impose.

To get on in politics you need the hide of a rhino and the social skills of a butterfly. The jury seems to be out as to whether either Miliband cuts the ice when it comes to gladhanding the various constituent parts of the Labour Party who get to vote in a leadership election. A friend of both the brothers has bad news for Ed, who he says is the 'less socially accomplished of the two.' He adds: 'If there's a room to work, Ed will get trapped in a conversation he's interested in, wheareas David will work the room relentlessly.' A Blairite Labour Minister concurs. 'Ed carries on the Brownite tradition of not deigning to speak to anyone he doesn't regard as a potential equal. David makes more of an effort. I can't imagine having a pint with Ed.' In a way, this illustrates the continuing divide between the Blairites and the Brownites. While the Blairite minister reckons Ed is a little aloof, there are plenty of witnesses to him leading the late night singing around the piano at party conferences and enjoying letting his hair down.

Ed Miliband has also gained the respect of trade union leaders, whose members still have a third of the votes in a leadership election. At a recent Labour Party Policy Forum he negotiated with the union general secretaries. One Labour Minister who was present said: 'He was much better, by that I mean steely and tough, than everyone expected. They were furious with him but he got their respect.'

Both the Milibands get their political kicks from ideas. They operate on the basis of 'if we are here, how can we get there'. They're never happier than when discussing how to develop a new policy one or other of them has thought up. David, in particular, loves wrestling with big, insoluble problems. A friend says: 'What he really likes is the discussion and debate before a decision. That's when he really comes to life.' When he was a minister at DEFRA his friend Brian Brivati used to organise lunchtime seminars for him on different issues of the day. Miliband repeatedly said they were the most enjoyable part of his jam-packed day.

Ed Miliband is particularly interested in the area of social justice and public service reform. His private staff has lost count of the times he's bounded into his office with a puppy-dog like enthusiasm and proposed some radical new idea to help a particular group of people. He restarted an online discussion forum in 2006 called the Left Book Club Online with the intention of sparking proper debate, although since he became a Minister it has disappeared.

They both get a lot of their ideas from their northern constituencies, Ed in Doncaster and David in South Shields. Their conversations are peppered with anecdotes. Just as they were both affected by their comprehensive schooling, they are deeply affected by a lack of aspiration among certain social groups in their constituencies. Where once most eighteen year olds would have gone down the mines, giving them a sense of discipline and community, now they have neither. Ed Miliband recently encountered a 17-year-old and asked him what job he would like. Quick as a flash, the teenager shot back: 'Yours.' Yet he was leaving school without a thought of going to university. No one had suggested it to him. Miliband was appalled.

The Miliband brothers are also living examples of the fact that the age of tribal politics is closing. The fact that party politics is now conducted entirely on the central ground plays into their hands. They're not especially interested in the old style arguments of left versus right. If the Tories agree with them they regard it as a plus. They have made it their business to cultivate friends in the Tory Party – people like Ed Vaizey, who was just ahead of Ed Miliband at Oxford and has a high regard for him. 'He has one of those faces which make you instantly like him,' says Vaizey. 'He'll happily have a gossip with you, but he knows there's a line which you don't cross.'

David Miliband has told friends he is closer to his brother than he has ever been, but despite the fact that they live within a stone's throw of each other in London's fashionable Primrose Hill, they rarely have time to meet socially to just chew the fat.

Their closeness was stretched this summer when Ed was nearly forced to choose between his brother and his inbuilt loyalty to Gordon Brown. One friend said Ed was 'torn by loyalty to the party and the loyalty of brothers'. It's probably not the last time his conscience will have to wrestle with that particular dilemma.

Opinion is sharply divided both in the Labour Party and the Westminster Village about which Miliband is more likely to become leader of the Labour Party. There's little doubt that in the current climate David is the better placed – he's been tested and emerged with his reputation enhanced. He's given the matter of leadership a good deal of thought and knows what needs to be done.

Ed, on the other hand, has only recently emerged from his older brother's shadow, and realised that he too has his chance for greatness. The question is: does he want it as much as his older brother?

With grateful thanks to GQ magazine for permission to reproduce this article.